T0418919

Cuban Music Counterpoints

Alejandro L. Madrid, Series Editor
Walter Aaron Clark, Founding Series Editor

Nor-tec Rifa!
Electronic Dance Music from Tijuana to the World
Alejandro L. Madrid

From Serra to Sancho:
Music and Pageantry in the California Missions
Craig H. Russell

Colonial Counterpoint:
Music in Early Modern Manila
D. R. M. Irving

Embodying Mexico:
Tourism, Nationalism, & Performance
Ruth Hellier-Tinoco

Silent Music:
Medieval Song and the Construction of History in Eighteenth-Century Spain
Susan Boynton

Whose Spain?
Negotiating "Spanish Music" in Paris, 1908–1929
Samuel Llano

Federico Moreno Torroba:
A Musical Life in Three Acts
Walter Aaron Clark and William Craig Krause

Representing the Good Neighbor:
Music, Difference, and the Pan American Dream
Carol A. Hess

Agustín Lara:
A Cultural Biography
Andrew G. Wood

Danzón:
Circum-Caribbean Dialogues in Music and Dance
Alejandro L. Madrid and Robin D. Moore

Music and Youth Culture in Latin America:
Identity Construction Processes from New York to Buenos Aires
Pablo Vila

In Search of Julián Carrillo and Sonido 13
Alejandro L. Madrid

Tracing Tangueros:
Argentine Tango Instrumental Music
Kacey Link and Kristin Wendland

Playing in the Cathedral:
Music, Race, and Status in New Spain
Jesús A. Ramos-Kittrell

Entertaining Lisbon:
Music, Theater, and Modern Life in the Late 19th Century
Joao Silva

Music Criticism and Music Critics in Early Francoist Spain
Eva Moreda Rodríguez

Carmen *and the Staging of Spain:*
Recasting Bizet's Opera in the Belle Epoque
Michael Christoforidis
Elizabeth Kertesz

Rites, Rights and Rhythms:
A Genealogy of Musical Meaning in Colombia's Black Pacific
Michael Birenbaum Quintero

Discordant Notes:
Marginality and Social Control in Madrid, 1850–1930
Samuel Llano

Sonidos Negros:
On the Blackness of Flamenco
K. Meira Goldberg

Opera in the Tropics:
Music and Theater in Early Modern Brazil
Rogerio Budasz

Sound-Politics in São Paulo
Leonardo Cardoso

Bossa Mundo:
Brazilian Music in Transnational Media
Industries
K.E. Goldschmitt

After the Dance, the Drums Are Heavy:
Carnival, Politics and Musical
Engagement in Haiti
Rebecca Dirksen

The Invention of Latin American Music:
A Transnational History
Pablo Palomino

Latin Jazz:
The Other Jazz
Christopher Washburne

Panpipes and Ponchos:
Musical Folklorization and the Rise of the
Andean Conjunto Tradition in La Paz,
Bolivia
Fernando Rios

Elite Art Worlds:
Philanthropy, Latin Americanism, and
Avant-garde Music
Eduardo Herrera

The Sweet Penance of Music:
Musical Life in Colonial Santiago de Chile
Alejandro Vera

Música Típica:
Cumbia and the Rise of Musical
Nationalism in Panama
Sean Bellaviti

Text, Liturgy, and Music in the
Hispanic Rite:
The Vespertinus Genre
Raquel Rojo Carrillo

Africanness in Action:
Essentialism and Musical Imaginations of
Africa in Brazil
Juan Diego Diaz

Inventing the Recording:
Phonographs in Spain, 1877–1914
Eva Moreda Rodríguez

Inca Music Reimagined:
Indigenist Discourses in Latin American
Art Music, 1910–1930
Vera Wolkowicz

Silvestre Revueltas:
Sounds of a Political Passion
Roberto Kolb-Neuhaus

Cuban Music Counterpoints:
Vanguardia Musical in Global Networks
Marysol Quevedo

Cuban Music Counterpoints

Vanguardia Musical in Global Networks

MARYSOL QUEVEDO

OXFORD
UNIVERSITY PRESS

Oxford University Press is a department of the University of Oxford. It furthers
the University's objective of excellence in research, scholarship, and education
by publishing worldwide. Oxford is a registered trade mark of Oxford University
Press in the UK and certain other countries.

Published in the United States of America by Oxford University Press
198 Madison Avenue, New York, NY 10016, United States of America.

© Oxford University Press 2023

All rights reserved. No part of this publication may be reproduced, stored in
a retrieval system, or transmitted, in any form or by any means, without the
prior permission in writing of Oxford University Press, or as expressly permitted
by law, by license, or under terms agreed with the appropriate reproduction
rights organization. Inquiries concerning reproduction outside the scope of the
above should be sent to the Rights Department, Oxford University Press, at the
address above.

You must not circulate this work in any other form
and you must impose this same condition on any acquirer.

Library of Congress Cataloging-in-Publication Data
Names: Quevedo, Marysol, author.
Title: Cuban music counterpoints: vanguardia musical in global networks / Marysol Quevedo.
Description: [1.] | New York : Oxford University Press, 2023. |
Series: Currents in Latin American and Iberian music | Includes bibliographical references and index.
Identifiers: LCCN 2023006130 (print) | LCCN 2023006131 (ebook) | ISBN 9780197552230 (hardback) |
ISBN 9780197552254 (epub) | ISBN 9780197552261
Subjects: LCSH: Music—Cuba—20th century—History and criticism. |
Avant–garde (Music)—Cuba—History—20th century.
Classification: LCC ML207.C85 Q34 2023 (print) | LCC ML207.C85 (ebook) |
DDC 780.97291/0904—dc23/eng/20230209
LC record available at https://lccn.loc.gov/2023006130
LC ebook record available at https://lccn.loc.gov/2023006131

DOI: 10.1093/oso/9780197552230.001.0001

Printed by Sheridan Books, Inc., United States of America

For Nico

Contents

List of Figures	xi
List of Music Examples	xiii
List of Tables	xv
Acknowledgments	xvii
Introduction: Mapping and Forging Musical Networks	1
1. Neoclassicism Meets 1940s Pan Americanism: The Grupo de Renovación Musical as the First Cuban School of Composition	27
2. The Sociedad Cultural Nuestro Tiempo: Precursor to the Cuban Revolutionary Cultural Projects, 1950–1958	65
3. A Decade of Revolution and Experimentation in Music: Grafting Experimentalism onto the Cuban Revolutionary-Socialist Trunk	106
4. Institutionalization and Fissures in the Cuban Classical Music Landscape: The 1970s	144
5. "Hacia nuevos horizontes": Electroacoustic Music and Globalization in 1980s Cuba	182
Epilogue: Unending and Repeating Coda—El "período especial" que nunca termina/The Never-Ending Special Period	212
Select Bibliography	237
Index	259

Figures

1.1 and 1.2. Invitation to June 20, 1942 Concert of Sonatas for Piano by Cuban Composers. 28

1.3 and 1.4. Concert Program of Aaron Copland's Presentation of Music by US composers in Cuba. 36

1.5 and 1.6. Invitation to concert of the Cuban-American Music Group, May 17, 1945. 47

2.1. Newspaper clipping from *El Mundo* February 12, 1950. The caption reads: "The image shows the directors of the Sociedad 'Amadeo Roldán,' who, with much enthusiasm promote the work of the novel institution. They are, Juan Elósegui, president, Odilio Urfé, Nilo Rodríguez, Ithiel León, Carmenchú Rodríguez, Josefina Elósegui, Edmundo López, and Pablo Iturrioz." From Sociedad Amadeo Roldán scrapbook at the Museo Nacional de la Música Cubana. 68

2.2. Harold Gramatges, image from *Nuestro Tiempo* Año 3, no. 14 (November 1956), n.p. 78

3.1. Stage layout for *Relieves* as provided in the OSN October 1969 concert program. 131

3.2. Juan Blanco, *Contrapunto Espacial III*. 133

4.1. Leo Brouwer, *Sonata "pian e forte"* (1973) manuscript, reproduced with permission of Leo Brouwer from his personal archive. 158

4.2. Aerial view of the roofs of the Instituto Superior de Arte. Photo courtesy of the Cuban Heritage Collection at the University of Miami. 171

Music Examples

1.1. León, *Sonatas a la Virgen del Cobre*, Sonata II, mm. 1–2.   56

1.2. León, *Sonatas a la Virgen del Cobre*, Sonata II, RL J.   56

1.3. León, *Sonatas a la Virgen del Cobre*, Sonata II, mm. 41–42, *tresillo* in the bass part.   57

1.4. León, *Sonatas a la Virgen del Cobre*, Sonata II, mm. 41–42, *cinquillo* in the piano.   57

1.5. León, *Sonatas a la Virgen del Cobre*, Sonata II, mm. RL D, *guajira* section.   59

1.6. Gramatges, *Serenata*, First Movement, mm. 1–10.   61

2.1. Blanco, *Quinteto*, "Allegro," mm. 1–14.   84

2.2. Blanco, *Quinteto*, "Allegro," mm. 68–82.   85

2.3. Blanco, *Quinteto*, "Pregón," mm. 1–17.   86

2.4. Blanco, *Quinteto*, "Allegro," mm. 109–114.   86

2.5. Blanco, *Quinteto*, "Allegro," mm. 183–193.   87

2.6. Gramatges, *Tres preludios a modo de toccata*, Preludio II, mm. 1–14.   90

2.7. Gramatges, *Tres preludios a modo de toccata*, Preludio III, m. 1–11.   91

2.8. Gramatges, *Tres preludios a modo de toccata*, Preludio I, m. 5.   92

2.9. Gramatges, *Tres preludios a modo de toccata*, Preludio III, mm. 1–2.   92

4.1. Gramatges, *La muerte del guerrillero*, xylophone and timpani part, mm. 7–10.   145

4.2. Gramatges, *Móvil I*, excerpt from page 6.   161

4.3. Gramatges, *Móvil I*, opening.   162

Tables

2.1. Members of the SCNT and their roles in the post-1959 cultural institutions.   99

4.1. Repertory recorded in the *Contemporáneos* series of the EGREM.   174

5.1. Programming of Primavera en Varadero Electronic Music Festival 1981.   201

5.2. LPs of electroacoustic music by Cuban composers released by the EGREM between 1979 and 1989.   203

Acknowledgments

This monograph is an extension of my doctoral dissertation, a product of several more years of research, writing, and revisions that is nevertheless indebted to that initial work; therefore, much of these acknowledgments reiterate my gratitude to individuals and institutions who have been supportive of my work for nearly fifteen years. Publications are the result of collective and collaborative work; in this section I wish to acknowledge the network of scholars who made my research and writing possible. This section cannot adequately reflect my deep appreciation and gratitude to everyone who has supported my work over the years.

First, I wish to thank key individuals from my alma mater, Indiana University's Musicology Department and Department of Folklore and Ethnomusicology. In particular, I'm grateful for the dedicated dissertation committee members who probed and pushed me to question my sources, J. Peter Burkholder, Phil Ford, Halina Goldberg, and Javier F. León, as well as other professors who provided constant support, Anke Birkenmaier, Melanie Burnim, Arlene Díaz, Daniel Melamed, Tina Muxfeldt, Massimo Ossi, Ayana Smith, and Ruth Stone. My years as a graduate student were made all the more fulfilling by my peer mentors, fellow doctoral students who offered intellectual and emotional support, Mollie Ables, Elise Anderson, Katherine Baber, Daniel Bishop, Sherri Bishop, Katie Chapman, Rodrigo Chocano, Lisa Cooper Vest, Liz Elmi, Dave Lewis, Rebekah Moore, Devon Nelson, Kerry O'Brien, Katie Rios, Molly Ryan, Derek Stauff, Laura Stokes, Kristen Strandberg, Nik Taylor, and Juan Eduardo Wolf, who all, at one point or another, read or heard some portion of the material present in this book.

I am eternally indebted to my dissertation advisor, Halina Goldberg. It was in my last doctoral seminar with her, "Music and Politics in Eastern Europe," that I became interested in this book's topic. She has challenged me to ask provocative questions and not shy away from situations and case studies that could not be easily interpreted. She has also pushed me to refine my thinking and writing and has been a mentor throughout my career; she has been a role model for how to be an engaging professor and a productive scholar.

IU's Latin American Music Center served as a home base for my professional activities over the last six years at Indiana University, thanks to its special collection of twentieth-century recordings and scores and for the intellectual support of the LAMC staff. Former LAMC directors Paul Borg, Erick Carballo, and the late Carmen Helena Téllez were unconditional supporters of my research. Erick

xviii ACKNOWLEDGMENTS

Carballo in particular was crucial in verifying my theoretical analysis of the compositions discussed in the first and second chapters. LAMC staff throughout the years—Juan Carlos Arango, Francisco Cortés-Álvarez, Emma Dederick, Carolina Gamboa, Luiz Lopes, Sofia Potdevin-Afanador, Yuriria Rodríguez, María José Romero, Daniel Stein—have also provided feedback on my research and fostered a supportive work environment where they have greatly nurtured my musicological skills. Carmen Téllez offered me invaluable opportunities that taught me how to be a public scholar and how to apply my research to performance contexts; this book is in part a testament to her work as a mentor, and I only wish she would have been able to see this book in print before her untimely death.

An academic's work is nearly impossible to conduct without grants and fellowships to fund their research. Several institutions provided such funds at various stages of my career, from graduate student to assistant professor. These include IU's Musicology Department's travel grants and the A. Peter Brown Research Travel Award; the Jacobs School of Music graduate student travel funds; IU's Latin American Music Center and IU's Office of the Vice-President of International Affairs' Latin American Fellowship; the University of Miami's Cuban Heritage Collection Goizueta Dissertation Fellowship; Florida International University's Diaz-Ayala Travel Grant; IU President's Diversity Dissertation Fellowship; University of Miami's Provost Research Awards (2018 and 2022); University of Miami's Fellowship in the Arts & Humanities Award; University of Miami Center for the Humanities Faculty Fellowship; and the University of Miami Institute for the Advanced Study of the Americas Faculty Grant.

I would not have been able to complete this book without the technical and intellectual support of the individuals who work at the various institutions and archives where I conducted research. These include Emma Dederick at IU's Music Library and librarian for the LAMC collection; at the Centro de Investigación y Desarrollo de la Música Cubana, director Laura Vilar, librarian Tamara Sevila, philologist Liliana Casanella Cué, and musicologists Ailer Pérez and Grizel Hernández; at the Museo Nacional de la Música de Cuba, director Jesús Gómez Cairo and librarians Daureen Alemán, Isabel Arrieta Álvarez, Roberto Nuñez Jauma, and Yohana Ortega; at Casa de las Américas, Music Department director María Elena Vinueza and musicologists Carmen Souto and Layda Ferrando; at the Instituto Superior de Arte Yianela Pérez Cuza, music librarian Mercedes del Sol Fernández, and composers Sigried Macías and Juan Piñera; at the Laboratorio Nacional de Música Electroacústica, director Enmanuel Blanco and composers Piñera and Macías; Miriam Escudero at the Gabinete de Patrimonio Musical Esteban Salas; at the University of Miami's Cuban Heritage Collection, former directors Esperanza B. de Varona and Maria Estorino Dooling, librarians

ACKNOWLEDGMENTS xix

Natalie Baur, Meiyolet Méndez, Amanda Moreno, Juan Antonio Villanueva, and Martin Tsang, and staff members Gladys Gómez-Rossié, Annie Sansone Martínez, and Rosa Monzón-Álvarez; at Florida International University's Díaz-Ayala Collection, director of the Cuban Research Institute Jorge Duany and librarians Verónica González and Tom Moore. I must also thank composers Héctor Angulo, Alfredo Diez Nieto, Guido López Gavilán, Sigried Macías, Juan Piñera, and Roberto Valera for taking time to discuss their careers and works with me; as well as Isabelle Hernández and Leo Brouwer for their personal communications and permission to reproduce Brouwer's manuscript of *Sonata pian e forte* in the fourth chapter.

My research and stay in Cuba were in part possible thanks to the vibrant and welcoming home of musicologist Prisca Martínez and her family. Prisca helped me connect with local musicologists and archivists and engaged in intellectual musicological discussions that helped me refine my interpretations of archival materials. Similarly, the late Danilo Orozco and his wife Purri opened their home to me. My conversations with Danilo changed the course of my research and the focus of this dissertation. Cuban musicologists Miviam Ruiz Pérez and Rolando Pérez also provided crucial contacts for my first trips to Cuba, as well as tremendous encouragement to pursue this research topic. My research in Miami would not have been the same had I not met the energetic and inquisitive anthropologist Martin Tsang, who has always been a sounding board for all my projects.

Since joining the faculty at the University of Miami (and even prior to my arrival) several scholars and programs have encouraged and supported me in various ways, from reading drafts of chapters to listening to presentations to pointing me to the right sources of funding. These include David Ake, my department chair, my Department of Musicology colleagues Melvin Butler, Gabrielle Cornish, Matteo Magarotto, Frederick Reece, Annie Searcy, and Brent Swanson, as well as the Frost School's Associate Dean of Research, Carlos Abril, and music theory faculty Juan Chattah. Through the University of Miami's Center for the Humanities Faculty and Dissertation Fellows program, Richard Chappell, Christina Civantos, John Funchion, Karl Gunther, Scott Heerman, Yolanda Martínez-San Miguel, Patricia Saunders, Helen Yetter-Chappell, Gabriella Faundez-Rojas, and Dainerys Machado-Vento all read and provided critical feedback on the fourth chapter of this volume. Colleagues Ava Brillat, Lilian Manzor, and Will Pestle, provided support and encouragement throughout these last years at the university. Although Michael Bustamante had only recently joined UM's faculty, he had been supportive of my research since we were Goizueta Fellows in the Fall of 2012 cohort; Mike read through the entire manuscript and provided detailed feedback as only a discerning historian would, and I cannot thank him enough for his time and effort in helping me make this book as accurate and clear as it can be.

XX ACKNOWLEDGMENTS

Over the last thirteen years I have presented material from this book at several conferences where I have received crucial feedback and provocative questions from colleagues in various disciplines. Ana Alonso Minutti, Eduardo Herrera, and Alejandro L. Madrid have helped me situate my work within a wider, Latin American context, encouraging my focus on avant-garde and experimental music practices. Danielle Fosler-Lussier, Carol Hess, and Susan Thomas have been great sources of encouragement and critical feedback for various projects and presentations that have made their way into this volume. I also thank Deborah Schwartz-Kates for her initial support of my research and career when I was conducting archival research at UM's Cuban Heritage Collection in 2012. She and her colleagues and students at the University of Miami welcomed me into their musicology department and provided a lively intellectual environment years before I would go on to officially become part of their community as an assistant professor of musicology. The list of mentors and colleagues in various disciplines who have provided encouragement and support includes (but I know that after this book goes to print I will remember someone's name whom I have left out) Noel Allende Goitía, Jacky Avila, Yurima Blanco, Joaquín Borges Triana, Chelsea Burns, Daniel Castro Pantoja, Xóchitl Chávez, Alexis Esquivel, Cesar Favila, David Garcia, León García Corona, Nora Lee García, Kaleb Goldschmidt, Bernard Gordillo, Jennie Gubner, Kunio Hara, Alisha Lola Jones, Benjamin Lapidus, M. Leslie Santana, Teresita Lozano, Ruthie Meadows, Iván César Morales Flores, Sergio Ospina-Romero, Alison Payne, Jillian Rogers, Elizabeth Schwall, Dan Sharp, Jason Stanyek, Noel Torres, Juan Fernando Velázquez, Jessie Vallejo, and Christine Wisch, thank you all for your feedback, stimulating conversations, and support over the years. I'd like to extend a special thanks to the editors and their team at Oxford University Press: Norman Hirschy, Elen Zigaite, Alejandro L. Madrid, Suzanne Ryan Melamed, and the copy editors and staff, as well as Robin Moore as one of the developmental editors who helped guide this project.

My parents, Ita and Néstor, encouraged and supported my music education at an early age and throughout all the years of changing interests, paying for lessons, driving us to music lessons, buying music instruments, taking us to music camps, and attending every single one of our performances; my siblings, Mariel, Néstor R., and Verónica; my grandparents, Julio, Felela, Irma, and Tato; and my extended family, aunts, uncles, cousins, and more, have all shown their support of my music and academic career throughout the years, making this work all the more satisfying and easier to do. I have to also thank my son, Nico (Domenic); his smile, beautiful and bright spirit, and his very existence fuel my soul and give me a reason to do this work when the work at times gets challenging.

Finally, I thank my partner, Mark Lomanno, for his emotional and intellectual support. He read and provided feedback on every portion of this volume. He

ACKNOWLEDGMENTS   xxi

probed and prodded my findings, conclusions, and assumptions. He encouraged me not only to write clearly, but to write beautiful and evocative prose, something I will continue to develop in future projects that he will undoubtedly also read and comment on.

A note about the cover art image:
The image featured on the cover is from the May–June 1959 issue of the cultural journal *Nuestro Tiempo* (discussed further in chapter two). The drawing was created by Roberto Juan Diago y Querol (1920–1955) and appeared with his other drawings that accompanied the article "Aporte negro a la música cubana: breves acotaciones a tan complejo como interesante tema" (Black contribution to Cuban music: Brief notes on such a complex and interesting topic), by Odilio Urfé the newly appointed director of the Instituto Musical de Investigaciones Folklóricas (Musical Institutes of Folkloric Research, one of the first institutions established after the 1959 Revolution for the promotion of folk music research). Roberto Diago was a black Cuban visual artist whose work was included in the Sociedad Cultural Nuestro Tiempo's inaugural exhibit on March 10, 1951. The image on the cover art is Courtesy of the Cuban Heritage Collection reproduced with permission from his grandson and visual artist Roberto Diago Durruthy.

Introduction

Mapping and Forging Musical Networks

Injértese en nuestras repúblicas el mundo;
pero el tronco ha de ser de nuestras repúblicas.[1]
(May the world graft itself onto our republics;
but the trunk ought to be of our republics.)

—José Martí

In a 2012 interview, Cuban composer Alfredo Diez Nieto (1918–2021) quipped that he "didn't belong to any groups," that most of his work had been as a music theory and composition professor, and that, because his music was largely excluded from concert programs of major ensembles, he primarily composed chamber and solo pieces for his students.[2] Diez Nieto was not exaggerating. Although his works were not performed very often in major national and international stages, he left an indelible mark on younger generations of composers and musicians who studied with him. He was one of the most respected music theory pedagogues in Havana, known for his clarity and meticulous method for teaching formal analytical techniques and their application in composition. In the last fifteen years, his music has received more attention, with new editions and recordings of his works by the music label Colibrí.[3] At the time of our interview, he was the only composer of his generation who was still alive (Juan Blanco, Harold Gramatges, Carlos Fariñas, among others, had passed away) and I could not corroborate his comments by interviewing the other composers. As I came across hundreds of concert programs in the Cuban archives, however, I noticed undeniable patterns: certain composer names surfaced again and again in major ensembles' programming, while other composers only appeared in programs of student recitals or chamber music concerts in the more intimate spaces of the conservatories' halls and the artists' union's headquarters (for example Diez

---

[1] José Martí, "Nuestra América," Published in *La Revista Ilustrada de Nueva York*, United States in January 10, 1981 and in *El Partido Liberal*, México, January 30, 1891.

[2] Alfredo Diez Nieto, interview with the author, July 2012.

[3] Alfredo Diez Nieto, *Capricho Cubano* CD. (Havana, Cuba: Colibrí, 2011).

Cuban Music Counterpoints. Marysol Quevedo, Oxford University Press. © Oxford University Press 2023.
DOI: 10.1093/oso/9780197552230.003.0001

2 CUBAN MUSIC COUNTERPOINTS

Nieto). Diez Nieto implicitly pointed to what would become the central focus of this book: there were very specific networks within the Cuban classical music scene and belonging to one "group" or another granted individuals access to resources that facilitated the dissemination of their music. As I looked at the stories the archival materials revealed (below I reflect on the limits of the archive), there were both loud protagonists and deafening silences. This book is mainly about the protagonists, those who accrued and deployed cultural capital within different political and social contexts to advance their work and that of aesthetically and politically like-minded composers. Throughout the 1940s and 1950s Cuban composers who gathered around two societies—the Grupo de Renovación Musical and the Sociedad Cultural Nuestro Tiempo—were afforded significant opportunities through the contacts they made in these groups. Each society promoted neoclassical aesthetics in the 1940s and modernist nationalism in the 1950s respectively. After 1959 a small collective of composers—led by Leo Brouwer, Juan Blanco, and Carlos Fariñas—promoted avant-garde and experimental music as the approach that could best represent socialist-revolutionary values and elicit in listeners social and political awareness. Composers who didn't adhere to the aesthetic-political agenda of the dominant voices were cast to the margins, relegated to teaching positions (like Diez Nieto), while those who did had their works published, premiered, and recorded and were given rare opportunities, such as scholarships and allowances to attend universities and festivals abroad. As the case studies I examine in this volume demonstrate, aesthetic and political points of view largely determined the degree to which individual composers engaged in various local and international artistic networks; and these networks were constantly being nurtured and shaped by their actors, who also had to contend with national and global, political and economic circumstances.[4]

Revolutions are often seen as points of rupture, inflection points in historical narratives that mark a before and an after. The Cuban Revolution is one of the most significant political events of the twentieth century, a series of military and political episodes that destabilized political alliances and shifted world powers and that still affect global politics as I write this introduction in the Spring of 2022. The political, economic, social, and historical precedents and repercussions of the Cuban Revolution have been the topic of hundreds, if not thousands of scholarly publications; what this book presents is not an analysis

---

[4] My use of the terms actor and network is indebted to Benjamin Piekut's discussion of actor-network theory's usefulness and limitations in music studies—following Bruno Latour, Annemarie Mol, Georgina Born, and Anna Tsing—as a method that grants agency not only to the human participants but also to the objects that are produced by these participants, objects that further various aesthetic and political ideas as they circulate beyond the actors' immediate context. Benjamin Piekut, "Actor-Networks in Music History: Clarifications and Critiques," *Twentieth-Century Music* 11, no. 2 (2014): 191–215.

INTRODUCTION 3

of how the classical music scene reflected or was affected by these political and historical events, but rather how, as part of a leftist intellectual elite, Cuban composers put their work and careers in the service of the Revolution and acted as the cultural workers needed to help build a new society. There is no denying that the Cuban Revolution was a seismic event in the island's history; however, the lives, careers, and musical activities this book sheds light on show that there was a great deal of continuity on the part of the cultural and intellectual elite, even if this elite was oppressed and marginalized in the years leading up to the Revolution. In the decade preceding the Revolution the leftists' activities of the members of the Sociedad Cultural Nuestro Tiempo (SCNT) led to their persecution under Batista's regime. Their activism, one focused on promoting local contemporary art as a remedy to their perceived threats of capitalist commercialism and imperialism, made SCNT members the ideal candidates for leading the new cultural institutions under the revolutionary government. Because of this continuity, this book is organized chronologically; it is a chronological narrative of the stories that came to the surface when examining archival materials.

Cuban Composers in and of the World

Cuban composers have always seen themselves as part of a global network of musical circulation. This viewpoint dates back to the nineteenth century when Italian opera companies and virtuosi toured the Western Atlantic ports of call that included Havana. Prominent Cuban musicians also toured the Western World, most notably the virtuoso violinist José White (1836–1918), whose international career included winning the Paris Conservatoire violin competition in 1856 and becoming a leading figure of the European classical music scene.[5] Later, in the first half of the twentieth century, composers like Alejandro García Caturla also traveled to Paris, while exchanging scores and correspondence with composers in the United States through the New Music Society and the Pan American Association of Composers. Amadeo Roldán and García Caturla shared interests with Edgar Varèse and Henry Cowell in promoting the music of living composers of the Americas through concerts, publications, and exchanges. They laid the foundations for what would become enduring bonds between Cuban and US-based composers, at least until the 1959 Revolution. *Cuban Music Counterpoints* traces the local and international artistic networks Cuban composers cultivated in order to promote their individual and collective aesthetic and political ideals between 1940 and 1991. I begin in 1940 with the deaths

---

[5] Yavet Boyadjiev, "Jose White Laffita (1835–1918): A Biography and a Study of His Six Etudes, Op. 13" (DMA document, City University of New York, 2015), 19.

4   CUBAN MUSIC COUNTERPOINTS

of Amadeo Roldán (1939) and Alejandro García Caturla (1940) as events that left a void in the Cuban classical music scene, which Catalan-born composer José Ardévol filled to a large degree. 1940 is also significant as the year of the ratification of the 1940 Cuban Constitution: one of the most progressive constitutions at the time, influenced by the collectivist spirit of the 1933 Revolution, it promised land, education, and labor reforms. The 1940 Constitution seemed to represent a new age for the Cuban people with the promise of multiparty democracy. However, the rise in corruption and the state's failure to implement the reforms outlined in the new Constitution set the stage for Fulgencio Batista's 1952 coup, the rise in popularity and power of Fidel Castro throughout the 1950s, and the eventual ousting of Batista by the rebel forces in 1959. The dissolution of the Soviet Union in 1991 serves as the end point of this book, an event that would mark the beginning of one of the most severe economic crises on the island. This crisis led to several composers leaving Cuba to pursue careers abroad and to the reduction or complete cessation of activities of the island's cultural institutions.

Although the book chapters are organized chronologically, rather than offering an overarching narrative of Cuban music history, the focus is on specific events (such as concerts and festivals) and objects (such as LP recordings and letters) that reveal the networks Cuban composers forged during these five decades. These case studies offer a microcosm of how composers enacted their individual agency within cultural and political institutions both locally and abroad. For example, in chapter 3, I will examine a 1969 symphony orchestra concert where composers Leo Brouwer, Juan Blanco, and Carlos Fariñas and conductor Manuel Duchesne Cuzán shocked audiences with a *happening* that included electronic music, actors, audience participation, and dissonant sound masses. Such an event would have been common fare in the New York experimental performance art scene but condemned practically anywhere within the Soviet Bloc. Yet, the composers framed their works as enactments of revolutionary and socialist ideals and as art that was most conducive to shaping the *hombre nuevo* (the socialist new man, but redefined, mainly by Ernesto Che Guevara, to fit the contexts and purposes of leftist political and social movements throughout Latin America and Cuba in particular). More broadly, through the works programmed in this concert, the composers, the orchestra, and its director placed themselves at the vanguard of classical music production in Cuba and in dialogue with likeminded composers within Cuba and abroad.

As the 1969 concert exemplifies, the networks are teased out by focusing on specific moments or objects that lead one to identify the connections between local and foreign cultural institutions, individuals, aesthetic preferences and discourses, and the state. The objects and moments selected allow us to then pan out from this microhistorical node and to the broader national and international music scenes or networks in which these individuals and compositions

INTRODUCTION 5

participated. This combined approach offers a multifaceted view of a network of actors who negotiated between their professional, aesthetic, and political interests and those of state cultural institutions and mid-level administrators.[6] Analysis of specific events and objects reveals not only that composers had greater individual agency than what may be assumed would be possible within a repressive totalitarian state, but also that their aesthetic and political viewpoints changed over time. Rather than reading the 1959 Revolution as a moment of complete rupture between an old guard and a new revolutionary future, through a microhistorical approach centered on specific moments and individuals, I reveal the complexity and nuance of a carefully crafted and previously unacknowledged continuity on the part of the Cuban classical music elite to obtain and maintain power before and after the Revolution.

Throughout the book I explore instances of tension, collaboration, and resistance between various Cuban composers, state cultural organizations, and foreign artists and institutions. Composers aligned themselves with like-minded individuals at both local and international levels, at times replicating the diplomatic and political relations between nation states, while at other times resisting and creating art that challenged official political agendas. In chapter 1, I examine the flourishing Pan American cultural initiatives of the 1940s, when Cuban composers heavily engaged with contemporary composers and music circles in the United States, continuing efforts initiated in the 1920s. These exchanges and relationships resulted in the cultivation of a neoclassical approach to composition, deeply informed by trends from Paris and Spain. After 1959 avant-gardist composers leveraged the cultural capital and artistic networks they had cultivated in the preceding two decades to promote avant-garde and experimental music as quintessentially Cuban, socialist, and revolutionary. Those who were most successful had either openly criticized Fulgencio Batista's regime and cultural institutions throughout the 1950s, avowed themselves as politically committed artists invested in building a new Cuban socialist-revolutionary society, or both. Notably, these composers' aesthetic predilections intersected with several forms of avant-garde and experimental art in service of the national-socialist project. The flourishing of avant-garde and experimental music in a socialist context was diametrically opposed to the Soviet government's official stance that deemed avant-garde art as too decadent and formalist.[7] Therefore, Cuban composers in their majority chose to forge connections with the more daring Polish music scene, where socialism and avant-garde art were not viewed as mutually exclusive, and where, as Lisa Cooper Vest notes, there were various

---

[6] Piekut, "Actor-Networks in Music History," 191–215.
[7] Pauline Fairclough, *Classics for the Masses: Shaping Soviet Musical Identity under Lenin and Stalin* (New Haven, CT: Yale University Press, 2016), 113.

6   CUBAN MUSIC COUNTERPOINTS

political forces (not just pro- or anti-Soviet camps) in the development of a post-World War II Polish avant-garde that included Polish nationalism.[8] As Cuban composers visited Warsaw during the Warsaw Autumn Music Festival and to further their formal compositional training, Poland also served as a third, liminal space where Cuban composers could continue to propagate the US connections they had already established through the Pan Americanist efforts of the previous two decades, but that had been officially discontinued due to the US-imposed embargo. Cuban composers' tenacity and the messy entanglements of their networks are examples of what Cubans and Cuban studies scholars identify as the "resolver" spirit, a mindset of making do with the circumstances and resources available at any given time.[9]

A Plurality of -isms

Because of the long time span covered in this book, I discuss several aesthetic tendencies and labels that facilitated composers' connections with several traditions and nascent trends from within the island and abroad. These include modernism, neoclassicism, *Afrocubanismo*, *Cubanía*, nationalism, *vanguardismo*, *dodecafonismo*, serialism, avant-garde, experimentalism, and postmodernism, among others. Some of these terms were employed by Cuban music critics, musicologists, and composers themselves, effectively creating sub-categories or internal groups within the Cuban classical music scene. Other terms may not have been used by Cuban music critics and composers themselves, yet I employ them to help readers understand how composers presented their works and the global music networks within which they inscribed themselves. For example, through the 1960s and early 1970s, Cuban composers rarely described their compositional approaches as "avant-garde" or "experimental"; instead, they deployed the term *vanguardia*. The term was loaded with leftist political meaning, and because of this, it was an efficacious term for linking aesthetically avant-garde and experimental works with the Cuban state's ideological rhetoric. It is useful to employ the terms "avant-garde" and "experimental" to describe these compositions and the aesthetic philosophies of these composers at that particular time because "the transnational and transhistorical flows of experimentalisms as particular ways of experiencing and performing

---

[8] Lisa Cooper Vest, *Awangarda: Tradition and Modernity in Postwar Polish Music* (Berkeley: University of California Press, 2020), 2.

[9] Judith Moris, "¿Resolver o robar? Cubanos opinan sobre la 'lucha' diaria," *CiberCuba*, February 3, 2017. https://www.cibercuba.com/videos/noticias/2017-02-03-u129488-resolver-o-robar-cubanos-opinan-lucha-diaria.

INTRODUCTION 7

cosmopolitanism and significant forms of belonging in the world"[10] allow us to connect various experimental music scenes throughout the region of Latin America and beyond through their shared practices. Furthermore, by adopting Alonso-Minutti et al's position that "the notion of 'experimentalisms' works as a performative operation of sound, soundings, music, and musicking that gives social and historical meaning to the networks it temporarily conforms and situates . . . [and that] the sonic result of experimentalism is always contingent to specific music traditions and shared habits of listening, an aural habitus"[11] we open such terms not to single definitions, but to a multiplicity of temporally, geographically, and socially contingent practices. In the case of some compositions discussed in this book, I employ the term "experimentalism" to refer to works in which composers set out to break from tradition and to stimulate a response of shock and questioning on the part of performers and audiences. As I demonstrate in chapter 3, they justified their daring approaches through both ideological and technical-scientific language of progress and *conscientización*.

Other music scholars have shown how the capitalist West promoted avant-garde music during the Cold War as proof that capitalism and democracy—more so than socialist models—allowed for greater individual artistic freedom and, therefore, more innovative art.[12] However, these Cuban composers and music institutions demonstrate the fluidity with which aesthetically daring approaches could be re-inscribed within varying, even diametrically opposed, political contexts during the Cold War. In the case of the term *avant-garde*, I sometimes use it interchangeably with experimentalism; yet, I often reserve it for works and practices that do not seek to break entirely from the tradition, but to push the limits from within the margins of the Western classical music tradition. In Cuba avant-garde practices often maintained close dialogue with similar developments in other cosmopolitan centers, such as Paris and New York, while experimental practices and practitioners oftentimes (although not always) positioned themselves in opposition to some of these foreign cosmopolitan avant-garde practices. In the decades prior to the 1960s "modernism/modernist" functioned as a broad category that encompasses several practices, from *Afrocubanismo* in the 1920s and 1930s that continued to influence the work of later generations of Cuban composers, to, as discussed in chapters 1 and 2, Cuban neoclassicism of the 1940s and 1950s that combined the formal, structural, and technical strictures of

---

[10] Ana R. Alonso-Minutti, Eduardo Herrera, and Alejandro L. Madrid, "The Practices of Experimentalism in Latin@ and Latin American Music," in *Experimentalisms in Practice: Music Perspectives from Latin America*, eds. Ana R. Alonso-Minutti, Eduardo Herrera, and Alejandro L. Madrid (New York: Oxford University Press, 2018), 10.

[11] Alonso-Minutti, Herrera, and Madrid, "The Practices of Experimentalism in Latin@ and Latin American Music," 3.

[12] Jennifer Iverson, *Electronic Inspirations: Technologies of the Cold War Musical Avant-Garde* (New York: Oxford University Press, 2018), 4.

8   CUBAN MUSIC COUNTERPOINTS

the neoclassical schools of composition of Paris, Spain, and New York, with local, national Cuban music elements.

By the end of the 1970s the experimental and avant-garde trends of the 1960s had nearly completely faded. In their place more accessible compositional idioms emerged, most of which included a renewed interest in local popular and folkloric musics as easily identifiable elements, and others that combined some of the local practices with techniques that some US-based music critics have attributed minimalist and postminimalist influences.[13] As discussed in chapter 5, this seemingly postmodern turn coincided with a time of increased globalization and foreign presence (through the renewed tourist industry and return of Cuban exiles to the island for family visits) and drastic political and economic changes. In employing the term "postmodern" I take into account how Cuban composers themselves, in particular Leo Brouwer, used the term to describe their work. In his essay "Música, folclor, contemporaneidad y postmodernismo" ("Music, folklore, contemporaneity, and postmodernism"),[14] Brouwer expanded upon how Cuban classical music could be categorized as postmodern, retroactively applied the term to works from the late 1960s, and, as I explain further in chapter 5, used Alejo Carpentier's concepts of *lo criollo* and *lo real maravilloso* to provide a Cuban epistemology for his and his peers' postmodern compositions. Because the term postmodernism helped Cubans composers translate their aesthetic approaches to the broader international classical music scene, I will use the term when discussing some of the works of the late 1970s and the 1980s. Cuban postmodernism in music is characterized by an eclectic use of sources, techniques, and media, often resulting in a collage or bricolage of sound sources, with multiple layers. In spite of the seemingly disparate origin of sources, most works have a clear form, usually binary, ternary, or rounded binary, that is articulated through returns of themes, timbres, or textures. Two other factors recur in these postmodern works: accessibility, wherein the works' sound is appealing or pleasing, not alienating, to listeners and audiences; and a ludic approach (could be humorous, a play on words and double-meaning, irony, satire, or parody) that correlates to the Cuban practice of *choteo*.[15] In a conference delivered in 1928, "Indagación del choteo" ("Investigation of the joke"), Jorge Mañach is one of the first Cuban intellectuals to probe the origins and nature of *choteo* (or Cuban wit and humor) as a Cuban habit, and provide a functional definition, stating that

---

[13] I would challenge notions that imply or overtly attribute the minimalist and postminimalist compositions of Steve Reich and fellow US composers as influences on Cuban composers.

[14] Leo Brouwer, "Música, folclor, contemporaneidad y postmodernismo," *Clave*, no. 13 (1989): 53–55.

[15] There are some overlaps with Kramer's categorization of postmodern musical practices, yet there are a few idiosyncratically Cuban elements that speak to international postmodern practices. Jonathan D. Kramer, "The Nature and Origins of Musical Postmodernism," *Current Musicology*, no. 66 (Spring 1999): 7–20.

"choteo—something familiar, small, and festive—is a form of relationship that we consider typically Cuban . . . it consists of 'taking nothing seriously' . . . 'turning everything into a joke' ['everything' and 'nothing' used hyperbolically] . . . an attitude erected into a habit, *choteo* does not take seriously anything that is generally taken seriously . . . a habit of disrespect, motivated by . . . a repugnance to all authority."[16] For Mañach, the basis of *choteo* stems from the *criollo* intermingling of cultural influences and practices from Southern Spain (Andalucía in particular) and Africa, making *choteo* a quintessentially Cuban practice. Humorous irreverence, although practiced by Cubans well before the postmodern turn in the West, coincides with Western postmodernist postures that rely on humor, satire, and irony to generate meaning and affect for performers and audiences.

From *Afrocubanismo* to *lo real maraviolloso*: Fernando Ortiz, Alejo Carpentier, and Cuban Intellectuals in the 1940s

This book begins in the early 1940s for several reasons. As Robin Moore and others have discussed, the 1920s and 1930s were dominated by the *Afrocubanista* aesthetic movement.[17] Although Amadeo Roldán and Alejandro García Caturla, the two composers associated with *Afrocubanismo*, never overtly labeled their approach as such, they were the leading figures in the Cuban classical music scene: their nationalist modernist compositional approach was categorized under the umbrella of *Afrocubanismo* by Alejo Carpentier in his seminal book *La música en Cuba* (1946) and all subsequent publications on Cuban music history replicate this chronological and aesthetic categorization. The untimely deaths of Amadeo Roldán and Alejandro García Caturla (in 1939 and 1940 respectively) left a void within the Cuban classical music scene that was quickly filled by Catalan-born José Ardévol. As I detail in the first chapter, these developments and other circumstances led to the formation of the first "group" of Cuban composers, the Grupo de Renovación Musical (the Grupo).

---

[16] "El choteo—cosa familiar, menuda y festiva—es una forma de relación que consideramos típicamente cubana . . . consiste en 'no tomar nada en serio' . . . 'tirarlo todo a relajo' . . . una actitud erigida en hábito [todo y nada se emplean hiperbolicamente] el choteo no toma en serio nada de lo que generalmente se tiene por serio . . . un habito de irrespetuosidad, motivado por . . . una repugnancia a toda autoridad." Jorge Mañach, *Indagación del choteo* (Barcelona: Editorial Linkgua, 2019), 12, 14, 15.

[17] Ramón Torres Zayas, "Afrocubanismo: algo más que una opción," *Comparative Cultural Studies—European and Latin American Perspectives* 7, no. 14 (March 15, 2022): 61–69; Belén Vega Pichaco, "La construcción de la música nueva en Cuba (1927–1946): del Afrocubanismo al neoclasicismo," *Revista de Musicología* 37, no. 2 (2014): 715–723; Robin D. Moore. *Nationalizing Blackness: Afrocubanismo and Artistic Revolution in Havana, 1920-1940* (Pittsburgh: University of Pittsburgh Press, 1998).

10 CUBAN MUSIC COUNTERPOINTS

In seminal works published and disseminated in the 1940s Fernando Ortiz and Alejo Carpentier outlined theories and terminology that explicated the development of Cuban and Latin American cultural identity, leaving an indelible mark on Cuban composers' approach to their craft and their political and cultural roles as Cuban artists. The title of this book, *Cuban Music Counterpoints*, is in part a nod to Ortiz's influential work *Contrapunteo Cubano del tabaco y el azúcar* (*Cuban Counterpoint: Tobacco and Sugar*, 1940), where he lays out for the first time his theory of transculturation in order to explain Cuban culture as a process of mutual influence between players from diverse racial and ethnic backgrounds. Yet my use of the term "counterpoint" in this book's title is also meant to evoke the compositional technique—a practice that was formative for young Cuban composers who had to master it as part of their composition curriculum, especially in the 1940s at the Conservatorio Municipal de La Habana under the tutelage of José Ardévol, who had a predilection for neoclassical compositional approaches—as a metaphor for how Cuban composers developed their own voices in relation to those of other actors in their artistic networks—or contrapuntal textures, to extend the metaphor—they created or in which they wished to participate. Another "counterpoint" I trace through the various case studies focuses on how composers strove for balance between the local and the so-called universal in their compositions and artistic networks.

I do not employ Ortiz's and Carpentier's theories in my own analysis of these composers' works and careers, but I do consider them essential for understanding why and how Cuban composers made certain aesthetic choices. Cuban composers were indelibly influenced by the writings of Ortiz and Carpentier, at times working with the two individuals as researchers and co-authors, and I would even argue that Ortiz and Carpentier would not have arrived at their cultural and aesthetic concepts without the influence of these young composers. In 1939 Fernando Ortiz gave a lecture titled "Los factores humanos de la cubanidad" ("The human factors of Cubanness") at the Universidad de La Habana, subsequently published in 1940 in *Revista Bimestre Cubana*. In the preface to a 2014 translation of Ortiz's original, João Felipe Gonçalves notes that the article "summarizes Ortiz's view that one could only understand Cuban culture by seeing it as a 'mestizaje of races, mestizaje of cultures' and by examining the various cultural elements that composed it. The text is thus a classic example of a Latin American anthropologist participating in the public imagination of nationhood based on a view of mestizaje."[18] Gonçalves asserts that "by using the culinary metaphor of the *ajiaco* (a typical Cuban stew made of several elements), by defining Cubanness as a process rather than an essence, and by distinguishing

---

[18] João Felipe Gonçalves, "The Ajiaco in Cuba and Beyond," *HAU: Journal of Ethnographic Theory* 4, no. 3 (December 1, 2014): 446.

INTRODUCTION 11

between Cuban culture and identity, Ortiz's conceptualization of cultural mixture may shed new light on processes occurring elsewhere."[19] Also in 1940, Ortiz published *Cuban Counterpoint: Tobacco and Sugar*, where, as Gonçalves adds, "Ortiz praised the tobacco industry for having fostered the most progressive—even revolutionary—factors in Cuban politics and for being based traditionally on small properties, national land ownership, and free labor. He contrasted this to the sugar economy, which he depicted as having a lasting conservative effect on the country due to its association with large estates, foreign capital, slavery, and the intense exploitation of labor."[20] Most significantly, in *Cuban Counterpoint* Ortiz introduced the term "transculturation," which would influence the fields of anthropology, sociology, and beyond as an alternative to the term "acculturation." With the term "transculturation" Ortiz critiqued the pervasive theories that posited that in moments of cultural encounter one culture assumes the traits of a dominant one, losing its essence. He argued that the process was multidirectional, that cultures that come into contact influence and transform each other. As influential as the term "transculturation" has been in international academic circles, within Cuba the term provided the theoretical grounding artists and intellectuals needed to justify their aesthetic choices. As late as the 1980s, as I discuss in the fifth chapter, Cuban composers deployed the term to explicate their omnivorous stylistic and aesthetic practices. "Transculturation" was an efficacious term and theory that allowed Cuban artists to play with artistic influences from abroad while still claiming to be cultivating an aesthetic grounded on Cuban identity and values. Ortiz's activities and publications are far too numerous to delve into in the space of this introduction,[21] yet it is also worth emphasizing his work in the field of anthropological research, which included several studies in Afro-Cuban religious musical and dance practices many of which he conducted with the assistance of Argeliers León, a composer and member of the Grupo who would go on to establish the field of musicology as an academic discipline in the island and train future generations of music researchers.[22]

Alejo Carpentier, one of the most influential writers in twentieth-century Latin America, also contributed to arts criticism—in particular music criticism (including the first book-length account of Cuban music history)—and coined the concepts of *lo real maravilloso* and *lo barroco americano* to describe the idiosyncratically Latin American traits of culture and art produced in the Western

[19] Gonçalves, "The Ajiaco in Cuba and Beyond," 447.
[20] Gonçalves, "The Ajiaco in Cuba and Beyond," 448.
[21] Robin D. Moore, "Preface," in *Fernando Ortiz on Music: Selected Writing on Afro-Cuban Culture*, ed. Robin D. Moore (Philadelphia: Temple University Press, 2018), viii.
[22] León loathed the term ethnomusicology.

12 CUBAN MUSIC COUNTERPOINTS

Hemisphere.[23] Through *lo real maravilloso* Carpentier aimed to explicate literary works in which the extraordinary does not need to be either beautiful or ugly, but can also be novel, unheard of: *lo real maravilloso* has the capacity to astonish by breaking away from preexisting models. Carpentier's article "Lo real maravilloso de América," first appeared in the newspaper *El Nacional* in 1948, and as the prologue to his novel *El reino de este mundo* a year later. For Carpentier, *lo real maravilloso* refers to specific events in Latin American history and ways of life that are surprising and that feed into the literary and artistic works of Latin American writers and artists; it "distinguishes it [Latin American art] from the rest of the world, and Europe in particular."[24] The marvelous "has to emerge from an unexpected alteration of reality . . . of an amplification of the scales and categories of reality, perceived with particular intensity in virtue of an exaltation of the spirit . . . [which] presupposes faith."[25] For Carpentier this was a unique aspect of Latin American culture because this faith and belief in the magical had been extinguished in Europe, while it was still present in Latin America.[26] It was Carpentier's theorization on a quintessentially Latin American faith and belief in the magical that allowed Cuban composers to delve into avant-garde and experimental musical practices while maintaining a connection to the local, as I show through the examples explored in chapter 3. Later in Caracas in 1975, he developed the concept of *lo barroco americano* to refer to a Latin American aesthetic preference for juxtaposing objects from various styles and epochs, items that seem to oppose or contradict one another, resulting in an artistic object that represents the height of artistic expression, an aesthetic approach that has been labeled as bricolage by several other cultural theorists.[27] Compositions from the

---

[23] Elsewhere, I have discussed in more detail Carpentier's role as an intellectual and his connections to the Parisian artistic and intellectual scenes. Marysol Quevedo, "Cubanness, Innovation, and Politics in Art Music in Cuba, 1942–1979" (Ph.D. diss, Indiana University, 2016), 60–62.

[24] "Sus teorías se centran en lo que define la cultura latinoamericana, y lo que la distingue del resto del mundo y de Europa en particular. Aunque hayan tenido una importancia sustancial, la legitimidad de ambos conceptos se ha puesto en duda. No queda muy claro, sin embargo, en qué exactamente consiste lo problemático." Victor Wahlström, "Lo real maravilloso y lo barroco americano" (M.A. Thesis, Medier vid Lunds Universitet, 2012), 4.

[25] "Lo maravilloso, según el parecer de Carpentier, no es algo que se puede hacer aparecer por trucos mágicos poco sofisticados, sino tiene que surgir de una 'inesperada alteración de la realidad, de una iluminación inhabitual [. . .], de una ampliación de las escalas y categorías de la realidad, percibidas con particular intensidad en virtud de una exaltación del espíritu' Además, y esto es unpunto fundamental en el prólogo, 'una sensación de lo maravilloso presupone una fe.'" Wahlström, "Lo real maravilloso y lo barroco americano," 19.

[26] "Carpentier propone que los elementos que gracias a una fe en lo mágico se pueden calificar de *maravillosos* han desaparecido por completo en Europa, mientras que abundan en la historia reciente de Latinoamérica, e incluso en su realidad presente. Esto se puede ver, según explica el autor, en los bailes de la santería cubana, que siguen teniendo un carácter mágico . . . En resumen, afirma Carpentier: 'América está muy lejos de haber agotado su caudal de mitologías.'" Alejo Carpentier, *Narrativa completa. Vol. 1* (Barcelona: RBA Coleccionables, 2006), 373, quoted in Ibid., 20.

[27] Alexis Márquez Rodríguez, "Alejo Carpentier: Teorías del barroco y de lo real maravilloso," *Nuevo Texto Crítico* 3, no. 1 (1990): 96.

INTRODUCTION   13

1960s and 1970s, discussed in chapters 3 and 4 respectively, possess many traits that align with Carpentier's concept of *lo barroco americano*.

Moreover, Leonardo Padura Fuentes has argued that Carpentier's preparation for writing and publishing *La música en Cuba* was crucial for the development of his concept of *lo real maravilloso*. I would add that this experience must have also influenced his development of *lo barroco americano*.[28] According to Padura Fuentes, Carpentier's detailed and deep research in Cuban archives and sources from cathedrals—church minutes and documents, in particular from the seventeenth through the nineteenth century—in which he had direct contact with Cuban historical sources, was not only important and influential in the development of his narrative works and style, but it was "a highly revealing and key piece in terms of the evolution of Carpentier's conception of Cubanness and Americanness, and in his comprehension of the two essential factors in his vision of continental reality."[29] Padura Fuentes goes a step further by connecting Carpentier's concepts to the development of a particularly Cuban national identity: "the first sketches of 'national distinction' and of what might be the essential element of a marvelous reality exactly as he would understand it: the determining presence of our peculiar *mestizaje* and the transculturation process of which our identities are the result."[30] Thus, *mestizaje* (the racial and cultural mixing of European and indigenous elements) and transculturation, both terms that focus on process rather than end result, became central to Cuban intellectual discourses on the formation of Cuban national identity and to the present discussion of Cuban art music throughout the following decades. As ideal as this conceptualization of *mestizaje* as ongoing process is, in practice, however, it has been deployed by members of the intelligentsia to silence ongoing discussions of racial difference and discrimination in order to project an image of a harmonious national culture in various Latin American contexts.[31]

---

[28] Wahlström, "Lo real maravilloso y lo barroco americano," 22–23.

[29] "Una pieza clave y altamente reveladora en cuanto a la evolución de las concepciones de cubanía y americanidad del autor, y en su comprensión de dos factores esenciales en su visión de la realidad continental." Leonardo Padura Fuentes, *Un camino de medio siglo: Alejo Carpentier y la narrativa de lo real maravilloso* (Miramar, Playa: Ediciones Cubanas, 2016), 117.

[30] "Los primeros esbozos de una 'distinción nacional' . . . lo que tal vez sea el elemento esencial de una realidad maravillosa tal y como él la entendería: la presencia determinante de nuestro peculiar mestizaje y el proceso de transculturación del cual son fruto nuestras identidades." Padura Fuentes, *Un camino de medio siglo*, 119.

[31] Joshua Lund has argued that the "mestizo state" in post-1910 Mexico is a modernity-driven political entity that conflates mixed-raced identity with Western modernity. As Mexico emrged from Spanish colonial rule into an independent nation, intellectuals and statesmen used the mestizo "as the symbolic protagonist of a new project of state formation." The obsession with mestizaje "would be brought to its greatest intensity with the publication of José Vasconcelos's megalomaniacal thesis about the 'cosmic race.'" Joshua Lund, *Mestizo State: Reading Race in Modern Mexico* (Minneapolis: University of Minnesota Press, 2012), ix–xv.

14 CUBAN MUSIC COUNTERPOINTS

Carpentier was also musically trained as a pianist, and was greatly influenced by the work of Fernando Ortiz. He conducted extensive archival work at various Cuban cathedrals, churches, and other colonial institutions between 1939 and 1943, as well as ethnographic fieldwork observing Lucumí and Abakuá rituals, aided by Fernando Ortiz. Carpentier's theories of *lo real maravilloso* and *lo barroco americano* were not only guided by his knowledge and experience with Spanish and Latin American literatures, but more profoundly by his experience and research of Cuban music. It is not a coincidence that Carpentier's seminal article, "Lo real maravilloso en América" ("The real marvelous in America"), appeared two years after the publication of *La música en Cuba*, a musicological volume that influenced his cultural and literary theories. These various interests—music, literature, and archival and ethnographic research— were matched by a gift for storytelling. The narrative of Cuban music history he outlined in *La música en Cuba* and his music criticism weighed heavily on composers in Cuban music circles during the 1950s, 1960s, and 1970s, as they replicated his narratives in later volumes.[32] Through *lo real maravilloso* Carpentier called for Latin American artists to find an individual voice, to study the European models in depth, analyzing them to gain technique, and to search and find a literary voice independent from European models. In addition to his work as a musicologist and novelist, Carpentier was one of the most influential music critics in Cuba and Latin America. Even when he lived in exile (in Paris from 1928 to 1939 and in Caracas from 1945 to 1959), he penned critical pieces for the arts and music columns of several Cuban periodicals, shaping the musical tastes of their cosmopolitan readers and influencing Havana's musical scene.

Notes on Archival Access and Research, Methodological Limits, and Lines of Inquiry for Future Research

Archives have been my guiding force throughout this project. The materials preserved, collected, organized, and made available to researchers at the most accessible and authoritative archives on the island reveal the individuals, institutions, and compositions that archivists and librarians consider worthy of occupying such scarce space and attention within these institutions. In Cuba, like in any other modern state, archives are repositories of power, they are made through power and in turn legitimize the power of those who constitute it.[33] My decisions to focus on certain composers, organizations, institutions, works, and

---

[32] José Ardévol, *Introducción a Cuba: La música* (Havana: Instituto del Libro, 1969); and Edgardo Martín, *Panorama histórico de la música en Cuba* (Havana: Universidad de La Habana, 1972).

[33] Francis X. Blouin Jr., and William G. Rosenberg, *Processing the Past: Contesting Authority in History and the Archives* (New York: Oxford University Press, 2011), 25.

INTRODUCTION 15

events (such as festivals) stems from their privileged place in the archives. In a way, this is as much a history of what has been deemed worthy of preserving for posterity, what has been regarded as national patrimony as it is about the individuals, music, and institutions themselves. There were certain types of information that were difficult to corroborate, such as salaries and the structures or procedures by which state institutions kept track of composers' work and employment; I chose to focus on how aesthetics and identity politics intersect with the artistic networks as traced by the archival documents, while the everyday, on-the-ground lives of individuals are largely unexplored in this volume, a compelling research topic for future projects.

Archival institutions in Cuba have to contend with a constellation of precarious situations, from a shortage of space to a lack of archiving materials (acid free paper and boxes), and from inadequate conditions for the control of humidity and temperature in a tropical climate to the lack of a robust digital infrastructure to catalog and digitize materials. In spite of the many challenges local musicologists, librarians, information technicians, and archivists contend with on a daily basis, they are eager to make their materials accessible to researchers, often apologizing for the conditions in which some of these materials are found. Thanks to these individuals (whom I thank in my acknowledgements), I consulted thousands of items, from published and manuscript scores to concert programs, from pedagogical materials to personal correspondence. As with any record, the archives only tell us a partial story, one that is shaped by what individuals considered worthy of saving in their personal archives in the first place, and by how their inheritors and the tropical climate have treated these materials over the years. In addition to the special collections held at these archives, journalistic print materials became another rudder for my analysis. Through these print publications, Cuban composers and music critics themselves guided the activities and tastes of music institutions, composers, and audiences; they promoted certain musics (while lambasting others) for their aesthetic proposals as well as their political significance. A looming question that I have yet to answer is what was the audience composition and public reception of avant-garde and experimental works. Most of the music reviews that appeared in public media emphasize the diverse class make up of audiences (housewives, factory workers, teachers, and doctors), and offer glowing reports of the quality of the music and performances; most of the mass media music criticism wasn't very critical as it was guided by the very composers whose works were being performed. But an attempt to attain information on audience reception via interviews presented another set of challenges. Although in my initial field trips to Cuba I did interview some composers, I found their memories of what took place forty to fifty years prior as idealist and nostalgic at best and rather murky and inconsistent at worst. As Kepa Artaraz has found through her experience in

16 CUBAN MUSIC COUNTERPOINTS

collecting oral histories of the Cuban intellectual elite,[34] the memories of events that took place decades ago, as told by my interlocutors, are often contradicted by the archival materials. I greatly value the testimonies of these composers; however, I found that basing my analysis on them necessitates a broader set of methodological and theoretical tools and would result in an entirely different project focused on memory and nostalgia—one I wish to embark on in the near future—but which is beyond the scope of this volume.

Another limitation of this volume is the cursory mention of race and gender as factors in the development of the classical music scene in Cuba. One of the reasons for this is the general lack of overt discussion of questions of race and gender in the archival and periodical sources. This is not to say that there were (are) no race and/or gender based discriminatory practices in Cuba; I—and other scholars—attribute this lack of discussion to a broad post-1959 attitude that the Revolution had "solved" many of the racial and gender inequalities.[35] Throughout the chapters, I note composers' race and/or gender when it is relevant, but many of the individuals themselves would resist being categorized through such terms, a similar attitude that Alejandro L. Madrid has noted in his biography of Tania León.[36] We do see an increase in the participation of women composers in the 1940s and then again in the 1980s; and beginning in the 1970s we see more composers who are phenotypically black, or who could be considered a "person of color" by US standards, gain access to music education and professional opportunities than in previous decades. There are several musicology theses and articles on Cuban women composers, however, most can only be found in Cuban libraries.[37] A more detailed study on the intersection of race and gender in the Cuban classical music scene would reveal an even more nuanced and complex picture than the one presented in this volume.

Two other lines of inquiry that are not explored are the pedagogical practices in Cuban conservatories, music schools, and arts institutes, and transnational comparisons to classical music scenes in other Caribbean and Latin America countries. Although many of the music education institutions are mentioned in relation to the careers of various composers, a discussion of the precise curriculum and repertory falls outside the purview of the present study. The José

[34] Kepa Artaraz, "Constructing Identities in a Contested Setting: Cuba's Intellectual Elite during and after the Revolution," *Oral History* 45, no. 2 (2017): 50–59.

[35] For further discussion on these topics see Johnnetta B. Cole, "Race Toward Equality: The Impact of the Cuban Revolution on Racism," *The Black Scholar* 11, no. 8 (1980): 2–24; and Sheryl L. Lutjens, "Reading between the Lines: Women, the State, and Rectification in Cuba," *Latin American Perspectives* 22, no. 2 (1995): 100–124.

[36] Alejandro L. Madrid, *Tania León's Stride: A Polyrhythmic Life* (University of Illinois Press, 2021), 2.

[37] See for example Mirelys Bringuez Acosta, "De mujeres y musica, algo mas que componer . . ." (Thesis, Instituto Superios de Arte, 2008); Alina Castro, "Acerca del estilo de creacion en la obra de Gisela Hernández" (Thesis, Instituto Superios de Arte, 1991).

INTRODUCTION 17

Ardévol Collection at the Museo Nacional de la Música Cubana offers valuable resources to researchers who wish to delve into the planning and operation of the music education system in Cuba, in particular after 1959, since Ardévol spearheaded the efforts to establish the Escuela Nacional de Arte (ENA) and the Instituto Superior de Arte (ISA). Many readers will be intrigued and curious about the involvement of Eastern European musicians and professors in the music education system in Cuba after 1959. The short answer is that yes, many music professors were recruited from socialist Eastern European countries to teach in Cuban music schools and to perform with the Orquesta Sinfónica Nacional de Cuba (OSN, Cuban National Symphony Orchestra); but their pedagogical methods and what repertory they used to teach music theory, music history, and performance lies beyond the goals of this book. Similarly, comparing the Cuban case to classical music scenes in neighboring countries presents a challenge, when many of those other local histories remain largely unexplored. With the exception of Mexico, Colombia, Chile, Argentina, and Brazil—some of the studies in these areas are mentioned below—there is a general dearth of critical studies of local classical music scenes, a basic barrier for cross-national comparisons. As future scholars engage with these topics, collaborative and co-authored research will illuminate the similarities and differences between countries.

Throughout the book I employ several methodological approaches, including: musical stylistic analysis; reception studies of periodical and printed materials; close readings of archival materials, such as official memoranda and private correspondence; as well as contextualizing these works and the composers' activities within the political milieu in which they were created. Due to the entangled nature of these networks, compositions, aesthetic and political values, institutions, and individuals, this diversified methodological approach is further informed by network theory, microhistory, and cultural studies more broadly. Beginning with Carpentier's *La música en Cuba* (1946), Cuban musicology has since continued to develop through various generations of scholars with a wide variety of methodological and theoretical approaches. My work is entirely indebted to this tradition and the indefatigable archival and musicological work of local Cuban scholars in institutions throughout the island, and would not be possible without the existing publications on Cuban composers and organizations. These institutions include the Dirección de Música of Casa de las Américas, the Centro de Investigación y Desarrollo de la Música Cubana, the Museo Nacional de la Música Cubana, and the Gabinete de Patrimonio Musical Esteban Salas.[38] My work is in dialogue with

---

[38] The individuals who work at these institutions and who have helped me throughout more than a decade are mentioned in the acknowledgements.

their publications, and it is also written from the perspective of a Puerto Rican musicologist who has received her training in US academic institutions. Here I would like to acknowledge the imbalance of power and access to resources, as I am able to travel to and from Cuba with relative ease in comparison to Cuban scholars who may want to conduct research outside of Cuba. As a Puerto Rican woman, my experience conducting research in Cuba needs to be understood through my intersectional identity and positionality. Born in Puerto Rico, I am a US citizen, a double-edged sword as I benefit from the rights and privileges of US citizenship while also always being in the position of second-class citizen in a white Anglo-Saxon male dominated country. I was born to a middle-class family and received a classical music education modeled after the Paris conservatoires starting at age three. My family has supported my music education and academic career at every stage, and that is an extremely privileged position to be working from. At the same time, as a Latina working in the United States, I also face numerous challenges when implicit biases prevent colleagues and students from seeing me as their intellectual equal. In the Cuban context, being Puerto Rican immediately elicited feelings of kinship and understanding. In post-1959 Cuba, Puerto Rico has served as an example of the continued colonial projects of the United States, of "imperialismo yanqui" ("Yankee imperialism"). Cubans who are committed to the socialist-revolutionary cause are sympathetic to the plight of Puerto Ricans as colonial subjects. Moreover, the slogan "Cuba y Puerto Rico son, de un pájaro las dos alas" ("Cuba and Puerto Rico are, two wings of the same bird") was often quoted by Cubans upon meeting me.[39] During one interview, one composer shared that if things ever got bad for me in the United States, I had a place at his home where I could stay. I also have the advantage of presenting as phenotypically white for Caribbean standards, which makes it easier to navigate certain social contexts. All of these conditions—in addition to what I believe is a general attitude of mutual respect and curiosity—seem to have facilitated my interactions with librarians, archivists, musicologists, composers, and musicians in Cuba. The institutions, their directors, librarians, archivists, and staff were generous in granting me access and support to conduct my research. Some individuals within and outside of Cuba may not agree fully or at all with my interpretation of the works and the events that I focus on throughout this book. One of my aims is to facilitate conversations where multiple viewpoints and stories can emerge.

---

[39] This phrase is from a poem by Puerto Rican poet and independence advocate Lola Rodríguez de Tió, which appeared in her 1893 collection *Mi Libro de Cuba: Poesías,* published in Havana by Imprenta Moderna.

INTRODUCTION 19

Cuban Classical Music Research in a Global Context

In addition to the networks Cuban composers nurtured, this book also places these developments in dialogue with existing research on musics of the Americas, Eastern Europe, and the Cold War, as well as those dealing with Cuban music and Cuban studies more broadly. This volume contributes to the growing body of scholarship on Pan American and Cold War diplomacy as explored by Amy C. Beal, Carol Hess, Danielle Fosler-Lussier, Jennifer Campbell, Stephanie Stallings, and Anne Searcy, among others.[40] Similarly, the recent work by Lisa Jakelski and Lisa Cooper Vest on the Polish avant-garde, with which Cuban composers heavily engaged in the 1960s and 1970s, deeply informs this book's accounting for the thriving musical avant-garde scene within a socialist context.[41] One of the key fields of recent scholarship upon which this volume builds is art music in the Soviet Union after Stalin's death (1953). Cuban composers, especially after 1959, had to contend with the state of art music production in the post-Stalinist Soviet Union, the Thaw, for, as Peter Schmelz notes, "unofficial art music engaged with the most pertinent transformations in Soviet aesthetics and society during the 1950s and 1960s."[42] During the 1950s and 1960s, young Soviet composers sought to engage with the avant-garde techniques of Western composers who had been off-limits during Stalin's rule. As Schmelz adds, they were eager to "catch-up" with their Western counterparts, "embarrassed by the belatedness" of their encounter with such techniques and they were able to produce such works thanks to a small group of performers who championed their music in the "unofficial concert subculture" and an avid audience seeking to hear new works.[43] In contrast to the purpose or motivations—as confrontation with or escape from the official Soviet artistic apparatus—behind Soviet composers' engagement with avant-garde techniques during the Thaw, Cuban composers who employed similar techniques worked within the official state cultural institutions and promoted avant-garde and experimental music as socialist-revolutionary.

---

[40] Danielle Fosler-Lussier, *Music in America's Cold War Diplomacy* (Berkeley, CA: University of California Press, 2015); Carol A. Hess, *Representing the Good Neighbor: Music, Difference, and the Pan American Dream* (New York: Oxford University Press, 2014); Stephanie N. Stallings, "Collective Difference: The Pan-American Association of Composers and Pan-American Ideology in Music, 1925–1945" (Ph.D. diss, The Florida State University, 2009); Jennifer L. Campbell, "Shaping Solidarity: Music, Diplomacy, and Inter-American Relations, 1936–1946," (Ph.D. diss, University of Connecticut, 2010); Amy C. Beal, *New Music, New Allies: American Experimental Music in West Germany from the Zero Hour to Reunification* (Berkeley: University of California Press, 2006); Anne Searcy, *Ballet in the Cold War: A Soviet-American Exchange* (New York, NY: Oxford University Press, 2020).

[41] Vest, *Awangarda*; Lisa Jakelski, *Making New Music in Cold War Poland: The Warsaw Autumn Festival, 1956–1968* (Oakland, CA: University of California Press, 2017).

[42] Peter John Schmelz, *Such Freedom, If Only Musical: Unofficial Soviet Music during the Thaw* (Oxford; New York: Oxford University Press, 2009), 4.

[43] Schmelz, *Such Freedom, If Only Musical*, 6.

20 CUBAN MUSIC COUNTERPOINTS

But Cuban composers didn't limit their artistic networks to socialist Eastern Europe, they also projected themselves as the leaders in Latin American leftist avant-garde circles. Alonso-Minutti's ongoing work on Mario Lavista and the Mexican avant-garde and experimental music scene of the 1960s and 1970s offers a complementary narrative to the events, composers, and works discussed in this book.[44] Alonso-Minutti argues for an examination of Lavista's early musical compositions as a search for a place within the international avant-garde as well as a response to the nationalist works by Mexican composers of the preceding decades. As such, it parallels the aesthetic and compositional approaches of Cuban composers discussed in the third and fourth chapters of this book, albeit within the specific political and social context of 1960s and 1970s Mexico. Another significant contribution to the field of Latin American avant-garde music of this period is Daniela Fugellie's work on the influence of the Vienna School (from Schoenberg and twelve-tone technique to serialism) in Brazil, Argentina, and Chile, and Luigi Nono's Latin American connections.[45] Eduardo Herrera similarly examines how cultural diplomacy and philanthropy intersected in Cold War US-Latin American music through his work on the Centro Latinoamericano de Altos Estudios Musicales (CLAEM) at the Torcuato Di Tella Institute in Buenos Aires, Argentina. As Herrera demonstrates, the CLAEM served as a crucial point of convergence for Latin American composers beginning in 1962, a particularly important node in the hemispheric network of avant-garde music composition. Like Herrera's work, this book also "contributes to the destabilization of narratives of art music that place Latin America on the peripheries of that tradition."[46] However, many of the nodes in the regional and global classical music networks that I trace through Cuban music case studies offer an alternative narrative to the one Herrera posits: while in the CLAEM's case avant-garde musical practices were promoted by US–Argentine philanthropy and the political, cultural, social, and economic elite of both countries, in Cuba the avant-garde aligned itself with the socialist-revolutionary cause, receiving support from the State, striving to bring avant-garde art to the masses, and supporting the political and social causes of the global left and Third World. Another salient set of contributions with which this volume dialogs is

---

[44] Ana Alonso Minutti, "Resonances of Sound, Text, and Image in the Music of Mario Lavista" (Ph.D. diss, University of California, Davis, 2008); Alonso Minutti, "Forging a Cosmopolitan Ideal: Mario Lavista's Early Music," *Latin American Music Review / Revista de Música Latinoamericana* 35, no. 2 (2014): 169–196; Luisa Vilar Payá and Ana Alonso Minutti, "Estrategias de diferenciación en la composición musical: Mario Lavista y el México de fines de los sesenta y comienzos de los setenta," *Revista Argentina de Musicología* 12–13 (2012): 267–290.

[45] Daniela Fugellie, "'Musiker Unserer Zeit': Internationale Avantgarde, Migration Und Wiener Schule in Südamerika" (Ph.D. diss, Berlin University of the Arts, 2018); "Las relaciones de Luigi Nono con los compositores latinoamericanos de vanguardia," *Boletín Música*, no. 35 (2013): 3–29.

[46] Eduardo Herrera, *Elite Art Worlds: Philanthropy, Latin Americanism, and Avant-Garde Music* (Oxford University Press, 2020), 3.

INTRODUCTION   21

the ongoing work by Alejandro L. Madrid on the art music of Mexico and Latin America. The time periods and aesthetic trends he has explored throughout his oeuvre are wide-ranging, from modernism and national identity in *Sounds of the Modern Nation*, to anti-biography and experimental music of Julian Carrillo and his most recent biography of Tania León.[47] My research is deeply indebted to his broadening of the methodological and theoretical tools for analyzing musics of Latin America and its diaspora.

In the last three decades, much of the musicological scholarship on the music and composers addressed throughout this book has been produced not only in Cuba but also by scholars working from Spain. Their research covers a wide array of topics: biographies of the members of Grupo composers (by Yurima Blanco); cataloging work on concert programming, radio broadcasts, and recordings (by Ailer Pérez); Cuban composers who seemingly worked on the margins of the state cultural institutions (such as Lilian González Moreno's work on Federico Smith); electroacoustic music (by Victoria Eli Rodríguez, Ileana Güeche, and Fernando Rodríguez Alpízar); and Cuban composers of the diaspora (by Iván César Morales Flores). This volume puts their writings in dialog with one another and into the context of the networks explored throughout this book. González Moreno's work on Federico Smith in particular points to some of the lesser acknowledged figures in the Cuban classical music scene discussed in this book. Through this book I do not attempt to paint a complete picture of musical life in Cuba from 1940 to 1991, an endeavor that would take up several volumes. My intent is to show how the most prominent composers accrued and used cultural capital in local and international networks of classical music making, and how these networks changed due to political and aesthetic shifts. Many composers and stories remain untold; others have been discussed by other scholars.[48] This book is also Havana-centric, given the city's significance as the island's political, economic, and cultural center. The better funded and state-supported ensembles and academic and cultural institutions operate out of Havana. Future studies on the classical music scenes of Matanzas, Santiago, and other cities throughout the island will reveal the complexity and variety of musical activity in Cuba.

---

[47] Alejandro L. Madrid, *Sounds of the Modern Nation: Music, Culture, and Ideas in Post-Revolutionary Mexico* (Philadelphia: Temple University Press, 2008); *Tania León's Stride: A Polyrhythmic Life* (University of Illinois Press, 2021); *In Search of Julián Carrillo and Sonido 13* (New York: Oxford University Press, 2015).

[48] Belén Vega Pichaco, *Ni la lira, ni el bongo . . .: La construcción de la música nueva en Cuba desde la órbita de Musicalia* (Granada: Editorial Comares, 2021); Victoria Eli Rodríguez, Elena Torres, and Belén Vega Pichaco, *Música y construcción de identidades: poéticas, diálogos y utopías en Latinoamérica y España* (Madrid: Sociedad Española de Musicología, 2018); Ailer Pérez Gómez, *Música académica contemporánea cubana: catálogo de difusión (1961–1990)* (Havana, Cuba: Ediciones Centro de Investigación y Desarrollo de la Música Cubana, 2011); and Yurima Blanco, "Impronta del compositor cubano: Hilario González en la cultura venezolana (1947–1960)," *Boletín Música*, no. 50 (December 2018): 79–113.

22   CUBAN MUSIC COUNTERPOINTS

Cuban Music Counterpoints also intersects with Cuban music and Cuban studies. Scholars of Cuban folk and popular music have focused on genres and artists that rose to fame before the Revolution (such as Ernesto Lecuona and Celia Cruz) or left Cuba, marking a strong before-and-after-1959 division in historiography. Few scholars outside of Cuba have focused on artists who stayed in Cuba and even fewer on those who participated in the classical music scene.[49] Cuban studies scholars in various disciplines (literature, history, anthropology) have focused on literature, film, visual arts, and ballet, providing compelling counterexamples in other artistic fields, as discussed in Yael Prizant's *Cuba Inside Out: Revolution and Contemporary Theater* (2014), Hector Amaya's *Screening Cuba: Film Criticism as Political Performance during the Cold War* (2010), and Sujatha Fernandes's *Cuba Represent: Cuban Arts, State Power, and the Making of New Revolutionary Cultures* (2006). This book offers a classical music counterpoint to these existing works and serves as a foundation for further studies not only on twentieth-century Cuban classical music, but also on Latin American classical music more broadly. *Cuban Music Counterpoints* highlights the tensions between world powers and so-called peripheral nations; it decenters dominant narratives that present individuals from the Third World as passive recipients of products and ideas from the center; and demonstrates how these composers deployed their agency and found ways not only to survive, but to thrive amid constantly shifting political circumstances.

Although I strive to challenge and problematize a chronological narrative throughout this book, the activities of composers and cultural promoters (what in Cuba and other Latin American countries is often referred to as "gestores culturales") revealed certain trends or tendencies that marked each of the five decades covered in this volume. Granted, when I say "each decade" I do not mean precise beginnings and endings to each trend within the delimitations of a ten-year span; some of these tendencies began before a decade's end and they all certainly overlap and did not vanish from one decade to the next. Moreover, the trends I identify cannot be applied to all creative individuals or institutions, they merely help conceptualize each decade through fifty years of musical and political events. I identify the 1940s as a period of "maturation," as most of the individuals who were to become the key players in the Cuban cultural scene in the 1950s and 1960s were students at the Conservatorio Municipal de La Habana and members of the Grupo. Within these two institutions, as well as several others discussed in chapter 1, these composers received focused training that

---

[49]   Robin D. Moore, *Music and Revolution: Cultural Change in Socialist Cuba* (Berkeley: University of California Press, 2006) is the first English language monograph to deal with post-1959 Cuban music in Cuba, and focuses on folk and popular music practices.

INTRODUCTION   23

emphasized a neoclassical approach and they were in constant dialogue with their counterparts in the United States.

By the 1950s, several of the members of this group of young composers who had spent the 1940s honing their skills became involved in politically leftist groups; therefore, I use the term "radicalization" to best describe some of the processes that took place throughout this decade. Many of the composers active in the Grupo were founding members and in leadership roles of the SCNT, an organization that was an incubator for the cultural agendas and institutions of post-1959 Cuba, as I discuss in further detail in chapter 2. The works from this period were performed in concerts and other events hosted by the SCNT and reflect an overt employment of Cuban folk and popular music elements incorporated with neoclassical forms and modernist harmonic language, a sort of reconciliation of the *Afrocubanista* trends of the 1920s and 1930s and the stricter neoclassicism of the 1940s.

In the third chapter I explore how composers and music institutions changed and adapted during the 1960s, a decade characterized by "experimentation." Just as the Cuban revolutionary-turned-socialist state experimented with economic, social, educational, and political reforms, so did composers and artists. Depending on the art form, some artists had more freedom to experiment aesthetically than others; due to classical instrumental music's lack of semantic stability, classical composers suffered less repression, censorship, and persecution than film makers, visual artists, novelists, and poets. A small group of composers succeeded in promoting experimental music as both socialist and revolutionary, accruing and wielding significant cultural capital. In the 1960s Cuban composers were also forced to abandon many of the connections with US composers and music circles due to the US-imposed embargo and internal pressures to distance themselves from US influences, turning to music festivals and composers in Eastern Europe as new nodes in their international music network. Paradoxically, non-Soviet Eastern European connections (in particular Poland) kept Cuban composers informed of developments in the United States and Western Europe.

In the fourth chapter, I delve into how artists struggled to adapt to a constantly shifting political and cultural landscape. Increasing political and economic pressures from Moscow on Havana and consequently from Havana to all national cultural institutions meant that artists had to contend with demands from various factions. Some institutions jumped at the opportunity to cultivate foreign ties, as I demonstrate through the case study of Casa de las Américas's Encuentro de Música Latinoamericana of 1972. Some individuals continued to experiment through works for piano, exemplified in this chapter by Leo Brouwer's *Sonata pian e forte* and Harold Gramatges's *Móvil I*. There was also a proliferation of festivals, *encuentros*, and *jornadas* intended to celebrate

24   CUBAN MUSIC COUNTERPOINTS

regional and international musical cooperation, much like the political and economic agreements forged by the Cuban state with other socialist nations. The festivals serve as a window into the kinds of relationships Cuban composers cultivated during these years. Although festivals were to a great degree products of the political-economic and diplomatic connections that the Cuban state invested in, they also reflect how Cuban composers wanted to present themselves to the world. Most notably, the 1970s began with a five-year period of artistic censorship and persecution known as the *quinquenio gris* (the five-year gray period), which affected all areas of cultural production in Cuba through increased centralization, institutionalization, and, according to some critics, even Sovietization. Beginning in the late 1960s and culminating in 1975 with the establishment of a Ministry of Culture, the Cuban Consejo Nacional de Cultura (CNC, National Culture Council) oversaw the centralization of cultural activities, dictating a Cuban bent of socialist realism that led to official censorship and unofficial self-censorship among the Cuban intellectual class. Ambrosio Fornet coined the term *quinquenio gris* to refer to the years 1971–1975, but in reality, he noted that the repressive and divisive measures against intellectuals were already underway in the 1960s. As Forent put it in his seminal 2007 lecture and essay, "Socialist realism—literature as pedagogy and hagiography, methodologically oriented toward creating 'positive heroes' and the strategic absence of antagonistic conflicts in 'among the people'—produced in us, my petit bourgeois friends and I, the same reaction someone experiences when a fly is found in the glass of milk."[50] Forent continued, "Socialist realism was not 'intrinsically evil,' what was intrinsically evil was the imposition of this formula in the USSR, where what could have been a school, one more literary and artistic current, suddenly became the mandatory official doctrine ... what we saw was that under that rigid and precarious artistic guidance model the line between art, education, propaganda and advertising was becoming blurred."[51] As I will discuss in further detail in the fourth chapter, this period of repression eventually abated after 1976 with the establishment of a Ministry of Culture and a renewed sense of artistic commitment to the revolutionary-socialist cause through nationalist symbols and a gradual attempt to rectify the extreme intellectual repression of the first half of the decade through rehabilitation of some of the intellectuals who had been blacklisted and/or persecuted.

In the fifth and final chapter I examine a series of developments in Cuban electroacoustic music production beginning in 1979. The effects of globalization and emerging postmodernist theories from Europe (theories that validated aesthetic

---

[50] Ambrosio Fornet, "El quinquenio gris: revisitando el término," *Revista Criterios* (January 2007); translated by Alicia Barraqué Ellison and others in *Translating Cuba*, https://translatingcuba.com/the-five-grey-years-revisiting-the-term-ambrosio-fornet/.

[51] Ibid.

INTRODUCTION 25

practices Cuban artists had been employing for decades prior to European theorizations of postmodernism) impacted how Cuban composers approached their craft, how audiences listened to classical music, and how composers engaged with audiences through their compositions. These shifts in aesthetics and worldviews took place when Cuba was undergoing drastic political, economic, and social changes, while also coinciding with the establishment of new institutions, festivals, and album releases that promoted new and electroacoustic music among national and international audiences. Over the course of the 1980s there is a proliferation of compositional approaches and techniques among a younger generation of Cuban composers. In an increasingly globalized postmodern world, Cuban composers, in spite of the effects of the US-imposed embargo on culture, drew from a wide range of techniques and influences, some local and many foreign, that—as José Martí professed in his famous quote reproduced in the epigraph to this introduction—they grafted onto their individual artistic Cuban rootstock. Some branches bore more fruits than others for certain composers, but all produced an eclectic oeuvre that challenged classification. The book closes not with a summarizing concluding chapter, but with an epilogue that presents more questions and lines of inquiry than it seeks to provide answers. In this final section I briefly explore developments in the post-Soviet Cuban music scene, in particular how changes in political and economic circumstances affected classical music. I close with how recent events have led to a new wave of repression of Cuban artists who openly protest the state's latest policies regarding the regulation of cultural and artistic work, as well as COVID-19 and the ensuing economic downturn's repercussions; and yet, much like in the preceding decades, I note how classical music and composers remain largely insulated from more general and pervasive repressive and censorship tactics with which artists in other fields have to contend.

Throughout this book I map the global networks of composers and performers in which Cuban musicians participated, providing a more nuanced picture of the vibrant role that cultural ambassadors from Third World countries played in the realm of international cultural diplomacy. This contrasts dramatically with dominant media representations of Cuba as an island isolated from the rest of the world. For example, Cuba held a recurring Latin American Music Festival (with Mexico, Brazil, and Uruguay) as well as a Music Festival of Socialist Countries (with the Soviet Union, Poland, Bulgaria, and Czechoslovakia). The Cuban Consejo Nacional de Cultura (and later the Ministry of Culture) also sent classical musicians to represent Cuba in festivals in Hungary, Poland, and Venezuela, among other countries. Through their connections with composers from Eastern Europe, Latin America, and non-aligned countries, Cuban composers developed diverse networks in counterpoint with their artistic counterparts, many of whom also sought to use the most innovative compositional techniques in the service of leftist or socialist politics, circumventing the limitations imposed by the US embargo and undermining US claims to cultural superiority afforded by capitalism. Cuban composers relied on their local as well as international connections, through a vast network of composers, ensembles, educational and cultural institutions, festivals, score publishing and audio recording projects, and cultural magazines that facilitated the dissemination of their work as well as their exposure to new music from abroad. It is to one of these foreign composers and festivals, Aaron Copland and the Berkshire Music Festival, that I first turn as a catalyst for a new school of Cuban composition in the 1940s.

1

Neoclassicism Meets 1940s
Pan Americanism

The Grupo de Renovación Musical as the First Cuban School of Composition

La presencia del Grupo de Renovación [Musical] inicia una nueva etapa de progreso en la conciencia artística cubana.[1]
(The presence of the Musical Renewal Group initiates a new era of progress in the Cuban artistic conscience.)

—Alejo Carpentier

On the evening of June 20, 1942, the Lyceum Lawn and Tennis Club of Havana—one of the most prominent women's clubs and an ardent supporter of culture and the arts in the city—hosted a recital of piano sonatas, all newly composed by students of the Conservatorio Municipal "Félix E. Alpízar." The invitation, reproduced in Figures 1.1 and 1.2 and sent on behalf of the Sociedad de la Orquesta de Cámara de La Habana, listed the works, composers, and performers to be featured that evening; notably, the program included two women composers, Gisela Hernández (1912–1971) and Virginia Fleites (1916–1966), pointing towards a more progressive era in Cuban classical music. In his opening remarks, José Ardévol (1911–1981), composition professor at the Conservatorio, explained the drive behind the concert. In 1942, US composer Aaron Copland (1900–1990), acting on behalf of the Berkshire Music Center, asked Ardévol to choose a young Cuban composer as the recipient of a scholarship to study composition with Copland and conducting with Serge Koussevitzky (1874–1951) at the Berkshire Music Festival at Tanglewood. These scholarships were established by the Office of Inter-American Affairs Music Committee (of which Copland was a member)

---

[1] Alejo Carpentier, "Panorama de la música en Cuba," originally published in *Conservatorio* 1, no. 2 (1944), reproduced in *La música en Cuba. Temas de la lira y del bongó* (Havana: Ediciones Museo de la Música, 2012), 363.

Cuban Music Counterpoints. Marysol Quevedo, Oxford University Press. © Oxford University Press 2023.
DOI: 10.1093/oso/9780197552230.003.0002

LVII

SOCIEDAD DE LA ORQUESTA DE CAMARA
DE LA HABANA

PRESENTA

SONATAS PARA PIANO

DE

COMPOSITORES CUBANOS

LYCEUM Y LAWN TENNIS CLUB
Calzada y 8, VEDADO
SABADO, 20 DE JUNIO, 1942
9.00 P. M.

INVITACION

Figures 1.1 and 1.2. Invitation to June 20, 1942, Concert of Sonatas for Piano by Cuban Composers.

Note: Box "Programas," Fondo Personal José Ardévol, Museo Nacional de la Música Cubana, Havana, Cuba.

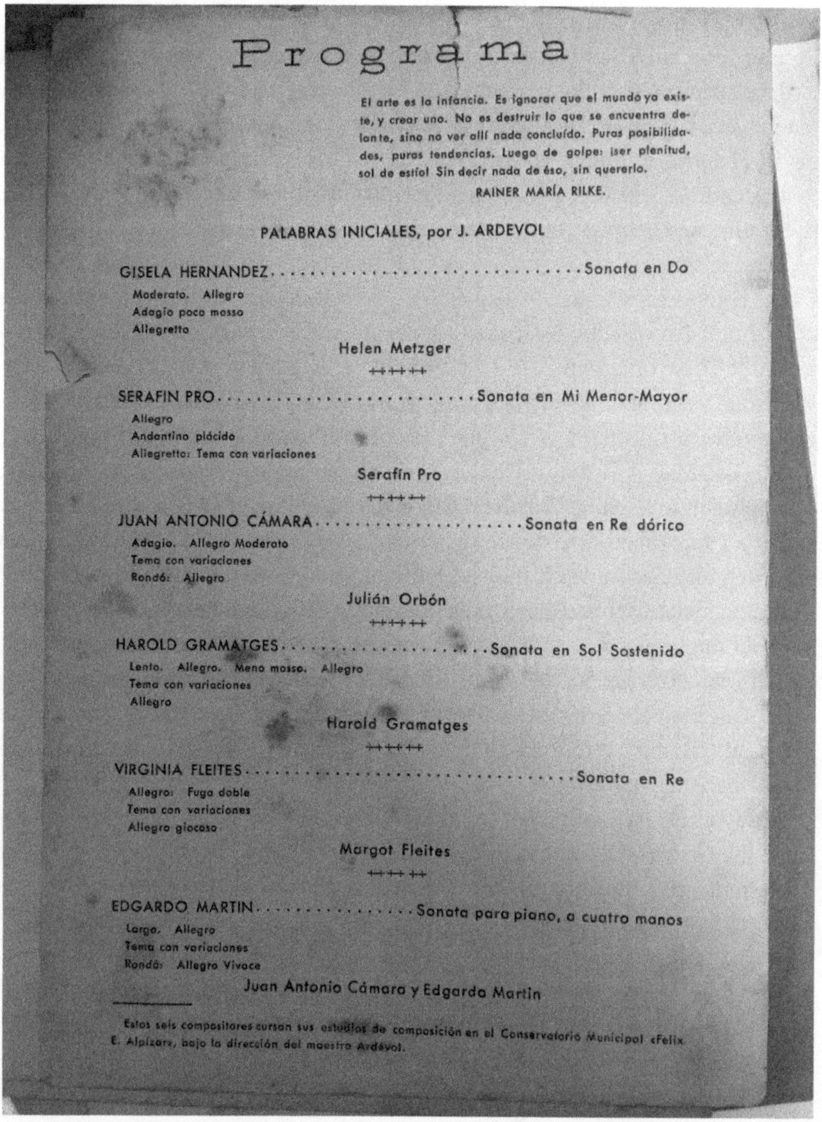

Programa

El arte es la infancia. Es ignorar que el mundo ya existe, y crear uno. No es destruir lo que se encuentra de-
lante, sino no ver allí nada concluído. Puras posibilidades, puras tendencias. Luego de golpe: ¡ser plenitud,
sol de estío! Sin decir nada de éso, sin quererlo.

RAINER MARÍA RILKE.

PALABRAS INICIALES, por J. ARDEVOL

GISELA HERNANDEZ . . . . Sonata en Do
Moderato. Allegro
Adagio poco mosso
Allegretto

Helen Metzger
+++++

SERAFIN PRO . . . . Sonata en Mi Menor-Mayor
Allegro
Andantino plácido
Allegretto: Tema con variaciones

Serafín Pro
+++++

JUAN ANTONIO CÁMARA . . . . Sonata en Re dórico
Adagio. Allegro Moderato
Tema con variaciones
Rondó: Allegro

Julián Orbón
+++++

HAROLD GRAMATGES . . . . Sonata en Sol Sostenido
Lento. Allegro. Meno mosso. Allegro
Tema con variaciones
Allegro

Harold Gramatges
+++++

VIRGINIA FLEITES . . . . Sonata en Re
Allegro: Fuga doble
Tema con variaciones
Allegro giocoso

Margot Fleites
+++++

EDGARDO MARTIN . . . . Sonata para piano, a cuatro manos
Largo. Allegro
Tema con variaciones
Rondó: Allegro Vivace

Juan Antonio Cámara y Edgardo Martín

Estos seis compositores cursan sus estudios de composición en el Conservatorio Municipal «Felix
E. Alpízar», bajo la dirección del maestro Ardévol.

Figures 1.1 and 1.2. Continued

30 CUBAN MUSIC COUNTERPOINTS

to foster positive music exchanges between the United States and Latin America.[2] Feeling it would be unfair for him alone to choose the recipient of the award, Ardévol explained at the beginning of the concert that instead he organized a piano sonata composition contest for his students at the Conservatorio Municipal de La Habana. The jury, which included Ardévol, María Muñoz de Quevedo, Joaquín Nín Castellanos, Diego Bonilla, and César Pérez Sentenat, would choose the winner and recipient of the scholarship to study at Tanglewood.[3]

This recital was the first instance where Ardévol referred to this group of young Cuban composers as a "school" or collective. He asked, "do we aspire to the formation of a school? Do we consider it already constituted? Is this concert its first manifestation?"[4] These questions reveal Ardévol's keen awareness of the concert's historical significance, and they served as a starting point for Ardévol's elaboration of the group's *ideario* (ideology). According to Ardévol, the young composers were united by a set of beliefs regarding art and culture and their role as artists; these included a commitment to learning "their craft" by studying and mastering all the techniques and procedures in order to develop a personal style that reflected "their times." Their approach included in depth study of Baroque and Classical forms and techniques, including sonatas, concertos, fugues, variations, string quartets, and symphonies. Without mastering these forms, Ardévol argued, then "very little will be expressed, even if what is carried inside is great; it is not possible in Cuba, as in so many other Latin American countries, to keep wasting musical talent due to the absence of true technical training."[5] Ardévol also observed that if their work did not reflect "their times" then they would be of "no times" and would never become part of history.

Ardévol's remarks provided the foundation of the manifesto for what soon became the *Grupo de Renovación Musical* (GRM, Group of Musical Renewal). The document was published in their periodical, *Boletín del Grupo de Renovación Musical,* first issued in February 1943, outlining the group's objectives:

> First, to organize concerts and conferences to make known, cultivate, and disseminate good music, according to the purest contemporary trends; second, to create in our country an artistic consciousness, through work that has as its goal to develop

[2] Jennifer L. Campbell, "Shaping Solidarity: Music, Diplomacy, and Inter-American Relations, 1936–1946" (Ph.D. diss, University of Connecticut, 2010), 94.

[3] Besides Ardévol, the jury included María Muñoz de Quevedo, Joaquín Nín [Castellanos], Diego Bonilla, and César Pérez Sentenat. See José Ardévol, "Sonatas para piano de compositores cubanos jóvenes (fragmentos)," reproduced in Radamés Giro and Harold Gramatges, *Grupo Renovación Musical de Cuba* (Havana: Ediciones Museo de la Música, 2009), 9.

[4] "¿Aspiramos a la formación de una escuela? ¿La consideramos ya contituida? ¿Es este concierto su primera manifestación?" See José Ardévol, "Sonatas para piano de compositores cubanos jóvenes (fragmentos)," reproduced in Radamés Giro and Harold Gramatges, *Grupo Renovación Musical de Cuba* (Havana, Cuba: Ediciones Museo de la Música, 2009), 10.

[5] "muy poco será posible decir, aunque sea mucho lo que se lleve dentro . . . no es posible en Cuba, como en tantos otros países latinoamericanos, se siga malogrando mucho talento musical por la ausencia de una verdadera formación técnica." Ibid., 11–14.

a musical concept that is typically of the 1900s, in other words "ours"; third, try to constantly produce constructive criticism on the most important problems of universal music, and particularly, regarding those extremes that in one way or another outdate our art.[6]

With this mission statement, the GRM became the first collective of Cuban composers to call themselves a "Cuban School of Composition," the first to gather around a specific composition professor (José Ardévol) and a core of institutions (Conservatorio, Sociedad de Música de Cámara, Lyceum, Orquesta Filarmónica de La Habana), and the first to proclaim shared musical and aesthetic values and to actively participate as a group in the cultural life of Havana. In spite of the collective efforts of the GRM, its members were occasionally at odds with one another in regard to their musical and aesthetic choices, leading to the eventual dissolution of the group in 1948. In this chapter I explore the activities of the GRM during the 1940s, first, by laying out the political and economic context, in particular 1940s Pan Americanism. I then delve into the group's aesthetic preoccupations and their efforts to reconcile neoclassical approaches with nationalist aesthetics. This is followed by a brief examination of the first book to present a chronological history of Cuban music, *La música en Cuba* written in 1946 by Alejo Carpentier, and its effect on Cuban music historiography and the contemporary music scene. Finally, I analyze two compositions, Argeliers León's *Sonatas a la Virgen del Cobre* and Harold Gramatges's (1918–2008) *Serenata* as prime exemplars of the group's compositional output. In spite of their differences, during the 1940s the members of the group shaped the Cuban classical music scene by cultivating a series of overlapping networks that allowed them to gain access to and control of resources and consequently promote their artistic agendas. They guided music directors on concert programming, audience taste through music criticism in the press and music appreciation courses, and they nurtured contacts with each other and foreign composers by exchanging music manuscripts and correspondence. Little by little they accrued the cultural capital that would make them the leaders of the Cuban music scene throughout the 1950s and the decades that followed the 1959 Revolution. This network consisted

---

[6] "1o. Organizar conciertos y conferencias para dar a conocer, cultivar y difundir la buena música, según las más puras tendencias actuales. 2o. Crear en nuestro país una conciencia artística, por medio de una labor que tenga como fin originar un concepto musical típicamente novecentista, es decir 'nuestro.' 3o. Tratar de hacer una obra constante de crítica orientadora y constructiva sobre los más importantes problemas de la música universal y, muy particularmente, sobre aquellos extremos que de una forma u otra atañan a nuestra arte." "El Grupo de Renovación Musical" published in *Boletín del Grupo de Renovación Musical*, no. 1 (1943), reproduced in Giro and Gramatges, *Grupo Renovación Musical de Cuba*, 24.

32   CUBAN MUSIC COUNTERPOINTS

of local musicians; international composers and performers; other local artists that included painters, sculptors, dancers, poets, novelists, and filmmakers;
and government institutions and the individuals who led them. It was in this
decade, the 1940s, that paths were chosen, alliances were forged, and aesthetic
preferences were explored and cemented that would determine the future of the
Cuban classical music composition tradition, a tradition that bears their legacy
to this day.

Cuba in the 1940s: Politics and Cultural Pan Americanism

The economic and political context in which Cuban composers operated during
the 1940s laid out favorable circumstances for art music production. The decade
was marked by relatively stable political and economic conditions—in spite of
rampant corruption and "gangsterism" in local politics—under which artistic
production enjoyed strong economic and social support from the rising upper-
middle class. First, a new Cuban constitution was ratified in 1940. In comparison with similar documents in other Latin American republics, it purported
extremely progressive social and political ideals. The Constitution was the cul-
mination of social and political reforms initiated in 1933 with the overthrow of
President Gerardo Machado. This rebellion stemmed from collectivist efforts
organized by university students and professors with strong connections to
Marxist thought, but which mainly defended left-wing nationalist ideology that
opposed the US presence on the island. Consequently, the Platt amendment,
which allowed the United States to intervene in local Cuban matters whenever
it saw its interests threatened, was repealed in 1934. The new 1940 Constitution
declared voting rights an obligation for all Cuban people; established the main
principles of Cuban government as republican, democratic, and representative; and granted individual and collective rights to Cuban citizens. One of the
biggest advances of the 1940 Constitution was the declaration of social rights
that protected family, culture, property, and labor. The 1940 Constitution, however, remained in effect only until 1952, when Fulgencio Batista's military coup
suspended many of the rights the Constitution had established. With the 1952
coup the relatively peaceful and prosperous period of the 1940s came to an end.

For many Cubans, the 1940s was not only an era of relative political stability
but also of economic development and security. The Cuban economy experienced rapid growth as the world sugar market relied more heavily on cane sugar
(produced in the tropics) rather than beet sugar from Europe, especially after
World War I and during World War II, when European beet sugar production
declined. Further economic growth was spurred by US businesses tapping into
the new consumer markets in Cuba, leading to the subsequent rise of a mostly

white, upper-middle class that could financially sponsor new music production. As Louis A. Pérez amply demonstrates in *On Becoming Cuban*, US manufactured goods and middle-class ideals of consumption were marketed to and embraced by the growing mostly white Cuban middle class.[7] Much of what defined US values and culture became synonymous with being Cuban; from dress codes to popular music, toiletry brands, and home appliances, Cubans increasingly consumed more and more US products and adopted US ways of life.[8] This is evident in classical music concert programs that advertised US products, including Goodall, Gerber's, Palmolive, Coca-Cola, Frigidaire, Cadillac, Ford Motor Company, Universal Music Co., Steinway, and RCA Victor.[9] Fewer young Cubans went to Europe to finish their education, as US colleges and universities offered a more appealing, relevant, and prestigious education to new generations, and political instability (and eventually World War II) made extended sojourns in Europe not only less attractive but downright dangerous. Following US models, civic support of the arts, mainly through women's societies and clubs, was one of the ways through which the upper-middle class asserted its rising social status.

However, as economic conditions worsened when sugar market demands and prices fell after World War II, the political circumstances in the island deteriorated. In the 1950s, living conditions for most Cubans declined, and the belief in upward social mobility through hard work and personal betterment, imported from the United States, was losing hold. This led to a general sense of disillusionment with the status quo that we will further explore in the following chapter. During the 1940s, however, the US government continued to promote US–Cuban relations, albeit in less overtly aggressive forms than it had employed in the past (such as the military interventions of 1906–1909, 1912, and 1917–1922), securing a profitable market for US investors on the island, and through the soft power of cultural diplomacy.[10] Cuba had also proved its loyalty to the United States during World War II, when it declared war on Germany and joined the United States as an ally. The island's contribution to wartime efforts included patrolling the Caribbean basin for the Allied forces, escorting Allied ships, and rescuing U-boat survivors.

---

[7] Louis A. Pérez, *On Becoming Cuban: Identity, Nationality, and Culture* (Chapel Hill: University of North Carolina Press, 1999), 62.

[8] Pérez, *On Becoming Cuban*, 76, 271.

[9] Box 1940–1944, Programas de Mano, Biblioteca Nacional José Martí, Havana, Cuba.

[10] Rita H. Mead, *Henry Cowell's New Music, 1925–1936: The Society, the Music Editions, and the Recordings* (Ann Arbor: UMI Research Press, 2002); Deane L. Root, "The Pan American Association of Composers (1928–1934)," *Anuario Interamericano de Investigación Musical* 8 (1972), 49–70; Stallings, "Collective Difference: The Pan-American Association of Composers and Pan-American Ideology in Music, 1925–1945" (Ph.D. diss, The Florida State University, 2009); Campbell, "Shaping Solidarity"; Carol Hess, *Representing the Good Neighbor: Music, Difference, and the Pan American Dream* (New York: Oxford University Press, 2013); Danielle Fosler-Lussier, *Music in America's Cold War Diplomacy* (Berkeley and Los Angeles: University of California Press, 2015).

34 CUBAN MUSIC COUNTERPOINTS

The US government established three organizations to promote Pan American music exchanges during these years: the Division of Cultural Relations of the State Department (1938), the Music Division of the Pan American Union (1941), and the aforementioned Office of Inter-American Affairs (OIAA). The US composers involved in these entities did not always overlap with the ones involved in the then defunct Pan American Association of Composers (PAAC, 1928–1934), and the exchanges were more unilateral than the ones organized by the PAAC.[11] Franklin D. Roosevelt's Good Neighbor policy encouraged US companies and entrepreneurs to invest in Latin American markets. US efforts in fostering strong economic and cultural relations with Latin American countries also served to protect other US interests: they helped contain what the United States viewed as politically subversive movements and protected the Western Hemisphere from infiltration of Nazi propaganda. After World War II the OIAA continued operations but shifted its focus to combat communist ideology in the Western Hemisphere. Jennifer Campbell has noted that although these US government organizations were meant to foster cultural diplomacy among the Western Hemisphere, concerns over the intentions of the Division of Cultural Relations of the State Department were raised by many individuals who questioned whether its work would serve as cultural diplomacy or rather propaganda.[12] The Music Division of the Pan American Union was established in 1941 with funding provided by a grant from the Carnegie Corporation, with Charles Seeger as chief of the Division. Their most significant publication was a series of catalogues of music by Latin American composers available for performance in the United States.

The Office of Inter-American Affairs (OIAA) was initially established in 1941 by US President Franklin D. Roosevelt to promote inter-American cooperation. According to Executive Order 8840 the Office of Coordinator of Inter-American Affairs was created "to provide for the development of commercial and cultural relations between the American Republics and thereby increasing the solidarity of this hemisphere and furthering the spirit of cooperation between the Americas in the interest of hemisphere defense."[13] Roosevelt named Nelson Rockefeller, who created a Cultural Division and its Music Committee, as the head of the agency. The OIAA's covert or implicit mission was to counter fascist propaganda (mainly Italian and German) prior to and during World War II by disseminating

[11] For a detailed account of the PAAC activities, see Stallings, "Collective Difference."
[12] Campbell, "Shaping Solidarity," 23.
[13] Franklin D. Roosevelt, "Executive Order 8840 Establishing the Office of Coordinator of Inter-American Affairs," July 30, 1941. Online by Gerhard Peters and John T. Woolley, The American Presidency Project, University of California, Santa Barbara. https://www.presidency.ucsb.edu/documents/executive-order-8840-establishing-the-office-coordinator-inter-american-affairs (accessed January 15, 2019).

NEOCLASSICISM MEETS 1940S PAN AMERICANISM   35

pro-US information to Latin American audiences through newsreels, films, radio broadcasts, and advertising.[14] According to Campbell, the main purpose of the cultural division was "to counter anti-American propaganda with materials that would create a pro-American image in the minds of the masses, but with a special emphasis on reaching the artistic and intellectual elite."[15]

Nelson Rockefeller also quickly established a Music Committee comprised of Marshall Bartholomew, William Berrien, Evans Clark, Carleton Sprague Smith, and Aaron Copland.[16] Thus, unlike the New Music Society (1925–1936) and the PAAC, these three entities were US state-sponsored and served to further the interests of the US government at the hemispheric level through cultural diplomacy, without direct input or feedback from Latin American composers.[17] One of the most publicized efforts in cultural diplomacy by the OIAA's Music Division was Aaron Copland's 1941 Latin American tour. The tour included a stop in Cuba with a concert of contemporary music by both Cuban and US composers, reproduced in Figures 1.3 and 1.4.[18] The visit must have also provided Copland with inspiration to compose *Danzón Cubano* in 1942. The works representing the Cuban composers, Gramatges's *Dos invenciones,* María Isabel López Rovirosa's (who would eventually marry Ardévol) Suite, and Ardévol's I Concerto Grosso, reflect the neoclassical turn in the Cuban school of composition, even though it would not coalesce as such until the June 1942 concert recounted at this chapter's opening. The works by the US composers, Copland's Sonata and *Quiet City* and Roy Harris's Trio, reflected a similar preoccupation with the use of classical forms and techniques. Although Ardévol had been involved in the PAAC and Henry Cowell's New Music Society, and had been in touch with US composers throughout the 1930s, it seems like Copland's 1941 visit cemented the relationship between Copland and like-minded US composers with the younger generation of Cuban composers that included Ardévol, Gramatges, and López Rovirosa. As mentioned earlier, in 1942 Copland extended an invitation and scholarship (funded by the Music Division of the OIAA) for a young Cuban composer to study with him in Tanglewood, leading to the sonata composition competition and the June 1942 concert at the Lyceum and Lawn Tennis Club.

Although Pan Americanist cultural diplomacy was fostered by initiatives that originated mostly from US state agencies, cultural and musical exchanges

---

[14] Initially the OIAA was named the Office of the Coordinator of Inter-American Affairs and was later renamed in 1945 as the Office of Inter-American Affairs, how it is better known.

[15] Campbell, "Shaping Solidarity," 57.

[16] Ibid., 55–56.

[17] Marysol Quevedo, "Exchanges: Modernist Approaches across Oceans and Borders" for Vol. 6 The Twentieth and Twenty-First Centuries edited by William Cheng and Danielle Fosler-Lussier. In *A Cultural History of Music in the Modern Age* (Bloomsbury).

[18] Box #4, Fondo personal José Ardévol, Museo Nacional de la Música Cubana, Havana, Cuba.

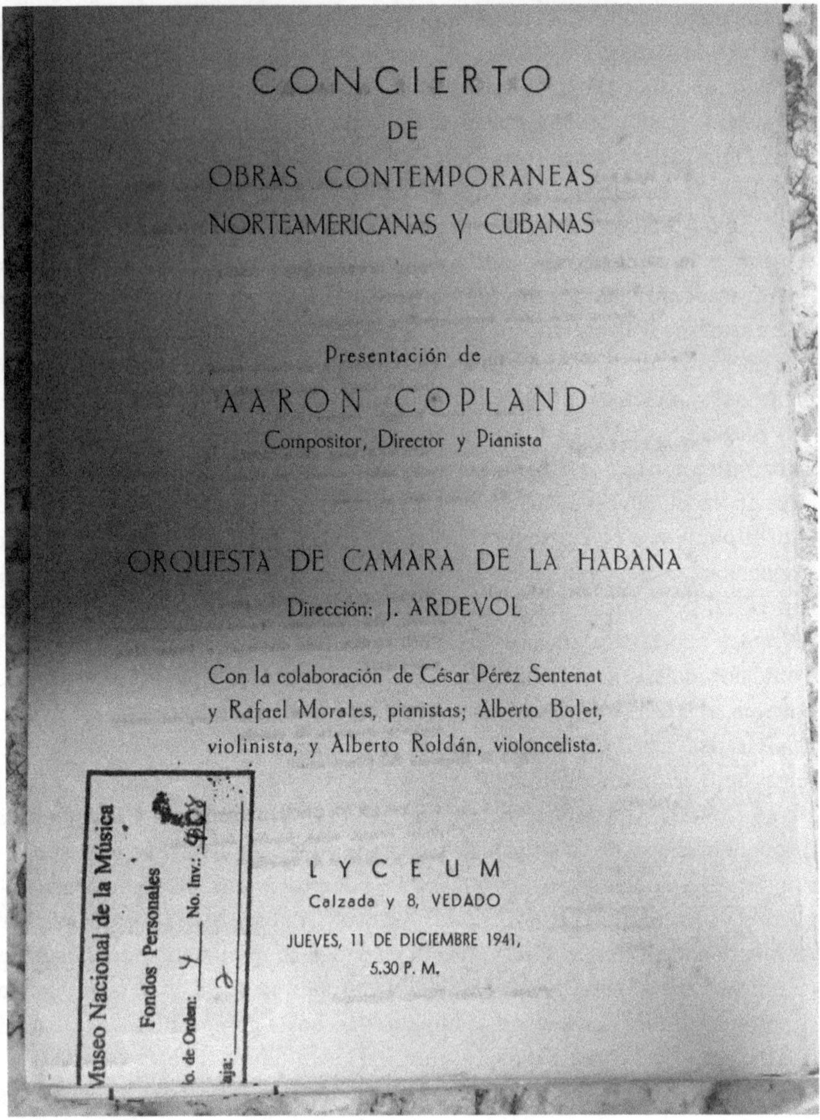
CONCIERTO
DE
OBRAS CONTEMPORANEAS
NORTEAMERICANAS Y CUBANAS
Presentación de
AARON COPLAND
Compositor, Director y Pianista
ORQUESTA DE CAMARA DE LA HABANA
Dirección: J. ARDEVOL
Con la colaboración de César Pérez Sentenat y Rafael Morales, pianistas; Alberto Bolet, violinista, y Alberto Roldán, violoncelista.
LYCEUM
Calzada y 8, VEDADO
JUEVES, 11 DE DICIEMBRE 1941,
5.30 P. M.
Museo Nacional de la Música
Fondos Personales

Figures 1.3 and 1.4. Concert Program of Aaron Copland's Presentation of Music by US composers in Cuba.

Note: Concert Program, Box #4, Fondo personal José Ardévol, Museo Nacional de la Música Cubana, Havana, Cuba.

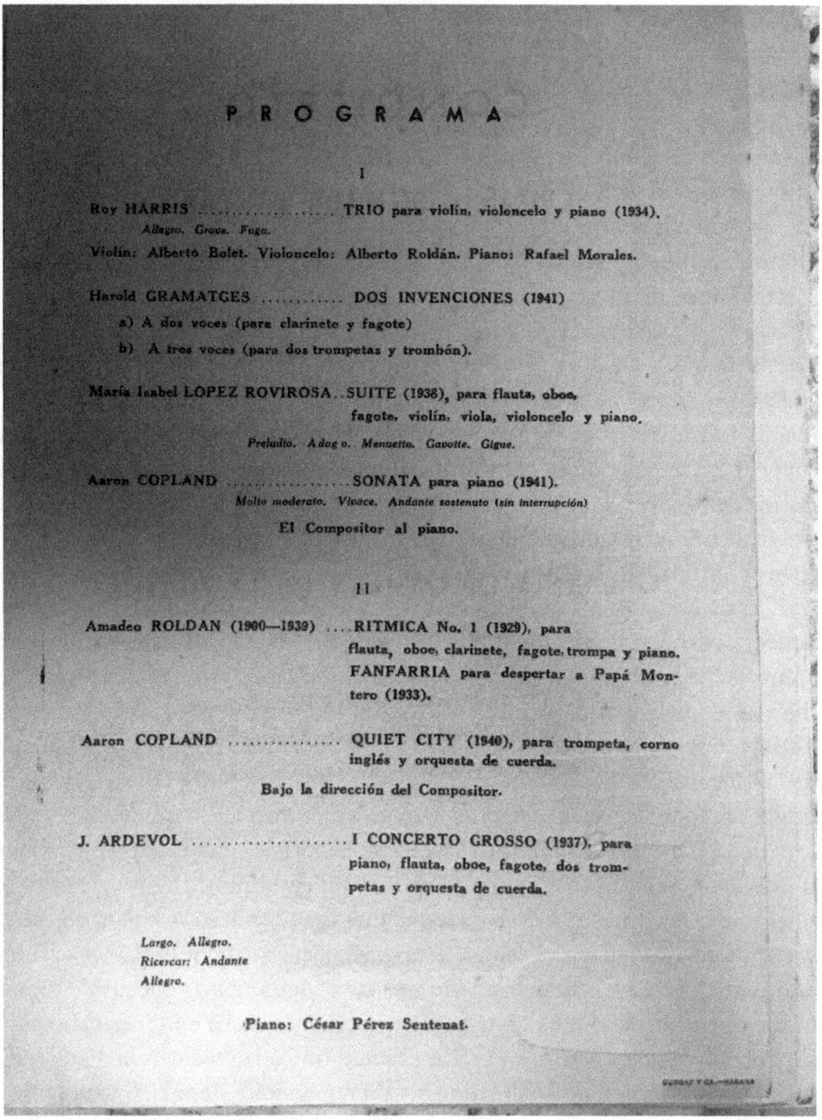

P R O G R A M A

I

Roy HARRIS .... TRIO para violín, violoncelo y piano (1934).
    Allegro. Grave. Fuga.
Violín: Alberto Bolet. Violoncelo: Alberto Roldán. Piano: Rafael Morales.

Harold GRAMATGES .... DOS INVENCIONES (1941)
    a) A dos voces (para clarinete y fagote)
    b) A tres voces (para dos trompetas y trombón).

María Isabel LOPEZ ROVIROSA..SUITE (1938), para flauta, oboe,
                                     fagote, violín, viola, violoncelo y piano.
         Preludio. Adag o. Menuetto. Gavotte. Gigue.

Aaron COPLAND ....SONATA para piano (1941).
       Molto moderato. Vivace. Andante sostenuto (sin interrupción)
          El Compositor al piano.

II

Amadeo ROLDAN (1900—1939) ....RITMICA No. 1 (1929), para
                             flauta, oboe, clarinete, fagote, trompa y piano.
                             FANFARRIA para despertar a Papá Montero (1933).

Aaron COPLAND .... QUIET CITY (1940), para trompeta, corno
                             inglés y orquesta de cuerda.
          Bajo la dirección del Compositor.

J. ARDEVOL .... I CONCERTO GROSSO (1937), para
                             piano, flauta, oboe, fagote, dos trompetas y orquesta de cuerda.

    Largo. Allegro.
    Ricercar: Andante
    Allegro.

         Piano: César Pérez Sentenat.

Figures 1.3 and 1.4. Continued

38   CUBAN MUSIC COUNTERPOINTS

were also of great interest to Cuban state cultural organizations. As Cary García Yero has shown, the administrations of Grau San Martín and Fulgencio Batista invested in foreign, hemispheric cultural diplomacy "because it was 'the duty of the government to stimulate all private efforts that lead to the development of our culture and its exchange with other people of our continent, promoting this way the strength of the spiritual ties that unite all American countries.'"[19] The individuals and projects they supported included the all-female jazz band Orquesta Ensueño (led by Guillermina Foyo) and composer and bandleader Moisés Simón, both popular music acts, as well as visual artists' travel and participation in modern art exhibits abroad.[20] During this period (1940–1959), as García Yero adds, Cuban "governmental support for the arts became a source of legitimacy, and cultural policies were used to evaluate government performance and effectiveness."[21] In spite of these efforts and state cultural agencies' support and regulation of music education institutions throughout the island, the initiatives of promoting new music composition and performance seemed to originate from non-governmental organizations and venues.

In addition to the Pan Americanist connections that led to the June 1942 concert, its invitation hints at a few other threads that constituted the fabric of the network of individuals, organizations, and ideals of the Cuban classical music scene. The concert was hosted by the Lyceum and Lawn Tennis Club, located in the Vedado neighborhood in Havana, one of the wealthiest areas of the capital. The Lyceum hosted concerts organized by the Sociedad de Orquesta de Cámara de La Habana (further discussed below) on a recurring basis. Fourteen women originally founded the Lyceum in 1929 to promote social and cultural activities, merging in 1939 with the "Tennis de Señoritas" and changing its name to the Lyceum and Lawn Tennis Club (effectively adding physical activity to their interests). Their 1929 bylaws stated that the organization's main objective was to "foment woman in her collective spirit, facilitating the exchange of ideas and guiding those activities that reinforce the benefits of the collective."[22] Some of their goals included the defense of democracy in Cuba and internationally, support of women's suffrage (a right granted to Cuban women in 1933), and world peace through understanding between peoples.[23] They claimed political and religious neutrality in order to include in their membership women from diverse social, political, and religious backgrounds. As a liberal and progressive

---

[19] Cary Aileen García Yero, "The State within the Arts: A Study of Cuba's Cultural Policy, 1940–1958," *Cuban Studies* 47, no. 1 (2019): 90.

[20] García Yero, "The State within the Arts: A Study of Cuba's Cultural Policy, 1940–1958," 90–91.

[21] Ibid., 91.

[22] Whigman Montoya Deler, *El Lyceum y Lawn Tennis Club. Su huella en la cultura cubana* (Houston: Ediciones Unos y Otros, 2017), 23.

[23] Ibid., 23.

organization they established the first free library in Cuba and offered the first librarian training courses in the island. In addition to chamber music concerts, they hosted lectures on botany, art, and culture and contemporary art shows, including a 1942 Picasso exhibit. Some of their activities had direct Pan American connections, such as the 1949 exposition "33 Artistas de las Américas" (33 Artists of the Americas), organized by the Pan American Union. They hosted the 1941 concert of US and Cuban music in which Aaron Copland participated as part of his US State Department Latin American tour, as well as the 1945 concert of the Cuban-American Music Group (discussed in more detail below). The Lyceum was heavily invested in raising the educational and cultural level not only of its members, but of the general public, and also supporting the local cultural scene. It continued operating after 1959, until it was dissolved in 1968, a rare occurrence given that most social clubs in Cuba "disappeared" after the Revolution (mainly because many of them discriminated on the basis of racial and social class and were seen as antithetical to the Revolution's socialist values) or simply ceased to exist when their members fled the island in the aftermath of the Revolution. The Lyceum often published catalogs of their art exhibits, and in the 1950s funded the first publication since the nineteenth century of a collection of Manuel Saumell's (1818–1870, edited by Harold Gramatges) *contradanzas*, considered the first truly Cuban classical genre. Composers Olga de Blank and Gisela Hernández were heavily involved in the Lyceum's activities contributing reviews and compositions published in the club's journal *Lyceum*. Other music critics for the journal included Edgardo Martín (composer, music critic, member of the GRM) and Antonio Quevedo (music critic for the broadly disseminated Cuban magazine *Bohemia* and husband to María Muñoz de Quevedo, choral director and founder of the Choral Society of Havana). The Lyceum and Lawn Tennis Club was an indispensable thread in the fabric of Havana's cultural scene, in particular during the 1930s, 1940s, and 1950s, and as a supporter of contemporary music. Evinced by the individuals and ensembles who collaborated with and at the Lyceum, the club was a space that reinforced the networks of musicians, ensembles, and music critics that extended to the Conservatorio Municipal de La Habana and publications such as the newspaper *Hoy*.

The very top of the invitation to the concert of June 20, 1942, that inaugurated the GRM announced: "Sociedad Orquesta de Cámara de La Habana . . . presents." By 1942, this society was one of the most respected musical institutions in Havana, if not in the entire island. Founded in 1934 by José Ardévol, who served as its music director and conductor for nearly two decades until its activities declined after 1952, the Orquesta de Cámara de La Habana's mission foreshadowed the cultural agenda of the GRM. The organization's main objective was to "stimulate the creation of Cuban classical music through dissemination, carried out in the

40   CUBAN MUSIC COUNTERPOINTS

best conditions, of the largest possible number of important national works."[24] Although the main goal was to promote Cuban music, throughout its existence the orchestra performed a varied repertory that included earlier works from the Baroque and Classical periods that had never been performed in Cuba, such as J.S. Bach's Brandenburg Concertos, several works by Girolamo Frescobaldi, Arcangelo Corelli, Giovanni Gabrieli, and Claudio Monteverdi, as well as contemporary pieces, such as Stravinsky's *Pulcinella* and *Apollon musagète*. It was the first ensemble to systematically present music of the Baroque and Classical European tradition that had rarely been performed or heard, if ever, in Cuban concert halls until the 1930s. In addition to focusing on pre-Romantic chamber music and works by Cuban composers, the society also promoted other lesser performed repertory: new compositions by contemporary composers from the United States, Europe, and Latin America.[25]

The orchestra performed the Cuban premieres of 200 works, and the world premieres of over fifty compositions, including Roldán's *Rítmicas* and *Tres toques* and García Caturla's *Primera Suite Cubana*. Most of the piano and chamber works composed by Grupo members throughout the 1940s were premiered in concerts organized by the Sociedad de la Orquesta de Cámara de La Habana, and eventually, Grupo members became involved in the society's board and program committee, along with other composers and musicians who were never officially affiliated with the GRM, such as Juan Blanco and Aurelio de la Vega. In 1953, the board and membership of the society were integrated not only by composers, but also by prominent individuals in various artistic fields, including anthropologist Fernando Ortiz, writer and music critic Alejo Carpentier, painter Wifredo Lam, writer and journalist Sara Hernández Catá, playwright Luis A. Baralt, poets Emilio Ballagas and Mirta Aguirre, dancer and choreographer Alberto Alonso, and writer-ethnographer Lydia Cabrera.[26] Several of these artists and intellectuals were also members of the Cuban Partido Socialista Popular (Popular Socialist Party, PSP), including Aguirre and Alonso, setting a precedent of leftist political involvement among some of the mainstream cultural elite who would later—as discussed in the following chapter—establish more overtly political and leftist cultural organizations. Involving individuals from several artistic

---

[24] "estimular la creación de la música culta cuabana mediante la divulgación, efectuada en las mejores condiciones, del mayor número possible de obras nacionales importantes." In "Memorandum sobre la Sociedad de la Orquesta de Camara de la Habana," sent by José Ardévol (president) and Juan Blanco (secretary) to the director of the Instituto Nacional de la Cultura, Dra. Vicentina Antuña, March 17, 1959, Box #4, Fondo personal José Ardévol, Museo Nacional de la Música Cubana, Havana, Cuba.

[25] Box "Programas," Fondo personal José Ardévol, Museo Nacional de la Música Cubana, Havana, Cuba.

[26] Certificate of the Society's election results from 1953, certified by Juan Blanco (secretary), Box #4, Fondo personal José Ardévol, Museo Nacional de la Música Cubana, Havana, Cuba.

and intellectual areas, as well as a wide range of political ideologies, the membership of the society reflected the same principles that Ardévol cultivated among his pupils in the Conservatorio Municipal, that to be a complete, well-rounded composer, the individual had to gain knowledge and understanding of all artistic and intellectual fields, which included anthropology, folklore, literature, visual arts, and philosophy.

Like the Conservatorio Municipal de La Habana and the various Pan American music organizations discussed above, the Sociedad de Orquesta de Cámara de La Habana functioned as a point of convergence for composers, performers, and audiences within and outside of Cuba. By pairing the music of contemporary composers from Cuba with those from Europe and the United States in one single event, composers, performers, and audiences could see themselves and the music they heard as part of a broader musical tradition that extended beyond the geographical and temporal boundaries of the island. They were part of an imagined community of artists and intellectuals who shared aesthetic and social values. They activated points of connection in a vast network of new music composition and performance that extended to New York, Paris, Mexico City, Argentina, Brazil, and beyond. The ensemble performed the Cuban premiers of seminal twentieth-century works Cuban audiences had only been able to read about in the press, or perhaps listen to in recordings. These included Stravinsky's *Pulcinella* and *Octect*, Darius Milhaud's *Quartet for the End of Time*, Béla Bartók's Children's Songs, and Paul Hindemith's *Chamber Music for Five Woodwinds* (1922).[27] The type of non-Cuban new music the ensemble performed (along with the pre-Romantic European repertory) reveals Ardévol's (and some of his protégés) aesthetic preferences: neoclassical forms and techniques. These served as a model for Ardévol's compositions from this time period and the compositional techniques he inculcated to his pupils in his composition studio.

Neoclassical in Form, Vernacular in Content

If Ardévol used the Sociedad de Orquesta de Cámara de La Habana as the vehicle through which to present Cuban audiences with works by pre-Romantic European masters and contemporary composers, then the Conservatorio Municipal de La Habana served as the training ground for a generation of composers who would study the "old masters" in order to perfect their craft while aspiring to universal and historical recognition. Prior to his arrival in Cuba Ardévol's aesthetic approach was informed by close study of Western European, in particular French,

[27] Concert programs, Box #4, Fondo personal José Ardévol, Museo Nacional de la Música Cubana, Havana, Cuba.

42 CUBAN MUSIC COUNTERPOINTS

modernist trends. He studied orchestral conducting with Hermann Scherchen in Paris in 1929, after he graduated from the Instituto Musical de Barcelona, where he was born. In Barcelona, he received thorough training in piano, chamber music, harmony, counterpoint and fugue, composition, and choral conducting.[28] This preparation points to his fascination with chamber music and imitative contrapuntal writing present in his works from the 1930s and 1940s, such as *Música de cámara* (1934). His admiration of Stravinsky's neoclassical works not only influenced his compositional approach but extended to his other professional endeavors. As director of the Ballet of the Society Pro-Arte Musical, he conducted the Cuban premiers of Stravinsky's *Petrushka* and *Apollon musagète*. In 1932 he presented the first concert of his own works in Cuba. At this event, Ardévol explained that Manuel de Falla's and Stravinsky's music offered great possibilities for Cuban composers to follow, citing two direct influences from his European training.[29] Therefore, it is not surprising that he led his composition students at the Conservatorio in in-depth studies of Baroque and Classical works as well as those by contemporary composers who had turned to these same models (mainly Stravinsky and Schoenberg). Additionally, in contrast to Roldán and García Caturla, who explicitly employed vernacular music in their compositions and promoted an American route to modernism, Ardévol preferred the modal language of Spanish folk music and Spanish medieval and Renaissance sources.

Finished in February 1936, *Música de cámara para seis instrumentos* exemplifies Ardévol's fusion of older forms and techniques with contemporary and vernacular elements in the decade prior to the activities of GRM.[30] The composer dedicated the work to the Lyceum feminine society and the piece was eventually published by the Music Division of the Pan American Union (in 1955). *Música de cámara* is scored for a sextet of flute, B-flat clarinet, bassoon, trumpet in C, violin, and cello, an instrumentation choice that resembles the *Pierrot* ensemble and Stravinsky's *Soldier's Tale*. Ardévol divides the ensemble into two groups according to instrument family, reminiscent of the polychoral canzonas and sonatas of sixteenth-century Venice in the style of Giovanni Gabrieli and of Stravinsky's chamber and orchestral writing in which he assigns certain instrumental groups to specific melodic motives and phrases in order to achieve textural and timbral variety. The neoclassical approach is immediately evident in the titles of the movements: I. Ricercare, II. Allegro [fugue], III. Quasi Habanera, IV. Fanfarria and Finale [rondo form].[31] These follow a

---

[28] José Ardévol, *José Ardévol: correspondencia cruzada*, ed. Clara Díaz (Havana: Editorial Letras Cubanas, 2004), 10.

[29] José Ardévol, *Música y Revolución* (Havana: UNEAC, 1966), 14.

[30] Díaz in Ardévol, *José Ardévol: Correspondencia Cruzada*, 21–22.

[31] The published score (1955) and the 1936 concert where it was premiered have slightly different movement numbers and titles.

NEOCLASSICISM MEETS 1940S PAN AMERICANISM   43

slow-fast-slow-fast-fast movement progression typical of Baroque Italian church sonatas, such as Corelli's and Tomaso Antonio Vitali's, consisting of short, tonally closed movements in alternating tempo and meter. A closer look at the construction of the individual movements reveals binary and rounded binary formal design, also reminiscent of Baroque sonata movements. Several of the movements contain extended passages of imitative counterpoint and even strict fugal writing. Ardévol's venture into neoclassical territory falls under the category of "eclectic" imitation in Martha M. Hyde's taxonomy of neoclassical imitation, which she divides (although at no point does she consider them mutually exclusive) into: reverential, eclectic, heuristic, and dialectical. Fitting Hyde's definition of eclectic imitation, Ardévol's composition contains "allusions, echoes, phrases, techniques, structures, and forms from an unspecified group of earlier composers and styles [that] all jostle each other indifferently."[32] Ardévol uses Renaissance and late-Baroque genres (ricercare and fanfare), Baroque and Classical forms (rondo and sonata), Baroque imitative and contrapuntal writing (ricercare and the Allegro), and an even more recent, yet highly codified Cuban genre, the nineteenth-century habanera.

As the title of the third movement suggests, Ardévol heavily employs the habanera base pattern, but unlike traditional habaneras, where the bass supports a more cantabile melody, the rhythmic pattern typically found only in the bass dominates the entire texture of this movement, frustrating listeners' expectations. Given that composers from the Baroque period introduced regional styles, mostly in the form of dances, in their sonatas, Ardévol's evocation of the habanera in the third movement is double-coded as both neoclassical and vernacular. However, he saw the introduction of a Cuban music genre in a sublimated manner and not necessarily as uniquely Cuban, one that evoked a more general Hispanic element. In a 1946 letter to Alejo Carpentier, Ardévol explains that "the third movement of *Música de cámara para seis instrumentos* (2/II/1936), work little localized, although within the general Hispanic root, is an *Andantio* (casi Habanera). I know that the Cuban aspects of this *casi* habanera are not very direct, and it is more evocative, as in the French style when it wants to capture Spain. Even as such, García Caturla saw in its last parts things of great interest with the most legitimate tradition of this Cuban form."[33] The habanera elements serve as markers of neoclassicism and the vernacular, referencing a genre of Cuba's (not too distant) past, connoting the archaic and the popular.

---

[32] Martha MacLean Hyde, "Neoclassic and Anachronistic Impulses in Twentieth-Century Music," *Music Theory Spectrum* 18, no. 2 (1996), 211.

[33] Ardévol and Díaz, *José Ardévol: Correspondencia Cruzada*, 114.

44 CUBAN MUSIC COUNTERPOINTS

The Cuban elements are also present in the rhythmic complexity of the faster finale, an Allegretto in rondo form with a coda, replete with hemiolas, syncopations, and meter changes. The first theme of the A section is characterized by hemiolas, while the second theme interrupts the established flow between 6/8 and 3/4 with irregular meters of 5/8 and 7/ 8. The alternation and overlapping of 3/4 and 6/8 in this context is reminiscent of the style of a *guajira*, a Cuban rural song and dance genre usually in 3/4 with alternating hemiolas or metric groupings of 6/8 with accents on the first, third, and fifth eighth notes. By referencing habaneras and guajiras Ardévol privileged white criollo genres, largely omitting Afro-Cuban influences at a time (the 1930s) when the two most prominent Cuban composers, Alejandro García Caturla and Amadeo Roldán, had achieved recognition for works that music critics associated with the *Afrocubanista* artistic movement. After Roldán and García Caturla's deaths, Ardévol became the leading figure, as composer, pedagogue, and music director, in the Cuban music scene and his neoclassical and Hispanist predilections become palpable in the GRM members' compositions.

The Grupo de Renovación Musical

GRM Members

The Grupo de Renovación Musical initially included Harold Gramatges, Julián Orbón, Hilario González, Gisela Hernández, Edgardo Martín, Serafín Pro, Virginia Fleites, and Esther Rodríguez. They were later joined by Juan Antonio Cámara, Enrique Aparicio Bellver, Dolores Torres, and Argeliers León. The presence of several women in its roster reflected a more open and progressive attitude among musicians and Cuban society in general than in previous decades. Harold Gramatges was selected as the recipient of the Tanglewood scholarship in 1942, after winning the composition competition that led to the GRM's formation. As a disciple of José Ardévol and member of the GRM, Gramatges followed in Ardévol's footsteps, writing piano works that relied on classical principles of form and phrasing, while also incorporating elements of Cuban popular and traditional music genres. He grew up in Santiago, and he first travelled to Havana to find scores for piano music by Stravinsky and Debussy that he needed for a piano audition in Belgium. At this point he met Amadeo Roldán, and began taking composition lessons. After Roldán's death, Gramatges continued taking lessons with José Ardévol at the Conservatorio Municipal de La Habana. A second scholarship and competition in 1945 resulted in the selection of Spanish-born Julián Orbón as the recipient of the Berkshire scholarship. Besides Gramatges and Orbón, other members of the group studied composition in the United States, such as Gisela Hernández who attended the Peabody Institute in 1944. The group's activities nurtured the careers of these young composers who would become central figures in the post-1959 Cuban music scene.

Grupo de Renovación Musical's Aesthetics

Modernism remained a central preoccupation of these composers and they continued to study contemporary works using materials brought to the island by individuals such as Alejo Carpentier, who returned from their European sojourns with scores and textbooks on composition. They closely studied and analyzed the compositions and treatises of Stravinsky and Schoenberg. But modernism was seen with suspicion by Ardévol, who cautioned that the young composers must first perfect their craft in order to engage with the "most up to date" compositional techniques. He also warned against unbridled use of vernacular musics to color classical compositions as nationalistic, preferring an approach in which local music elements would lead to a "universal" musical language and historical recognition.

The embrace of neoclassicism by Ardévol and his students was not only the result of growing interest in and contact with foreign composers who had famously cultivated that approach. Falling under the umbrella of modernism, neoclassicism shared with other "-isms" of the time a general disdain for the musical styles that had immediately preceded it, mainly Romanticism, searching for and finding in the models of a more distant past (Renaissance, Baroque, and early Classical works) forms, structures, and basic compositional devices as a foundation upon which they could try out modernist techniques, such as twelve-tone and bi- and polytonality. In Cuba, the neoclassical turn also coincided with a turn away from *Afrocubanismo* and other ethnic and racial "-isms" in various arts in other countries in the 1940s. Towards the end of the 1930s, *Afrocubanismo* as an artistic movement was in decline, and in classical music in particular, after the deaths of Roldán and García Caturla, there were no major figures left to champion it. Furthermore, *Afrocubanista* writers and visual artists had been presenting a racialized view of Cuban identity that clashed with the dominant narratives of racial homogeneity purported by the white Cuban political and intellectual elite. By bringing racial difference to the center of aesthetic and national discourse, *Afrocubanista* art was read as a threat to national unity and the enduring discourse of national identity as racially homogeneous.[34] An alternative path in the realm of music was to draw inspiration from musical sources of

---

[34] Robin Moore, *Nationalizing Blackness: Afrocubanismo and Artistic Revolution in Havana, 1920–1940* (Pittsburgh, PA: University of Pittsburgh Press, 1997), 18.

46   CUBAN MUSIC COUNTERPOINTS

Cubanness outside purely Afro-Cuban practices, turning to *criollo* and *mulato* traditions. Although the GRM's aesthetic views were marked by an initial rejection of the overt nationalist approach to composition taken by their predecessors Roldán and García Caturla, the founders of the GRM never denied Roldán and García Caturla's legacy and continued to celebrate their work as a necessary step in the evolution of a Cuban school of composition. The members of the group acknowledged Roldán and García Caturla as visionaries in their own time, bringing Cuban music up to date with contemporary music developments in the United States, Latin America, and Europe and for introducing the use of vernacular Cuban music elements to contemporary art music, particularly the use of Afro-Cuban rhythms and percussive instrumentation. Ardévol and his pupils considered the approaches taken by Roldán and García Caturla significant in regard to establishing an idiosyncratically Cuban music idiom, but in their writings they expressed that Cuban composers could not extract the full potential contained within the Afro-Cuban idiom without first mastering the compositional techniques of the past and the present. Neoclassicism in twentieth-century music was marked by the intentional use of pre-Romantic music styles and genres in order to forge a new, modern music aesthetic that merged elements from the old models with new compositional styles and techniques.[35] This working definition allows us to identify the seemingly disparate musical forms, styles, genres, and sources that Cuban composers used and alluded to in their works as a quintessentially modernist approach.[36] Neoclassicism offered Cuban composers a path within modernism through which they would "master the old forms and techniques" while trying out compositional devices drawn from current harmonic practices (such as bitonality and polytonality) and vernacular Cuban traditions (such as odd meters, frequent meter changes, and syncopations).

Cuban-American Music Group

In May 17, 1945, the Orquesta de Cámara de La Habana presented a concert in collaboration with the Cuban-American Music Group (CAMG)—a collective of Cuban and US composers who exchanged correspondence and scores and promoted each other's music in their respective countries—at the Lyceum and Lawn Tennis Club, the invitation is reproduced in Figures 1.5 and 1.6. The

[35] Scott Messing, *Neoclassicism in Music: From the Genesis of the Concept through the Schoenberg/Stravinsky Polemic* (Ann Arbor: UMI Research Press, 1988), 154.

[36] This definition is distilled from my readings on the origins and definitions of neoclassicism found in the works of Richard Taruskin, "Back to Whom? Neoclassicism as Ideology," *19th-Century Music* 16, no. 3 (1993): 286–302; Scott Messing, *Neoclassicism in Music*; and Martha M. Hyde, "Neoclassic and Anachronistic Impulses," 200–235.

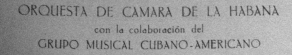

Figures 1.5 and 1.6. Invitation to concert of the Cuban-American Music Group, May 17, 1945.

Note: Box "Programas," Fondo personal José Ardévol, Museo Nacional de la Música Cubana, Havana, Cuba.

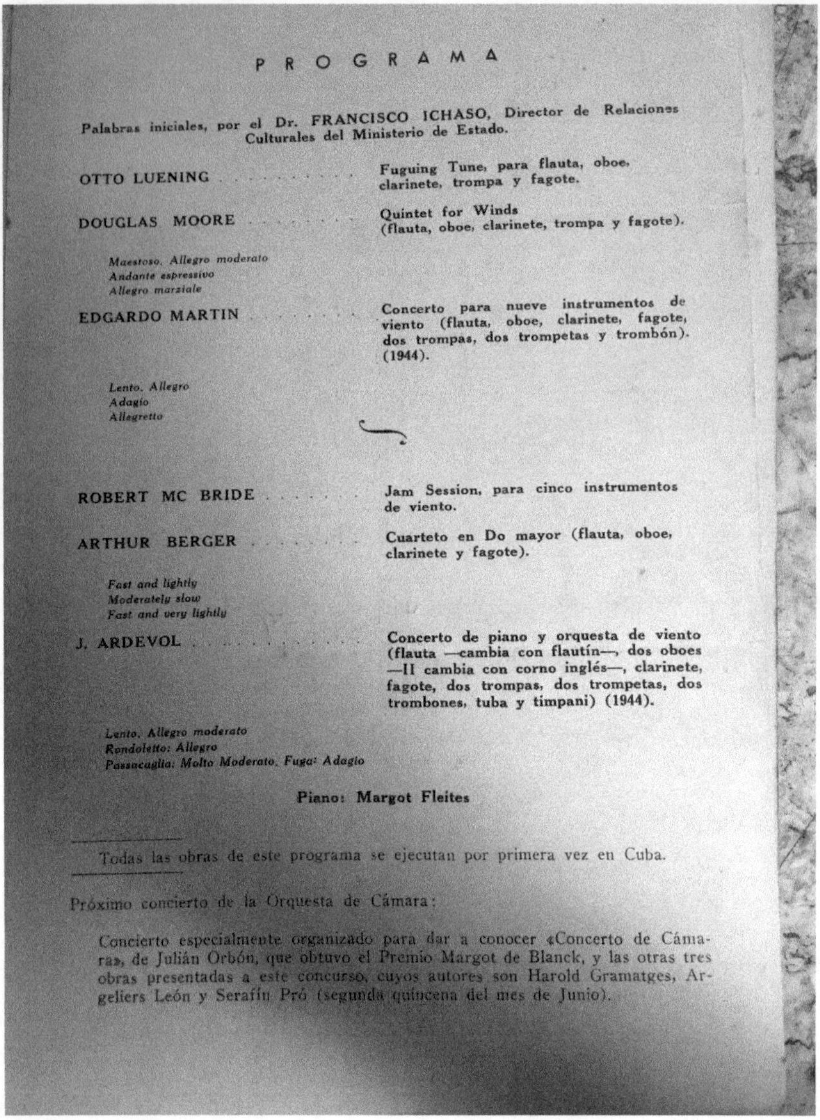

PROGRAMA

Palabras iniciales, por el Dr. FRANCISCO ICHASO, Director de Relaciones Culturales del Ministerio de Estado.

OTTO LUENING . . . .
Fuguing Tune, para flauta, oboe, clarinete, trompa y fagote.

DOUGLAS MOORE . . . .
Quintet for Winds
(flauta, oboe, clarinete, trompa y fagote).

Maestoso. Allegro moderato
Andante espressivo
Allegro marziale

EDGARDO MARTIN . . . .
Concerto para nueve instrumentos de viento (flauta, oboe, clarinete, fagote, dos trompas, dos trompetas y trombón). (1944).

Lento. Allegro
Adagio
Allegretto

ROBERT MC BRIDE . . . .
Jam Session, para cinco instrumentos de viento.

ARTHUR BERGER . . . .
Cuarteto en Do mayor (flauta, oboe, clarinete y fagote).

Fast and lightly
Moderately slow
Fast and very lightly

J. ARDEVOL . . . .
Concerto de piano y orquesta de viento (flauta —cambia con flautín—, dos oboes —II cambia con corno inglés—, clarinete, fagote, dos trompas, dos trompetas, dos trombones, tuba y timpani) (1944).

Lento. Allegro moderato
Rondoletto: Allegro
Passacaglia: Molto Moderato. Fuga: Adagio

Piano: Margot Fleites

Todas las obras de este programa se ejecutan por primera vez en Cuba.

Próximo concierto de la Orquesta de Cámara:

Concierto especialmente organizado para dar a conocer «Concerto de Cámara», de Julián Orbón, que obtuvo el Premio Margot de Blanck, y las otras tres obras presentadas a este concurso, cuyos autores son Harold Gramatges, Argeliers León y Serafín Pró (segunda quincena del mes de Junio).

Figures 1.5 and 1.6. Continued

orchestra was celebrating its eleventh anniversary, and the concert program featured contemporary works for chamber wind ensembles by Cuban and US composers: Otto Luening (*Fuguing Tune*, 1938), Douglas Moore (Quintet for Winds), Edgardo Martín (Concerto for nine instruments), Robert McBride (*Jam Session*), Arthur Berger (Quartet in C Major, which was not performed because one of the performers was "indisposed"), and José Ardévol (Concerto for piano and wind instruments).[37] The concert was also co-sponsored by the Dirección de Cultura of the Ministry of Education (The Ministry of Education's Culture Department). The program opened with remarks by Dr. Francisco Ichaso, Director of Cultural Relations of the Cuban State Department.[38] In his review of the concert, Carpentier noted that the US composers had distanced themselves from their predecessors of the 1920s, who, according to Carpentier, had committed themselves indiscriminately to atonality for novelty's sake. Carpentier seemed confused by Luening's *Fuguing Tune*, which, instead of presenting a fugue, was actually lyrical in character (Carpentier was not familiar with the fuguing tune tradition of the First New England school of psalmodists that Luening was referencing in his title). Carpentier then described Moore's *Quintet* as efficient with vigorous dramatic accent, while he admired McBride's *Jam Session* as bringing to a "serious level" the "prodigious rhythmic, interpretative, and expressive findings of jazz musicians."[39] He similarly praised, in a more extended passage, the works by the two Cuban composers, Edgardo Martín and José Ardévol, for their clarity and solid construction. Under the banner of the CAMG, the May 1945 concert formalized the ties between composers of both countries who shared an interest in exploring vernacular themes through neoclassical models, while also embodying the Good Neighbor policy that was bandied in the local Cuban press as the US involvement in World War II increased.

World War II was coming to an end, yet few composers would have anticipated the role that cultural diplomacy, which had been nurtured by the US State Department and through many non-state sponsored Pan American programs, was to play at the onset of the Cold War and into the following decades. While the end of World War II disrupted the previous world order as new alliances formed, intellectuals in the "periphery" sought to forge paths forward and define their national and cultural identities while negotiating new and contradictory political interpretations of aesthetic matters, in which overtly nationalist music

[37] Box "Programas," Fondo personal José Ardévol, Museo Nacional de la Música Cubana, Havana, Cuba.

[38] Francisco Ichaso would remain in this position after the 1952 military coup and continue to serve in this capacity under Fulgencio Batista.

[39] Alejo Carpentier, "El Grupo Musical Cubano-Norteamericano. Concierto de la Orquesta de Cámara," *Conservatorio* no. 5 (1945), 11–14.

50   CUBAN MUSIC COUNTERPOINTS

was increasingly viewed with suspicion. The CAMG concert was not particularly outstanding or exceptional, but rather, it was a continuation, under a new banner and organization (the CAMG), of the Pan American ties that stretched back at least a decade and a half. The works included in this program and in many others organized by the Orquesta de Cámara de La Habana and the CAMG demonstrate that Cuban composers asserted their Cuban identity by sublimating particularly Cuban musical markers into a neoclassical modernist framework, cultivated by the senior members of the group and also favored by a particular group of US composers. By the 1940s the sublimation of nationalist traits in modernist composition was gaining traction among several Latin American composers—most famously Alberto Ginastera—who wished to move away from the "postcard" nationalism that had become emblematic of the Latin American school. For these composers nationalist musical idioms were subsumed under a broader modernist language as they strove for "universality."

Although the Pan American Association of Composers had ceased to exist by the 1940s, the Cuban and US composers continued their exchange of music scores and the promotion of each other's work through the CAMG. Erminie Kahn directed the CAMG from its headquarters in New York, receiving and forwarding correspondence and music scores for performance and publication. The CAMG members included Aaron Copland, Henry Cowell, John Cage, Paul Bowles, and Carl Ruggles from the United States, as well as Cubans Joaquín Nin-Culmell, Harold Gramatges, Hilario González, Julián Orbón, José Ardévol, and others belonging to the GRM. In 1946 the CAMG published *English biographies of Cuban Composers*, edited by Kahn herself.[40] The CAMG received support for the publication of the pamphlet from the American Steel Corporation of Cuba and the American Tropical Products Corporation of Cuba. The seventeen-page booklet listed short biographies of twenty-eight Cuban composers, some from the nineteenth century while most were from the first half of the twentieth century, including the members of the GRM. Written in English, the booklet was to be disseminated in the United States to promote the work of the Cuban composers. In Cuba, Ardévol and the Sociedad de Orquesta de Cámara de La Habana presented a few concerts "in collaboration with the Cuban American Music Group." Several music score manuscripts housed at the Museo Nacional de la Música Cubana bare the official "Cuban-American Music Group" stamp, showing that the manuscripts Cuban composers sent to the New York City headquarters of the group were returned bearing the mark of the exchange. Though short-lived (1945–1947), the CAMG was created with a clear goal: to establish

---

[40] Erminie Kahn, *English Biographies of Cuban Composers* (New York: Cuban-American Music Group, 1946).

an archive of scores created by Cuban and US composers, with the purpose of preserving and disseminating said materials, either through live concerts or publishing edited scores, and awarding scholarships to young Cuban composers for advanced training in composition in the United States.[41] In 1946, the CAMG funded the second scholarship for a Cuban composer to study in Tanglewood with Copland. Julián Orbón was selected as the winner through a competition. The selection of Orbón and his quick rise to prominence among the GRM members would prove divisive and problematic, as he would go on to disavow the Cuban influence in his music once he was in Tanglewood while at the same time Carpentier praised him as the most promising young composer in Cuba in his music criticism and his 1946 book.[42]

Carpentier's *La música en Cuba*

In 1946, the much-anticipated volume by Alejo Carpentier, *La música en Cuba* was published by the Fondo de Cultura Económica in Mexico. By this point, Carpentier had established himself as a major influence in Cuban culture as music critic whether he was residing in Cuba or in exile. He served as music critic for *La Discusión, El Heraldo de Cuba, Social, Carteles* and *Diario de la Marina*, and his involvement since the 1920s with the Grupo Minorista and his contributions to their journal *Revista Avance* during Gerardo Machado's presidency led to his political persecution, detention, and eventual self-imposed exile in Paris and later Venezuela. The time spent in Paris in self-imposed exile (1928–1939) due to his leftist political activities was instrumental for Carpentier and Cuban music in several ways: artistic movements and new technologies influenced his theories and concepts of Cuban and Latin American culture and history; the emerging field of anthropology equipped him with the tools to examine and write about vernacular music; and his involvement in artistic circles allowed him to write about new music trends in Paris for Cuban magazines and promote the works of modernist Cuban composers in Paris. He became acquainted with the surrealist circle and worked for French radio stations. He eventually distanced himself from the surrealist artists, and devoted himself more fully to writing and producing radio programs.[43] During this period he met influential poets, painters, and composers, most significantly Edgar Varèse, for whom he co-wrote, with French poet and journalist Robert Desnos (who had lent Carpentier his passport and papers so he could escape Cuba), a libretto for the

---

[41] Carpentier, "El Grupo Musical Cubano-Norteamericano," 11–14.

[42] Letter from Ardévol to Carpentier, October 15, 1946, reproduced in Ardévol, *José Ardévol: correspondencia cruzada*, 111.

[43] Anke Birkenmaier, *Alejo Carpentier y la cultura del surrealismo en América Latina* (Madrid: Iberoamericana, 2006), 156.

52 CUBAN MUSIC COUNTERPOINTS

opera *The One All Alone*, although it was never published or staged.[44] While in Paris he wrote for the Cuban cultural magazine *Carteles*, where he kept Cuban readers informed of the latest Parisian cultural, but in particular musical, trends. Carpentier became the French connection for aspiring Cuban composers, including Alejandro García Caturla, who visited Paris in 1928, and was introduced to Nadia Boulanger by Carpentier. Carpentier also circulated new unedited music scores by Cuban composers among his French music circles. Varèse was particularly interested in their work, as he was exploring new ways for organizing sound through rhythm and timbre. Cuban composers explored these two musical parameters throughout the 1920s and 1930s and their developments led to the birth of a Cuban school of composition headed by Roldán and García Caturla, more rooted in local traditions than the work of previous generations of composers.

Carpentier returned to Cuba from Paris in 1939, continuing his activities as music critic for several magazines and newspapers. He embarked on two exploratory journeys that would drastically redefine his role as a cultural figure in Cuba: a 1943 trip to Haiti where he gathered material and information he used to write his novel *El reino de este mundo* (1949, in its preface he would flesh out his theory of *lo real maravilloso*); and extensive archival research in Cuban institutions for his seminal treatment of Cuban music history in *La música en Cuba*. Carpentier was residing in Venezuela (again in self-imposed political exile from 1945 to 1959) while he worked on the final draft of the Cuban music history volume. He corresponded with the Cuban composers of the GRM, who eagerly awaited its release. He sent drafts of the sections on the GRM to Ardévol and Edgardo Martín. In spite of receiving ample feedback from these individuals, the chapter on the contemporary composers in the final version of the 1946 edition was heavily criticized by several members of the GRM. In the last chapter of the book, "Estado Actual de la Música Cubana" (Current State of Cuban Music), Carpentier provided a brief overview of musical activities in the 1940s, focusing on the GRM. After a substantive introduction in which he focused on Ardévol, Carpentier presented in more detail four of the composers of the younger generation: Julián Orbón, Hilario González, Harold Gramatges, and Gisela Hernández. The rest of the members of the GRM were treated in passing in a shorter section. Carpentier's treatment of Orbón stands out in length and characterization. The section on Orbón is nearly twice as long as that of any other composer (other than Ardévol) in this chapter, and opens "Julián Orbón is the most singular and promising figure of the young Cuban school [of composition]" later stating, "always willing to break from everything and everyone, he passed through the *Grupo Renovación* like a meteor, before declaring himself a dissident."[45] In regards to Orbón's penchant for forms, composers, and

[44] Ibid., 182.
[45] Carpentier, *La música en Cuba,* 259.

influences from Spain, Carpentier noted "at least, Orbón situated himself in a point of departure more reasonable and historically justified than those who pretended to depart, in Cuba, from Prokofieff or from Schoenberg."[46] Carpentier continues praising Orbón for two more pages, describing his music with decisively masculine terms: "virile beauty," "rhythmic violence," "coarsness of discantus," and "risk taker." Knowing that some Cuban composers and music critics had their doubts about Orbón as a *Cuban* composer (given his Spanish birth and music influences), Carpentier closes "Shouldn't we give him our complete trust?" By comparison, Carpentier did not use this laudatory language when describing the compositions of Hilario González (whom he describes as "el criollo"), Harold Gramatges (as the most austere, clean, precise, *seriedad estatuaria,* and a stranger to folklore), and Gisela Hernández (profoundly feminine sensibility).[47]

Edgardo Martín, who was treated in passing even though he was a close acquaintance of Carpentier, disapproved of Carpentier's treatment of the GRM in private correspondence with Carpentier. Similarly, Ardévol also felt that Carpentier's brief mention of the other members of the GRM stemmed, not from their lack of compositional skills, but from Carpentier's unfamiliarity with their work, which he communicated through private letters.[48] Argeliers León wrote a review of *La música en Cuba* for *Conservatorio,* in which he noted that a more detailed study of contemporary composers would change the last chapter, where he notes an absence of "direct treatment with the music and its authors, basing [its content] on incomplete references and impressions."[49] Whatever fissures were already present and fragmenting the GRM when *La música en Cuba* was published, they were severe enough to lead to its complete dissolution by 1948. This was followed by the formation of new groups in the 1950s, setting the stage for whom within the Cuban classical music scene would support the revolutionary ideals and receive the support of the state's cultural institutions after 1959.

Embracing Vernacular Music in a Modernist Context

Throughout the 1940s, most of the members of the GRM tended to imbue their compositions with elements of Cuban vernacular music, even if they refrained from this practice in their early compositions. They used melodic and rhythmic elements from popular and traditional music within a modernist compositional

---

[46] Ibid., 260.

[47] Ibid., 262–268.

[48] Ricardo R. Guridi, *Edgardo Martín/Alejo Carpentier correspondencia cruzada* (Havana, Cuba: Ediciones Museo de la Música, 2013), 91.

[49] Argeliers León, "[Review]," *Conservatorio,* no. 8 (1947), 29.

54 CUBAN MUSIC COUNTERPOINTS

framework and vocabulary heavily informed by the neoclassical training they received from Ardévol and through the study of music scores by contemporary composers from Europe and the United States. By the late 1940s, these composers arrived at a more mature style that balanced neoclassical approaches with a subtler incorporation of vernacular elements. They continued using terms that aligned their works with classical forms, such as the use of "serenata" (serenade), suite, and sonata in composition titles, and labeling movements by their tempo markings in Italian. They also resorted to more creolized or mulato vernacular forms, such as the *son* and the *contradanza*, as sources of local musical markers, instead of the overtly Afro-Cuban genres, such as rumba, that their predecessors Roldán and García Caturla favored. Harold Gramatges's *Serenata* and Argeliers León's *Sonatas de la Virgen del Cobre* illustrate how composers took the technical skills they developed during this decade as the foundation for their personal compositional voices, an approach in which Cuban elements were seamlessly woven into a modernist fabric. They did, however, incorporate some of the compositional devices that Roldán and García Caturla had employed in their Afro-Cuban compositions. But now these elements went beyond coloristic accents, as Ardévol put it; they were intrinsic to the language of their modernist compositions.

On June 20, 1947, the Sociedad de Orquesta de Cámara de La Habana presented the first of two concerts of Contemporary Cuban Music. The program included Edgardo Martín's *Fugas*, for string chamber orchestra (1947); Harold Gramatges's *Serenata*, for string chamber orchestra (1947); Ardévol's, V Sonata a tres, for two clarinets and bass clarinet (1945) and his VI Sonata a tres, for three horns (1946); as well as Argeliers León's *Sonatas a la Virgen del Cobre*, for chamber orchestra and piano (1947). León's composition was the only one that overtly alluded to any specifically Cuban extramusical elements. In the title of the work, the Virgen de la Caridad del Cobre—the patron saint of Cuba, who is also revered by Lucumí practitioners as the orisha Oshún—León immediately alerts performers and listeners that they are about to experience a particularly Cuban composition. In the program notes for a 1949 concert by the same ensemble, León explained that the first and second sonatas "were conceived within the sonorities of the old **contradanzas**, while the third is nothing more than a **son**."[50] But, at the beginning of the notes on this work, León posed two rhetorical questions "Folklore? Nationalism?" which led him to explain his views on what motivates an artist, "la **realidad hombre** [the reality mankind] . . . one's reality . . . a need for expressing oneself," adding that the musical work "is not the

---

[50] Argeliers León, "Notas al Programa," Concert program of the Sociedad Orquesta de Cámara de La Habana, June 22, 1949, Box "Programas," Fondo personal José Ardévol, Museo Nacional de la Música Cubana, Havana, Cuba. Emphasis from the original.

collector or exhibitor of a climate, of a landscape, but it is a product of a people that has made a complex way of sounding (modo de sonar) and, more circumstantially, a way of believing (*modo de creer*)." León's use of the term "sonata," he explained, connotes a return to its original use and meaning (for early instrumental pieces), closer to his concept of "ways of sounding." In this sense, his adoption of the term sonata aligns with neoclassical approaches in music composition shared by his contemporaries. However, León's work also bares traces of late Classical sonata form procedures, as well as concertante style. León imbues the work with particularly Cuban "ways of sounding," mainly through references to the *contradanza* and *punto guajiro*.

León's *Sonata* also shares several traits with Manuel de Falla's approach in his Harpsichord Concerto, including the use of polychordal harmonies, short and memorable thematic motives, playful gestures, and chamber music instrumentation.[51] De Falla's Concerto was admired and closely analyzed in Ardévol's composition and analysis courses and had been performed by the Orquesta de Cámara de La Habana with Julián Orbón as soloist in 1942. Considering Ardévol's admiration of de Falla and Spanish neoclassicism and his role as teacher and mentor of León and his colleagues, it is not surprising that de Falla's approach would have influenced León's work. León relies on the classical sonata as well as the Baroque and Classical concerto to structure the work. The sections alternate between tutti (ripieno/ritornelli) and solo piano passages (episodes), yet, León also infuses the work with dissonances that create polychordal moments, which recall Manuel de Falla's and Charles Ives's harmonic writing and impart his work with a modernist sound that distinguishes it from the traditional nineteenth-century Cuban *contradanza*. An example of this juxtaposition is apparent at the very opening of the second sonata, where León begins the movement with an E-seven chord (the dominant of A Major), but in addition to the E dominant sonority in the piano, he adds the pitches of A and C-natural, creating a polychordal sonority of E dominant and A minor. León "corrects" the C-natural to a C-sharp in the next measure, where an A major chord is juxtaposed with G#-B-D-F#, shown in Music Example 1.1. A similar moment of polychordal juxtaposition occurs at letter J; here the piano drops out while the violins, cellos and basses play a B Major chord and the violas play D-naturals, the lowered third of the chord, at the same time as we hear D-sharps in the violins, shown in Music Example 1.2. These polychordal moments sound as though one of the instrumentalists or entire sections (the viola section in the second cited example) have made a mistake in reading the key signature. Bitonality and odd phrasing instill the work with

---

[51] Carol Hess, *Manuel de Falla and Modernism in Spain, 1898–1936* (Chicago: University of Chicago Press, 2001), 236–239.

Music Example 1.1. León, *Sonatas a la Virgen del Cobre*, Sonata II, mm. 1–2.

Music Example 1.2. León, *Sonatas a la Virgen del Cobre*, Sonata II, RL J.

tongue-in-cheek moments of musical humor, while at the same time marking the work as modernist.

In this Sonata, León evokes Cubanness through the use of rhythmic and melodic elements from two Cuban genres: the *contradanza* and the *guajira*. The *contradanza*, a formal dance and salon genre from the mid-nineteenth century in binary form, survives as publications of piano sheet music, but the genre was performed in upper-middle-class social gatherings by instrumental ensembles. León employs syncopation typical of the *contradanza*: the *tresillo*, shown in Music Example 1.3; the *cinquillo*, shown in Music Example 1.4; and the *habanera*. León also uses imitative phrases and contrasting sections more closely associated with the classical style in combination with the rhythmic and melodic devices from the *contradanza*. León's use of the musical figures associated with *contradanza* and its younger relative, the *danzón*, is not simply nationalist but a particularly Cuban approach to neoclassicism, a modernist engagement with a local tradition from the past, offering an idiosyncratically Cuban approach within a neoclassical framework.

Combining the French contredanse form, harmonic language, and instrumentation, with African-influenced rhythmic patterns, the *contradanza* encapsulated the dominant narrative of Cubanness as the homogeneous result of

Music Example 1.3. León, *Sonatas a la Virgen del Cobre*, Sonata II, mm. 41–42, *tresillo* in the bass part.

Music Example 1.4. León, *Sonatas a la Virgen del Cobre*, Sonata II, mm. 41–42, *cinquillo* in the piano.

58 CUBAN MUSIC COUNTERPOINTS

the process of transculturation blending the most desirable aspects of European and African cultures to create distinctly Cuban art where neither the African nor the European elements dominate the others. In *La música en Cuba,* Carpentier went to great lengths to explain the "arrival" and popularization in Cuba of the creolized French contredance from Haiti in the wake of the slave revolt that led the mostly white creole elite and their slaves to flee Haiti and arrive in Eastern Cuba.[52] Throughout his book, Carpentier credited New Orleans native, Louis Moreau Gottschalk with encouraging local Cuban composers to work with local genres and for promoting "concert" versions of music that had largely been relegated to dance halls. Carpentier noted that the quintessential element that made this music "creolized" was the presence of the *cinquillo* rhythmic pattern, which he traced to ritual and drumming practices of Afro-descendants in the Caribbean (he specifically mentions voudun), and he hypothesized that it was probably present in early nineteenth-century dance music of several Caribbean islands, including Puerto Rico and the Dominican Republic.[53]

The contradanza was the immediate predecessor of the danzón, which, as Alejandro L. Madrid and Robin Moore have shown, developed in the late 1800s and early 1900s in a transnational context in which composers, musicians, and dancers from Cuba, Mexico, and beyond experienced danzón through sonic and embodied practices. Rather than categorize the danzón as a music genre or generic complex (*complejo genérico*) Madrid and Moore discuss it as a performance complex, "a particular kind of music and dance that exists within unique cultural web of production, circulation, and signification."[54] As the immediate predecessor of the danzón, we can also include the contradanza within the transnational performance complex. When idiosyncratic and identifiable musical traits of the contradanza are evoked and reconfigured in modernist works by composers such as León, musical works also gain a transhistorical agency, acting as nodes in a web of musical references that cut across chronological and national boundaries.

In the Sonata II, León disrupts the *contradanza's* 2/4 dance pattern on two occasions (at RL D and I) by inserting a twenty-measure section in the style of a *punto guajiro,* a rural song and dance genre usually in 3/4 with alternating hemiolas or metric groupings of 6/8 with accents on the first, third, and fifth eighth notes, seen in Music Example 1.5. Although the section is in 3/4, León places the

---

[52] As Peter Manuel has demonstrated, the contredance arrived in Cuba in both Santiago and Havana prior to the Haitian revolution, but Carpentier did not have access to these older sources that Manuel and other scholars have examined in more recent years. Peter Manuel, *Creolizing Contradance in the Caribbean* (Philadelphia: Temple University Press, 2011).

[53] As Peter Manuel and Díaz Díaz have explored recently, Carpentier's intuition was correct. Edgardo Díaz Díaz "Puerto Rico: The Rise and Fall of the Danza as National Music," and Peter Manuel, "Cuba: From Contradanza to Danzón," in *Creolizing Contradance in the Caribbean* (Philadelphia: Temple University Press, 2009).

[54] Alejandro L. Madrid and Robin D. Moore. *Danzón: Circum-Caribbean Dialogues in Music and Dance* (New York: Oxford University Press, 2013), 10.

Music Example 1.5. León, *Sonatas a la Virgen del Cobre*, Sonata II, mm. RL D, *guajira* section.

accents in 6/8 in the left hand of the piano and the cellos. At the same time, the violas and right hand of the piano have rhythmic figures that bring out the 3/4 division of the measure. The 3/4–6/8 dance patterns are still popular not only in Cuba, but throughout most of Latin America, from several varieties of Mexican *sones* and the *joropos* of Venezuela to the *cuecas* and their related genres in Chile, Argentina, Peru, and Bolivia, and the *malambo* in Argentina. By engaging with a vernacular tradition that shared features with other Latin American dances, León also tied his work to broader Latin American musical practices. Alberto Ginastera had used similar rhythmic devices in several of his overtly nationalist works, such as his "Danza final (malambo)" from *Estancia* (1943).

León's adoption of rhythmic, melodic, and formal musical features drawn from popular music practices was not only motivated by his nationalist and modernist sensibilities as a classical music composer. His engagement with Cuban vernacular traditions stemmed from in-depth study and ethnographic fieldwork. In the 1940s, León studied ethnology and folklore with Fernando Ortiz and María Muñoz de Quevedo in the University of Havana's summer courses. By this point, León was well-versed in Ortiz's theories on cultural hybridity not only as a student, but eventually as a collaborator. León conducted ethnographic fieldwork on Afro-Cuban religious music with Ortiz and eventually offered his own courses and lectures on

60 CUBAN MUSIC COUNTERPOINTS

the topic starting in the late 1940s. León's research activities demonstrate that interest in Afro-Cuban music and culture never disappeared; instead of serving as a source of rhythmic cells and motives for modernist works, Afro-Cuban music had become the subject of anthropological and systematic study. Between 1947 and 1949, the very same years when he worked on the *Sonatas*, León collaborated with Ortiz on the first publication on Afro-Cuban folk music, researching and editing *Preludios étnicos de la música afrocubana*. In 1952, León published *El Patrimonio Folklórico Musical Cubano* as part of the series *Cuadernos del Folklore*.[55] The stylistic analysis of Sonata II, when framed by León's broader intellectual pursuits and Carpentier's account of the *contradanza's* history in *La música en Cuba*, helps us locate León's *Sonatas a la Virgen del Cobre* as a neoclassical, modernist, and Cuban work that strove to dialog with compositional circles within and outside of Cuba.

Gramatges's *Serenata*

Succinctly titled *Serenata*, Gramatges's composition for string orchestra offered performers and listeners a highly stylized interpretation of Cuban vernacular idioms within neoclassical forms and procedures. In the program notes for a 1949 concert, Gramatges opined that an artist could not "reach the ultimate truth in their work if they don't fully identify themselves with their people."[56] Regarding his compositional output, Gramatges explained that beginning in 1944, with his Trio for clarinet, cello, and piano, "Cuban stylistic elements appear in [his] music."[57] Yet at the core of his artistic intentions, he strove for a balance between the "universal" and the "local": "guided . . . by a constant aspiration: to situate our [Cuban] music within a universal level because of its technical elaboration, and that said Cuban stylistic elements, sometimes present in essence . . . or treated in more direct ways, are fully recognizable, in this way affirming our present in the Cuban musical tradition."[58] Gramatges further explained that his *Serenata* responded "in spirit" to a "Cubanness that [Gramatges] tried to shape more deeply in [his music]" in each movement.[59] He noted that he elaborates the rhythmic traits of a *guajira* in the first movement, clarifying that "the character of the theme shows that it is not self-imposed, but rather, a natural musical need, completely spontaneous."[60] The time signature lets the performers know

---

[55] Fernando Ortiz, "Preludios étnicos de la música afrocubana," *Revista Bimestre Cubana* LIX (1947); Argeliers León, *El patrimonio folklórico musical cubano* (Havana: Cámara & León, 1952).

[56] Harold Gramatges, "Notas al Programa," Program Concert of the Sociedad Orquesta de Cámara de La Habana, June 22, 1949, Box "Programas," Fondo personal José Ardévol, Museo Nacional de la Música Cubana, Havana, Cuba.

[57] Ibid.

[58] Ibid.

[59] Ibid.

[60] Ibid.

immediately that they will be dealing with the juxtaposition of the duple and triple subdivision of the beats, indicated as 3/4 = 6/8. Although Gramatges limits his comment on the influence of the *guajira* to rhythmic parameters, upon closer examination we can see and hear that the melody also follows the melodic contour conventions of guajira figurations usually improvised by the *tres* player in an ensemble: alternating ascending thirds or fifths with descending stepwise motion, as seen in the opening measures in Music Example 1.6. This opening motivic gesture serves as the basis for the entire movement, developed in various

Music Example 1.6. Gramatges, *Serenata*, First Movement, mm. 1–10.
Note: Harold Gramatges, *Serenata, orquesta de cuerdas* (Havana: Editora Musical de Cuba, 1988), 1.

62   CUBAN MUSIC COUNTERPOINTS

modes and in sequences, set in different instrumental combinations, and treated contrapuntally through points of imitations at the octave, almost in *Fortspinnung* manner. Although lacking a clear secondary theme or section, the motivic material is transformed and treated in distinct ways in the middle section of the movement where two other key areas are explored, returning to the home key of G major and the movement's opening gesture at rehearsal number 15, resulting in a rounded binary form. Gramatges grafted the Cuban element, the *guajira* rhythm and melody, to the form and techniques he acquired through his neoclassical training. Two other characteristics align this composition with the neoclassical contemporaries and models he admired (Schoenberg, Stravinsky, Bartók, Hindemith, and de Falla): the avoidance of thirds and leading tones, which gave the harmonic and melodic writing a more modal sound, and the pervasive use of quartal and quintal harmonies, both of which he employed in the middle and last movements.

Gramatges opened the slow middle movement with a series of points of imitation of a melody that featured several rhythmic patterns present in various genres of vernacular Cuban music, such as the *cinquillo*, amphibrach, *tresillo*, and other syncopated figures. Because he sets them in a slow tempo, the effect is more lyrical rather than dance-like. The final "Allegro" returns to the 6/8 = 3/4 rhythmic and metric pace set up in the opening movement. This final movement is structured in rondo form, in which the A consists of a fast 3/4 = 6/8 guajira-like material, while the alternating sections are slower and in 3/4, without the alternating and overlapping 6/8 subdivision of the faster sections. In his program notes, Gramatges explained that these slower sections were "inspired by popular songs of *nuestro medio habanero* [our Havanan scene] (I [Gramatges] think of the so-called **boleros**, which are really like habaneras)."[61] These slower middle sections lacked the imitative contrapuntal writing Gramatges used in the faster sections, providing contrast not only through tempo but also in their part writing.

Both compositions, Gramatge's *Serenata* and León's *Sonatas de la Virgen del Cobre,* became regular fixtures in the Orquesta de Cámara's programing. Although they were not recorded or published until the following decade, eventually both works would be treated as classic examples of this time period, the neoclassical period of both composers, published by the Editora Musical de Cuba and recorded in more recent years by Cuban ensembles and projects dedicated to "rescue" these relatively "forgotten" works from the 1940s. The emphasis on

---

[61] Gramatges, "Notas al Programa," Program Concert of the Sociedad Orquesta de Cámara de La Habana, June 22, 1949, Box "Programas," Fondo personal José Ardévol, Museo Nacional de la Música Cubana, Havana, Cuba. Emphasis in original.

elements from vernacular Cuban music shows Gramatges's and León's individual interests and concerns and sheds light on how intellectuals dealt with the broader Cuban cultural and political context. By combining what they considered more contemporary compositional techniques of "universal" music with *criollo* musical traits, these composers engaged in the nation-building project and presented their views on Cubanness through music. In order to be respected as composers on par with their US and European counterparts Cuban composers had to engage with international modernist approaches, such as neoclassicism, atonality, or bitonality, while cultivating an individual sound that was also representative of their Cuban national identity. Using the *guajira* and *contradanza* imbued León's work with Cubanness, but one that was more "civilized," more "modern" than that associated with purely Afro-Cuban elements, speaking to broader Cuban interests and desires to be viewed as "modern" by outsiders. By incorporating *criollo* and mulato genres—genres that intellectuals like Caprentier and León claimed to encapsulate the Cuban racial and cultural mixture that Ortiz identified as transculturation—into the neoclassical forms and modernist harmonic language, Gramatges and León reconciled seemingly opposing goals: national and universal, traditional and modern. León's musical conceptualization of Cubanness was firmly rooted in Ortiz's concept of transculturation and on a legacy of nation-building that upheld Cubanness as the eclectic result of hundreds of years of racial and cultural mixing, and always positioned in reference to foreign views of Cubanness.

Throughout the 1940s the members of the GRM continued to mature and develop their individual compositional voices. While having José Ardévol and Alejo Carpentier as their mentors and champions, these young composers forged lasting bonds internally as a group and with foreign composers. These connections would prove crucial to the success of their artistic careers in the subsequent decades, as I explore in the following chapters. By 1948 the GRM ceased to exist, but its former members took the helm of the Havana music scene. The connections and networks they engaged with throughout these years continued to provide opportunities to educate audiences through public lectures and music criticism in the press, and promote their music in the ensembles and with performers involved in the Sociedad de Orquesta de Cámara de La Habana. A neoclassical training and approach allowed them to hone their compositional tools and to write music that composers outside of Cuba, particularly in the United States, would view as clear, modern, and refined. However, their blend of structural clarity and vernacular idioms began to be viewed with suspicion, especially as European emigrés who settled in cities throughout the Americas during and after World War II promoted twelve-tone composition among their New World pupils. In the United States, populist idioms also began to be associated with a new threat and enemy, communism, especially after Copland's

64 CUBAN MUSIC COUNTERPOINTS

and Bernstein's involvement in the 1949 Cultural and Scientific Conference for World Peace and the House Un-American Activities Committee (HUAC) trials that red-listed Copland.[62] The Golden Years of Cuban–US cultural exchange would come to a close as Fulgencio Batista's repressive regime would censor and persecute leftist and communist artists and intellectuals in the 1950s. The generation of the GRM would face arduous political circumstances throughout the 1950s. These composers had to decide with which intellectual groups to align themselves and how to continue producing work that was individually and collectively meaningful while running the risk of being labeled and persecuted as communists or anti-Batista.

---

[62] For more on US composers' political engagement before and after World War II and during the Cold War see Emily Abrams Ansari, *The Sound of a Superpower: Musical Americanism and the Cold War* (New York: Oxford University Press, 2018); Jennifer DeLapp-Birkett, "Aaron Copland and the Politics of Twelve-Tone Composition in the Early Cold War United States," *Journal of Musicological Research* 27, no. 1 (2008): 31–62.

2

The Sociedad Cultural Nuestro Tiempo

Precursor to the Cuban Revolutionary Cultural Projects, 1950–1958

On December 27, 1949, a new organization of musicians, the Sociedad Amadeo Roldán (SAR), presented a concert comprised entirely of music by Cuban composers at the Teatro "Normal" (Teatro de la Escuela Normal de Maestros) in Havana. The program included *Danzas Números 1 y 2* by Ignacio Cervantes (1847–1905), *Página de un album* by Gonzalo Roig, and *Fugas para Cuerdas* by Edgardo Martín. When compared to the programming of the Sociedad de Música de Cámara, this concert does not seem unusual or particularly outstanding. As discussed in the previous chapter, the Sociedad de Música de Cámara, led by José Ardévol, was one of the primary musical institutions that promoted new music by contemporary Cuban composers throughout the 1930s and 1940s. However, the SMC did so as part of a broader objective of disseminating music that was seldom heard in Cuban concert music spaces. Consequently, Cuban composers' works comprised only a fraction of the concert programming that also included Renaissance, Baroque, and early Classical European works, and contemporary music (mainly in the neoclassical vein) by composers from Europe and the Americas. In contrast, the concert at the Teatro Normal was the inaugural event of a new organization, the Sociedad Amadeo Roldán (SAR), devoted exclusively to the promotion of classical compositions by Cuban composers. This inaugural concert marked the beginning of a Cuban centered cultural organization that would expand its purview to include local literature, theater, visual art, ballet, and film as an antidote to a lack of support from the Instituto Nacional de Cultura (INC, National Institute of Culture) and the preponderance of popular music genres in radio broadcasts, recording studios, and entertainment venues due to the commercial ventures of multinational corporations.

In the program notes for the SAR concert, composer Ithiel León wrote that the group came into being when two colleagues, Nilo Rodríguez and Juan Elósegui, (pictured in Fig. 2.1 along with other members of the SAR), approached him at the Conservatorio Municipal with the idea of organizing a concert society that would program concerts comprised solely of works by Cuban composers. I. León pointed to the untimely deaths of Roldán and García Caturla as the moment when Cuban music was finally "up to date" (puesta al día), a labor that had begun,

Cuban Music Counterpoints. Marysol Quevedo, Oxford University Press. © Oxford University Press 2023.
DOI: 10.1093/oso/9780197552230.003.0003

66   CUBAN MUSIC COUNTERPOINTS

according to I. León, with Roldán's *Obertura sobre temas cubanos* (Overture on Cuban themes) from 1925. Roldán's widow, Rita Robaina, was named the honorary president of the SAR, and the top leadership included Juan Elósegui as president, Odilio Urfé as vice-president, Nilo Rodríguez as secretary, and Juan Blanco as treasurer. A lawyer by training, Juan Blanco was a relative newcomer to the Conservatorio circle, yet he would become one of the leading cultural figures of the 1950s and after. Odilio Urfé had made it his mission to revive the *danzón*, a dance genre that had enjoyed great popularity in the Caribbean basin in the preceding decades but that had been displaced as outmoded by the 1950s thanks to the chachachá and mambo crazes in cosmopolitan ballroom and dancehall circles.[1] His revival efforts repackaged the *danzón* as an elegant salon genre and as national patrimony (when in fact, it had been criticized as "barbaric" and "improper" when it emerged in the late nineteenth century).[2] Although other SAR concerts consisted mainly of vocal, piano, and chamber works by Cuban composers, they also performed some wind band transcriptions of compositions by Ludwig von Beethoven, Alexander Borodin, and Pytor Ilyich Tchaikovsky, and they programmed the first Cuban performance of J.S. Bach's *St. Matthew's Passion*, in a way breaking with or contradicting their stated mission of only performing music by Cuban composers. I. León added to his notes, a sort of mission statement for the SAR:

> We are convinced that [the public] has the right to be made aware of what they do not know and we approach them with the best honesty, free from preconceived judgments, with the extraordinary faith that gives sight to a generation that moves and raises in order to procure the establishment of our own values, of the musical language of our time (nuestro tiempo), breathing the atmosphere of the minute in which—luckily—we have had to live.[3]

Here, I. León indicates two main concerns that would shape the activities of this and a subsequent society throughout the 1950s: the dissemination of unknown music to a broader audience and a preoccupation with the current context, *nuestro tiempo* (our time). The music of the past, as far back as the nineteenth century (as with the works of Ignacio Cervantes and Manuel Saumell) and into

---

[1] Alejandro L. Madrid, and Robin D. Moore, *Danzón: Circum-Carribean Dialogues in Music and Dance* (New York: Oxford University Press, 2013), 35.

[2] Ibid., 5.

[3] "Estamos convencidos de que este [el público] posee el derecho de ser enterado de lo que ignora y a él nos acercamos con la mejor honradez, libres de juicios preconcebidos, con la fe extraordinaria que da ver a una generación que se mueve y levanta en procura del establecimiento de nuestros valores propios, del idioma musical de nuestro tiempo, respirando la atmósfera del minuto en que—por suerte—nos ha tocado vivir." Concert program in Sociedad Amadeo Roldán (SAR) scrapbook, Museo Nacional de la Música Cubana, Havana, Cuba.

THE SOCIEDAD CULTURAL NUESTRO TIEMPO 67

the 1930s (with the works of Amadeo Roldán and Alejandro García Caturla), although not of "their time" became synonymous with Cuban musical and cultural identity. In the face of a cultural state apparatus—first under Carlos Prío Socarrás's Dirección de Cultura under the Ministry of Education and later under Fulgencio Batista's Instituto Nacional de Cultura (INC)—that broadly ignored the Cuban classical music these composers valued, to revive and promote any classical music by Cuban composers was to go against the grain. And by promoting Cuban music of a particular vein (nineteenth-century salon music in the case of Cervantes and Saumell and *Afrocubanismo* in the case of Roldán and García Caturla) this new generation of composers created a historical narrative in which they placed themselves as the inheritors of a Cuban nationalist music tradition, a narrative that had been well-established by Alejo Carpentier in his 1946 *La música en Cuba*. Their efforts were just as much about legitimizing themselves as part of the arch of Cuban music history as it was about "rescuing" the forgotten old masters. As we shall see in the next chapter, even when composers "broke" from tradition or the norm, they placed themselves within this narrative, as part of a legacy of Cuban music history that justified their aesthetic and social views. To be of "our time" always meant to have a keen sense of the past and a desire to leave a mark and be remembered in the future.

The individuals and organizations we encounter in the Cuban classical music scene of the 1950s overlapped significantly with those from the 1940s, with a few notable additions. Although contacts with salient US composers were maintained—young Cuban composers continued to travel to the United States to further their compositional training—connections with Latin American music circles expanded. This was in part thanks to Alejo Carpentier's role as music critic in Caracas, Venezuela, and the Latin American Music Festivals held in that same country. Musically, as the SAR suggests, there was also a return to vernacular music as a source of rhythmic, melodic, and structural elements in their compositions. They grafted the Cuban music elements onto the solid trunk of compositional training they received at the Conservatorio Municipal under José Ardévol. By the late 1940s and early 1950s, some of the young composers who had been pupils of Ardévol (such as Gramatges) had become music theory and composition professors at the Conservatorio. A new facet of their overall activities in the 1950s was the politicization of their discourse and the synthesis of their cultural and artistic work with political activism. This model of the artist–activist was certainly not new in Cuba. The intellectuals from the Grupo Minorista[4] were still active among the Cuban intelligentsia. For many of these composers and artists, to be an artist of "our time" was to be an *artista comprometido*: a socially and

---

[4] See Ana Cairo Ballester, *El Grupo Minorista y su tiempo* (Havana, Cuba: Editorial de Ciencias Sociales, 1978).

Figure 2.1. Newspaper clipping from *El Mundo*, February 12, 1950. The caption reads: "The image shows the directors of the Sociedad 'Amadeo Roldán,' who, with much enthusiasm promote the work of the novel institution. They are, Juan Elósegui, president, Odilio Urfé, Nilo Rodríguez, Ithiel León, Carmenchú Rodríguez, Josefina Elósegui, Edmundo López, and Pablo Iturrioz." From Sociedad Amadeo Roldán scrapbook at the Museo Nacional de la Música Cubana.

politically committed artist, an intellectual who sought to address the political and social issues of their people through their artistic production, an artist who was not indifferent to the people living at the margins, an individual with strong political ideals who would not shy away from openly criticizing the state for its failures to address the needs of its people or social and racial inequalities. These composers and other artists promoted both local vernacular traditions and modernist art works while also engaging with international artistic trends. The "enemy," it seems, was a field of cultural production that ignored or threatened these two areas, and in 1950s Cuba this was represented by a multi-national music industry that promoted popular music through capitalist and commercial

THE SOCIEDAD CULTURAL NUESTRO TIEMPO   69

consumption as well as an INC that ignored the practical needs of Cuban artists. The SAR was the beginning of a cultural movement in 1950s Cuba that was committed to promoting a national music tradition that had been largely ignored by commercial music enterprises and state cultural institutions. This is not to say that there were no state cultural institutions in the decades leading up to the 1959 Revolution. On the contrary, as Cary García has argued the four administrations that preceded the Revolution "aimed to regulate arts education by controlling its content, its academic structure, the art personnel, and student financial aid. Each government built on the works of its predecessor to further expand and consolidate music and a visual arts education. These continuities were embedded in institutional structures that lasted past specific directors and governments . . . and [each government] understood and used the power of the arts in similar ways to bring legitimacy to the state by promoting the image of a modern and progressive Cuba."[5] Prior to World War II, the Partido Socialista Popular (Popular Socialist Party, PSP) worked with artists' unions and made significant gains in terms of legislative measures to protect artists' rights and work. It wasn't until the repressive, anti-communist/socialist measures of the Cold War, epitomized by Batista's coup and regime, that we see leftist Cuban artists being censored and persecuted as well as their activities becoming more organized and overtly political.[6] Throughout this chapter we'll explore how the SAR evolved into the Sociedad Cultural Nuestro Tiempo (SCNT, Cultural Society of Our Time) as the composers who founded it collaborated with artists in other fields, expanding their activities to other artistic manifestations. The SCNT activities also coincided with the leftist political agenda of the ensuing Revolution, in fact many of the SCNT members were also active members of the PSP. The overlap in political and social ideology of SCNT members with that of the revolutionary leaders would result in SCNT members becoming the leaders of the post-1959 cultural organizations, such as Edgardo Martín in music and Alicia Alonso, Fernando Alonso, and Alberto Alonso in ballet.

New Music and the Ballet Nacional

Edgardo Martín's *Fugas para Cuerdas*, the only contemporary composition performed in the first SAR concert discussed above, also served as the musical backdrop for a new production by a relatively young organization that would go on to become one of the most celebrated cultural jewels in the crown of the

---

[5] Cary Aileen García Yero, "The State within the Arts: A Study of Cuba's Cultural Policy, 1940–1958," *Cuban Studies* 47, no. 1 (2019): 85.

[6] Ibid., 86.

70   CUBAN MUSIC COUNTERPOINTS

Cuban artistic scene, the Ballet Nacional. In the first public performance of the new Ballet Nacional of Cuba, on April 23, 1950, *Fugas* was choreographed by Alberto Alonso, with set and costume design by René Portocarrero, in a ballet titled *Cuatro Fugas* (Four Fugues), which received subsequent performances as part of the Ballet Nacional's repertoire. The other works in this first program were *Concerto* (music by Vivaldi–Bach keyboard concerto; set and costume design, by Fico Villalba; and choreography, Alberto Alonso); and *Panoram* (music by Brahms *Variations on a Theme by Haydn*; set and costume design by Andres; choreography by Elena de Cueto). The three ballets were non-representational and not programmatic, setting choreographies to musical compositions that were not initially intended to be danced or choreographed, and that had strong connections to quintessentially Baroque and Classical forms (a Concerto and a set of Variations from the Baroque and Classical/Romantic periods respectively). This neoclassical approach to music selection and choreography shows a clear influence from the New York-based ballet companies Ballet Theatre (later known as American Ballet Theater) and Jerome Robins, where Ballet Nacional founders and choreographers (the Alonsos) had trained in earlier decades, as well as the influence of the Ballets Russes from Paris, a company in which Alberto Alonso (Fernando Alonso's brother) danced principal roles for works choreographed by Michel Fokine in the 1930s. The individuals and institutions with which the Cuban dancers and choreographers interacted outside of Cuba was eerily similar to the ones with which the Cuban composers engaged in their musical and artistic networks, Paris and New York.

Although this was the first official performance of the Ballet Nacional under this name, the company had been active since 1947–1948 as the Ballet Alicia Alonso. The concert program's synopsis of *Cuatro Fugas*, although brief, explains that Cuban popular dance elements served as the inspiration for the non-narrative work: "The choreography of this work, like its music, has been extracted from our purest popular source, acquiring our plebeian dances, a letter of definitive aristocracy, in this ballet without narrative/plot."[7] Which Cuban popular dance elements Alberto Alonso incorporated in the choreography is not entirely clear. However, the description of Portocarrero's set and costume designs specifies which aspects of Cuban folklore were invoked in the work:

[Portocarrero] based his set and costume designs for the ballet *Cuatro Fugas* on the atmosphere of the *Cuarto Fambá*, the secret room of the ñáñigo ceremonies. In the costumes, inspired by Afro-Cuban signs, and in the sets of the ballet *Cuatro Fugas*,

---

[7] "La coreografía de esta obra, al igual que su música, ha sido extraída de nuestra más pura fuente popular, adquiriendo nuestras danzas plebeyas, carta de definitiva aristocracia, en este ballet sin argumento." Concert program notes for Ballet Nacional performance, April 23, 1950, Box 1950–1951, Collection Programas de Mano, Biblioteca Nacional José Martí, Havana, Cuba.

THE SOCIEDAD CULTURAL NUESTRO TIEMPO   71

Portocarrero's intimate idea has been to project the models that he has physically seen according to his emotional reactions and visions, faithful to his aesthetic of not reproducing the nature or things as seen by the senses. The dancers represent the altars, the beads, etc. The artist has used pure, "clean" colors, as he states.[8]

This description points to a modernist, mediated, and sublimated interpretation of the Afro-Cuban religious visual aspects for the set and costume design. This approach to the visual components of the ballet was not unlike that of the Cuban composers, whose work incorporated Afro-Cuban music elements within the clear and clean structures of neoclassical forms, in this case Baroque fugues. As a non-representational ballet, we can assume that the choreography did not attempt to replicate or reference any specific religious rituals. However, later in life Alberto Alonso pointed to this period in his career as a time when he was heavily influenced by Abakuá and other Afro-Cuban religious dance traditions. He was also influenced by Jerome Robins's Americanist approach to choreography and he was in the same artistic circles as the leading Cuban anthropologists and ethnographers, including Fernando Ortiz and Argeliers León (León would compose the music for Alberto Alonso's 1952 Afro-Cuban ballet *Toque*). The Ballet Nacional, however, was taking a risk in including Afro-Cuban elements in this work. As ballet historian Elizabeth Schwall has noted, the company had been heavily criticized for exploring and incorporating Afro-Cuban music, dance, and costume elements in previous productions, most notably their 1947 *Antes del Alba* (Before Dawn) choreographed by Alberto Alonso, with music by Hilario González (another member of the Grupo de Renovación Musical).[9] In *Cuatro Fugas,* the Cuban vernacular reference could have been perceived as even more incendiary, since Portocarrero's designs were inspired by the secret room used in the religious ceremonies of one of Cuba's most infamous secret Afro-religious societies, the Abakuá. But reviews of the two 1950 performances (April and October) were not critical of the Afro-Cuban elements. In fact, the reviewer for *Diario de la marina* of the April performance made no mention of the Afro-Cuban elements, and criticized the ballet as "the least fortunate" of the three works performed that evening, either because the choreographer was uninspired, or because the music itself was uninspiring, noting that Martín's composition lacked contrast of color and drama that ballets need. In her view, Martín's music was well-suited for a chamber concert performance, but not for ballet.[10] In contrast, the October review described *Cuatro Fugas* as a work that

[8] Concert program notes for Ballet Nacional performance, October 15, 1950, Box 1950–1951, Collection Programas de Mano, Biblioteca Nacional José Martí, Havana, Cuba.
[9] Elizabeth Schwall, "Dancing with the Revolution: Cuban Dance, State, and Nation, 1930–1990." (Ph.D. diss, Columbia University, 2016), 93–95.
[10] Review of April 27, 1950, performance of the Ballet Nacional. Nena Benítez, "Fué un exito la presentación del Ballet Nacional en el Auditórium," *Diario de la Marina* (April 28, 1950): 15.

72   CUBAN MUSIC COUNTERPOINTS

showed what Ballet Nacional could offer that no foreign ballet company could, a true Cuban ballet; the reviewer made several positive comments about the Afro-Cuban influences and called the work "essential for Cuba and revealing for other countries."[11] There was one significant difference between the October and the April performances; in October 1950, the Musicians' Syndicate was negotiating musicians' contracts, and pulled the musicians of the Orchestra of the Instituto Nacional de la Música from the performance, leaving all the works to be performed to a piano accompaniment. Perhaps the orchestral version from April was not as well-rehearsed by the orchestra musicians and the piano reduction performance from October was more precise, or the work, both music and choreography, had been edited and tightened for impact and accuracy for the October performance. Either way, the October version was received as a triumph in comparison to the April premiere.

Dancers and choreographers Fernando and Alberto Alonso and composer Edgardo Martín were founding members of the SCNT, ardent supporters of the Ballet Nacional, and, after 1955, staunch critics of Batista's regime and the INC for their lack of financial support of the Ballet Nacional.[12] The Alonsos found in the composers who had been trained by Ardévol both ideological and aesthetic counterparts. Both composers and dancers promoted European art forms they considered to be universal, their starting point was a strong neoclassical training (both in dance and composition) that was reflected in their artforms (writing and choreographing fugues), and they were preoccupied with imbuing their "universal" art forms with identifiably Cuban elements. Martín's *Fugas* was not the only collaboration between the Ballet Nacional and the SCNT composers. In 1952, the Ballet Nacional produced *Toque*, another Afro-Cuban-inspired work, with music by Argeliers León.

The program notes for the music by Martín neatly encapsulate these aesthetic preoccupations on how to balance the universal with the Cuban:

> The desire to produce Cuban music within the most prestigious universal norms and principles is present in them [*Fugas para Cuerdas*]. The attitude is not that of a folkloric and closed nationalism, but that of taking advantage, within those principles, of the rich quarry of sonorous elements created by our country, our splendid national quality of sounding in our own way that contributes to the world an inventiveness, a popular creation, music that is unfailingly Cuban and amazingly abundant in quality features. It is clear that for anyone born on this island the spell of its musical language works with a sometimes hypnotic

---

[11] Review of October 15, 1950, performance of the Ballet Nacional. Regina, "Escnario y Pantalla: Teatro Auditorium: Ballet Nacional," *Diario de la Marina* (October 17, 1950): 15.

[12] *Nuestro Tiempo* journal.

THE SOCIEDAD CULTURAL NUESTRO TIEMPO   73

power; but in the *Fugues* efforts have been made to overcome "the tropical," "the jungle" [selvático-savage], "the typical" [folkloric], in favor of a more ambitious creation. Because of this, all the themes of the Fugues are completely original; that is to say, if they are conceived in the style of our popular music, none comes from this or that song or dance of the people. Because, after all, the source is the same, and both the one who makes a simple popular song and the one who composes a symphony can be equally faithful to the sonorous idiosyncrasy of his own country. The difference is only in the goal, be it the immediate popular creation, or to aspire to the creation of greater art, of universal art.[13]

In spite of an attempt to legitimize popular music, the writer (most likely Martín himself), shows their biased opinions that regard "universal" art as superior to folkloric or popular music. The composer "overcomes" the tropical, the savage, the folkloric in order to create something "more ambitious that aspires to be 'universal.'" Vernacular music elements are treated as raw material that can be exploited by a well-trained composer, even referring to this music as a "rich quarry" that can enrich the rest of the world. The writer also emphasizes the originality of the themes, reminding listeners that they are not mere copies of popular music, but rather inspired by it. Similarly, the Ballet Nacional's commentary on its mission, found in the same concert program, emphasized ballet's universal appeal and capacity to reach the people while elevating the local to the level of the universal,

> that we succeed in making ballet, Cuban ballet, one more index that indicates the height of our artistic-cultural level . . . That this love of dancing transcends the great mass of the people, and surpasses the current limits that surround them to that of the privileged minorities . . . raising our "standard" as a nation and as a human conglomerate . . . that we be helped in this endeavor, in every way, not only individually, but by the powers of the State as well, who, after all, sooner or later, will have to recognize and see in these activities of ours, a movement worthy of their protection and encouragement, thus fulfilling the sacred duties for which it is precisely constituted . . . that we achieve the goal that we pursue, for the good of art, of the hidden wealth that we contain, and of our country, which we want to see stand out in all its aspects and occupy its rightful place in the universal concert.[14]

[13] Concert program notes for Ballet Nacional performance, October 15, 1950, Box 1950–1951, Collection Programas de Mano, Biblioteca Nacional José Martí, Havana, Cuba.
[14] Ibid.

74 CUBAN MUSIC COUNTERPOINTS

Here, as in the case of the musical composition, "universal" implied an artform derived from a Western European tradition (ballet) that was cultivated in all of the major cosmopolitan centers of the Western Hemisphere. In keeping with the SCNT's mission (discussed below), to be truly of "our time" was to engage with art forms and aesthetic practices that would be understood by audiences and critics outside of Cuba, to be of "our time" was to be "universal." Martín's *Fugas para Cuerdas* also had a life that extended beyond the artistic networks within the island. In 1952, the work was conducted by Colombian composer Guillermo Espinoza at the Konserhuset in Goeteborg, Sweden.[15] And in 1954, the Pan American Union published the work through Peer International Corp. This remains the only edition of the work. Later, we will explore the connections Cuban composers cultivated in their international and hemispheric networks in further detail. These international connections, however, heavily depended on the internal, local networks of artists and intellectuals, especially through groups that focused on artistic and cultural production.

The Sociedad Cultural Nuestro Tiempo

By 1951, the SAR, briefly discussed at the beginning of this chapter, seemingly ceased to exist, but on further inspection it becomes clear that it was folded into another, newer, more all-encompassing cultural society. According to Harold Gramatges, one of the objectives of the SAR was to present music to audiences outside the usual and familiar venues, offering concerts in spaces where these had rarely taken place. Many of the SAR concerts took place in the theater of the Escuela Normal de Maestros, a venue that rarely showed up in the concert programs of the Sociedad de Música de Cámara de La Habana (which performed mostly at the Lyceum and Lawn Tennis Club). As the members of the SAR interacted more frequently with artists and intellectuals outside the Conservatorio Municipal and the Lyceum (the usual institutions that hosted classical music concerts), their circle of collaborators expanded to include painters, poets, playwrights, dancers, and film critics, to the extent that the Sociedad was completely transformed from an exclusively musical organization to a cultural one.[16] They began promoting not only Cuban classical music, but all Cuban art forms, and had grown to include among its membership artists and

---

[15] "Cuba en el Extranjero:. . . El director colombiano Guillermo Espinoza presentó las <u>Fugas para Orquesta de Cuerda,</u> del mismo compositor [Edgardo Martín], en el concierto que dirigió el 17 de febrero en la Konserhuset de la ciudad de Geoteborg, en Suecia." *Boletín de música y artes visuales* 24–23 (1952).

[16] Gramatges, "La Sociedad Cultural Nuestro Tiempo" reproduced in *Sociedad Cultural Nuestro Tiempo: resistencia y acción*, ed. Ricardo Luis Hernández Otero (Havana: Letras Cubanas, 2002), 282.

THE SOCIEDAD CULTURAL NUESTRO TIEMPO   75

intellectuals of all stripes; with this expansion in cultural scope, view, and mission, the group became the Sociedad Cultural Nuestro Tiempo (SCNT, Cultural Society of Our Time). I. León's initial remarks about the SAR's mission, "to procure the establishment of our own values, of the musical language of *our time*" [my emphasis], was the germinal idea for a cultural society of "our time." Their many activities included establishing an art gallery where they held expositions of modern art (focusing on Cuban artists) as well as exhibits of Cuban folk music instruments. They promoted national production of ballet, theater, literature, film, and music through subsections within the SCNT devoted to each artistic expression. Their focus was on modern, contemporary Cuban art. Yet, they also published letters and articles by or for foreign artists, such as Aaron Copland's 1956 essay "La Música como aspecto del espíritu humano" and a 1931 letter by Amadeo Roldán addressed to Henry Cowell.[17] By publishing contributions by foreign intellectuals in *Nuestro Tiempo*, the SCNT fostered a sense of cosmopolitanism and universality, of being in touch with influential individuals outside of Cuba. These foreign connections legitimized the SCNT's work in the eyes and minds of local audiences and readers. This was a significant process, for it served as a tool for acquiring cultural capital during Batista's regime, cultural capital that several members of the SCNT would exert in the initial years of the Revolution. In a 1997 article on Juan Blanco (founding member of the SCNT), Neil Leonard III compared the SCNT to the group of artists who gathered at Black Mountain College in Asheville, North Carolina, which included John Cage, Merce Cunningham, and Robert Rauschenberg.[18] The SCNT's aesthetic predilections, however, were tame and conservative by comparison to those artists at Black Mountain College; although later, after the 1959, the SCNT members would explore artistic experimentation along the lines of happenings that took place at Black Mountain, as we'll see in the following chapter.

As the 1950s progressed SCNT members became increasingly critical of Batista's regime and his INC. According to Jorgelina Guzmán Moré "the INC emerged as the result of political conjuncture caused by the coup d'état of March 10, 1952, when Batista took control of the country; therefore, his regime used the INC as an instrument of domination and legitimation." The INC programming also reflected the interests of its administrators, who belonged mainly to Havana's bourgeoisie.[19] Although members of the PSP had made considerable gains in terms of labor and union legislation in the 1940s, by the mid- to late

---

[17] Aaron Copland, "La música como aspecto del espírtu humano," *Nuestro Tiempo* Año 3, no. 14 (1956), n.p.; Amadeo Roldán, "Carta a Henry Cowell," *Nuestro Tiempo* Año 3, no. 10 (1956): 2–3.

[18] Neil Leonard III, "Juan Blanco: Cuba's Pioneer of Electroacoustic Music," *Computer Music Journal* 21, no. 2 (1997): 11.

[19] Jorgelina Guzmán Moré, *De Dirección General a Instituto Nacional de Cultura* (Havana: Editora Historia, 2014), 15–17.

76 CUBAN MUSIC COUNTERPOINTS

1950s the SCNT grew more and more dissatisfied with the INC's programming and activities. SCNT members refused to comply with what they viewed as capitalist and imperialist threats on local Cuban culture and artists. By examining the activities of the SCNT we can begin to understand that what seems like a dramatic cultural revolution after 1959 in Cuba, was actually the implementation of cultural policies that the members of the SCNT had been planning and advocating for nearly a decade prior. During the 1950s, through their artistic criticism and activities, the SCNT defined what cultural manifestations and aesthetics were in line with leftist-socialist ideology and would be promoted by the Cuban revolutionary state after 1959. Some of the key individuals involved in the SCNT were composers Harold Gramatges, Argeliers León, and Juan Blanco. In addition to their constant criticism of Batista's regime and state cultural institutions for their lack of support of contemporary national artists, several SCNT members belonged to the PSP. This connection drew the attention of the US embassy and Batista's regime, and resulted in the state's surveillance of SCNT activities. The SCNT's work was at times censored or blocked from public presentation. According to Gramatges, in some instances, Batista's police detained, incarcerated, and even killed SCNT's members whose leftist political views threatened the regime.[20] Because the members of the SCNT had shown their commitment to promoting and producing politically engaged art and had opposed Batista's regime, many of them were placed in key administrative roles in the post-1959 revolutionary state's cultural institutions.

In their "Manifesto," most likely drafted by Harold Gramatges and Juan Blanco, the SCNT laid out the group's motives and objectives, declaring that "we arise to bring the people to art, bringing [the people] closer to the aesthetic and cultural concerns of our time, precisely now that, already sensing the realities [of our times], [the people] demand a vehicle that allows it to appreciate and assimilate [art] for [the people's] quickest cultural formation and maturing." These statements foreshadowed the cultural policies of the Cuban Revolution after 1959,[21] most strikingly making art accessible to the masses as one of the main goals of state-sponsored cultural institutions. Initially, SCNT members claimed to be politically neutral, stating that they did not align with any particular political ideology or creed. In reality, however, their leftist and communist leanings (and in some cases, downright official political affiliations) became apparent in the wording of their manifesto and in their writings. In the final

---

[20] Harold Gramatges, *Yo ví la música: vida y obra de Harold Gramatges* (Havana, Cuba: Editorial Ciencias Sociales, 2009), 64–67.

[21] "Surgimos para traer el pueblo al arte, acercándolo a las inquietudes estéticas y culturales de nuestro tiempo, precisamente ahora en que, intuyendo ya estas realidades, demanda un vehículo que le permita palparlas y asimilarlas para su más rápida formación y madurez cultural." "Manifesto," *Nuestro Tiempo* no. 1 (1951): 1–2. Reproduced in Hernández Otero, *Sociedad Cultural Nuestro Tiempo,* 19.

THE SOCIEDAD CULTURAL NUESTRO TIEMPO   77

sentences of the manifesto, we can see the first traces of their discontent with the current political climate: "we are the voice of a new generation that arises in a moment during which violence, despair, and death want to take over as the only solutions."[22] They claimed to offer an alternative, through art and culture, to the negative environment Cubans experienced in the early 1950s. During the SCNT's existence its members constantly criticized and challenged official cultural institutions (mainly the INC), lambasting the "conservative" art and music promoted by these organizations.[23] For instance, the music programming of the Orquesta Filarmónica de La Habana (OFLH, Havana Philharmonic Orchestra) primarily consisted of works by European composers from the late Classical to the Romantic period—such as Wolfgang Amadeus Mozart, Beethoven, Franz Schubert, and Johannes Brahsm—and largely excluded compositions by living composers of any nationality and most Cuban composers of the twentieth century.

One of the constant targets of the SCNT's criticism was the Instituto Nacional de Cultura (INC), which was charged with managing all cultural matters. Established in 1955, one of the INC's covert goals was the legitimization of Batista's government, which it achieved partly by repressing intellectual and artistic activities that undermined the regime.[24] In the September 1955 issue of the SCNT's journal, titled *Nuestro Tiempo*, they decried the seemingly unwarranted expulsion of several professors from the faculty ranks at the Universidad de Oriente, allegedly due to an anti-communist witch hunt led by Robert M. Hallet through the articles he penned for the *Christian Science Monitor*.[25] In March 1956, another "Editorial" piece bemoaned the lack of payments of royalties in local theatrical productions and its dire effects on the national theater scene.[26] The SCNT and its members were frequently accused by the INC and Batista's regime of communist activities. On several occasions, their libraries and publishing facilities were raided by local police to confiscate books and other publications that threatened the status quo; SCNT members claimed that the orders for the raids originated from the US embassy and that Batista's police enforced local anti-communities measures, although I have not been able to corroborate these claims.[27] Gramatges and Blanco responded to the attack, defending the SCNT's

---

[22] "Somos la voz de una nueva generación que surge en un momento en que la violencia, la desesperación y la muerte quieren tomarse como únicas soluciones." "Manifesto," *Nuestro Tiempo* no. 1 (1951): 1–2. Reproduced in ibid., 19.

[23] Nuestro Tiempo used the term "conservative" mainly to describe musical programming of concerts that consisted mainly of music from the late eighteenth- and nineteenth-century European musical canon and excluded new works by Cuban and American composers.

[24] Jorgelina Guzmán Moré, *De Dirección General a Instituto Nacional de Cultura* (Havana: Editora Historia, 2014), 15–17.

[25] Editorial, "La Universidad de Oriente," *Nuestro Tiempo* Año 2, no. 7 (September, 1955): 1.

[26] Editorial, "Amenaza a Nuestro Teatro," *Nuestro Tiempo* Año 3, no. 10 (March, 1956): 1.

[27] Gramatges, *Yo vi la música*, 64–69.

Figure 2.2. Harold Gramatges, image from *Nuestro Tiempo* Año 3, no. 14 (November 1956), n.p.

activities in an article titled "La pupila del sabueso" ("The bloodhound's pupil/eye"). Gramatges and others insisted that their activities were purely cultural in nature, their goal was to elevate and disseminate Cuban art, they were open to all ideologies without adhering to any single one, and none of their activities could be labeled or identified as communist or antidemocratic.[28] As I have already mentioned, however, many of the artists and intellectuals were members of the PSP, and they were all united by strong anti-imperialist, nationalist ideals. Therefore, although the SCNT claimed political neutrality—a claim they could not support given several SCNT members' affiliation with the PSP—their activities implicitly supported a leftist cultural agenda that promoted Cuban high art, literature, and music of and for the people while they explicitly opposed and criticized the cultural policies of Batista and the INC.

While Blanco was active in less visible roles within the SCNT as treasurer and editor, as president of the SCNT, composer Harold Gramatges (pictured in Figure 2.2) noticeably contributed to *Nuestro Tiempo* with general articles and pieces on music criticism. He led most of the SCNT's music activities,

---

[28] Harold Gramatges, "Conferencia en la Escuela de Cuadros del Consejo Nacional de Cultura (14 de marzo de 1974)," reproduced in Hernández Otero, *Sociedad Cultural Nuestro Tiempo*, 298–302.

THE SOCIEDAD CULTURAL NUESTRO TIEMPO   79

organizing concerts of new music by young composers. In his reviews of these concerts, Gramatges promoted specific views on the composer's responsibility in society and the citizens' role as concertgoers, defined what constituted "good" new music, and criticized concerts that failed to meet the SCNT's standards. On several occasions, Gramatges criticized the OFLH for not programming new music or Cuban music.[29] In 1954, on the thirtieth anniversary of the OFLH, Gramatges wrote an article in *Nuestro Tiempo*, that, rather than serve as a positive commemorative piece instead offered a scathing review of its activities since the death of Amadeo Roldán (who had been its conductor during the 1930s). Gramatges recounted the ways in which the OFLH conductors, administration, and musicians fell short of meeting expected standards. According to Gramatges, three factors—conductors, administration, and musicians—needed to be remedied in order for the orchestra to present its audience with good quality repertory. In his view, this repertory should include new music by composers from around the world, but more specifically Latin American and Cuban ones. He listed the various conductors that followed Amadeo Roldán, noting their lack of interest in promoting new and Cuban symphonic repertory. In his view

> Erich Kleiber (1943–1944) arrived, with the undisputed capacity for the position of the main conductor, but affected, in his Germanic arrogance, by a certain contempt towards Latin American music and for national symphonic production. The orchestra, under his direction, reached unforeseen quality, but this was accompanied, unfortunately, by a traditionalist repertory, depriving the people of contact with good contemporary music and the symphonic scores of the country [Cuba].[30]

Here Gramatges criticized Kleiber for not programming works by Latin American and Cuban composers and for performing pieces that Gramatges regards as "traditionalist," meaning from the European musical canon. In addition to conductors' "traditionalist" preferences, Gramatges opined that the low salary the musicians received from the OFLH led them to seek employment in theater and cabaret orchestras, which resulted in a lack of musicianship and questionable professional conduct. The root cause for the decline in musicians'

[29] Harold Gramatges, "Treinta Años de la Orquesta Filarmónica de La Habana" (Thirty years of the Havana Philharmonic Orchestra), *Nuestro Tiempo* Año 1, no. 2 (November, 1954): 1, 14, reproduced in Hernández Otero, *Sociedad Cultural Nuestro Tiempo*, 32.

[30] "Erich Kleiber (1943–1944), con capacidad indiscutible para el cargo de director propietario, pero afectado, en su arrogancia germánica, por cierto desprecio hacia la música latinoamericana y la producción sinfónica nacional. La orquesta, bajo su mando, alcanzó calidades insospechadas, pero esto iba acompañado, desdichadamente, de un repertorio tradicionalista, privando al pueblo del contacto con la buena música contemporánea y las partituras sinfónicas del país." Gramatges, "Treinta Años de la Orquesta Filarmónica de La Habana," reproduced in ibid., 32.

80 CUBAN MUSIC COUNTERPOINTS

aptitude and behavior, for Gramatges, was the lack of financial support from the state; Gramatges's complaints are sustained by the fact that government support of artists had declined after 1948, in comparison to the 1940–1948 period, which included Batista's first presidency and Grau San Martín's term. The PSP's influence on state cultural policy and support of artists as workers was so significant that even a change in government, from Batista to Grau San Martin, did not elicit major changes.[31] It wasn't until Prío Socarrá's and Batista's second presidency, under post-World War II/Cold War anti-communist attitudes and measures, that we see a decline in governmental support of artists when the PSP begins to lose power and is officially banned in 1953.[32] In his article Gramatges condemned the government for having failed to see the effect that a high quality symphonic ensemble had on the country's reputation and morale:

> Because there hasn't been a government capable of understanding that we cannot call ourselves a civilized people without the existence of a symphonic ensemble that keeps [the people] in touch with the great music of all time periods, and composers with an instrument which is the only medium to deliver to their people the efforts of his work.[33]

This statement points to Gramatges's Western European values of culture and civility as he hoped Cuban culture could rise to the standards set by music institutions in Europe and the United States; in order to be a "civilized" people, Cubans had to do so under the terms of other "civilized" nations. In addition, the only way to remedy the orchestra's quality was for the government to take legal measures to guarantee a stable income for the orchestra musician "so that he can regain his discipline."[34] By proposing that the government should be responsible for funding the national symphonic ensemble, Gramatges implicitly points to his (and the SCNT members') leftist political leanings, foreshadowing the initiatives he was to support after 1959.[35]

In the September 1955 issue of *Nuestro Tiempo*, Juan Blanco penned an article where he criticized the lack of music by Cuban composers in concert programming.[36] But Blanco went a step further than Gramatges had in other writings, he

---

[31] García Yero, "The State within the Arts," 94.

[32] Ibid., 97.

[33] "Porque no ha habido un gobierno capaz de comprender que no podemos llamarnos un pueblo civilizado sin la existencia de un conjunto sinfónico que lo mantenga en contacto con la gran música de todos los tiempos, y a los compositores con un instrumento que es el único medio para entregar a ese pueblo el esfuerzo de su trabajo creador." Gramatges, "Treinta Años de la Orquesta Filarmónica de La Habana," reproduced in Hernández Otero, *Sociedad Cultural Nuestro Tiempo*, 33.

[34] Ibid., 33

[35] Gramatges would serve as Cuban ambassador to France and as music advisor and director of several cultural organizations after 1959.

[36] Juan Blanco, "En torno a nuestra música," *Nuestro Tiempo* Año 2, no. 7 (September, 1955): 21.

THE SOCIEDAD CULTURAL NUESTRO TIEMPO   81

also questioned the validity of the neoclassical tendencies—a somewhat ironic criticism given his compositional approach in *Quinteto No. 1* analyzed later—that were cultivated in the 1940s by Catalan-born composer José Ardévol, composition professor to Gramatges and to Blanco himself. Although he admitted that this training resulted in a solid musical foundation, he argued that most composers tended to engage with some musical practices that were not intrinsic to Cuban music making. He called for searching within Cuban music traditions to find the sources of new music composition.

Blanco's activities in the SCNT during Batista's regime led to his imprisonment on several occasions. In spite of all the artistic and intellectual repressions of leftist-leaning individuals by the state, Blanco continued to direct activities for the SCNT until 1959. Although Blanco is better known for his post-1959 experimental works in electroacoustic music, his compositions from the 1950s evince a lesser-known stage in his career in which he composed for conventional ensembles, such as symphony orchestra and chamber groups, and engaged with the overtly nationalistic idioms of Roldán and García Caturla. Some of his works from the 1950s make explicit reference to the revolutionary cause, such as *Elegía (Homenaje a los caídos en la lucha revolucionaria)* (Elegy, Homage to the fallen in the revolutionary fight), for symphonic orchestra (1956); and *Cantata de la Paz (Cantata for peace) for choir, bass solo, and orchestra* from 1950, which won the 1952 Premio del Movimiento por la Paz (Prize from the Peace Movement, a Soviet-sponsored organization with connections in Cuba to the PSP), awarded by the Comité Nacional de la Paz (now Movimiento Cubano por la Paz).[37] *Cantata de la Paz* is an example Blanco's engagement with social causes as a young composer, almost a decade prior to the triumph of the Revolution, after which he became even more involved in promoting social change through art. With this particular work he supported the national movement for peace that had formal ties to the World Peace Council (WPC), an international organization founded by communist groups.[38]

---

[37] The work is organized in three movements, played without interruption: "Introducción," "Exordio," and "Canto a la Paz." For the text, Blanco used excerpts of the poem "Que despierte el leñador" (May the lumberjack wake up) by Pablo Neruda, the celebrated Chilean poet and communist revolutionary. For more on the Peace Movement and cultural connections between the Soviet Union and Latin America see Patrick Iber, *Neither Peace nor Freedom: The Cultural Cold War in Latin America* (Cambridge, MA: Harvard University Press, 2015).

[38] The international World Peace Council was founded in 1948 in an international meeting in Wrocław, Poland. It was founded on the principles of world peace and de-weaponing, seeing US military intervention throughout the world as a threat to world peace. Their principles were based on the Communist Information Bureau's doctrine that dived international forces into two camps: the peaceful communist international community and the warmongering capitalist powers, led by the United States. Among the initiatives sponsored by this international organization were protests against the US invasion of Korea and the Korean War, tributes to the victims of the bombings of Hiroshima and Nagasaki, and denouncements of the development of atomic bombs in general. "Movimiento Cubano por la Paz y la Soberanía de los Pueblos (MOVPAZ)," http://www.ecured.cu/

82   CUBAN MUSIC COUNTERPOINTS

The SCNT's activities were not limited to "high art" manifestations, such as ballet, modern art, and classical music. As part of their mission, they also organized events through which the public could come in contact with Afro-Cuban religious and musical practices as valuable cultural forms that merited scientific research and had aesthetic value. This in particular would become a central line of research and cultural production after 1959, with SCNT ethnographers and folklorists, such as Fernando Ortiz, Argeliers León, and María Teresa Linares taking the helm of institutions such as the Unión Nacional de Escritores y Artistas de Cuba (UNEAC, National Union of Writers and Artists of Cuba), the Institute of Ethnology and Folklore at the Academy of Sciences of Cuba, the Folklore Department at the National Theater of Cuba, the Music Department of the José Martí National Library, and the Music Department at Casa de las Américas.[39] Afro-Cuban music and religious practices were heavily featured in the SCNT's fifth anniversary celebrations, which included special concerts and exhibits. In their gallery space, the Galería Nuestro Tiempo (located on the corner of 23 and 4 in Vedado, the most affluent urban neighborhood in Havana), they held an exhibit between November 16 and November 30 of "Instrumentos Típicos Cubanos" ("Cuban Folk Instruments"). The exhibit was inaugurated with a lecture by Fernando Ortiz, and it was accompanied by a catalog listing all the instruments on display. The exhibit was the product of the collaborative efforts of individuals from several institutions who donated and collected instruments and curated the exhibit. A related event was chosen in 1957 by the music critics and journalists of the Cuban press as one of the best musical performances of the year. The event, which took place at the Lyceum and Lawn Tennis Club in July 1956, was a recital of Afro-Cuban religious ritual chants by Ñica Drake, with a lecture component by Argeliers León.[40] This is ironic considering that performances of Afro-Cuban religious rituals were practically banned by the *Comision revisora de los Programas Novelizados Radiales y Televisados* of the Commission on Radio Ethics (CRE), yet the Cuban press recognized it as the best musical performance that year.[41] These events show that the SCNT's members were not only focused on promoting "high" art, but also the cultural expressions of the people, in particular those of the marginalized Afro-Cuban class. Their interest in both art and traditional

index.php/Movimiento_Cubano_por_la_Paz_y_la_Soberan%C3%ADa_de_los_Pueblos (accessed February 19, 2015).

[39] Most of Fernando Ortiz's research and publications date from before the Revolution decreased in his later years before his death in 1969. Nevertheless, he continued to be an influential figure in Cuban anthropology and ethnography after 1959; his legacy was honored in 1995 with the establishment of the Fundación Fernando Ortiz.

[40] "La crítica musical y Nuestro Tiempo," *Nuestro Tiempo* Año 4, no. 16 (March–April, 1957): 14, reproduced in Hernández Otero, *Sociedad Cultural Nuestro Tiempo*, 62.

[41] Yeidy Rivero, *Broadcasting Modernity: Cuban Commercial Television, 1950–1960* (Durham; London: Duke University Press, 2015), 79–92.

THE SOCIEDAD CULTURAL NUESTRO TIEMPO   83

forms of music aligned with leftist, socialist leanings, and eventually became a significant focus that was further developed in the various cultural organizations established after the Revolution, with Argeliers León (composer and father of Cuban ethnomusicology, though he loathed the term) becoming the director of the Music Department of Casa de las Américas and the head of the folklore division of the National Theater. This interest in all Cuban artistic expressions, "high" and "low" (but never "middle-brow"), guided the activities of the SCNT members well after 1959, when SCNT members would continue to focus their efforts on promoting these types of cultural manifestations as directors, advisors, and artists (composers/performers, too) in revolutionary institutions.

In addition to the exhibit of "Instrumentos Típicos Cubanos," the fifth anniversary celebrations of the SCNT included a concert of contemporary Cuban music at the Lyceum and Lawn Tennis Club (also located in Vedado) on November 30, 1955. The works performed at this concert exemplify SCNT's and its composers' compositional approaches; a close look at the contributions by A. León and Blanco will illustrate this point. This chamber music concert included N. Rodríguez's Sonata-Trio (for flute, clarinet, and viola), Serafín Pro's Capriccio (for flute, oboe, clarinet, and bassoon), A. León's Sonata (for flute, clarinet, and bassoon), and J. Blanco's *Quinteto No. 1* (for flute, oboe, clarinet, bassoon, and cello). In the titles and forms used in these works, we can still detect José Ardévol's influence and neoclassical training; all works followed the "universal" models that the GRM had mastered in the 1940s, and all also infused their compositions with rhythmic and melodic traits that evoked various Cuban vernacular traditions. Juan Blanco's *Quinteto No. 1* (1954) serves as an exemplary case study for examining the compositional approaches of SCNT members. In this work Blanco employed vernacular Cuban musical elements within clear formal structures based on binary and ternary Baroque and Classical forms (similar to Edgardo Martín's *Fugas* discussed above), further combined with a harmonic and rhythmic language that engaged with modernist compositional trends.[42]

In the first movement of *Quinteto*, "Allegro," Blanco establishes a clear formal structure through textural changes and the roles assigned to each instrument. In the opening measures, the cello, bassoon, and clarinet trade melodic lines, which he further develops through imitative passages between the oboe and clarinet (mm. 30–48). By m. 68, Blanco also establishes an ostinato figure in the cello and

---

[42] Blanco indicates that the piece is dedicated "A Curujey," but the meaning of this dedication is elusive, as the *curujey* is a parasitic tropical plant, that because, of its shape, reserves water in its cups. The plant has symbolic importance for Cuban struggles for independence and rebellion, as *mambises* (nineteenth-century Cuban revolutionary soldiers) and the anti-Batista armies relied on the water supply saved in these plants to drink water while walking and moving through the forests. Blanco's dedication, therefore, may be connected to the plant's important role in providing water for the revolutionaries.

Music Example 2.1. Blanco, *Quinteto*, "Allegro," mm. 1–14.

bassoon, which he layers with rhythmic accents in the clarinet and syncopated thematic material in the flute and oboe, shown in Music Example 2.2. The ostinato of the bassoon and cello at m. 68 consists of alternating measures of straight eighth-notes with *tresillo* rhythmic figures (two dotted eighth notes followed by a sixteenth note). Blanco's layering of ostinatos with other rhythmic motives as well as melodic passages and fragments reminds one of earlier modernist composers' approach to texture and musical development (such as those found in works by Bartók and Stravinsky) as well as Mexican composer Silvestre Revueltas's approach in works such as *Ocho por radio*. But Blanco's idiosyncratically Cuban style can be detected in the contour of his melodies and rhythmic figurations. The opening theme consists of four descending sixteenth-notes that lead into a *cinquillo* in the following measure, seen in Music Example 2.1. As already mentioned in the previous chapter's discussion of A. León and Gramatges's compositions, the *cinquillo* is a syncopated rhythmic figure resulting in a long-short-long-short-long rhythmic pattern found in many genres and styles of Cuban vernacular music. The pitches set to the *cinquillo* rhythm (scale degrees 5-3-6-5-2-1) result in a melodic turn of phrase often found in Cuban *son* and other genres, which serves to outline and establish the key or tonal center. Blanco uses the *cinquillo* as a recurring rhythmic motive that drives the whole movement. Many of the vertical sonorities in this movement are built on quartal and quintal chords, showing Blanco's engagement with modernist harmonic practices that other Cuban composers also employed.

Music Example 2.2. Blanco, *Quinteto*, "Allegro," mm. 68–82.

The movement also shows Blanco's use of older musical practices cultivated by the members of the GRM, such as imitation, thematic unity, and ostinatos.

Blanco labels the second movement, "Andante-Allegro-Andante," a "Pregón," or "street-seller's cry," a practice found in the Caribbean and much of Latin America, by which vendors sing, shout, or yell vocalizations advertising the products or services they offer to potential customers.[43] In this movement Blanco uses a ternary form to depict a street seller's typical day: beginning and ending slower and quieter, with faster and louder activity in the middle section. In 6/8 meter, the movement opens with a call-and-response passage between the cello and the flute. The cello's arpeggiated motive in C Major is answered by a similar motive in the flute in E Major, shown in Music Example 2.3. Other instruments join in the call-and-response action, replying to the cello's line, each in their own keys. The dynamic indications going from *f* to *p*, from *mf* to *p*, from *p* to *f* and back to *p*, give the impression of movement through space and time, the same sonic effect one would experience when hearing a *pregonero* walking and chanting through the streets. The cello always plays in C Major, while the rest of the instruments' melodic range and key shift throughout the movement. This creates a sonic depiction of the cello

---

[43] The most famous and commercially successful *pregón* is *El manisero* or "The Peanut Vendor," arranged as a *son* and popularized through recordings and sheet music publication in 1943.

86 CUBAN MUSIC COUNTERPOINTS

Music Example 2.3. Blanco, *Quinteto*, "Pregón," mm. 1–17.

Music Example 2.4. Blanco, *Quinteto*, "Allegro," mm. 109–114.

as the unchanging voice of the *pregonero*, while the other instruments represent the different people or situations he encounters as he moves through the city.

Blanco also employs the *cinquillo* rhythmic motives in the third movement, "Allegro," as well as other techniques present in the previous movements, including the use of ostinatos and layering of rhythmic and repetitive motives, shown in Music Example 2.4. He also recalls the first movement's opening of descending sixteenth-notes followed by a *cinquillo*. The coda is a tour de force in 5/8 meter that leads into ascending sixteenth-notes and the *cinquillo* pattern in a homophonic setting marked *fff* that concludes the piece, shown in Music Example 2.5. Blanco's use of similar rhythmic and melodic motives in the first and third movements provides unity throughout the work. The rhythmic and melodic traits of these figures mark the work as identifiably Cuban, much like

Music Example 2.5. Blanco, *Quinteto,* "Allegro," mm. 183–193.

Ginastera's *Malambo* (1940) captures rhythms and figures strongly associated with Argentine musical identity. But Blanco's use of ostinatos, imitative passages, layering of rhythmic and melodic motives, and quintal and quartal vertical harmonies also aligns this work with the modernist works of Carlos Chávez, Heitor Villa-Lobos, Silvestre Revueltas, Stravinsky, and Aaron Copland. In this piece, Blanco demonstrates a keen awareness of the compositional techniques his predecessors and contemporaries used to imbue conventional classical musical forms with both modernist and national elements. In composing *Quinteto,* which was performed at a concert in celebration of the SCNT's fifth anniversary, Blanco evinced a compositional aesthetic that encapsulated the values of the SCNT: it was both Cuban and "universal," timeless through its use of neoclassical forms and of "our time" through its harmonic language and textural writing.

The SCNT's manifesto also pointed to another focus of their activities, to connect with artists of the Americas: "our aesthetic is that of an American art, free of political or religious prejudices, extoled above concessions, [art] that is a synthesis of what is current and permanent in America."[44] By using "American," the group highlighted its connections to US and Latin American artistic circles.

---

[44] "Nuestra estética es la de un arte Americano, libre de prejucios políticos o religiosos, enaltecido por encima de concesiones, que sea síntesis de lo que estimamos vigente y permanente en América." "Manifesto," *Nuestro Tiempo* Año 1, no. 1 (1951): 1–2. Reproduced in Hernández Otero, *Sociedad Cultural Nuestro* Tiempo, 19.

88 CUBAN MUSIC COUNTERPOINTS

They published Spanish translations of essays by several US writers as well as essays by Latin American intellectuals. As mentioned above, in an effort to make further connections with US music circles they published letters and essays by US composers Henry Cowell and Aaron Copland.[45] The latter was not surprising given the well-established connections between the former members of the GRM and Copland (discussed in the previous chapter). SCNT members also programmed music by living composers from throughout the Americas in special concerts meant to showcase Pan American solidarity through music. This exchange of compositions was also multi-directional, as the Cuban composers' works were also performed and published abroad. For SCNT members it was not enough to promote modern art by local artists and composers; in order to cultivate "universal" aesthetic values, they had to locate their art within the broader context of Hemispheric artistic scenes.

Harold Gramatges's *Tres preludios a modo de toccata* exemplifies the composer's mature compositional style and helps us examine the Hemispheric networks Cuban composers participated in during the 1950s. In 1956, US pianist Harry McClure premiered Gramatges's *Tres preludios a modo de toccata* (1952– 1953) at the Hall of the Americas (the concert hall of the Pan American Union) in Washington D.C.[46] The work was published in 1955 by the Pan American Union through Peer International Corp. (of New York), just as Martín's *Fugas para orquesta de cuerdas* in the previous year.[47] Gramatges's participation and publication through the Pan American Union/Organization of American States (OAS) is ironic considering his and the SCNT's links with the PSP. After 1959 Cuban composers refused to cooperate with the OAS's cultural diplomacy, particularly the Inter-American Music Festival (IAMF) and the OAS's publication of works catalogs of composers of the Americas. *Tres preludios* marked Gramatges's career as one of his first mature compositions and has become a staple of the Latin American piano repertory, having received multiple editions by presses in Cuba and Europe in recent decades. As such, it is one of the most influential works for the piano by a Cuban composer of his generation. *Tres preludios a modo de*

---

[45] Amadeo Roldán, "Carta a Henry Cowell," *Nuestro Tiempo* Año 3, no. 10 (March, 1956): 2–3; the editors reproduced a letter by Amadeo Roldán, addressed to Henry Cowell, dated from June 1931; Aaron Copland, "La música como aspecto del espíritu humano," *Nuestro Tiempo* Año 3, no. 14 (November, 1956): n.p.

[46] Amanda Virelles del Valle, "Stylistic Analysis of Six Pieces for Solo Piano by Rodion Shchedrin and a Stylistic Analysis of Tres preludios a modo de toccata, Dos danzas cubanas, and Estudio de contrastes by Harold Gramatges" (DMA Thesis, University of Southern Mississippi, 2008), 48.

[47] Prior to 1959, Cuban composers faced several challenges in the dissemination of their work, specifically the lack of means for publishing classical music in the island. This challenge was noted several times by composers and music critics, as nearly all new works were edited and published outside of Cuba because there was no music editor or publishing house in the island until all publishing industries were nationalized after the Revolution.

THE SOCIEDAD CULTURAL NUESTRO TIEMPO   89

toccata combined the neoclassical procedures Gramatges mastered throughout the 1940s with rhythmic and melodic elements from Cuban folk and popular music. It was composed in a more dissonant and modern harmonic language than Gramatges's earlier pieces, but it is connected to all of Gramatges output by a strong rhythmic drive and a penchant for lyrical melodies. Following the Baroque trio sonata movement sequence of fast-slow-fast, Gramatges titled each movement a "Prelude." Using common compositional devices of preludes and toccatas, Gramatges was aware of the contemporary use of terms for genres— sonata, toccata, or prelude—and that these terms had flexible and changeable meanings for modern composers who used them to allude to older genres.[48] By pointing to a specific form in a title, contemporary composers set up an expectation that they usually broke or avoided fulfilling, in this way challenging performers' and audiences' preconceived notions of genres and forms. Both the first and third movements are in rounded binary form and the characteristics of the toccata are evident in their fast-moving figurations of scales, arpeggios, repetitive motives presented in sequences that span the entire range of the instrument, and texture, which combines two lines in parallel or contrary motion of continuous sixteenth notes.

Gramatges incorporates Cuban musical traits in several ways in the three movements. Throughout the work, the driving sixteenth notes are interrupted by syncopations in the form of the *cinquillo, tresillo,* and habanera rhythmic patterns.[49] Gramatges constantly changes the meter, switching from 2/4 to 5/8 to 3/4 in quick succession. The short, two-measure-long melodic motives have a wide range, spanning almost two octaves, which require the performer to quickly change articulation and dynamics. These features align the work with the tradition of the toccata as a vehicle for displaying virtuosic technique. The presence of virtuosic figurations and the use of rhythmic patterns from folk and popular music had a precedent in other pianistic works by Latin American composers where syncopations and dance rhythms are combined with fast tempos and constant scales and arpeggios, such as Silvestre Revueltas's *Toccata sin fuga* (1933) for chamber ensemble, and Villa-Lobos's fourth movement of his *Bachianas Brasileiras No. 2*, IV. Toccata (1951), for orchestra, in which he imitates the locomotion of a train through repetitive driving rhythms, and later Ginastera's *Toccata Concertante* (1961) for piano and orchestra. The second prelude is distinct from the first and third in featuring a lyrical melody in a slow tempo. The melody travels between the right and left hand, while a contrasting recurring *cinquillo* rhythmic pattern appears in the other

---

[48] Milvia Rodríguez, "Eclecticism in Modern Cuban Music as Reflected in Selected Piano Works by Harold Gramatges: An Investigative Analysis" (DMA document, University of Nebraska, Lincoln, 2006), 68.

[49] Ibid., 53.

Music Example 2.6. Gramatges, *Tres preludios a modo de toccata*, Preludio II, mm. 1–14.

accompanying hand, shown in Music Example 2.6. In this example we also see the metric displacement of the *cinquillo* figure, each time entering on a different part of the measure. Gramatges's metric displacement of an iconic rhythmic figure from Cuban popular music as well as setting it in parallel fourths in dissonance with the right-hand melody transforms the figure into an intrusive and modernist element; this combination fulfilled musically SCNT's aesthetic vision: to seamlessly yet purposefully combine the Cuban with the "universal."

In the third movement, Gramatges invokes elements from the *guajira*, a genre from the Western part of the island, rooted in the Hispanic music traditions from Andalusia and the Canary Islands.[50] The *guajira* is characterized by the use of guitar, percussion, and the Cuban *tres*.[51] Not to be confused with the urban *guajira* that developed in the 1930s, which combines aspects of the *punto cubano* with elements from the Cuban *son* and changes its metric organization to 4/4, the rural *guajira* is in 3/4 or 6/8 and the guitar or *tres* part outlines the chords

---

[50] Argeliers León, *Del canto y el tiempo* (Havana: Editorial Letras Cubanas, 1984), 95.

[51] Virelles del Valle, "Stylistic Analysis of Six Pieces for Solo Piano by Rodion Shchedrin and a Stylistic Analysis of Tres Preludios a Modo De Toccata, Dos Danzas Cubanas, and Estudio De Contrastes by Harold Gramatges," 56.

Music Example 2.7. Gramatges, *Tres preludios a modo de toccata*, Preludio III, m. 1–11.

by picking the strings instead of strumming them, alternating the accents between groupings of three and two, creating the distinctive hemiolas that characterize *punto cubano* and *guajiras*.[52] Gramatges replicates this guitar technique of picking or plucking instead of strumming the chords most often used in *guajiras*, which can be seen in the metric changes in Music Example 2.7. Gramatges plays with the typical rhythmic patterns of the *guajira*, omitting or adding beats, and constantly changing the meter between 6/8, 5/4, 1/4, 5/8, 12/8, and 9/8.

Like in Blanco's *Quinteto*, the modernist musical elements are evident in Gramatges's treatment of harmonic and melodic material and ambiguous tonal centers. *Preludes I* and *II* use a pentatonic pitch collection (GABDE, 0,2,4,7,9) in the right hand and the inverted form (BC#EF#G# 0,2,5,7,9) in the left, present in the opening motive shown below in Music Example 2.8. Gramatges challenges the player and listeners by stacking these two pentatonic scales, which created clashing vertical dissonances. Another element that contributes to the first movement's tonal ambiguity is Gramatges's use of two possible tonal centers, as he opens and closes the first prelude with stacked Es and Ds. The tonal centers of the movements are separated from one another by major and minor seconds, D and E for the first movement and C# for the second and third movements. In *Prelude III*, Gramatges employs a D major scale but the tonal center is C#, which appears in the first two measures of the movement, seen Music Example 2.9.

---

[52] Ilan Stavans, *Latin Music: Musicians, Genres, and Themes* (Santa Barbara, CA: Greenwood, 2014), 303; Peter Manuel, "The 'guajira' Between Cuba and Spain: A Study in Continuity and Change," *Latin American Music Review* 25, no. 2 (2004): 149–150.

Music Example 2.8. Gramatges, *Tres preludios a modo de toccata*, Preludio I, m. 5.

Music Example 2.9. Gramatges, *Tres preludios a modo de toccata*, Preludio III, mm. 1–2.

In *Tres preludios a modo de toccata* we can observe how Gramatges played with the incorporation of Cuban themes within ternary formal schemes, as well as with elements of modernist compositional practices, such as the simultaneous use of pentatonic scales that resulted in dissonances, quartal and quintal harmonies, and ambiguity of tonal center. Throughout the work Gramatges incorporates Hispanic influences in the contour of the melodies, while Afro-Cuban influence is evident in his use of rhythmic patterns. The piece features rhythmic motives from the *son*, *guajira*, and *contradanza*, but in less overt ways than in his earlier works, as he plays with Cuban listeners' expectations by varying the meters and rhythmic accents.[53] Like in Martín's *Fugas* and Blanco's *Quinteto*, Gramatges engaged with both local and universal musical practices

---

[53] Virelles del Valle, "Stylistic Analysis of Six Pieces for Solo Piano by Rodion Shchedrin and a Stylistic Analysis of Tres Preludios a Modo De Toccata, Dos Danzas Cubanas, and Estudio De Contrastes by Harold Gramatges," 50.

THE SOCIEDAD CULTURAL NUESTRO TIEMPO   93

that allowed him and SCNT members to forge connections locally and abroad among like-minded artists, intellectuals, and composers such as Copland, Villa-Lobos, and Ginastera. Over the decades, Gramatges continued to explore new compositional techniques and to experiment with extended techniques, indeterminacy, twelve-tone technique, and graphic scores in his compositions for the piano. This instrument was the composer's preferred vehicle for experimentation and his piano works became known in new music circles outside of Cuba thanks to pianists who specialized in new music performance (such as Ninowska Fernández-Brito). But Gramatges, like many of the composers of his generation, also wrote works for the stage, such as the incidental music for *Calígula* (1955), several choral and solo vocal works, as well as compositions for solo guitar. He also went on to compose film scores for several revolutionary films after 1959 (including Tomás Gutiérrez Alea's *Historias de la Revolución*, 1960). Collaborations between the film makers and the composers of the SCNT set the stage for their work throughout the 1960s and 1970s once the Instituto Cubano de Artes e Industrias Cinematográficas (ICAIC, Cuban Film Institute) was established by the revolutionary government in 1959.

Nuestro Tiempo and the Beginning of Revolutionary Film

In 1955, Juan Blanco worked on the production of the film *El Mégano,* directed by Julio García Espinosa and Tomás Gutiérrez Alea (Titón). Conceived and produced with a neorealist visual aesthetic, the film depicts the life of the "carboneros," rural workers who dig wood out of wetlands and then burn this wood to make charcoal, in an area in the south of Cuba called "El Mégano," also known as the Zapata Swamps. Most of the individuals involved in the production of the film were either members of the SCNT or frequently participated in the SCNT's activities: José Massip, Alfredo Guevara, Moisés Ades, Jorge Haydu, and Pedro García Espinosa. Not only did Blanco compose the music for the film, he was also involved in drafting the script, shooting, and post-production. In one of his memoirs, Gutiérrez Alea recalled that the film was only screened once, after which Batista's police confiscated the reels and negatives, and brought in its creators for interrogation (which, as previously mentioned, was a common occurrence with SCNT events), but other than that, there was no major scandal.[54]

---

[54] However, Edgardo Martín's review of the music for the film in *Nuestro Tiempo* in 1955 recounts at least two screenings, the second of which had a revised musical score with more musical material than the first screening (it is quite possible that the first screening that Martín was referring to would have been a private screening after which changes were made for the first public screening). Evora and Gutiérrez Alea, *Tomás Gutiérrez Alea* (Madrid: Cátedra: Filmoteca Española, 1996), 20.

94   CUBAN MUSIC COUNTERPOINTS

The January–February 1959 issue of the journal *Nuestro Tiempo* included an article titled "*El Mégano*" by Julio García Espinosa, the film's writer and director. Published after the triumph of the Revolution, it was the first time that the director shared publicly an account of the production and subsequent interrogation by the police. He opened the article with a dialogue:

—Esta es una pelicula comunista/This is a communist film

—Es un filme neorrealista./It is a neorealist film

—Neo . . . qué?/neo . . . what?

—Neorrealista./Neorealist

—No importa. El caso es que enseña la miseria./It doesn't matter. The thing is that it shows poverty.

—Si, enseña la miseria. La miseria existe en nuestro país./Yes, it shows poverty. Poverty exists in our country.

—Pues usted se me pone a fotografiar las obras del gobierno o se va a hacer cine a . . . /Well you are going to start photographing the works of the government or you are going to make films at . . . [55]

This dialogue, allegedly took place between García Espinosa and a police detective when the film was confiscated. According to García Espinosa, the government repressed the film because for the first time it showed the authentic reality of a specific Cuban: it showed a peasant without making a spectacle out of it, a small reality that was not made up by the producers. According to García Espinosa, the film had no theatrical additions, it presented a Cuban reality and it could be understood by the rest of the world. In the article, he explained that he and the other film makers considered this neorealist approach as the only way for Cuban film makers to gain recognition outside of Cuba.[56] He closed the article by sharing his hopes that with the Revolution, reason would be reestablished and film makers would be able to produce films that reflected the realities of the Cuban people and that the Cuban people would enjoy.[57] Here we see a member of the SCNT, at the dawn of a new revolutionary government, condemning the previous administration's censorship and abuses of power and sharing his hope and faith in the promises of the new regime. As we'll see later, the SCNT members strongly backed the revolutionary government; their support was rewarded in the new cultural institutions where they continued their artistic-political work,

[55] [a similar dialog took place, sadly, in the offices of the Servicio de Inteligencia Miliar (Military Intelligence Service), when they ceased from us *El Megano*.] Julio García Espinosa, "El Mégano," *Nuestro Tiempo* Año 6, no. 27 (January–February, 1959): 27.

[56] Cuban filmmakers saw the success of the Italian film industry as a model for what Cuban filmmakers could achieve.

[57] García Espinosa, "El Mégano," 27.

THE SOCIEDAD CULTURAL NUESTRO TIEMPO   95

such as the ICAIC, where Julio García Espinosa and Tomás Gutiérrez Alea went on to produce and direct many documentaries and feature films after 1959.

When *El Mégano* was first screened, composer and music critic Edgardo Martín wrote a review of Juan Blanco's score, published in *Nuestro Tiempo* in December 1955. In his review Martín praised Blanco for not making "mere background" music, for writing music that adequately underscored the scenes, and not being excessively thematic nor merely suggestive, "atmospheric" or "ornamental." Martín emphasized the film score's originality, "not of the sonorities employed but more of the creation itself, its motives, its rhythms, its fluidity, and its adaptation to the events on screen . . ."[58] Martín concluded that "future producers of Cuban films will have to think about Juan Blanco."[59] About two-thirds into the film, the *carboneros* meet the buyers of the charcoal and receive paperwork and payment. This scene is followed by one of the final moments where the family around which the plot centers is frantically attempting to cool one of the ovens that is overheating. Blanco expertly underscores the two moments, building tension in the payment scene, showing the discomfort of the transaction for the *carboneros*, and setting the frenetic pace in the next scene as they all hurry to tend to the fire [18:58]. In this last scene, Blanco employs rhythmic ostinatos with irregular accents and melodies inspired by folk songs evocative of the Cuban son, which usually consists of syncopated arpeggios that shift between major and minor modes. The hectic activity of the individuals who are tending to the fire is mimicked by Blanco by layering several melodies; all techniques we saw in a smaller scale in his *Quinteto*. The dissonant, syncopated, and repetitive texture provided by the strings and woodwinds is topped with longer and more sustained lines in the trumpets that reinforce this moment as the climax of the film, emphasizing the neorealist footage and editing.

The film ends with two scenes, after the main male character realizes everyone is safe and walks back into his hut. Blanco underscores the return of hunters, who appeared earlier in the film leisurely navigating down the swamp on a small boat with their hunting gear and with the same musical accompaniment: dissonant, jazz-like music featuring dotted rhythms, an almost boogie-woogie piano, drum-set, and solo clarinet and trumpet, sonically marking the hunters as outsiders to the *carbonero* community. The hunters could be foreigners (Americans) or simply Habaneros (from the capital). As the foreign woman nonchalantly applies makeup and waves at them completely unaware

---

[58] "when it highlights the drama that can be seen, when it takes the lyrical form of a guajiro song, or even in the two moments in which it ironically imitates jazz to accompany the passing of the foreign hunters . . . The music has come to fill with energy filmic moments where the dramatic strength was not explicit enough [without the music]." Edgardo Martín, "La música de El Mégano," *Nuestro Tiempo* Año 2, no. 8 (December, 1955): 23.

[59] "los realizadores de próximos filmes cubanos tendrán que pensar en Juan Blanco." Ibid.

96   CUBAN MUSIC COUNTERPOINTS

of the family's recent ordeal we hear an ironic, outdated recreation of jazz. In this instance, jazz represents a cosmopolitan view that is out of touch with the realities of rural Cuban communities. Once the hunters disappear, the man pulls his paperwork out of his pocket, gripping and bunching it up. In this final moment, we first hear a solo clarinet playing the *son*-like melody, but as the man looks out, stoic, Blanco builds the main theme by adding the brass, and finally incorporating the full orchestra and increasing the dynamics. The music for the concluding scene is also reminiscent of Copland's *Fanfare for the Common Man* (1942) and Blanco's orchestration and treatment of the melody in this final moment could have been a nod to the well-known work by the US comrade.[60] There is a vast contrast between the jazz that accompanies the hunters and the final, grand, yet stoic iteration of the Cuban son melody that we have heard in various forms throughout the film. If Blanco's music is the narrative voice, the final message is that the common Cuban man will stand strong in the face of exploitation and indifference of outsiders. *El Mégano* is often credited as the first Cuban revolutionary film.[61] In a way, the film was a proto-ICAIC production, since all of the individuals involved in its creation went on to become the founding and core members of the ICAIC, further discussed in the following chapter). Much like the Ballet Nacional's staging of Martín's *Fugas, El Mégano* was the result of a collaboration of like-minded individuals who strove to create Cuban modernist art that engaged with universal themes and aesthetics and who gathered around the SCNT (although the SCNT didn't exist at the time of the ballet production in 1950, the composers, choreographers, and costume and set designer all became involved in the SCNT once it was established). *El Mégano* included some of the key features that became synonymous with ICAIC films: black and white footage, neorealist aesthetic, "imperfect" cinematic production, protagonists that represented the common man, depiction of class struggles and exploitation of the lower classes, as well as tongue in cheek criticism of capitalist values, all underscored by music that employed Cuban folk genres, modernist and avant-garde language, and foreign popular music elements in the service of the dramatic situation.

Blanco serves as a prime example for how the aesthetic and political involvement of SCNT members during the 1950s was rewarded once Batista's regime was overthrown. After 1959, Juan Blanco quit his job at a law firm where he had worked throughout the 1950s representing US businesses. The revolutionary

---

[60] Through the 1930s and early 1940s Copland was active in the Popular Front and many of his compositions dealt with themes of the common folk not only in the United States, but also in Cuba and Mexico. This populist style, however, fell out of favor after World War II and Copland found himself under scrutiny for his leftist associations, most famously his participation in the 1949 World Congress for Peace in New York.

[61] Michael Chanan, *Cuban Cinema* (Minneapolis: University of Minnesota Press, 2004), 36, 109.

THE SOCIEDAD CULTURAL NUESTRO TIEMPO   97

government immediately offered him several prominent positions. Blanco served in various administrative capacities in cultural state institutions until his death in 2008. After 1959, he composed scores for twenty-five films produced by the ICAIC. In the program notes for a 1964 Cuban National Symphony Orchestra concert, Blanco noted that his journey into experimental and electronic music began with his musical score for the film *El Mégano*, but that he was limited at the time by standard music notation. For Blanco, the artistic projects of the 1950s that centered around SCNT laid the foundation for future developments that engaged with avant-garde and experimental compositional techniques that were circulating among international music circles. In 1961 Blanco began experimenting with electronic music, and finally in 1964, in his work for orchestra and magnetic tape *Texturas* (1963–1964), he was able to convey through new graphic notation borrowed from the Polish Sonorist school what he had started to develop while working on the score for *El Mégano*.[62]

The End of Batista's Regime and Nuestro Tiempo in 1959

In January 1959, the latest issue of the Cuban cultural magazine *Nuestro Tiempo* included a leaf insert where the members of the SCNT proclaimed the revolutionary forces' intervention as a welcome change in the local political and cultural climate and declared their support of the revolutionary leaders. The SCNT congratulated the new administration in overthrowing Fulgencio Batista's regime, and took the liberty to speak for all Cuban artists and intellectuals who had opposed the dictatorship. The article's unnamed authors followed the initial congratulatory remarks with a list of goals the new administration should keep in mind in order for "the transformative Revolution of our civil life to be reflected in the cultural [realm]."[63]

- Complete reorganization of the National Institute of Culture and its placement in the hands of the most responsible exponents of our art, our science, and our letters;
- Tight links between the country's high cultural manifestations within an intensive popular educational divulgation;
- Complete respect for the free broadcasting of thinking in all of its creative manifestations;

---

[62] OSN Concert Program, April 19, 1964, OSN Concert Program Collection, Museo Nacional de la Música Cubana, Havana, Cuba.

[63] "Cultura Libre en Cuba Libre," *Nuestro Tiempo* Año 5, no. 26 (November–December, 1958), inserted page, reproduced in Hernández Otero, *Sociedad Cultural Nuestro Tiempo*, 25. My emphasis.

98 CUBAN MUSIC COUNTERPOINTS

- Moral and material support by the State of the country's artistic and cultural organizations in their work, and strict respect of their independence of criteria and action;
- Free cultural exchange in the international [realm], without any sort of crippling restrictions;
- Channeling of Cuban culture through revelatory paths of our best liberal and revolutionary traditions that promote our national character;
- Battle against disfiguring cosmopolitanism that damages the national cultural heritage as tends to happen, for example, in the realm of popular music.[64]

The article closed with a very specific statement regarding who should be involved in building the new cultural programs: "*Nuestro Tiempo* hopes that all the intellectuals and artists and all the cultural institutions *that did not tarnish themselves with embarrassing alliances with the dictatorship* will unite so that 1959 marks, in the cultural as well as in the political [realm], the beginning of a new, higher, and memorable stage for Cuba."[65] With these words the author(s) excluded from the revolutionary cultural efforts those individuals and institutions who collaborated with Batista's regime, in particular the INC. The declaration finally overtly revealed the group's political leanings, their views on the role of culture in civil society, and the relationship between the state, cultural institutions, and artists and intellectuals. This letter articulated a utopic cultural agenda that, although appealing in theory, was never fully realized by the revolutionary cultural institutions in practice. In light of this document it should come as no surprise that several of the members of the SCNT became involved in establishing the new revolutionary cultural institutions soon after 1959, summarized in Table 2.1.

In a 1974 lecture on the SCNT's history and legacy, Harold Gramatges noted that with the triumph of the Revolution the SCNT's activities and existence were no longer necessary because the government fulfilled the functions the SCNT provided during the 1950s. Gramatges added that at the beginning of the 1960s the most outstanding members of the SCNT held administrative positions and developed their creative activities to the fullest.[66] Furthermore, he listed a series of presentations and lectures organized by the SCNT throughout the 1950s that were crucial in supporting the revolutionary cause. These presentations included Ernesto Che Guevara's "Proyecciones del Ejército Rebelde"; Comandante Faure Chomón's "La juventud y la Revolución"; Capitán Antonio Núñez Jiménez's "Reforma Agraria"; Alfredo Guevara's "La creación del Instituto Cubano del

---

[64] Ibid., 25.
[65] Ibid., 26. My emphasis.
[66] Gramatges, "Conferencia en la Escuela de Cuadros del Consejo Nacional de Cultura (14 de marzo de 1974)," reproduced in Hernández Otero, *Sociedad Cultural Nuestro Tiempo*, 305.

THE SOCIEDAD CULTURAL NUESTRO TIEMPO 99

Table 2.1. Members of the SCNT and their roles in the post-1959 cultural institutions.

Mirta Aguirre: Driector of Sección de Teatro y Danza of the Consejo Nacional de Cultura	Manuel Duchesne Cuzán: Director of National Symphony Orchestra (OSN)
Sergio Aguirre: Asesor Ministerio de Educación, History Professor at the Universidad de La Habana	Julio García Espinosa: ICAIC
	Harold Gramatges: Cuban Ambasador to France (1960–1964) Founder of the Music Department of Casa de las Américas (1965–1970). Composition Professor at various music schools.
Yolanda Aguirre: Consejo Nacional de Cultura	
Alberto Alonso: Choreographer, Ballet Nacional de Cuba	Tomás Gutiérrez Alea (Titón): ICAIC
	Alfredo Guevara: Director of ICAIC
Fernando Alonso: Founder & Choreographer, Ballet Nacional de Cuba	Argeliers León: Director of the Departamento de Folklore del Teatro Nacional de Cuba and the Music Department of the Biblioteca Nacional José Martí
Santiago Alvarez: ICAIC, Radio Station CMQ	
Marta Arjona: Director of Visual Arts at the Dirección Nacional de Cultura and National Director of Museums and Monuments of the Consejo Nacional de Cultura	José Massip: ICAIC
	Serafín Pro: Founder and Director of the Cuban National Choir
Juan Blanco: Director of the Ministry of Education's radio broadcasting station, CMZ; Music director of the Consejo Nacional de Cultura; Director of the military band of the Ejército Rebelde	

Arte e Industria Cinematográficos."[67] Through its publications and activities the SCNT set the foundation upon which many of the Revolution's cultural policies and initiatives were built. The intellectuals who had shown a commitment to the Revolution in the early years (mainly the 1950s) and who showed an unwavering commitment to the revolutionary government after 1959 went on to occupy highly privileged positions within the Cuban revolutionary government— Gramatges as the Cuban ambassador to France, Blanco as Music Director of CMZ the Ministry of Education's radio station, both were cofounders of the UNEAC—promoting both their cultural and aesthetic agendas.[68]

---

[67] Gramatges doesn't provide full details on when and where these lectures took place. It is possible they were held in the early years of the Revolution or, if prior to 1959, that they were held clandestinely. Ibid., 306.

[68] This meant that not all composers and musicians enjoyed the same level of support from the government, as Liliana González has demonstrated in her monograph on Federico Smith. Liliana González Moreno, *Federico Smith, cosmopolitismo y vanguardia* (Havana, Cuba: Ediciones CIDMUC, Centro de Investigación y Desarrollo de la Música Cubana, 2013).

100   CUBAN MUSIC COUNTERPOINTS

Musically, composers involved in the SCNT developed individual styles that incorporated Cuban vernacular elements within a modernist language that focused on structural unity, bitonality, modal scales, and twelve-tone and serial techniques, among others. For these Cuban composers, engaging with current international musical styles and techniques was also a form of resistance against the pervasive colonial mentality and cultural imperialism they experienced during Batista's dictatorship. Like previous generations of leftist Cuban artists and intellectuals, the members of the SCNT conflated aesthetic *vanguardismo* with political *vanguardismo*. Through their art they criticized Batista's regime for its political failures, social injustices, and lack of support for the work of contemporary Cuban artists. With the end of Batista's regime and the onset of the Revolution, SCNT members were already exemplary models of the *artista comprometido* (committed artist) that would legitimize the Cuban Revolution through the arts and culture.

Cultivating Foreign Musical Networks and the Cessation of Official Cuba–US Music Exchanges

Throughout the 1950s, Cuban composers and performers maintained existing contacts with their counterparts outside of Cuba and cultivated new connections with foreign individuals and organizations. One of the recurring activities that facilitated an increased familiarity with music by composers outside of Cuba were guided listening sessions hosted by members of the SCNT. Thanks to new developments in sound recording technology, most significantly the LP, which allowed for longer pieces to be recorded and played back with less interruptions than the shorter 78s rpm format, classical music of all time periods received further dissemination than in previous decades. Cuban composers, musicians, and audiences interested in new music gathered to listen to the latest recordings and discuss contemporary music's challenges and opportunities. Additionally, they coordinated efforts with new international and Pan American organizations to perform new music, exchanged letters and scores with fellow composers and music critics abroad, and traveled to foreign countries to participate in music festivals. For instance, in 1951, SCNT member and conductor Enrique González Mántici traveled to Berlin where he conducted Mozart's Serenade in G Major, E. Martín's *Fugas para Cuerda*, Félix Guerrero's *Homenaje al Sóngoro Cosongo*, and Amadeo Roldán's *Tres Pequeños Poemas* as part of the Berlin Youth Festival for Peace.[69] Harold Gramatges's *Serenata* (1947) for string orchestra was conducted by Walter Goehr in London for the British Broadcasting

---

[69] Concert Program, September 27, 1951, Box 1950–1951, Collection Programas de Mano, Biblioteca Nacional José Martí, Havana, Cuba.

THE SOCIEDAD CULTURAL NUESTRO TIEMPO   101

Corporation.[70] Beginning in 1952, several of the chamber music concerts held at the Lyceum were presented in collaboration with the Cuban section of the International Society for Contemporary Music (ISCM). In keeping with the ISCM's aim to promote new music of diverse aesthetic stripes, the concerts included works that ranged from the overtly nationalistic to dodecaphonic compositions by composers from Mexico, France, the United States, Germany, and Cuba.[71]

The Cuban composers eagerly participated in the first Latin American Music Festival of Caracas in 1954 and coordinated concerts to promote music by American composers through the Cuban section of the Inter-American Music Association (IAMA).[72] The first Latin American Music Festival of Caracas was organized by Venezuelan developer, impresario, art collector, cultural promoter, and musicologist Inocente Palacios. According to Palacios, the idea of the Caracas Festivals was first suggested by none other than Alejo Carpentier, who was living in Caracas at the time and working as music critic.[73] Both Carpentier and Palacios opined that the musicians in Caracas lived in relative isolation and, although they knew of what was being produced in Europe, they were totally ignorant of what was being produced in the Western Hemisphere. The festival also led to the foundation of the IAMA, which, similar to the ISCM, had individual sections by country and region. At the first IAMA Cuba Section concert, which took place on July 1955 at the Lyceum, audience members were treated to Chilean Juan Orrego-Salas's *Rústica*, USian Aaron Copland's *Blues*, Mexican Blas Galindo's *Cinco preludios*, Argentine Juan J. Castro's *Intrata y Danza*, Spanish-Mexican, Rodolfo Halffter's *Feliciano me adora*, Venezuelan Vicente Sojo's *Pastoral*, Uruguayan H. Tosar-Errecart's *Tres Canciones*, Argentine Alberto Ginastera's *Cancion de la luna lunatica*, and Brazilian Francisco Braga's *Seresta*. This focus on Hemispheric music making would become central to post-1959 musical activities, as will be discussed in the next two chapters.

According to Cuban saxophonist and music critic Leonardo Acosta, who attended the second Caracas Festival, the Cuban composers were somewhat divided in their assessments of the works performed and awarded in the festivals.[74] Although several aesthetic tendencies were represented by the variety of works included, the praise of Panamanian Roque Cordero's twelve-tone work *Segunda Sinfonía* was questioned by some of the Cuban composers, mainly Julián Orbón,

---

[70] n.a. "Música de Gramatges en Londres," *Nuestro Tiempo* (September 1955): 10.
[71] Concert Program, January 16, 1952, Box 1952–1955, Collection Programas de Mano, Biblioteca Nacional José Martí, Havana, Cuba.
[72] Concert Program, July 27, 1955, Box 1952–1955, Collection Programas de Mano, Biblioteca Nacional José Martí, Havana, Cuba.
[73] A.S.D., "A word with Inocente Palacios" *Américas* 10, no. 1 (January 1958): n.p.
[74] Leonardo Acosta, "Testimonio de Fe," *Clave—Revista Cubana de Música* 6, no. 1–3 (2004): 75–76.

102   CUBAN MUSIC COUNTERPOINTS

who claimed that a technique that developed in Vienna was alien to Latin American composers. Cordero on his part, defended his use of twelve-tone composition, stating that "I don't wish to classify my music as tonal, polytonal, or atonal... What is needed is to find the essence of our nationalism in the melodies and rhythms of our typical songs and dances, in order to create from them a *personal* art, which, precisely because it *is* personal, will be Panamanian without having to 'beat the drum' to proclaim nationality."[75] Cordero's *Segunda Sinfonía* was subsequently performed and further lauded in the first IAMF held in 1958 in Washington D.C. and organized by the Music Division of the Organization of American States, headed by Colombian composer and conductor Guillermo Espinosa.[76] Both the Caracas Festivals and the IAMF facilitated dialog and exchanges between composers of the Americas; as Cordero's *Segunda Sinfonía's* critical acclaim attests, the festivals also served as wind vanes for the direction classical music would take in the following decades, when composers eschewed overt nationalism and more tonal and compositionally conservative approaches in favor of so-called universal techniques, such as serialism and indeterminacy.

One of the Cuban composers who remained in the "conservative" camp and came to represent a sort of "old-school" in Cuban composition was José Ardévol. The 1958 IAMF would be his last involvement in US-based Pan Americanist music activities, one year before the Cuban Revolution. Out of the twenty-one works presented in the 1958 festival, two were by Cuban composers: Ardévol's *Music for Little Orchestra* and Aurelio de la Vega's *String Quartet*.[77] In a review for *The Musical Quarterly* Richard Franko Goldman observed that Ardévol's *Music for Little Orchestra*, commissioned by International House of New Orleans, although not as "portentous" as some of the other works, still suffered from "trouble with motion and length."[78] This first edition of the IAMF was the first large-scale

[75] Cordero quoted in Gilbert Chase, "Composed by Cordero," *Américas* 10, no. 6 (1958): 10–11.

[76] The organizing committee also included Venezuelan impresario, art collector, cultural promoter, and musicologist Inocente Palacios; Cuban-born Gilbert Chase, whose mother was Cuban and had been a fervent advocate of Latin American music throughout the 1940s and 1950s; and Samuel R. Rosenbaum, the founder and trustee of the Recordings Industries Music Performance Trust Funds, which provided the highest monetary sum in support of the IAMF. In an interview for the OAS's cultural magazine *Américas*, Inocente Palacios explained that the IAMF was in part modeled after the Latin American Music Festivals that he founded and organized in Caracas, Venezuela, because "The Cuban musicologist Alejo Carpentier [Cuba] began to promote the idea [of a festival of Latin American music] in the press." Similarly, Guillermo Espinosa, chief of the Music Division of the OAS, had founded the Cartagena Music Festival with a comparable focus. Therefore, the IAMF was not only a product of Washington, D.C. and the OAS, but also a project in which key figures from various Latin American countries collaborated to create a truly Hemispheric event.

[77] The information regarding the Inter-American Music Festival concerts was gathered from a database compiled be Emma Dederick, music librarian at Indiana University, and special collections curator of its Latin American Music Center. The data was collected from the Espinosa Collection of the LAMC. I am very grateful to Ms. Dederick for her work and her help.

[78] Richard Franko Goldman, "Current Chronicle," *The Musical Quarterly* 44, no. 3 (1958): 384.

event to take place on US soil where music by US and Latin American composers was presented side by side. Later editions of the IAMF included music by Cuban composers who no longer resided in Cuba, excluding compositions by Cuban composers who still lived in the island. Unlike Aurelio de la Vega, who moved to Mexico in 1960 and settled in the United States in 1964 and whose music was performed in subsequent years at the IAMF, Ardévol did not participate in post-1960 editions of the IAMF. This is not surprising considering Ardévol's support of the Cuban Revolution and strong commitment to the island's cultural and educational reforms. After 1959 he continued teaching at the Conservatorio Amadeo Roldán and the Escuela Nacional de Arte. Although he was heavily involved in Pan Americanist exchanges throughout the 1940s and 1950s—his music was published in the *New Music Quarterly* and later by the Pan American Union—he was an ardent supporter of the Revolution. It is probable that the programmers of the IAMF did not consider Ardévol's political leanings exemplary of a Pan American composer. The geo-political bias was also exerted from the Cuban side in relation to the Cuban composers who settled in the United States. As mentioned in the previous chapter, Julián Orbón's music has only recently been "rediscovered" by Cuban musicologists who are currently exploring the activities of the GRM.[79] Aurelio de la Vega remains practically unknown to Cuban musicians and audiences, although some composers and musicologists are aware of his career, most are not familiar with his music.

The exclusion of Cuban composers from the IAMF reflected the souring political relations between Cuba and the United States. As we will encounter in the following chapter, to counteract the isolation of the US embargo, Cuban composers and the revolutionary government established institutions to foster exchanges with other Latin American countries and socialist Eastern Europe. The pre-revolutionary exchanges discussed in this chapter determined which composers and traditions would be exalted as emblems of Cuban identity reinterpreted through the lens of socialism after 1959. When Pan Americanism no longer stood as one of the dominant *political* objectives after 1959, the change in ideology also shifted the sites of modernist aesthetic from the United States and Western Europe to socialist Eastern Europe, Poland in particular, where Cuban composers found new modernist and avant-garde models through which they could articulate their identity.

---

[79] This includes a recent thesis by José Luis Fanjul completed at the Instituto Superior de Arte, Havana, Cuba.

104 CUBAN MUSIC COUNTERPOINTS

Conclusion

Through the activities of the SCNT we have gained a better sense of the foundation the leftist artistic and intellectual elite of Havana established in the decade leading up to the 1959 Revolution. Ballet, film, solo piano, and chamber music all showcase the collaborative efforts of composers and artists in other disciplines and their desire to forge enduring bonds with like-minded individuals in Cuba and abroad. Their leftist views, which focused on cultural manifestations of the common man as well as in collective action, garnered them unwanted attention and persecution from Batista's regime as well as praise and respect from Castro's revolutionary government. Rather than rupture with a pre-revolutionary past, this decade and the SCNT activities help us see the continuities in Cuban cultural production. In the works of Martín, Gramatges, and Blanco, all vital members of the SCNT, we find a continuation of the nationalist works of Roldán and García Caturla through the incorporation of rhythmic and melodic elements drawn from Cuban vernacular genres into works based on Baroque and Classical forms, such as the fugue, sonata, toccata, and prelude. Through the use of modal melodic writing, non-functional, quartal, and quintal harmonies, bitonal passages, pitch cells, ostinato, and layering of rhythmic and melodic motives, these composers engaged with modernist compositional approaches that dialogued with the works of their contemporaries in Europe, Latin America, and the United States. The diversity of the musical elements that these composers combined—from the past and the present, from Cuba and from abroad—was itself a characteristically Cuban approach to making art and music. This musical eclecticism continued into later decades, becoming increasingly marked as Cuban composers interacted with composers and musicians from avant-garde and experimental music scenes from Eastern Europe and Latin America.

Overtly evoking Cuban musical elements in their compositions was not only an aesthetic feat, but also a political one, as celebrating the local and national, in particular those elements from musics that were linked to the racialized lower classes, was an act of defying a local repressive government that censored artists and intellectuals who asserted their independence and national identity through art. These composers resisted cultural colonialism by using vernacular musical elements to create modernist works that aimed to both serve local needs and dialogue with foreign composers and music scenes. However, by aspiring to compose "universal" classical music Cuban composers engaged with a literate tradition with rules, codes, and expectations set forth by mostly male composers from European and US economic, political, and cultural centers. As the local political situation changed, Cuba's foreign relations affected the local music scene; Cuban composers continued to define their compositional voices vis-à-vis the expectations and influences of foreign music circles. After 1959, Cuban composers shifted their attention from US music circles and composers to leftist and avant-gardist composers of Eastern and Western Europe and Latin America.

If in the 1940s we saw a "formalization" of compositional studies in Cuba, through a thorough training in theory, counterpoint, and Baroque and Classical forms and techniques, then in the 1950s we find that those composers who had been students at the Conservatorio Municipal under Ardévol in the early 1940s took the reins of musical and cultural production. They returned to some of the aesthetic ideals of the 1930s, through a focus on vernacular elements as a source of inspiration for their modernist art. They also became highly preoccupied with bringing art to the people and to a broader audience beyond the social and cultural elite of Havana, a process I identified as "radicalization" in this book's introduction. These composers established and led the most influential cultural organizations of the 1950s, and they also became more politically active and radicalized. Many of them were members of the PSP, and openly criticized Batista's regime and what they viewed as cultural imperialism, the imposition of the values (aesthetic and commercial) of the US capitalist market on the cultural production of the island. Their concern over national and modernist cultural production with a leftist political agenda set the foundation for what would become the cultural organizations and priorities of the cultural leaders under the new socialist and revolutionary regime after 1959.

3

A Decade of Revolution and Experimentation in Music

Grafting Experimentalism onto the Cuban Revolutionary-Socialist Trunk

Creo que si esto no hubiera ocurrido todavía estaríamos haciendo habaneras.[1]
(*I think that if this hadn't happened we'd still be writing habaneras.*)
—Juan Blanco

In 1960, José Ardévol delivered a lecture on contemporary music to listeners of radio station CMZ, where he recounted his experience while attending a series of concerts in the United States in 1958, noting that most of the compositions he heard in these concerts employed serial technique. Although he doesn't specify where and when the concerts had taken place, he was more than likely referring to the first Inter-American Music Festival (IAMF) in Washington D.C. Ardévol traveled to Washington to attend the premiere of his *Music for Little Orchestra* at the IAMF, for which the International House of New Orleans had commissioned the work. He described the use of serial techniques that he witnessed in his 1958 US visit as lacking the personality and individuality of the composer, resulting in "an academism of a new stamp that says nothing and means nothing in relation to our times—because to be up to date, to reflect contemporary man, is something much deeper and riskier than to change techniques [as one] changes shirts."[2] If Ardévol warned against facile use of serialism, then the US critics found Ardévol's composition stale.

---

[1] Marta Ramírez, "Juan Blanco: Aún a la vanguardia," *Clave—Revista Cubana de Música* 4, no. 3 (2002): 35.

[2] "Un academismo de nuevo cuño que nada dice ni nada significa en relación con nuestra época—porque estar al día, relfejar al hombre contemporáneo, es algo mucho más profundo y arriesgado que cambiar de técnica como se cambia de camisa. [. . .] creo que es una posición falsa buscar el serialsimo como una salida fácil a la ausencia de estilo personal y como demostración de que se está al día; pienso, en cambio, que puede ser fecundo cuando un compositor lo use por necesidades de su evolución y desarrollo técnico, y de sensibilidad [. . .]." Ardévol, *Correspondencia curzada*, 40–41.

Cuban Music Counterpoints. Marysol Quevedo, Oxford University Press. © Oxford University Press 2023.
DOI: 10.1093/oso/9780197552230.003.0004

A DECADE OF REVOLUTION AND EXPERIMENTATION   107

US music critic Richard Franko Goldman observed that *Music for Little Orchestra* seemed "to fall in love with itself and to go long after it had declared itself in full. The scoring . . . produced a variety of delightful sounds, not entirely unknown, but these, after a time, lost all promise of surprise or freshness . . . it, too, had trouble with motion and length."[3] Goldman found the Symphony [No. 2] by Mexican composer Blas Galindo the least pretentious of the works offered in the same concert, which also included Juan José Castro's Concerto for Piano and Orchestra. Of the two symphonic concerts that Goldman reviewed for the *Musical Quarterly* he commented, "it is evident, and had been for some time, that the countries of South and Central America can show a large number of professional composers who can be considered on their own merits without reference to local mannerisms or international derivations. There is no more provincialism than there is among composers of the United States."[4] Similarly, just a few pages before Goldman's review, Irving Lowens quipped that "the 'rum and coca-cola' school of Latin American composers was, happily, not represented, and the quality of the music offered was, for the most part, unusually high."[5] For Lowens, the Julliard String Quartet concert "provided what was the undoubted sensation of the entire Festival, Ginastera's String Quartet No. 2," which Lowens further described as "gripping, full-blooded music of striking originality . . . Polytonal and serial techniques are used throughout with the utmost virtuosity, but with a distinctively personal touch . . . magnificent vitality and controlled turbulence mark [the fast movements]."[6] The use of serialism that Ardévol viewed with suspicion for its potential to trap composers into an impersonal and unrooted musical style was the very trait that US music critics found appealing in Ginastera's String Quartet No. 2. Additionally, the absence of provincialism, i.e., overt use elements derived from folk or vernacular music or nationalist composition, and an overall international musical style were praised by Lowens and Goldman. Yet, this would be the only IAMF, which continued until 1986, that would include works by Cuban composers who resided in the island.

In this chapter I explore the dramatic shifts in international artistic networks Cuban composers maneuvered after the 1959 Revolution and with them the changes in aesthetic and compositional preferences. First, I discuss the political and economic changes in Cuba in the early years of the Revolution and their consequences in the realm of classical music. A report by Juan Blanco on a visit to Cuba by Soviet and East German composers and musicologists sheds light

[3] Richard Franko Goldman, "Washington D.C." in "Current Chronicle," *Musical Quarterly* 44, no. 3 (1958): 384.
[4] Ibid., 382.
[5] Irving Lowens, "Washington D.C." in "Current Chronicle," *Musical Quarterly* 44, no. 3 (July 1958): 378.
[6] Ibid., 378–379.

108   CUBAN MUSIC COUNTERPOINTS

on the tensions and conflicts between the Cuban composers and their Eastern European socialist counterparts. This is followed by an examination of the emergence of a socialist and revolutionary discourse regarding the arts in the early years of the revolution, one in which innovation, *vanguardismo*, socialism, and Cubanness gained importance and acquired new meanings. I then look at specific developments in the Cuban classical music scene through several moments that marked this decade: the 1962 Latin American Music Festival, the establishment of the Unión Nacional de Escritores y Artistas de Cuba (UNEAC, National Union of Writers and Artists of Cuba) and its role in hosting the 1964 concerts of experimental and electronic music, and the foundation of the Orquesta Sinfónica Nacional de Cuba (OSN, Cuban National Symphony Orchestra) and its October 1969 concert of orchestral experimental works. Finally, the chapter concludes with a discussion of a book by José Ardévol and a pair of essays by Leo Brouwer (b. 1939) that hint at the mixed opinions on avant-garde and experimental music among Cuban composers at the close of the decade, which set the stage for the following chapter on the institutionalization and centralization of culture and the arts in Cuba in the 1970s.

From US Allies to Reluctant Soviet Comrades

In 1958, Cuban and US composers were still in constant communication, exchanging scores and recordings. By 1960 the situation had drastically changed; after the triumph of the Cuban Revolution and subsequent US embargo on Cuba, interactions between US and Cuban composers and musicians lessened dramatically. The use of serial and twelve-tone techniques became closely associated with certain US composition circles and, as the music criticism that followed the IAMF attests, some Latin American composers. These approaches were closely tied to ideals of individual freedom and technical achievements the Capitalist West extolled as paramount conditions to modern advancement and truly creative endeavors. Additionally, composers and music critics from Cuba's new major ally, the Soviet Union, had deemed these techniques as "formalist," bourgeois, capitalist, and decadent, even though there was a relative relaxation of official policies against composers who explored these compositional approaches in the aftermath of Stalin's death. Although Ardévol was not alone in his resistance to serialism (and he eventually employed the technique in his *Noneto* from 1966) among his Cuban peers (Edgardo Martín was also skeptical), not all Cuban composers were so dismissive of serialism or other techniques that were being explored and promoted among music circles in the "capitalist West" or so keen on siding with Soviet composers and musicologists on which compositional devices were politically or ideologically appropriate.

A DECADE OF REVOLUTION AND EXPERIMENTATION   109

In 1961, a group of Soviet and Eastern European composers and musicologists visited Cuba and met with local composers, studying Cuban music as part of a cultural exchange agreement between Cuba, the German Democratic Republic (GDR), and the Soviet Union. The Music Section of the UNEAC organized a series of listening and discussion sessions of Cuban, German, and Soviet music. The decision to host the meeting at the UNEAC must have been strategic on the Cuban composers' side. The UNEAC was founded on August 22, 1961 with the goal of preserving national independence and promoting social justice in Cuban artistic and literary creation. Founding members included Nicolás Guillén, Alejo Carpentier, José Lezama Lima, René Portocarrero, Roberto Fernández Retamar, Lisandro Otero, Pablo Armando Fernández, José A. Baragaño, Fayad Jamís, and Luis Martínez Pedro and composers Harold Gramatges, Argeliers León, and Juan Blanco, among others. Over the years individual sections (eventually reconfigured as associations) were created to oversee and organize activities within specific fields, including literature, visual arts, theater and scenic arts, and music. The UNEAC grants several awards and honors and publishes *La Gaceta de Cuba* as well as several other magazines and journals in specialized areas. The UNEAC served as a legitimate space for artistic debate, a Cuban counterpart to the artists' unions with which their Soviet and German counterparts would have been familiar. According to a report written by Juan Blanco and published in Casa de las Américas's magazine, the discussion sessions held at the UNEAC with the German and Soviet visitors facilitated sincere, fraternal, and fruitful discussions that benefited all attendants. Yet, Blanco noted that

> the most polemic attitude of our visitors was captured in [their reaction] to the position of the most advanced Cuban composers who presented their view that the development of new styles and techniques, such as twelve-tone compositions, aleatoric music, microtonalism, athematism, electronic and concrete music, etc., constitute achievements of humanity, that stripped of all orthodoxy or dogmatism can be put to good use by composers of our time to enrich their works.[7]

Blanco's description of the foreign visitors' attitude toward the Cuban composers' judgment of new music techniques as 'polemic' implicitly defended the Cuban composers' stance. For Blanco and several other Cuban composers these

---

[7] "la actitud más polémica de los visitantes se plasma frente a la posición de los compositores cubanos más avanzados que expusieron su criterio de que el desarrollo de nuevos estilos y técnicas como la dodecafonía, el aleatorismo, el microtonalismo, el atematismo, la música concreta y electrónica, etc. constituyen conquistas de la humanidad, que despojadas de toda ortodoxia o dogmatismo, pueden ser aprovechadas por los compositores de nuestro tiempo para enriquecer sus trabajos." Juan Blanco, "La música," *Revista Casa de las Américas*, no. 9 (1961): 121–122.

110   CUBAN MUSIC COUNTERPOINTS

techniques could be used by any composer to enrich his or her language, as long as they are stripped of "orthodoxy and dogmatism," code terms for bourgeois capitalist decadence. This would not be the only instance in which Cuban composers defended their use of new, avant-garde and experimental techniques.

The East German and Soviet visitors were Nathan Notowicz, musicologist and Secretary General of East Germany's Composers' Union; Günter Kochan, East German composer; and Vladimir Fere, Soviet composer and, at the time, composition professor at the Chaikovsky Conservatory in Moscow. Nathan Notowicz was a member of a group of musicologists active in East Germany during 1950s and 1960s, who were dubbed "the mighty handful." According to Laura Silverberg, these scholars "ardently supported the SED [Socialist Unity Party of Germany] program of building a socialist culture, enjoyed considerable authority in musical matters, and were well positioned to influence the development of East German musical life."[8] The group's artistic views aligned with Stalinist-Zhdanovist aesthetics denouncing "serialism, atonality, and harsh dissonance as too complex for the general public and inadequate for relaying an appropriate ideological message."[9] Fere had served the Soviet Union in the Kyrgyz Republic as part of the efforts to unify local national art music with a musical language that reflected socialist aesthetics.[10] During their time in Cuba, these visitors held sessions devoted to listening to and discussion of new music. Unsurprisingly, they opposed the employment of new techniques in contemporary art music, which differed greatly from Cuban composers' stance on modernist and avant-garde techniques. The visiting composers, staunch ideologues in their respective countries, were probably sent to Cuba by the Soviet Union to promote aesthetically conservative compositional techniques and to guide Cuban composers on aesthetic matters. Juan Blanco did not agree with their aesthetic goals and encouraged Cuban composers to experiment with styles and techniques deemed unacceptable by the visiting composers and musicologists who promoted musical conservatism. The visit ended on a positive note, as the various parties signed a cultural exchange agreement by which all countries would share and exchange recordings, scores, and musicians.

Blanco's report documents how Cuban composers' networks were changing and shifting after the 1959 Revolution, especially in comparison to the spaces and moments of music exchange with Latin American and US composers exemplified by the 1958 IAMF. As tensions between Cuba and the United States increased—eventually leading to the US embargo on Cuba—and the Cuban

---

[8] Laura Silverberg, "Between Dissonance and Dissidence: Socialist Modernism in the German Democratic Republic," *The Journal of Musicology* 26, no. 1 (2009): 49.

[9] Ibid., 49–50.

[10] Marina Frolova-Walker, "'National in Form, Socialist in Content': Musical Nation-Building in the Soviet Republics," *Journal of the American Musicological Society* 51, no. 2 (1998): 349.

A DECADE OF REVOLUTION AND EXPERIMENTATION   111

government established new political and economic agreements with the Soviet bloc, Cuban artists also found themselves in positions where they had to sever ties with some of the networks and relationships they had built with US-based composers and begin to cultivate new networks with composers and organizations in Eastern European socialist countries as well as new ways to maintain contact with fellow Latin American composers. Cuban composers were also well aware of the decades-long history of political and aesthetic debates composers and the cultural elite had wagered in the Eastern bloc; as Blanco's account reveals, Cuban composers staunchly resisted aesthetic dicta from Eastern European cultural institutions or figures and defended their abilities to maintain artistic freedom and an idiosyncratically national and Cuban tradition.

Blanco's article appeared in a cultural magazine published by Casa de las Américas, one of the most important state cultural organizations that encourages cultural exchanges with foreign countries. Its founder and director, Haydée Santamaría, was one of the few women heavily involved in the early revolutionary efforts and one of the key players and organizers in the attacks of July 26, 1953. Casa was founded by the revolutionary government on April 28, 1959, through Law 288 as an autonomous non-governmental agency that would promote cultural activities between Cuba and the people of Latin America, the Caribbean, and the rest of the world. Its objectives reflected Santamaría's vision to spread the culture of the American continent, foster international cultural exchange and dialog, and fight against isolation imposed upon Cuba by the US embargo.[11] In 1965 Casa created an internal Music Department, with Harold Gramatges as its director. Since its inception, the Music Department has hosted visits by composers, musicians, and musicologists from other Latin American countries, conferences, concerts, festivals, and workshops on various topics, including folk, popular, art, and experimental music. The Music Department has also organized contests and competitions in the areas of composition and musicological research, the result of which has been the publication of new music and academic articles and books.[12] Throughout the years the Music Department of Casa de las Américas has collected scores and recordings of works by composers from all of the Americas, creating a valuable music collection, and becoming an epicenter of cultural exchange for leftist Latin American artists. As my account of other moments after 1959 unfolds, Casa de las Américas and its Music

---

[11] Bernardo Flores, *Perfiles culturales: Cuba 1977* (Havana: Editorial Orbe, 1978), 49.

[12] The Music Department established the Premio de Musicología (musicology prize) de Casa de las Américas in 1979, which they later paired with the Coloquio Internacional de Musicología in 1999. The Music Department also held a short-lived Concurso de Composición (composition contest) between 1966 and 1967 that was resumed in 2004 as the Premio de Composición (composition prize) de Casa de las Américas, which would include the Primer Taller Lationamericano de Composición (first Latin American music workshop) in 2009, in conjunction with the Music Section of UNEAC.

112 CUBAN MUSIC COUNTERPOINTS

Department will continuously surface as key nodes in the networks in which Cuban composers circulated.

In the same 1961 review, Blanco complained that Cuban ensembles should promote more new and local music. Although Blanco served in an advisory capacity for the OSN, he did not shy away from criticizing the Orchestra's programming. The Cuban OSN was founded on October 7, 1959, with Manuel Duchesne Cuzán and Enrique Gonzàlez Mantici as its directors; one of its main objectives was to promote national and contemporary classical music.[13] But two years after its foundation, in Blanco's assessment, it had failed to fulfill its mission. Blanco made three specific recommendations for improving the OSN's offerings:

a) Programming enriched with contemporary works by composers from all over the world. b) More music by Latin American composers. c) Absolute omission of transcriptions, adaptations, arrangements or whatever other distortions of great musical works that, under the appearance of simplicity, mislead the people.[14]

Blanco justified his criticism by reminding readers that the lack of new compositions and works by Cuban and Latin American composers, as well as the inclusion of transcriptions or arrangements of works that according to him "mislead the people," were remnants of bourgeois tastes and society. Regarding the OSN's national tour, where they performed for audiences from farms, factories, co-ops, schools, and mines, Blanco complained that the orchestra was watering down its musical program by including mostly works that were easy to listen to; yet, Blanco believed that "precisely, this segment of the population, uninitiated in the practice of listening to good music, should be offered programs that, as much as possible, expose them to the works of the most important time periods, including the contemporary period, so that everyone's sensibility, imagination, and taste are fully developed and do not end up dissolutely isolated in determined moments of music history."[15] For Blanco, these programs did not contribute

---

[13] For a more detailed account of OSN programming see Marysol Quevedo, "The Orquesta Sinfónica Nacional de Cuba and Its Role in the Cuban Revolution's Cultural Project," *Cuban Studies* 47, no. 1 (2019): 19–34.

[14] "a) Programación enriquecida con obras comtemporáneas de compositores de todas partes del mundo. b) Más música de compositores latinoamericanos. c) Omisión absoluta de transcripciones, adaptaciones, arreglos o cualesquiera otras tergiversaciones de grandes obras musicales que, bajo la apariencia de la facilidad, desorienten al pueblo." Blanco, "La Música," 118. Blanco's inclusion of compositions that distort "great musical works" in this list points to a broader attitude in Cuban cultural politics of avoiding watered-down culture in order to reach the masses. On the contrary, Cuban officials spoke of elevating the education level of the people, of the common man, so that he could appreciate "high" art.

[15] "Creemos que, precisamente, a esta parte del pueblo no inicado en la práctica auditiva de la buena música debe dársele programas que, en lo posible, sean exponentes de las épocas más importantes, incluyendo la contemporánea, para que la sensibilidad, la imaginación y el gusto de

to the formation of the socially conscious citizen and promoted a neocolonial mentality.

If Ardévol's radio broadcast from 1960 casted doubts over the indiscriminate use of serial techniques he witnessed at the 1958 IAMF and implicitly called into question the US-backed pre-1959 Pan Americanist activities, then Blanco's 1961 review exemplified the early revolutionary years by criticizing ongoing cultural practices within Cuba that reflected pre-revolutionary, bourgeois tastes and values. Blanco's assessment also demonstrated Cuban artists' willingness to question any aesthetic rulings that originated from Soviet and Eastern European officials or artists, while they constantly sought to carve an independent and Cuban path. Blanco's review marks a particular moment in the early years of the Revolution that connects several individuals and organizations, as well as ideas of aesthetic validity. By writing the review, Blanco established himself as a crucial member of a new cultural elite under the revolutionary government; in spite of the socialist regime's purported goals of democratizing access to all forms of artistic production, these efforts were still organized by administrators at the various cultural institutions that oversaw artistic programming, creating a cultural elite comprised of individuals who showed a strong commitment to the Revolution and to promoting national cultural forms. The government had already accredited Blanco in the early years of the Revolution by naming him Music Director of CMZ (the Ministry of Education's radio station, where Blanco created a radio symphony orchestra and several chamber music groups), professor at Conservatorio Alejandro García Caturla, chief of the band of the Estado Mayor del Ejército Rebelde, as well as founder of the OSN and the UNEAC. But even from his privileged position, he did not refrain from criticizing what he viewed as a lack of progress in musical programming, nor did he avoid voicing his disagreement with the aesthetic positions of the Soviet visitors. This review also helps us identify further nodes in the new network of composers and institutions in post-1959 Cuba, one that had connections to some pre-revolutionary precedents (after all, Blanco was an important player in the Sociedad Cultural Nuestro Tiempo in the 1950s), local composers, conductors, ensembles, and cultural institutions as well as new foreign music circles. Further documents and moments of the 1960s reveal more connections among composers and institutions within and outside of Cuba, and the political and aesthetic values they purported to promote: Cuban, socialist, revolutionary, and innovative.

---

todos se desarrollen íntegramente y no queden viciosamente enclaustrados en determinados momentos de la Historia de la Música." Blanco, "La Música," 118.

Cuban, Revolutionary, Socialist, and Innovative

Juan Blanco was one of many artists who, during the 1950s, criticized the lack of support for local contemporary art from the cultural institutions during Batista's regime, had been persecuted for their political leanings and "subversive" art, and saw the Revolution as an opportunity to contribute to the revolutionary project through their artwork. Political leaders and composers introduced and reinforced new revolutionary and socialist values through their political discourse by relying on pre-revolutionary national symbols. These new values were articulated through the purported goals of cultural institutions and the aesthetic principles they sought to promote. Composers were not passive or complacent participants in the nation-building project, but rather active actors in the revolutionary-socialist experiment of 1960s Cuba. The majority of active composers sought to shape the new man and enact the Revolution through their compositions; after enduring political persecution and artistic repression during Batista's regime, they actively engaged in the cultural agenda of the Revolution, shaping cultural policies, music education programs, artistic programming, ensembles and cultural organizations, and artistic exchange with their foreign counterparts. However, the composers who assumed leadership roles in the new state cultural organizations did not always agree among themselves on which musical aesthetics were best suited for the new revolutionary society. A group of composers who accrued cultural capital during the 1950s and at the onset of the Revolution in the early 1960s (including Juan Blanco) had a decisive role on which composers and types of works would be promoted and supported by state institutions. This resulted in privileging avant-gardist and experimental compositions at the highest rungs of the intellectual elite ladder and excluding from it works and composers that did not engage with the same aesthetic language.

As the examples discussed throughout this chapter demonstrate, key concepts and terms were deployed in concert program notes, journalistic pieces of music criticism, and several other types of public documents that were meant to speak for and to cultural producers, the state, and the people. In the first years of the Revolution, political as well as cultural leaders went to great lengths to portray the Revolution as a quintessential Cuban, i.e., national, phenomenon. They were largely successful by heavily relying on pre-revolutionary national symbols and placing them alongside new ones that carried symbolic capital both as socialist and nationalist icons. They drew from a pre-existing Cuban revolutionary tradition rooted in the legacy of the nineteenth-century poet and political activist José Martí. In the realm of classical music, composers and music educators extolled Amadeo Roldán as the symbolic figure of the revolutionary spirit in pre-revolutionary art music. Once the state nationalized education, the former Conservatorio Municipal de La Habana (where Roldán had taught in the 1930s and where the Grupo de Renovación Musical gathered in the 1940s) was renamed Conservatorio Amadeo Roldán. His music continued to be promoted and performed after 1959 as Cuban, revolutionary, modern, and universal. These were the core values to which music should aspire and to which composers adhered after 1959. But how to define these values musically was not as clear or straight forward.

Artists and intellectuals conflated aesthetic *vanguardismo* with political *vanguardismo*. Although it would be logical to equate or translate the term *vanguardia* or *vanguardista* to avant-garde, in post-1959 Cuba it did not always imply aesthetic avant-gardism. However, in the realm of classical music, some of the staunchest supporters of the revolutionary government and socialist ideals were also avowed musical avant-gardists and experimentalists. Throughout the decade the state's agricultural and educational reforms were framed by language that emphasized the importance of "technical" development and advancement, with "innovation" as a key component of socialist and revolutionary society. Engaging with international Cold War politics entailed a need to demonstrate the virtues of socialism and its superiority to capitalism through the system's ability to foster innovation. If we scan through Cuban periodicals of the 1960s, we find numerous photographic magazine spreads that feature the new techno-logical advancements from the Soviet Union, and in the late 1960s with a focus on imported agricultural or factory equipment and Cuban workers learning how to operate the new technology that would increase productivity and benefit the people. In 1960, the Soviet Exhibition of Science, Technology, and Culture arrived in Havana after its 1959 stop in Mexico City, drawing an estimated 800,000 visitors with displays that included the Lunik and Sptunik spacecrafts.[16] As Austin Yost has argued, these exhibitions "intended to 'normalize' the USSR in the minds of visitors—to make the Soviet Union seem inviting, unthreat-ening, and friendly—while simultaneously drawing attention to the exceptional achievements of Soviet science and industry."[17] Another recurring topic covered in the Cuban press was the Soviet Union's cosmonautical program as one of the great technical and scientific achievements of their socialist ally. Several Cuban composers defended musical avant-gardism and experimentation as *technolog-ically* innovative and therefore, revolutionary. This aesthetic stance also allowed them to claim universality in their work; in other words, because they were in-novative and revolutionary, they were also producing music that was universal. At the close of the decade, Leo Brouwer connected music composition and

---

[16] Austin Yost, "Exposiciones Soviéticas: Selling Socialist Modernity in the US's Backyard" (M.A. Thesis, University of Chapel Hill, 2015), 2, 14.

[17] Yost, "Exposiciones Soviéticas," 3.

116   CUBAN MUSIC COUNTERPOINTS

Cubanness with the revolutionary spirit and innovation in his 1970 article "La música, lo Cubano, y la innovación" ("Music, Cubanness, and Innovation"), in which he argued that "to innovate is, without a doubt, one of the most difficult things to achieve in a moment of great richness of means as is our century. It is also, radically, one of the conditions of revolutions."[18] Brouwer was also aware of the potentially dangerous implications of employing experimental approaches that were closely tied to composers and music circles in capitalist countries. Brouwer concluded that "the solution for a colonized country is in *suppressing defining traits of the oppressive culture and not [suppressing] the common traits of the universal culture.*"[19] For Brouwer and some of his colleagues, there was a shared universal music culture Cuban composers could be a part of through the use of innovative (i.e., avant-garde and experimental) techniques.

Another way in which classical music could meet the demands of a revolutionary and socialist society was through the values of *collectivism, hard work, and economic egalitarianism.*[20] These three tenets are closely tied to one another, for the Cuban socialist state needed individuals to think of themselves as part of a larger, national collective (collectivism), in which, through citizens' voluntary participation in the national project (work), the national wealth could be equally distributed (egalitarianism), benefiting all Cubans. Voluntarism and hard work were at the core of state ideology, and composers such as Brouwer and Blanco described themselves and fellow composers as cultural "trabajadores" (workers) in most of their writings. Art music was one public platform through which artists and audiences, i.e., civil society, negotiated definitions of *Cubanness, socialism, revolutionary*, and *vanguardismo* with the state. Composers constantly praised the ability of classical music (and avant-garde and experimental music) to be shared with the masses through mass media and to serve the people by educating them and encouraging them think critically, in essence shaping the *hombre nuevo* (new man). Brouwer compared the situations between capitalist and socialist models for composers vis-à-vis audiences, "when there is a mutual relationship between the creative elite and the minority [who is in control] of the economic power, then we see a rupture between art and the masses. In a country like revolutionary Cuba, there isn't the slightes reason for the superstructure (political power) to yield power of action for self-identification, since its work is a reflection of the masses for which it exists."[21] Brouwer had a utopic view that

[18] "Innovar es, sin duda, una de las cosas más arduas de lograr en un momento de gran riqueza de medios como el de nuestro siglo. También es, radicalmente, una condición de las revoluciones." Leo Brouwer, "La música, lo cubano, y la innovación," *Cine Cubano* (1969–1970): 32–33.
[19] "La solución para un país colonizado está en *suprimir rasgos definidores de la cultura opresora y no los rasgos communes de la cultura universal.*" Ibid., 35.
[20] Sujatha Fernandes, "Reinventing the Revolution: Artistic Public Spheres and the State in Contemporary Cuba" (Ph.D. diss, University of Chicago, 2003), 3.
[21] "Al relacionarse mutuamente el fenómeno 'élite creadora' con la minoría del poder económico, viene la ruptura entre arte y masa. En un país como Cuba revolucionaria, no la más minima razón

A DECADE OF REVOLUTION AND EXPERIMENTATION   117

placed the socio-economic socialist framework above that of capitalist countries in regards to music production and consumption: in Cuba, the state did not need to impose itself in art, because the people and the art they produced reflected the state. Brouwer's stance reflected Fidel Castro's *Palabras a los intelectuales,* his often-cited speech to Cuban intellectuals on June 30, 1961, where he pronounced the now famous phrase "within the revolution everything against the revolution nothing."

Finally, tied to these values was the idea of the *artista comprometido,* the politically and socially committed artist. Revolutionary intellectuals saw artistic creation as intrinsically connected to the political and social conditions in which it was created. For influential individuals, like writer and critic Roberto Fernández Retamar (1930–2019), the *vanguardista* artist had to be an *artista comprometido.* In *El socialismo y el hombre en Cuba,* Ernesto Che Guevara accused many members of the intellectual class (formed prior to 1959) of not being true revolutionaries, labeling their work as decadent. Fernández Retamar defended the older generation by drawing a distinction between "decadent" and "*vanguardia artística*" (artistic avant-garde). For Fernández Retamar, Guevara had erroneously conflated the two, because, although there were avant-garde artists that did partake in the decadence of capitalism and bourgeois tastes, the true avant-garde artist was the *artista comprometido.*[22] Composers went to great lengths to position themselves and their works as committed to the Revolution, as *artistas comprometidos.* And the state needed the work and support of these artists and intellectuals to legitimize the regime and function as mediators between the state and the people.

Launching Official Music Exchanges: The 1962 Latin American Music Festival

One of the most overt forms of cultural diplomacy and demonstrations of political commitment was to foster musical exchange through focused programs, including music festivals.[23] In October of 1962, the OSN held a Festival of Latin

---

para que la superestructura (el poder político) quiera ejercer la acción de poder para autoidentificarse, pues su trabajo es de acción refleja con la masa por y para la cual existe." Brouwer, "La música, lo cubano, y la innovación," 33.

[22] Roberto Fernández Retamar quoted in Jorge Cabezas Miranda, *Proyectos poéticos en Cuba, 1959–2000: algunos cambios formales y temáticos* (San Vicente del Raspeig: Publicaciones de la Universidad de Alicante, 2012), 102–105.

[23] These festivals were part of a broad attempt to organize and mobilize musicians on the part of the National Arts Council, under a new state regime after the departure from Cuba of most artistic managers and producers. Robin D. Moore, *Music and Revolution: Cultural Change in Socialist Cuba* (Berkeley: University of California Press, 2006), 70–71.

118 CUBAN MUSIC COUNTERPOINTS

American Music, performing works by Alberto Ginastera, Heitor Villa-Lobos, José Ardévol, Blas Galindo, José Pablo Moncayo, García Caturla, Silvestre Revueltas, and Amadeo Roldán, and with the participation of Mexican composer and conductor Blas Galindo.[24] As discussed in the previous chapters, Cuban composers had been active participants in Pan Americanist music programs and efforts led by US-based composers and organizations throughout the 1930s, 1940s, and 1950s. Yet, after 1959, to promote musical Pan Americanism from Cuba was to support an alternative path to hemispheric unity and collaboration that not only excluded, but blatantly opposed US-led Pan Americanist efforts. Additionally, the 1962 Festival in Cuba also coincided with the Cuban Missile Crisis, a thirteen-day period in October when the United States mobilized a naval blockade around the island to pressure the Soviet Union and Nikita Khrushchev to remove the nuclear missiles they had stationed in Cuba. Read in the context of one of the tensest moments in Cold War political history, especially in terms of the nuclear threat within the Western Hemisphere, the festival in Cuba showed their Latin American counterparts and the United States that what happened in Cuba had broader implications and Cubans were willing and ready to take the lead within Latin America, even if politically, Castro had been undermined by the Soviets when they agreed to pull the misiles from Cuba without consulting with Castro. The 1962 Festival was not the first of its kind; as discussed in the previous chapter, it was preceded by two Latin American Music Festivals held in Caracas in 1954 and 1957 and two Inter-American Music Festivals organized by the Music Section of the Organization of American States and held in Washington D.C. in 1958 and 1961, all of which included works by Cuban composers in their programs. However, in the last of these, only one Cuban composer was included, Aurelio de la Vega, who had emigrated to the United States after the Revolution; no Cuban composers who remained in Cuba after 1959 were ever included in future Inter-American Music Festivals, which ran until 1986. Nor did the Cuban composers want to be included in a music festival organized by the OAS, given that Cuba's membership to the organization was suspended in 1962 and that the Cuban revolutionary government considered the OAS an agent of US imperialism and a threat to Latin American nations' ability to self-govern. Therefore, the 1962 Latin American Music Festival functioned as an alternative space organized and hosted outside of the United States, a festival from, for, and by Latin Americans.

At the heart of the 1962 Festival was the OSN, which, in addition to conductors Manuel Duchesne Cuzán and Enrique González Mántici, included in tis advisory board composers Juan Blanco and Harold Gramatges. Both composers were

[24] OSN Concert Program (October 1962), Fondo Orquesta Sinfónica Nacional, Museo Nacional de la Música Cubana, Havana, Cuba.

A DECADE OF REVOLUTION AND EXPERIMENTATION 119

former members of the Sociedad Cultural Nuestro Tiempo, which had criticized the former Orquesta Filarmónica de La Habana for its lack of inclusion of Cuban and contemporary music in its concert programming during the 1950s. Manuel Duchesne Cuzán had been a long-time supporter of the new music scene in Cuba, performing in new music concerts organized by Ardévol's Orquesta de Cámara de La Habana in the 1940s and actively participating as a member of the Sociedad Cultural Nuestro Tiempo in the 1950s. Duchesne Cuzán was an ardent promoter of new, avant-garde and experimental symphonic music, conducting most of the OSN concerts that featured this repertory, while González Mantici, a composer himself, conducted repertory in a more conventional language, and new works, many times his own compositions, written in an overtly nationalistic vein. In comparison to its predecessor, the Orquesta Filarmónica de La Habana, the OSN programmed more works by Cuba, Latin American, and contemporary composers. It also helped foster goodwill and cultural understanding between Cuba and its new socialist allies, programming concerts of Czech, Hungarian, Polish, Soviet, and Chinese symphonic music during visits to the island of diplomatic delegations from each country.[25] The 1962 Latin American Music Festival was in keeping with the OSN's mission of promoting new music while also cultivating positive cultural relations with other Latin American countries. But the Festival not only served as a vehicle to promote cultural understanding and hemispheric unity; the program notes highlighted the underlying commonalities among the Latin American composers.

The concerts of the 1962 Festival in Cuba included works by composers who had participated in the first two Inter-American Music Festivals in Washington D.C., Blas Galindo, Alberto Ginastera, Heitor Villa-Lobos. However, the compositions included in the 1962 Latin American Music Festival in Cuba were aesthetically [as well as chronologically] far removed from the works those composers presented in Washington D.C. All of the works performed in the Cuban festival had been written much earlier, and were markedly more nationalist and conventional in their musical language than the more-recently composed works by the same composers that were performed in Washington D.C. in 1958 and 1961. The works of the 1962 Festival in Cuba dated from the 1940s or earlier and exhibited the nationalist-modernist style for which some composers, such as Alberto Ginastera in his *Obertura para el Fausto Criollo* (1943–1944), had become known. But, by the late 1950s and early 1960s, Ginastera, and several other Latin American composers, had moved away from the overt nationalism exhibited in their early works, and developed a style in which they "sublimated" nationalist musical traits and incorporated twelve-tone and serial techniques

---

[25] Quevedo, "The Orquesta Sinfónica Nacional de Cuba and Its Role in the Cuban Revolution's Cultural Project," 19–34.

120   CUBAN MUSIC COUNTERPOINTS

into their musical language. As noted in the opening of this chapter, Ginastera's serial approach in his String Quartet no. 2, which was commissioned for and premiered at the 1958 IAMF, was praised by US music critics. This led to a series of prominent commissions that catapulted Ginastera's US and international career.[26] US critics' approval of Ginastera's use of twelve-tone and serial techniques was presented as proof that he was a "universal" composer, who had mastered "universal" techniques. Coincidentally, in the program notes for the 1962 Latin American Music Festival in Cuba, composer Edgardo Martín also emphasized the Argentine composer's ability to move beyond musical nationalism by projecting his music toward the universal. Martín observed that Ginastera was influenced by Stravinsky, Bártok, Hindemith, and Prokofiev, and his work is distinguished by a self-assured, robust, and vigorous style and treatment. Although Martín did not delve into Ginastera's more recent explorations into twelve-tone and serial technique and his *Obertura para el Fausto Criollo* was overtly nationalist in character, Martín's program notes praised Ginastera in very similar terms as had the US music critics who reviewed the 1958 and 1961 IAMF in Washington D.C.: universal, vigorous, devoid of facile nationalism. Ginastera's example shows how the same composer was viewed as a successful figure by both Cuban and US music critics, in spite of the obvious political divisions between Washington and Havana. Aesthetically, universality, clarity of forms and musical language, and the clearly masculine trait of vigor, were all praised as desirable compositional traits by both US and Cuban critics. However, when it came to which economic and political systems provided the ideal conditions for these traits to be developed by composers, the Cuban sources show an overt politicization of composers and symphonic compositions that was absent in the US press.

In the program notes, Cuban composer Edgardo Martín extolled the virtues of socialist revolutions in Latin America and the beneficial conditions these revolutions presented for composers and classical music. In the notes for the Mexican music concert, conducted by Blas Galindo, Martín highlighted the revolutionary conditions that allowed the Mexican composers to produce works with a "rebel spirit" integrated in a structure of "universal character."[27] Martín credited Lázaro Cárdenas's nationalization of the oil industry as part of the social reforms that allowed Mexican artists and composers to fully develop a style that reflected the "rebel" and "revolutionary" spirit.[28] The concert included Blas Galindo's *Cantata Homenaje a Juárez*, which used as its text Benito Juárez's

---

[26] Hess, *Representing the Good Neighbor*, 153; Alyson Payne, "Creating Music of the Americas during the Cold War: Alberto Ginastera and the Inter-American Music Festivals," *Music Research Forum* 22 (January 1, 2007): 57–79.

[27] OSN Concert Program (October 1962), Fondo Orquesta Sinfónica Nacional, Museo Nacional de la Música Cubana, Havana, Cuba.

[28] Ibid.

A DECADE OF REVOLUTION AND EXPERIMENTATION   121

manifesto for the declaration of the 1857 Constitution of Mexico.[29] Martín concluded in his notes, "in revolutionary Cuba, what better Mexican voice than that of Benito Juárez could we listen to, who can affirm the common ideals between both countries [Cuba and Mexico]?"[30] Martín made an explicit connection between the Cuban and the Mexican revolutions through musical works that featured revolutionary sentiments. This was not unique to the Mexican case. Program notes for concerts featuring music by composers from other socialist countries were presented with similar language, especially those that included music by contemporary composers from Eastern European socialist countries, in which the socialist and revolutionary conditions were highlighted as important elements in the formation of composers, and in informing their aesthetic viewpoints and creative endeavors.

The 1962 Festival would not be the only one dedicated to music by Latin American composers. As we will see in the next chapter, Casa de las Américas organized a much larger and all-encompassing festival in 1972. Yet, here, as early as 1962, we can already detect the Cuban composers' and cultural institutions' efforts to foster musical exchanges with composers of Latin America by circumventing the musical Pan Americanism emanating from the United States and the OAS, exemplified by the Inter-American Music Festivals. Throughout the 1940s and 1950s, Cuban composers were fervent promoters of the type of musical Pan Americanism that took place through official state channels—such as the Pan American Union and the US State Department tours—and "unofficial" organizations or simply through private contact between composers (as was the case of Aaron Copland). After 1959, these exchanges were no longer tenable, and the Cuban Revolution aimed to become a leader among the Third World and Latin America. By hosting a Latin American music festival in 1962, Cuban composers and conductors positioned themselves at the helm of hemispheric music production. They placed Cuba at the center of a new Pan American music network that did not rely on US initiatives or funding and that openly criticized US interventionism—whether military, political, or cultural—in Latin America.

1964: A Year of Firsts in the Cuban Music Scene

In 1964, the Unión Nacional de Escritores y Artistas de Cuba (UNEAC) hosted a concert of Leo Brouwer's *Sonograma I* (1963), for prepared piano, and two weeks later another of electroacoustic music by Juan Blanco, both concerts the

---

[29] Ibid.

[30] "En Cuba Revolucionaria, que mejor voz Mexicana que la de Benito Juárez podemos escuchar que nos ratifique la comunidad de ideales entre ambos pueblos?" OSN Concert Program (October 1962), Fondo Orquesta Sinfónica Nacional, Museo Nacional de la Música Cubana, Havana, Cuba.

122   CUBAN MUSIC COUNTERPOINTS

first of their kind (prepared piano and indeterminacy and electronic music respectively) in Cuba.[31] Brouwer is one of the youngest composers to garner prestige in post-1959 Cuba. He rose to prominence initially as a guitar virtuoso who revolutionized classical guitar technique in the twentieth century. In 1959 he traveled to the United States under a scholarship from the Cuban revolutionary government (this was before US–Cuba relations had completely soured) studying at the Hartt College of Music in Connecticut and the Julliard School where he studied composition under Vincent Persichetti and Stefan Wolpe. One of his most important roles in the 1960s was as director of music at the Instituto Cubano de Artes e Industrias Cinematográficas (ICAIC, Cuban Film Institute) where he encouraged young composers to experiment with new techniques and the technology available at the Film Institute's studios and where he also mentored the members of the Grupo de Experimentación Sonora.[32] Months after the 1964 UNEAC concerts, the OSN, under the direction of new music champion Manuel Duchesne Cuzán, performed a concert of new music by Tadeusz Baird, Grażyna Bacewicz, and Juan Blanco. In a 1970 essay, Brouwer points to this year and these events as a turning point in Cuban music after a few years of maturing that had begun with his attendance at the Warsaw Autumn Music Festival in 1961 and his return to Cuba with scores and recordings from the festival, which he shared with fellow Cuban composers, noting "that listening in Warsaw was a vital impulse, a definitive point of departure for the Cuban vanguardia."[33] In addition to Juan Blanco, some of the other composers who Brouwer mentions in his overview of 1960s Cuban musical vanguardia were Carlos Fariñas, Héctor Angulo, Roberto Valera, Sergio Fernández [Barroso], Carlos Malcolm, and Calixto Álvarez. Their inclusion in Brouwer's account cemented these composers' place and identity as part of the Cuban musical avant-garde. The list excluded several prominent composers—Edgardo Martín, Argeliers León, José Ardévol, Hilario González— some of whom even called themselves part of a *retaguardia*. The *retaguardia* composers where not at the margins, neglected, or cast aside. Politically, they were some of the staunchest supporters of the regime, and throughout the 1960s served the state as directors, advisors, and professors in several music schools and education programs. They were members of the UNEAC, music critics, wrote program notes, and taught music theory, music history, and composition courses; and their compositions were performed by several prominent ensembles, even recorded by the new EGREM, the national recording label. But

[31] Brouwer, "La vanguardia en la música cubana," *Boletín Música* no. 1 (1970): 3.

[32] For more on the Grupo de Experimentación Sonora del ICAIC (GESI) see Tamara Levitz, "Experimental Music and Revolution: Cuba's Grupo de Experimentación Sonora Del ICAIC," in *Tomorrow Is the Question*, ed. Benjamin Piekut (Ann Arbor: University of Michigan Press, 2014), 180–210.

[33] Brouwer, "La vanguardia en la música cubana," n.p.

A DECADE OF REVOLUTION AND EXPERIMENTATION   123

composers who belonged the vanguardia claimed aesthetic experimentation as the most authentic expression of the Revolution, implying that musical conservatism [of the retaguardia] was a remnant of pre-revolutionary capitalist culture and an outdated mode of expression for the new socialist-revolutionary society.

The concerts that took place in 1964 pointed to a rather different, if unexpected to some readers, turn in the development of artistic networks. As the moments discussed up to this point in this chapter recount, after the 1959 Revolution ties had been severed with US music circles, the Soviet approach and stance on musical avant-gardism and experimentation was kept at arm's length, and contact with Latin American composers was maintained as the Cuban composers sought to forge hemispheric alliances that circumvented US involvement. But it was the Polish avant-garde and the Warsaw Autumn Music Festival that offered Cuban composers an alternative path to musical experimentation that was not devoid of the political commitment to socialism that the Revolution and the people required of *artistas comprometidos*. The Warsaw Autumn not only exposed Brouwer and, by consequence, Cuban composers to the Polish avant-garde, but to a wide array of avant-gardist and experimental composers from all over the world. If Cuban composers could not make direct contact with composers from the United States and other countries that had severed diplomatic ties with Cuba, then they could at the very least keep abreast of developments in the United States and much of Western Europe through the Warsaw Autumn Festival.

The Polish school offered Cuban composers an alternative to the more conservative music education institutions in Moscow, Leningrad, and East Berlin. As part of diplomatic cultural exchange agreements, Cuban music institutions and ensembles received professors and performers from the Eastern Socialist bloc; this was reciprocated and reversed by sending Cuban music students to continue their education in university institutions throughout Eastern Europe, mainly Moscow, Leningrad, and East Berlin. However, the young Cuban composers who showed the most promise and tended to prefer the more avant-gardist approach of Brouwer, Blanco, and Fariñas, furthered their formation as composers at schools in Poland. These included Roberto Valera, José Loyola, and Carlos Malcolm (who traveled to Poland later than Valera and Loyola, and made Poland his permanent home in 1990). Cuban composers incorporated the use of extended instrumental techniques, employing new notation and music symbols also used by the Polish sonorist school, in particular the omission of time signatures and indicating duration by marking minutes and seconds as well as the use of blocks of black lines to represent sound masses of indeterminate pitches in orchestral scores. Roberto Valera also recalled that his experience of Polish avant-garde theater left an indelible mark on him as a composer, changing his approach to artistic creation, opening him to what was possible as an artist. Valera and his younger contemporaries (although he is one year older than Brouwer)

124 CUBAN MUSIC COUNTERPOINTS

had the support of their older counterparts through organizations such as the Brigadas Hermanos Saíz. Founded by Blanco from his position as secretary of Public Relations for the UNEAC, the Brigadas Hermanos Saíz (which became the Asociación Hermanos Saíz in 1986) sponsored the promotion and collective efforts of young artists and intellectuals on their way to becoming official *artistas comprometidos* and card-carrying members of the UNEAC.

The Unión de Escritores y Artistas de Cuba (UNEAC) was one of the key institutions that hosted new music concerts of experimental works for small chamber ensembles, piano, and electroacoustic music. They also hosted meetings between Cuban intellectuals and their counterparts who visited from Eastern European socialist countries. Among its purported goals, the UNEAC strove to

> reject and fight all activity contrary to the principles of the Revolution; con-
> tribute to the preservation and dissemination of the artistic and intellectual
> values of the Cuban people, and that which is most representative of the cultures
> of peoples around the world; and participate in the defense of humanity, cul-
> tural diversity, Latin American and Caribbean integration, and fight against
> culture's and art's canalization [standardization] and commercialization.[34]

Its organizational structure consists of a general presidency and board that oversees sections or associations that focus on the specific artistic disciplines, including a Music Section. The Music Section was established in 1961, with Juan Blanco as its president and César Pérez Sentenat, Leo Brouwer, Félix Guerrero, Antonieta Henríquez, Ivette Hernández, and Roberto Valdés Arnau as secretaries. According to Blanco, the Music Section of UNEAC's main concerns included:

> a) Cultural exchange with other similar organizations. b) Organize an archive
> of scores, recorded music and specialized literature. c) Rescue our musical pat-
> rimony. d) Editions. e) Study circles. f) Conferences, lectures, and discussions
> about aesthetic aspects and music technique. g) Economic concerns of
> composers and performers. h) Study of general aspects of popular music ed-
> ucation: radio, television, [and] concerts. i) Collaboration with the Cultural
> Departments of the Revolutionary Government. In regard to this last point

[34] "Rechazar y combatir toda actividad contraria a los principios de la Revolución. Favorecer el estudio, la valoración crítica y difusión, tanto nacional como internacional, de las obras representativas de la cultura cubana. Contribuir a la preservación y difusión de los valores intelectuales y artísticos del pueblo cubano y a lo más representativo de las culturas de los pueblos del mundo. Participar en la defensa de la humanidad, de la diversidad cultural, de la integración latinoamericana y caribeña y luchar contra la canalización y mercantilización de la cultura y el arte." "UNEAC," http://www.ecured.cu/index.php/Uni%C3%B3n_de_Escritores_y_Artistas_de_Cuba (accessed May 18, 2015).

A DECADE OF REVOLUTION AND EXPERIMENTATION   125

and in representation of the Union, members of the Section will be part of the National Commission of the Music of the National Culture Council of the Revolutionary Government.[35]

The Music Section has also focused on safeguarding copyrights and work remuneration for composers and performers, holding competitions, and granting awards to individuals in the areas of performance, composition, and musicology. In 1997 it initiated the publication of the magazine *Música Cubana*, publishing articles on national music production.

The Music Section of UNEAC has also served as space for composers to engage in debates regarding artistic and political matters, and facilitate meetings and discussions with foreign composers. A short report on the 1964 concert of electroaoustic music by Blanco in the UNEAC's official journal, *Unión,* noted that the concert was an "important event," well-attended, and the audience was interested or enthusiastic. After the performance, Blanco delivered a lecture on "The technical revolution of concrete music," where he described electroacoustic music as "a phenomenon of our time and direct consequence of the development of science."[36] The space and people at the UNEAC was significantly more intimate (smaller performing forces and smaller and more selective audience of the Cuban intelligentsia) making it an ideally suited context for the more experimental works of Leo Brouwer and Juan Blanco. Unlike the concerts of the OSN and other major ensembles (choirs, ballet), the UNEAC concerts, although opened to the public, were attended by the Cuban intellectual elite—writers, visual artists—and served as a relatively safe space for artistic experimentation. In contrast to some of the other moments I have explored in this chapter so far, in which Cuban composers forged ties with music circles outside of Cuba, the UNEAC concerts fostered an internal, local network of composers and artists and served as a platform for a circle of composers to define their voice and reputation as experimentalists.

The aforementioned connections with the Polish avant-garde concretize themselves overtly beginning with the OSN concerts in 1964 that included works by Blanco, Tadeusz Baird, and Grażyna Bacewicz and in later years with concerts that included compositions by Witold Lutosławski and Krzysztof

[35] "a) Intercambio cultural con otras organizaciones similares. b) Organización de un archivo de partituras, música grabada y literatura especializada. c) Recuperación de nuestro patrimonio musical. d) Ediciones. e) Círculos de Estudio. f) Conferencias, charlas y discusiones sobre aspectos estéticos y de técnica musical. g) Aspecto económico de los compositores e intérpretes. h) Estudio de aspectos generales de la educación musical popular: radio, televisión, conciertos. i) Colaboración con los Departamentos Culturales del Gobierno Revolucionario. En base de este último punto y en representación de la Unión, miembros de la Sección formarán parte de la Comisión Nacional de Música del Consejo Nacional de Cultura del Gobierno Revolucionario." Juan Blanco, "La Música," *Revista Casa de las Américas* no. 9 (1961): 121.
[36] n.a., "Commentarios" *Unión* no. 1, Year 3 (1964): 170.

126 CUBAN MUSIC COUNTERPOINTS

Penderecki. One of the salient features of the OSN concerts in which Polish new music was performed is that they almost always paired the Polish repertory with works by Cuban composers. This wasn't unique to concerts with music by Polish composers; the OSN had a similar programming tactic of including Cuban compositions in concerts featuring music by Czech and Soviet composers or that had the participation of Czech and Soviet guest conductors or soloists.[37] However, those concerts often included works that were more conventional, nationalist, and conservative (such as the older compositions of Roldán, García Caturla or Gilberto Valdés, or newer works by *retaguardia* composers such as González Mántici) than the more avant-garde compositions of Brouwer, Blanco, and Fariñas that were programmed in concerts with contemporary Polish music. In March 28, 1965, the OSN performed Witold Lutosławski's *Postludio*, Stravinsky's *Petrushka* and premiered Leo Brouwer's *Sonograma II* and Juan Blanco's *Episodio*. The program notes were written by Edgardo Martín, and they discuss the composers' careers and works within the ideological framework and language of socialist and revolutionary values.[38] Martín, introduced Lutosławski as one of the most important contemporary Polish composers, noting that "this possibility that a composer exclusively dedicates his time to his creative work is quickly becoming a daily reality in socialist countries, in which all human endeavor has its place in the production and improvement of the wellbeing of the people. This is the case in Poland, the Soviet Union, Hungary, Czechoslovakia, East Germany, etc. And without a doubt it will also be one day in Cuba."[39] Martín here was projecting a utopic ideal into Cuban composers' futures, one in which they would be unencumbered by other responsibilities—teaching and administrative duties (as was the case for many of the Cuban composers in the first decade of the Revolution)—and would be free to compose thanks to full financial support from the state.

The rest of the program notes introduced the listener to new compositional techniques employed by Brouwer and Blanco. Martín presented the two composers as part of a recent movement of musicians in Cuba who cultivated concrete, electronic, and aleatoric music, as well as twelve-tone and serial techniques. In addition to Brouwer and Blanco, Martín included among them Argeliers León, Roberto Valera, and Manuel Duchesne Cuzán. In the description of Brouwer's *Sonograma II*, written by Brouwer himself, he highlighted the

[37] Quevedo, "The Orquesta Sinfónica Nacional de Cuba and Its Role in the Cuban Revolution's Cultural Project," 19–34.

[38] Edgardo Martín, "Notas al Programa," OSN Concert Program (March 28, 1965).

[39] "Esta posibilidad de que un compositor se dedique exclusivamente a su trabajo creador se está convirtiendo rápidamente en una realidad cotidiana en los países socialistas, en los cuales todo trabajo tiene su lugar en la producción y en la incrementación [sic] de los bienes del pueblo. Ello es así en Polonia, URSS, Hungría, Checoslovaquia, RDA, etc. Y sin duda lo será algun día también en Cuba." Ibid.

A DECADE OF REVOLUTION AND EXPERIMENTATION   127

importance of having a conductor who is willing and able to perform music such as his, meaning avant-garde works that feature controlled indeterminacy; for this reason, Brouwer dedicated the piece to Duchesne Cuzán. This demonstrates the close ties and significant relationship between composer and conductor at the time. As we saw in the previous chapter, Gramatges had singled out the lack of a conductor willing to perform the contemporary works of the Cuban composers as one of the major challenges to Cuban composers' creative output during the 1950s. Brouwer also placed the work in the same vein as preceding works, such as his *Variantes, Sonograma I,* and his film score for *La Estructura.* He described the work in one movement as "belonging to the so-called 'continuous forms' of serial music, with an interlude in the form of a multiple 'cadenza,' for flutes, cembalo, harp, and guitar."[40]

The program notes also include a transcription of Juan Blanco's commentary on his work, which Martín pointed out are solely Blanco's opinions and could be considered polemic by some readers. Blanco noted that his journey into experimental and electronic music began with his musical score for the film *El Mégano* (1955, Blanco states he wrote the music in 1953), but he was limited at the time by standard music notation. In 1961 he began experimenting with electronic music, and finally in 1964 he was able to convey through new graphic notation in his work for orchestra and magnetic tape *Texturas,* what he had envisioned since working on the score for *El Mégano.* Blanco credits three major events and circumstances that contributed to his musical development: (1) the Cuban Revolution, (2) the 1962 Cuban Music Festival—in which he noticed that most Cuban art music compositions up to that point consisted in reworking traditional and popular Cuban musics, that, according to Blanco, the people did not sing or dance to anymore, and that some Cuban popular musicians were using twelve-tone rows in their improvisatory *descargas* (jam sessions), and (3) the delayed encounter with twelve-tone and serial technique—delayed because, according to Blanco, in the past the works of Schoenberg and Anton Webern had been ignored, but thanks to the Revolution's promotion of artistic freedom and renovation, the "blinds had been lifted," benefiting Cuban composers.[41] Here I would like to note that the so-called "artistic freedom" brought on by the Revolution was described and defended as such by artists and intellectuals like Blanco, who saw themselves as part of the revolutionary movement and fully committed to the cause. The cases of state censorship are numerous, most famously, the *P.M.* incident, when Orlando Jiménez Leal's and Alberto Cabrera Infante's film *Pasado Meridiano* was blocked from public screening in 1961. Regarding *Episodio,* Blanco claimed that

---

[40] "Pertence a las llamadas 'formas continuas' de la música serial, con un **interludio** a modo de 'cadenza' múltiple, para las flautas, el cembalo, el arpa y la guitarra." Brouwer quoted in ibid.

[41] "Hemos logrado despojarnos de las vendas con que habían cubierto nuestros ojos." Blanco quoted in ibid.

128 CUBAN MUSIC COUNTERPOINTS

it was one more composition in a series that started with *Texturas*, in which he attempted "from his condition of Cuban—of human being—in revolution, give faith of his times through the best suited means, in other words, of those [means] that bring him the incorporation precisely of that time period."[42]

The notes on Stravinsky are also quite revealing, praising the newfound popularity of Stravinsky in the Soviet Union after he was invited to return to his homeland by the Soviet Composers Union in celebration of his eightieth birthday. Martín commented on the Soviet press's antagonistic coverage of Stravinsky's visit, noting that the reports took one of two sides, in favor or against the composer. But Martín pointed out that the "cult of personality" (by this I think Martín was referring to the cult of personality of Stalin) had been overcome in the Soviet Union, allowing for a well-deserved welcome of Stravinsky and his music, which resulted in the increase of performances and recordings of his works by Soviet ensembles.[43] Martín heavily criticized the Soviet Union and its Composers Union for having framed Stravinsky's music as reactionary, Western degenerate, and bourgeois decadence in the past. Composers like Martín, including Blanco and Brouwer, were not above critiquing the staunch conservatism of the musical establishment of past decades in Eastern European socialist countries. They went to great lengths to defend their artistic freedom and to credit the Cuban Revolution for setting up the ideal conditions for them to freely pursue musical creation without compromising their individual voice. In future concerts of avant-garde and experimental new music by Cuban composers, concert organizers, most likely Duchesne Cuzán and Juan Blanco, included works by composers from the Polish avant-garde, mainly Lutosławski, Bacewicz, and Penderecki, therefore creating a direct connection between the most "up to date" Cuban composers and their Polish counterparts.

The Height of Cuban Experimentation

As the 1960s came to a close, compositional experimentation would reach its climax, at least in terms of large works for orchestra performed by the OSN. On October 10, 1969 the OSN premiered three works—*Relieves* by Carlos Fariñas, *Contrapunto Espacial III* by Juan Blanco, and *La tradición se rompe . . . pero cuesta trabajo* by Leo Brouwer—that epitomized Cuban contemporary and experimental music. The concert would test the limits of what was aesthetically permissible within the Cuban revolutionary-socialist framework at a time when the

---

[42] "En la que intentaré, desde mi condición de cubano—de ser humano—en revolución, ir dando fe de mi época a través de los medios más idóneos, es decir, de aquellos que me brindan la incorporación de las técnicas de esa época precisamente." Blanco quoted in ibid.
[43] Ibid.

A DECADE OF REVOLUTION AND EXPERIMENTATION   129

Cuban state felt increasing pressure to meet the demands of the Soviet Union (in particular regarding economic productivity). One of the major national projects Fidel Castro and his Ministry of Agriculture envisioned was the *zafra de los 10 millones,* the sugar cane harvest of the 10 million, that is 10 million tons. All efforts from various industries were diverted to producing the promised 10 million tons of sugar, which had been planned over several years, but officially "began" with Fidel Castro's speech to the Cuban Communist Party on October 27, 1969, less than a month after the October 10 OSN concert. According to Juan Blanco, the 1969 concert was so scandalous that the person within the Consejo Nacional de Cultura (CNC, National Culture Council) "responsible" for allowing these pieces to be performed was fired, and that soon after the "administration grew more concerned about works that expressed independent political views, and it made attempts to control artists who were critical of the system."[44] After the scandal caused by the concert settled, Brouwer's, Blanco's, and Fariñas's music continued to be performed by the OSN, but only as part of concerts that included less experimental works. Given the heightened economic and political tensions that drove the entire country to focus its energies into the sugar cane harvest (even popular music groups were tapped to write and record songs to encourage massive participation in the sugar harvest), it is not surprising that experimental art and music that did not outwardly show support of the economic and political projects the majority of the island faced were indirectly repressed through strategic concert programming. In the next chapter we will delve further into the state's overt repression of counter-revolutionary art and artists in what became known as the *quinquenio gris*; the seeds of this heightened state repression of the arts had already been planted in the late 1960s.

The peak of musical experimentation in a symphonic setting came to a head in October 1969; the accompanying programs notes evince the composers' concern with connecting their experimental approaches to the socialist and revolutionary cause. The program consisted of Brouwer's *La tradición se rompe. . . pero cuesta trabajo,* Fariñas's *Relieves* for five groups of instruments, and Blanco's *Contrapunto Espacial III* for twenty-four groups of instruments, magnetic tape, and twenty actors. The ensemble was led by conductor Manuel Duchesne Cuzán, the more daring of the two principal conductors of the OSN. The program notes for this concert introduce the three composers with the heading "Time: Affirmation and Development," leading into Angel Vázquez Millares's description of Brouwer, Fariñas, and Blanco as "the first Cuban composers who tackled, with audacity and efficacy, the current expressive resources and techniques . . . They speak the language of **today** and open infinite possibilities of our musical creation's

---

[44] Neil Leonard III, "Juan Blanco: Cuba's Pioneer of Electroacoustic Music," *Computer Music Journal* 21, no. 2 (1997): 15.

130   CUBAN MUSIC COUNTERPOINTS

future."[45] The notes focus on the composers' accomplishments as the firsts, the *vanguardia*, to bring the Cuban music scene up to date with current composition techniques that were being employed by composers abroad. The experimental music practices present in these works included the consideration of space and spatial placement of musicians within a performance hall; the use of graphic scores and graphic notation; participation of actors; electroacoustic magnetic tape tracks amplified through speakers; and participation of the audience as part of the performance.

Relieves

In *Relieves* (Reliefs or Terrains), Carlos Fariñas (1934–2002) manipulated sound perception through the physical placement of groups of musicians in the concert hall and explored controlled indeterminacy. The concert program included a hand-drawn diagram of the spatial placement of the instrumental groups, transcribed in Figure 3.1. Fariñas's goal was to envelop the audience in sound. In addition to spatial placement of instrumentalists, the work featured "free aleatorism" and focused on the audience's role "as listener in a **vital and living** way for the end result, but also in [the composers'] search to liberate [the audience] from the traditional inhibitions and limitations secularly established during the listening in the concert hall."[46]

Fariñas had a very similar educational background to Gramatges and Blanco and common compositional interests and aesthetic concerns; in fact, he shared Blanco's interest in electroacoustic composition and was responsible for the establishment of the first electronic music laboratory in an academic institution in Cuba, the Instituto Superior de Artes's Electroacoustic and Computer Music Laboratory in 1989. Like Gramatges, Fariñas attended Aaron Copland's composition courses at Tanglewood (1956). His composition professors in Cuba included Ardévol, Gramatges, and Enrique González Mántici. Between 1961 and 1963, he also attended the Moscow Conservatory, where he studied with Alexander Pirumov and Dmitry Kabalevsky. Upon his return from his studies in the Soviet Union, Fariñas was named Director of the Conservatorio Alejandro García Caturla, where he also taught composition and served in the first Committee on Educational Reform. Like, Gramatges, Blanco, and Brouwer, Fariñas took on

---

[45] "Los primeros creadores cubanos que abordaron, con audacia y eficacia, las técnicas y recursos expresivos actuales . . . hablan la lengua de **hoy** y abren infinitas posibilidades al futuro de nuestra creación musical." Emphasis in original. Vázquez Millares, OSN concert program (October 10, 1969), n.p.

[46] "Oyente como posible elemento **vital y vivente** en el resultado sonoro, por otra parte, buscar una forma de liberarlo de las tradicionales inhibiciones y limitaciones establecidas secularmente durante la audición en la sala de conciertos." Ibid.

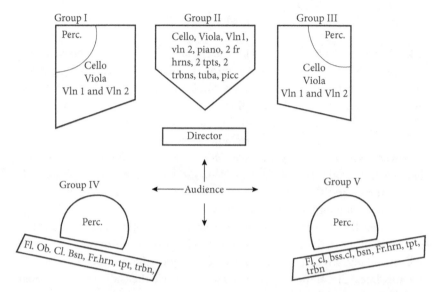

Figure 3.1. Stage layout for *Relieves* as provided in the OSN October 1969 concert program.

Note: This is my transcription of a hand-drawn diagram provided in the OSN concert program. Ibid.

leading administrative posts within Cuban revolutionary cultural and educational institutions. These posts rewarded his early loyalty to the revolutionary cause—in 1959, as a member of the Ejército Rebelde (Rebel Army), Fariñas participated in the culture and arts section, writing the music for the Ejército Rebelde's first film, *¿Por qué nació el Ejército Rebelde?* (Why was the Rebel Army born?, 1960), directed by José Massip. Fariñas showed his commitment to the Revolution by composing for ideologically charged projects like Massip's film and the 1964 Soviet film, directed by Mikhail Kalatozov, *Soy Cuba*.[47] Working in film and electroacoustic music also linked Fariñas to Brouwer's and Blanco's work as *artistas comprometidos*.

---

[47] *Soy Cuba* was a cinematic milestone as the first Soviet-Cuban co-produced film. In contrast to the Cuban-made and censored film *P.M.* (mentioned earlier), where Havana nightlife was uncritically depicted as hedonistic, *Soy Cuba* portrayed the capital city's nightlife as problematic within the new socialist-revolutionary political context. As Marc Olivier Reid argues "*Soy Cuba* muestra y critica el lado oscuro de las noches habaneras pero lo corrige apoyándose en un contenido ordenado (donde se les da dirección política a las masas) y una estética ordenada (en la cual, en la cinematografía y la dirección artística, se dirigen física y espacialmente a las masas)." Marc Olivier Reid, "Esta Fiesta Se Acabó: Vida Nocturna, Orden y Desorden Social En P.M. y Soy Cuba," *Hispanic Research Journal* 18, no. 1 (2017): 31.

132   CUBAN MUSIC COUNTERPOINTS

Contrapunto Espacial III

Like *Relieves*, *Contrapunto Espacial III* featured the spatial placement of musicians throughout the hall. Moreover, in this work Blanco engaged with several other experimental techniques that included the use of a graphic score, actors, magnetic tape, and controlled indeterminacy.[48] The performing forces for *Contrapunto Espacial III* included twenty-four instrumental groups, twenty actors, one child, saxophone soloist, and two magnetic tapes. In a 1970 article, Brouwer described *Contrapunto Espacial III* as "Effective noise-ism, **happening** between the components of the work (actors and musicians), a saxophone walks among the actors. The recorded voice of a boy recites a philosophical text. The actors move among the audience. The weight of this work falls on the staged [component]."[49] The graphic score, reproduced in Figure 3.2, is functioned as *particelle* (individual performing parts for each performer). The piece of paper itself was cut into an octagon with six geometric figures that are cut out (rectangles, squares, lines) that allow the performer to read it on either side (recto and verso). Depending on which of the eight sides the individual musician places the score, there are sixteen possible versions of each part. Because the score can be flipped and turned on any of its eight sides, Blanco built into it its retrograde and inversion. Blanco also leaves the choice of dynamics, intervals, and articulation up to the players, but does require each player to maintain the same dynamics and articulation through each single reading of the score. For Blanco, the work should elicit a psychobiologic response in the performers and the listeners through the spatial placement of the performers and speakers.[50]

[48] Later, Blanco reused the graphic score and conceptual framework of the piece in his *Contrapunto espacial III-b* (for two or more pianos) and *III-c* (for two or more guitars). Blanco renamed *III-b* and *III-c*, giving them the title *Octagonales*. These were his first works in a series he titled "estímulos para sonar" (Stimuli for sounding), which also included *Tridimensionales* (1971). All the works in the series were experimental in nature, but on a smaller scale than *Contrapunto espacial III*, for smaller performance forces and settings, most for chamber groups or soloists, and were performed at smaller performance spaces of Casa de las Américas or UNEAC, which were usually attended by artists and intellectuals, and less so by the general public.

[49] "Ruidismo efectivo, **happening** entre los componentes de la obra (actores y músicos), un saxofón camina entre los actores. La voz de un niño grabada directamente dice un texto filosófico. Los actores se mueven entre el público. El peso de la obra recae en lo escénico." Original emphasis. Brouwer, "La vanguardia en la música cubana," n.p.; Juan Blanco, *Contrapunto Espacial No. 3* (1969) http://www.fondation-langlois.org/html/e/oeu.php?NumEnregOeu=o00003332 (accessed December 12, 2014); My discussion of this piece is based on the graphic score reproduced in the concert program, provided in Figure 3.2, an article by Argeliers León on Blanco's compositions, and the manuscript of the graphic score, located at the Museo Nacional de la Música Cubana, that also included specific directions on how to read the score and perform the piece.

[50] OSN Concert Program (October 10, 1969), Fondo Orquesta Sinfónica Nacional, Museo Nacional de la Música Cubana, Havana, Cuba.

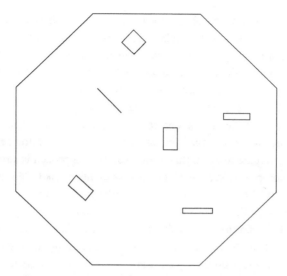

Figure 3.2. Juan Blanco, *Contrapunto Espacial III*.
Note: Transcribed from Argeliers León, "Del acto y el resultado," *Boletín Música*, no. 26 (n.d.): 11.

Brouwer's *La tradición se rompe... pero cuesta trabajo*

In *La tradición se rompe... pero cuesta trabajo*, Leo Brouwer engaged with several compositional techniques that aligned him with Blanco, Fariñas, and the international experimental music scene: quotation, collage, extended techniques, audience participation, and controlled indeterminacy. The liner notes of the 1970 LP release of *La tradición se rompe...* note that by requesting the audience's participation, Brouwer turned the concert into a "POP" event, a happening.[51] Brouwer assigned individual instrumentalists excerpts from the classical orchestral and solo repertory and instructed them to play these excerpts "de pié" ("standing up"). The collage resulting from the simultaneous and consecutive layering of excerpts of pre-composed works presented the composer's sonority overtaking that of the "masters." Sometimes the quotations are easily identifiable; but in other instances Brouwer juxtaposes them creating a sense of chaos due to the clash of tonal centers, meters, rhythms, tempos, and timbres. Some of the material Brouwer quoted include the "Presto" of J.S. Bach's Violin Sonata in G, the main theme of Dvorak's Cello Concerto, excerpts from the Scherzo of Beethoven's *Eroica* in the oboe, Ravel's *Daphnis et Chloé* in the flute, Mozart quintet and Stravinsky's *Rite of*

---

[51] The LP cover for the 1970 recording for the EGREM's label Areito includes the notes, written by Angel Vázquez Millares. These same notes were also included by Brouwer in the 1970 article "La vanguardia en la música cubana."

134   CUBAN MUSIC COUNTERPOINTS

Spring in the clarinet, Cimarosa's Oboe Concerto, and Tchaikovsky's *Nutcracker* in the piccolo, the opening of Beethoven's Fifth Symphony, the Lutheran hymn *Ein feste Burg*, an "Allegro" by Handel, the horn solo from Richard Strauss's *Till Eulenspiegel*, and Liszt's *Paganini Etudes*. By layering excerpts from a broad collection of styles and epochs Brouwer creates a sense of timelessness; all of the different time periods are experienced synchronically by the performers and the audience, or as Isabelle Hernández conceptualizes it, a "historic multidimensionality."[52] Brouwer challenged the concept of time by layering several historical epochs simultaneously. In this sense Brouwer's approach is similar to other avant-garde composers such as Stockhausen's in *Telemusik* (1966) and *Hymnen* (1966–1967) and Berio's in *Sinfonia* (1968–1969), all composed shortly before or around the same time Brouwer composed *La tradición se rompe* . . . . But "collage" doesn't fully capture the work's spirit, as Brouwer has noted, "what is fundamental of a structure such as *La tradición se rompe . . .* is not its apparent 'collage,' it is about capturing a poetic vision: the transformation of great cliches into a contemporaneity. It is a vision of the sonorous universe of all times, coexisting in the same moment."[53] The work is about the struggle and the unity of apparently contradictory elements.[54] Brouwer also employed graphic notation for extended techniques and effects, including clusters, glissandi, progressive accelerando, and indeterminate pitches, similar to the new music notation symbols used by Penderecki and Lutosławski, two Polish composers whom Brouwer admired.[55]

In addition to the use of quotations and layering, Brouwer writes passages of twelve-tone sound clusters (RL C), repetitive motives played by the percussion section, and sustained dissonances in the woodwinds (RL D). Other experimental devices Brouwer deployed in the work include: sound masses and glissandi in the strings; percussive motives in the brass, percussion, and woodwinds; dissonant clusters; harsh attacks and articulations; and wide variation in dynamics within short time spans. The piece ends with what Brouwer describes as an " 'infinite' medieval chord that, because of its open structure, allows the incorporation of sound."[56] The infinite "medieval" chord Brouwer refers to consists of stacked fifths in the strings, played *pppp*. In Brouwer's description we see that he used this sonority to "allow for the incorporation of sound," in other words, any

[52]   Isabelle Hernández, *Leo Brouwer* (Havana, Cuba: Editora Musical de Cuba, 2000), 134.

[53]   "Lo fundamental de una estructura como la de *La tradición se rompe* . . . no es el aparente 'collage,' se trata de apresar una visión poética: la transformación de los grandes 'clisés' en una contemporaneidad. Es una visión del universo sonoro de todos los tiempos, conviviendo en un mismo instante." Brouwer quoted in ibid.

[54]   Ibid.

[55]   Leo Brouwer, *La tradición se rompe . . . pero cuesta trabajo*. MS, 35, Museo Nacional de la Música Cubana, Havana, Cuba. For a more detailed discussion of this work see Quevedo, "Experimental Music and the Avant-garde in Post-1959 Cuba: Revolutionary Music for the Revolution," 251–278.

[56]   "Un acorde medieval 'infinito' que, por su estructura abierta, permite incorporación de sonido." Liner notes, *La tradición se rompe . . .* (Areito LDA-7009, 1970).

A DECADE OF REVOLUTION AND EXPERIMENTATION   135

ambient noise or other sounds naturally occurring at the performance's final moment could also be considered part of work. Finally, Brouwer's experimentalism extended to audience engagement and participation. At different moments the audience is shown signs instructing them to make a soft "Shhhhh" sound with the conductor or to clap. Audience participation aligned the work with experimental music practices of happenings, but also with the Cuban Revolution's ideological goals of collectivism and shaping the *hombre nuevo*.

The polystylistic effect obliterates the hierarchies of classical music that had been established and preserved by the Cuban cultural elite in the decades that preceded the Revolution. In the liner notes, the language is even more combative by describing the performers "attacking" the great masters. The "classics" are explicitly attacked and interrupted, "broken," by Brouwer's original material. As Isabelle Hernández observes, within *La tradición se rompe . . .* "there is a will, or rather, a way of articulating languages that is physical and corporeal, almost paroxysmal: the struggle for identity of the sound itself."[57] The work is *vanguardista* both aesthetically and ideologically; it brings into question the aesthetic hierarchies that canonized the compositions Brouwer quotes— hierarchies inherited through the colonial, political, and social processes that the Cuban Revolution sought to overturn. Moreover, the irreverent treatment of the quoted material engaged in musical *choteo*—the idiosyncratically Cuban sense of humor through which authority figures and values are made fun of or satirized—and thus marks Brouwer's experimental approach as characteristically Cuban. The work's rebellious tone situated Brouwer at the *vanguardia* of Cuban classical music; *La tradición se rompe . . .* not only opposed the traditional classical music repertory, but also secured Brouwer's place within the Revolution as an *artista comprometido* who enacted the Revolution's rebellious spirit through his work; it represents "one of the most significant works of the entire decade of the sixties where the world and the language of the composer are synthesized."[58] In Brouwer and *La tradición se rompe . . .* we find one of the central paradoxes of experimental music in Cuba: the work and the composer rebel against established norms, cementing their place as aesthetically revolutionary; the composer claims that aesthetic experimentation is the result of the revolutionary environment and supports revolutionary values; aesthetic experimentation creates tension between the composer as individual and the political and cultural establishment, which in spite of calling itself revolutionary, does not allow certain forms of dissent. Brouwer was labeled the *enfant terrible* of Cuban

---

[57] "Hay una voluntad, o mejor, una forma de articular lenguajes que es física y corpórea, casi paroxística: la lucha de identidad del propio sonido." Hernández, *Leo Brouwer*, 135.

[58] "Una de las obras más significativas de toda esa década de los sesenta donde se sintetiza el mundo y el lenguaje del compositor." Ibid., 136.

136 CUBAN MUSIC COUNTERPOINTS

classical music; such a label granted him legitimacy, for he challenged the norms from a position of relative privilege.

These three compositions aligned with contemporary concerns over art music's alienation of the public. Like US composers John Cage and Morton Feldman, Brouwer, Blanco, and Fariñas presented audiences with a different paradigm of what constituted art.[59] Although these works challenged audiences, the goal of these composers was to bring experimental music to the people, and to take part in the socialist and revolutionary project through the betterment of the common man. The hybrid nature of these works meant that, while they were undeniably *vanguardista*, they could be read at the same time as Cuban-national *and* innovative-international-postmodern. The spatial placement of instrumental groups, use of magnetic tape, graphic score, indeterminacy, and audience involvement in *Contrapunto Espacial III* were features shared with the experimental composers of New York, and Western and Eastern Europe. Blanco wrote his piece with goals and values similar to those promoted by his contemporaries in other countries who challenged preconceived notions of what constituted art and music and blurred the line between performer and audience. According to the program notes and Brouwer's writings on the Cuban musical *vanguardia*, the three compositions presented in the October 1969 concert were meant to stimulate the listener to be more critical of the art they consumed and be a more involved, socially conscious citizen. Like some experimental performance art by composers in other countries (such as La Monte Young, Yoko Ono, and John Cage), these works had an implicitly *collective* bent. Compositional authority was downplayed by the freedom given to performers to choose many of the musical parameters, making them collectively created works to be collectively experienced. But the focus on collective music making and experience also aligned these compositions with Cuban political and social ideology that emphasized collectivism as a key value of the Revolution, a value that was particularly emphasized during the *zafra de los 10 millones* campaign. Shared music making fulfilled two purposes: it brought Blanco's, Brouwer's, and Fariñas's aesthetics in line with the aesthetic goals of the international experimental music scene, and aligned their music with national revolutionary ideology.

By describing these works as a "happening," Brouwer connected them to the experimental works of the international group of artists Fluxus, John Cage, and other composers and groups. The fact that happenings were closely tied to collective music making in Western experimental music circles linked them not only to the socialist values of collectivism promoted in revolutionary Cuba, but also to similar compositional practices outside of Cuba. Their graphic scores utilized

---

[59] Brouwer would later spend two years in West Germany through a DAAD scholarship at the same time as Morton Feldman. In Germany, Brouwer closely collaborated with Hans Werner Henze.

A DECADE OF REVOLUTION AND EXPERIMENTATION 137

notational concepts established by Bogusław Schaeffer, Karlheinz Stockhausen, György Ligeti, and Iannis Xenakis. Cuban composers' awareness of international compositional trends and conscious engagement with the musical language and aesthetics of composers abroad is itself a particularly Cuban trait. For decades, Cuban composers had been purposely grafting foreign musical styles, techniques, and aesthetics into their works, as long as these musical devices helped them deliver their message and define their voice. Although the Cuban composers' works challenged audiences and made them question the composers', the performers', and the listeners' roles, the goal was for those who experienced this music to become more conscious citizens who would contribute to society. At least this was the rationalization Brouwer offered in published essays and, based on their ardent support of the Revolution and socialist values, it showed the composers' commitment to the transformative power of avant-garde and experimental music to develop critical thinking in the listeners. Collectivism, however, was an implied aspect of the work and it is not clear whether audiences and state officials understood the compositions in those terms. Because the aesthetic meaning of *vanguardia* was also inextricably intertwined with its political meaning in Cuba, the collective aspect of these works must be read jointly through the ideological meaning of collectivism in revolutionary Cuba and the international practice of happenings.

The spatial placement of musicians, use of actors or acting cues, and audience participation aligned this concert with events presented by international theatrical and experimental music circles. Blanco's piece required twenty actors who moved throughout the concert hall in a "happening"-like fashion. Fariñas's placement of the instrumental groups enveloped the audience in sound. Brouwer asked the instrumentalists to play standing up and gave instructions on how to react to each other. Brouwer also engaged the audience in a way that turned them into participants and not just passive listeners. These traits were typical of Brechtian theater and 1960s experimental performance art. Bertolt Brecht's plays and his dramaturgical approaches were admired by Cuban artists and intellectuals, and his reputation as a politically committed artist, in particular in relation to his agitprop plays, granted him the approval of political leaders.[60] Happenings and politically engaged theater were meant to disrupt the status quo; they created a collective aesthetic experience that opposed a commercial culture that relied on passive consumers. In this sense, the OSN event of 1969 could have been read in two ways: (1) as aligned with leftist art that protested the usual modes of music consumption in capitalist countries, or (2) as a protest against passive cultural consumption in revolutionary Cuba itself. Given that,

[60] Humberto Arenal, "Presencia de Bertolt Brecht en el teatro cubano," *La jiribilla* (November 11–17, 2006) http://www.lajiribilla.co.cu/2006/n288_11/288_14.html (accessed April 4, 2016).

138 CUBAN MUSIC COUNTERPOINTS

according to Blanco in a 1993 interview with Neil Leonard III, the person at the CNC responsible for the concert was removed from their position (he doesn't specify who this was), it seems like some cultural or political leaders found the concert problematic.[61] However, in a 1998 interview with Isabelle Hernández, Blanco noted that "the concert was accepted in such a way that it was repeated in its entirety in the same concert hall the following week."[62] These seemingly contradictory remarks point to what may have been a split between audience and state reception.

Brouwer's *La tradición se rompe . . .*, although recorded for a 1970 LP of Brouwer's music, only received two OSN performances and has not been edited for publication, Blanco's *Contrapunto Espacial III* was performed once more by the orchestra of the radio station CMBF, and Fariñas's *Relieves* has not been performed since its premiere. None of the works performed in this concert have been published, and only Brouwer's piece has been recorded and released in a commercial LP by the EGREM (the national Cuban music label) as part of an LP of Brouwer's experimental music. The work has reached mythical status as the sound of the Cuban avant-garde among younger generations of composers throughout Latin America.[63] In spite of only having been performed twice by the OSN (it was performed again on July 8, 1970), *La tradición se rompe . . .* has reached an international community of experimental music followers through digitized versions shared on YouTube.

Opiniones Encontradas

Published the same year as the highly experimental and controversial OSN concert, José Ardévol's *Introducción a Cuba: La Música* offered readers a succinct introduction to Cuban music history. The book was part of a series published by Cuba's Instituto del Libro (Book Institute) that presented brief accounts on Cuban history, geography, and visual arts to local non-specialist readers. Like other general texts on music, the book was influenced by Carpentier's *La música en Cuba*. In fact, all music textbooks published after 1959 drew mainly from Carpentier's book and research and most repeated his narrative, especially in regard to developments up to 1940. However, it is in the sections on musical events in Cuba after 1940 that we see one of the first writings where a Cuban composer

---

[61] Neil Leonard III, "Juan Blanco: Cuba's Pioneer of Electroacoustic Music," *Computer Music Journal* 21, no. 2 (1997): 15.

[62] "El concierto tuvo tal aceptación que se repitió completó a la semana siguiente en el mismo teatro." Blanco quoted in Hernández, *Leo Brouwer*, 134.

[63] I have learned this from conversations with several Latin American composers, most recently with Colombian composer and professor Rodolfo Acosta (September 25, 2015).

A DECADE OF REVOLUTION AND EXPERIMENTATION   139

questioned the avant-garde and experimental approaches of composers such as
Brouwer and Blanco. Ardévol's chronological account concludes with an overview of music after the Revolution in which he attempts to hold back on his negative judgement of certain experimental approaches (which he overtly criticized
in his radio broadcasts when discussing works he heard in the United States in
1958). When discussing Juan Blanco's use of post-serial techniques and electronic
composition, Ardévol adds, "whatever may be the definitive value that time will
grant these works, it is unquestionable that this composer has been, in the last
years, an important factor in terms of awakening interests and search for new
horizons."[64] Although Ardévol had reservations regarding the "definitive value"
of Blanco's work, he acknowledged that Blanco had stirred curiosity among the
younger generation of composers. This is one of the first instances in which we
see a public expression of skepticism on the part of one of the Cuban composers
toward the experimental techniques of Blanco or his colleagues. Ardévol valued
the curiosity, in other words, innovation that Blanco's approach brought to the
Cuban art music scene. Because innovation was equated with revolutionary art,
even if the value of Blanco's music seemed dubious, at the very least the motives
and approaches to composition were in line with revolutionary values.

Roughly a year after Ardévol's book and the infamous OSN concert, Brouwer
penned two essays on contemporary Cuban classical music: "La vanguardia en
la música cubana," which appeared in the first number of a new journal, *Boletín
Música*, published by the Music Department of Casa de las Américas; and "La
música, lo cubano, y la innovación," for *Cine Cubano*.[65] When placed within the
context of Ardévol's book publication and Blanco's account of the state's reaction
to the OSN's October 1969 concert, Brouwer's articles read as a response to a lack
of understanding of the political and aesthetic value that experimental music
brought to Cuban socialist-revolutionary society on the part of state officials and
fellow composers—such as Ardévol and Edgardo Martín, who also penned a
book on Cuban music history published in 1971 in which he questioned the aesthetic choices of the experimental composers in Cuba and proudly called himself
a member of the musical *retaguaria* or old-guard, discussed in more detail in
the following chapter. Brouwer's background provides some insight into how his
artistic formation informed how he positioned himself and his contemporaries
within Cuba and at an international level. He was too young during the 1950s
to fully partake in the activities of the Sociedad Cultural Nuestro Tiempo, but

---

[64] "Cualquiera que sea el valor que, en definitiva, el tiempo otorgue a estas obras, es indudable que
este compositor ha sido, en los últimos años, un importante factor en cuanto a despertar inquietudes
y buscar nuevos horizontes." José Ardévol, *Introducción a Cuba: La música* (Havana, Cuba: Instituto
del Libro, 1969), 111.

[65] Brouwer, "La música, lo cubano, y la innovación," 28; Brouwer, "La vanguardia en la música
cubana," 22.

140   CUBAN MUSIC COUNTERPOINTS

began to associate with its members toward the end of Batista's regime. He became involved in post-1959 state cultural institutions early on in his career. By showing a strong commitment to the Revolution through his music and his writings, Brouwer positioned himself and other like-minded composers at the helm of the Cuban art music scene. He studied composition with Isadore Freed at the Hartt College of Music of the University of Hartford, Connecticut, and with Vincent Persichetti at the Juilliard School of Music, under a scholarship from the Cuban revolutionary government in 1959, before relations between the United States and Cuba soured and the US embargo was put in place in October of 1960. While in the United States he was in direct contact with avant-garde music and composers, an experience that would mark his compositions and aesthetic thinking. As mentioned above, in 1961 Brouwer traveled to Warsaw, Poland, to attend the Warsaw Autumn Music Festival, which he singled out in the *Boletín Música* essay as a decisive event in his and Cuban composers' aesthetic development. Upon his return to Cuba from his studies in the United States in 1960, Brouwer was appointed director of the newly created music section of the Instituto Cubano de Artes e Industrias Cinematográficas (the Cuban Film Institute, ICAIC). Throughout his career he has provided music scores for over one hundred films, including the Mexican adaptation of *Como agua para chocolate* (Like Water for Chocolate, 1992). In 1968 he composed the music for one of the most critically acclaimed films produced by the ICAIC during the first decade of the Revolution, *Lucía*.[66]

In the *Boletín Música* essay, Brouwer placed experimental music within the context of the Cuban Revolution, pointing out that "the *vanguardia* in Cuba has the two major obstacles for composers resolved: liberty of creation and the 'reason for being' of this immediate liberty: the audience."[67] According to Brouwer, composers are fully immersed in the social realities of the people and the non-prejudiced audience is accepting of this new experimental music as a point of departure for shaping a "cultura propia" (one's own culture). Brouwer lists the instances in which Cuban composers provided avant-garde music for contexts in which it reached the masses: Juan Blanco's electronic compositions for the national sports games and commemorative acts; Brouwer's *Conmutaciones* performed for the thirteenth anniversary (in 1966) of July 26, 1953; and collaborative compositions for the Cuban pavilion for the Expo-1967 in Montreal and the Expo-1970 in Osaka. Brouwer also identifies film music by himself, Roberto

---

[66] Marysol Quevedo, "Music in Cuban Revolutionary Cinema: Musical Experimentation in the Service of Revolutionary Ideology," in *Experiencing Music in Visual Cultures: Threshold, Intermediality, and Synchresis*, eds. Antonio Cascelli and Denis Condon (Oxford, UK: Routledge, 2021), 131–141.

[67] "La vanguardia en Cuba tiene resuleta la doble problemática del compositor actual: la libertad de creación y la 'razón de ser' de esa libertad inmediata: el público." Brouwer, "La vanguardia en la música cubana," 24.

A DECADE OF REVOLUTION AND EXPERIMENTATION   141

Valera, Blanco, and Fariñas for the films and documentaries produced by the ICAIC as one of the ways in which composers met the demands of the public and the Revolution. He added that their compositions respond to current society's needs better than "standardized" compositions: "It is obvious that the demand for this is the result of its functionality in today's world, where mass communication media acquire an important dimension, and avant-garde music becomes more functional—in this sense—than the *standardized* products."[68] By "*standardized* products" Brouwer alluded to commercial and popular music from the United States and Cuban popular music that assimilated some of the traits of US commercial pop music. He then described in detail the three compositions from the OSN concert of October 10, 1969, as examples of the Cuban musical vanguardia.

Finally, we should also consider the intended audience of the new music journal in which Brouwer's essay appeared. *Boletín Música* was published by Casa de las Américas, which, as discussed above, aimed to maintain cultural ties among all Latin American intellectuals and artists. Therefore, Brouwer was not writing for an exclusively local audience, but rather for a hemispheric and even international readership. In describing the Cuban musical *vanguardia* and the political circumstances that were favorable for this type of music to be composed and performed, Brouwer celebrated the Cuban Revolution's success in the field of music, particularly as an alternative to capitalism, because, according to him, the music of revolutionary Cuban composers was not being produced for and by an intellectual elite or for commercial purposes, but for the masses, for the Revolution, and by socially committed composers who were in touch with the people and their needs. The Revolution was, by nature, *vanguardista*; it challenged and broke from the prevailing status quo. Additionally, according to Brouwer, artistic innovation and experimentation was only truly possible under socialism and the Revolution. The freedom of experimentation that allowed Cuban composers' music to reach the masses was, according to Brouwer, a testament to the Cuban revolutionary and socialist system's superiority over capitalism and consumerism.

Concert programs, music criticism, institutional changes through the establishment of new ensembles and cultural organizations, as well as the compositions themselves, demonstrate the shifts that took place in the musical and cultural networks that Cuban composers inhabited and cultivated in the first decade of the Revolution. This decade was marked by an overall sense of experimentation: musical, cultural, technical, diplomatic, economic, and ideological.[69]

---

[68] "Es obvio que la demanda de nuestra obras es resultado de la funcionalidad de esta música en el mundo actual, donde los medios masivos de comunicación adquieren una importante dimension y la música de vanguardia se hace más funcional—en ese sentido—que los productos *standarizados* [original emphasis]." Ibid., 24–25.

[69] For further discussion on how this experimentation manifested in the realm of popular and folk music see Moore, *Music and Revolution*, 63.

142   CUBAN MUSIC COUNTERPOINTS

This observation of generalized "experimentation" does not apply equally to all sectors of society, as many facets of Cuban life became increasing dogmatic as the decade progressed, such as the overall homophobic environment in the arts and culture as well as growing hostility toward artists and writers who did not conform to the socialist-revolutionary ideology and values. The two most dramatic transformations were the severing of ties between Cuban and US compositional circles and the move of many composers from the margins of the local cultural scene—a position they held through the 1950s, where they were ignored or persecuted by Batista's regime—to the center of the state's cultural program where composers were placed in key administrative roles. The internal, local networks were in part determined by which foreign compositional circles individual composers felt most akin to in terms of aesthetic approaches. A more moderate or conservative group that aligned itself with the overtly nationalist works of Ginastera, Villa-Lobos, Galindo, and Khachaturian (and other Soviet composers)—such as Martín, Ardévol, Hilario González, González Mantici— were considered as somewhat outdated and out of touch with current trends by Cuban composers who aligned themselves with the approaches of the Polish and Western European avant-garde—such as Brouwer, Blanco, Fariñas, Valera, and Héctor Angúlo. Local and foreign music networks continued to determine whose compositions were performed, edited for publication, and recorded. Acquisition of cultural capital through the cultivation of these connections and networks had real, tangible results in terms of the monetary and material capital state institutions would invest in the promotion of certain musics and certain composers. Cuban composers were remunerated not through individual commissions, but through a yearly salary that stipulated that they complete a certain number of works for various performing forces within a calendar year. Beyond the required compositions, they were free to write other works. Additionally, the state provided housing, transportation (vehicles and chauffeur), and other basic needs as they did for other professionals, such as doctors and engineers.[70] Prominent composers received scholarships, travel funds, and other forms of professional support that enabled them to maintain and develop professional contacts within and outside of the island and facilitated their creative work.

Through cultural journals, institutions—including Casa de las Américas, the UNEAC, the OSN, the ICAIC—and the use of state funding for prizes and scholarships, Cuban composers defined what was politically and aesthetically relevant and worthy of state investment. As we saw through the examples and moments described in this chapter, the composers who were able to demonstrate a commitment to the revolutionary-socialist agenda were the most successful

---

[70] José Ardévol Collection, Museo Nacional de la Música Cubana, Havana, Cuba.

at gaining state support. The *vanguardistas* demonstrated their commitment to the Revolution's projects through a particularly socialist internationalism that criticized capitalist models of cultural production and consumption. But they also furthered their individual aesthetic agendas by aligning themselves with a permissible and existing form of musical avant-gardism and experimentation present in specific Eastern European socialist countries, namely Poland. The music and writings discussed in this chapter fulfilled several aesthetic and political goals: they legitimized the Revolution and socialism as *Cuban* by fostering exchanges with musicians from foreign socialist countries, increased Cuba's international presence and served the state's agenda through cultural diplomacy, and promoted local, new music production within the context of the Western European art music tradition through a carefully selected music repertory. In the next chapter we will explore how, after a decade of experimentation, new political and economic pressures led to dramatic changes in the 1970s that would reaffirm the dominance of a particular group of composers. In the following decade, composers aligned their avant-garde and experimental compositions more overtly with socialist and revolutionary rhetoric—through less abstract and more blatantly political titles and texts—therefore curtailing any ambiguity as to the political commitment of their creative work. Throughout the 1970s we will also witness a new, younger generation of composers who came of age after 1959, rise among the ranks and also question the aesthetic and ideological impetus of the previous generation and compete for the same resources of cultural production that were dominated by the older composers who had acquired preeminent status in the 1960s.

4
Institutionalization and Fissures in the Cuban Classical Music Landscape
The 1970s

Almost a year after the October 1969 concert of avant-garde works by Brouwer, Fariñas, and Blanco, discussed in the previous chapter, the Orquesta Sinfónica Nacional de Cuba (OSN) presented a performance on August 17, 1970, that also consisted entirely of premieres. The concert opened and closed with memorial pieces: the first, Arnold Schoenberg's *A Survivor from Warsaw*, a tribute to the Jewish victims at the hands of Nazis and fascism, and the last, Harold Gramatges's *La muerte del guerrillero* (The Death of the Guerrilla [Fighter]), a homage to Ernesto Che Guevara who had died fighting for the revolutionary cause in Bolivia on October 9, 1967. Unlike the October 1969 OSN concert discussed in the previous chapter, the ideological significance of the compositions was not subtly suggested through the collective act of music making or employment of avant-gardist techniques. Instead, Gramatges's composition was a memorial piece dedicate to Ernesto Che Guevara and Roberto Valera's *Devenir*, with its suggestive title (Transformation), referenced the transformative process Cuba underwent after the triumph of the Revolution. Although Bartók's Piano Concerto No. 3 (the fourth work on the program) is an apparent outlier in terms of its lack of ideological engagement, this piece, along with Schoenberg's *Survivor,* served to contextualize the Cuban compositions within an international, *vanguardista* musical aesthetic, one marked by the use of serialism and twelve-tone technique.

The moments further discussed throughout this chapter show that the 1970s was a decade during which artists struggled to adapt to the shifting political and cultural landscape. Increasing political and economic pressures from Moscow on Havana and consequently from Havana to all national cultural institutions meant that artists had to contend with demands from various factions. Some institutions jumped on the opportunity to cultivate foreign ties, as we'll see through Casa de las Américas's Encuentro de Música Latinoamericana of 1972. Some individuals continued to experiment through works for piano, exemplified in this chapter by Leo Brouwer's *Sonata pian e forte* and Harold Gramatges's *Móvil I*. There was also a proliferation of festivals, *encuentros*, and *jornadas* intended to celebrate regional and international musical cooperation, much like

Cuban Music Counterpoints. Marysol Quevedo, Oxford University Press. © Oxford University Press 2023.
DOI: 10.1093/oso/9780197552230.003.0005

the political and economic agreements forged by the Cuban state with other socialist nations. Most notably, the decade began with a five-year period of artistic censorship and persecution known as the *quinquenio gris* (the five-year grey period), which affected all areas of cultural production in Cuba through increased centralization, institutionalization, censorship, marginalization, and, according to some critics, even sovietization. I contend that composers of classical music were mostly spared from this wave of censorship and persecution due to three main factors. First, high-ranking officials and cultural leaders lacked the musical knowledge to interpret avant-garde and experimental music language as an act of dissention or opposition. Second, without overt text or plot, instrumental classical music's polyvalent capacities enabled various parties to read it in diverse ways. And third, because of instrumental music's semantic malleability, Cuban composers overtly connected their compositions to the socialist-revolutionary cause by adding texts, titles, or program notes to accompany their pieces, such as Gramatges's *La muerte del guerrillero*. Before delving into the national political and cultural shifts that mark the first half of the decade, let's examine the works of the OSN concert of August 17, 1970, more closely.

Gramatges's *La muerte del guerrillero* and Valera's *Devenir*: Socialist-Revolutionary-Vanguardista Orchestral Music

In the program notes for the OSN's concert of August 17, 1970 , Gramatges's *La muerte del guerrillero* was described as employing "open serialism." The row (A-flat, G-flat, G, B, B-flat, D-flat, C, D, F, A, D-sharp, E) first appears in the xylophone, which Gramatges then transforms through inversions and transpositions. Additionally, the timpani alternates between E, F, B and B-flat, creating two pairs of minor seconds separated by a tritone that evade any sense of tonal center, shown in Music Example 4.1. Other new techniques used by Gramatges throughout the work include the lack of meter, extended instrumental

Music Example 4.1. Gramatges, *La muerte del guerrillero*, xylophone and timpani part, mm. 7–10.

Note: Harold Gramatges, *La muerte del guerrillero: para recitante y orquesta* (Havana: Editora Musical de Cuba, 1972).

146 CUBAN MUSIC COUNTERPOINTS

techniques, use of rhythmic patterns of five against two against four, a dissonant rhythmic palindrome in the woodwinds, and clusters played by the strings along with pointillistic writing in the percussion parts. By this point, Cuban composers touted twelve-tone and serial techniques among the most advanced compositional practices, and as evidence of music's "technification."[1]

Additionally, by setting a poem about one of the most iconic revolutionary figures (Ernesto Che Guevara) written by one of the most revered national poets (Nicolás Guillén), Gramatges created a work that was ideologically committed to the revolutionary socialist cause.[2] Through his use of serialism in *La muerte del guerrillero* Gramatges proved that Cuban composers could utilize new music techniques, including dodecaphony, to deliver a revolutionary message. Legitimization went both ways: Gramatges circumscribed these techniques within the ideological sphere of *vanguardismo* in Cuba making these techniques viable options within a socialist-revolutionary context. As Cuban composers utilized them in works that had overt political meanings, these techniques gained legitimacy as tools Cuban composers could use as committed artists. Consequently, composers themselves gained legitimacy by employing techniques that were considered "universal" and advanced by their foreign contemporaries. As we will discuss further, in the early 1970s the Cuban government had begun to tighten the reins on artists by centralizing the administration of cultural organizations and institutions and exerting stronger control over artists who were sending conflicting messages abroad with their "decadent" creations. Therefore, Gramatges's subject matter and text selection played into the increasingly politicized cultural climate of the early 1970s.

The other Cuban work and premiere in the concert, Roberto Valera's *Devenir* (Transformation, written in 1969), employed slightly more daring musical techniques than Gramatges's composition, but not as experimental as the compositions performed in the October 1969 concert discussed in the previous chapter. In the program notes, Ángel Vázquez Millares tells concert goers that Valera's "interest in expressing himself through the most modern techniques in musical language was reinforced by his studies in Poland under the tutelage of Witold Rudziński and Andrzej Dobrowolski."[3] By emphasizing Valera's studies in Poland and his use of the "most modern techniques" Millares ties musical

---

[1] Juan Blanco, "La Música," *Revista Casa de las Américas*, no. 9 (1961): 121–122.

[2] In informal conversations with Cuban musicologists some of them consider *La muerte del guerrillero*, as well as other works with overtly revolutionary titles and texts, as engaging with socialist realism. However, I think that these are fairly recent readings of Cuban compositions from the 1960s and 1970s, which focus solely on the political context and do not take into account the aesthetic issues that concern these works' musical style.

[3] "Su interés en expresarse mediante las más modernas técnicas del lenguaje musical se vió reforzado con los estudios realizados en Polonia bajo la dirección de Witold Rudzinski y Andrzej Dobrowolski." Ángel Vázquez Millares, OSN program notes (August 17, 1970).

INSTITUTIONALIZATION AND FISSURES   147

innovation or *vanguardismo* to internationalism, further legitimizing the relatively young composer for Cuban audiences. In the style of Polish avant-garde composers, as well as that of Brouwer and Gramatges, Valera provided a key to reading the graphic notation he used throughout the piece. In keeping with the Polish school, durations and time are indicated in seconds between "measures" instead of numbers of metered measures. The program notes also indicate that Valera developed *Devenir* through a technique in which every musical moment derives from the previous one, which explicates the work's title (to become or to transform).

Presenting *vanguardista* music in an overtly politicized context secured a composition's greater acceptance and dissemination. Valera's *Devenir* was so well received that it was later included in the 1972 Festival of Latin American Music and its LP release, discussed below in more detail. Gramatges's *La muerte del guerrillero*, although not recorded for commercial release, was edited and published by the Editora Musical de Cuba as a special edition in collaboration with the Music Section of UNEAC (Unión Nacional de Escritores y Artistas de Cuba), performed by the OSN again in 1978, 1984, 1986, and 1988, and broadcasted through the radio in 1978 and 1984.[4] By comparison, Brouwer's *La tradición se rompe . . .* , although recorded for a 1970 LP of Brouwer's music, only received two public performances and was not edited for publication, and Blanco's *Contrapunto Espacial III* and Fariñas's *Relieves* have neither been performed nor published since their premieres.

Throughout the early 1970s, the OSN continued to include works by Cuban composers, but most of these compositions were not in the experimental vein of the works immediately discussed above or in the previous chapter. Most of the Cuban works performed by the OSN after 1970 consisted of overtly Cuban-sounding compositions and pieces that had a popular appeal, such as the works of Roldán and García Caturla from the 1920s and 1930s, as well as other pieces written before 1959.[5] In spite of the relatively conservative turn in OSN concert programming, Cuban composers continued to write avant-garde compositions, but these were destined for contexts that required smaller scale means of

---

[4] Ailer Pérez Gómez, *Música académica contemporánea cubana, Catálogo de difusión (1961–1990)* (La Havana, Cuba: Ediciones CIDMUC, 2011), 113–114.

[5] A concert held on May 4, 1970 included José Ardévol's *Tres Ricercari* from 1936, Amadeo Roldán's *Tres pequeños poemas* from 1926, and Enrique González Mantici's *Obertura "Cuba."* The works by Mantici and Roldán were more conventional—using tonal language, Cuban folk and popular rhythms and melodies—in their writing and included overtly Cuban musical elements drawn from traditional and popular music, while Ardévol's work is in the neoclassical vein of his compositions from the 1930s and 1940s. Later that same year, on October 19, a concert consisting entirely of Cuban music was offered. It included García Caturla's *Obertura Cubana* (1938) and *Bembé* (1929), Felix Guerrero's *Homenaje al Songoro Consongo* (1950), González Mantici's *Obertura "Cuba,"* and Blanco's *Texturas* (1964). With the exception of Blanco's piece, all of the works employed musical elements from vernacular Cuban music and were written in a tonal language.

148   CUBAN MUSIC COUNTERPOINTS

dissemination and performing forces, or pieces in which the avant-garde techniques were used in the service of a political event or message. As the 1970s progressed, large organizations and institutions that had greater visibility within and outside of Cuba needed to promote musical styles that reflected overtly socialist ideals, which, in turn, mirrored both internal shifts in the relationship between the Cuban state and cultural producers and changes in the relationship between Moscow and Havana.

The *quinquenio gris*

The term *quinquenio gris* was first used by Ambrosio Fornet to refer to a five-year period in Cuban cultural history from 1971 to 1975.[6] Recent official Cuban historiography looks back at these years as a time when Cuban officials "deviated" from the originally purported cultural politics of the Cuban Revolution by cracking down on dissent.[7] Some of these changes were partly driven by economic concerns, as Cuba had failed to deliver the *Zafra de los 10 millones* (the Sugarcane harvest of 10 million tons) in 1970 and entered the Council for Mutual Economic Assistance in 1972. As Luis Martínez-Fernández has noted, "the 1970 watershed separated the early idealist phase of the Revolution from a new fifteen-year period of pragmatic institutionalization during which a sugar-centered economy, Soviet-style reforms, dependent development, and material incentives became guiding policies."[8] The *quinquenio gris* began in part with superficial readings of texts, such as *Condenados de Condado* by Norberto Fuentes and *Los Pasos en La Hierba* by Eduardo Heras León, as subversive and critical of the state; other writers were simply marginalized because of their sexual orientation, including José Lezama Lima and Virgilio Piñera. Most significantly was what historians and literary critics have dubbed "el Caso Padilla," in reference to the scandal surrounding Casa de las Américas awarding its literature prize in 1968 to Heberto Padilla for his novel *Fuera de juego*. The novel was read as a criticism of the Soviet process, but some read it as a veiled criticism of the Cuban state. When it was published by the UNEAC, the organization annexed a preface where it voiced its dissidence with the work and the prize and rejected the work

---

[6] Doreen Weppler-Grogan, "Cultural Policy, the Visual Arts, and the Advance of the Cuban Revolution in the Aftermath of the Gray Years," *Cuban Studies* 41 (2010): 155.

[7] Emily J. Kirk, Anna Clayfield, and Isabel Story, eds. *Cuba's Forgotten Decade: How the 1970s Shaped the Revolution* (Lanham, MD: Lexington Books, 2020), 23.

[8] Luis Martínez-Fernández, *Revolutionary Cuba: A History* (Gainesville, FL: University Press of Florida, 2014), 128. Martínez-Fernández prefers to use the term "personalistic" rather than "institutionalization" to refer to this period because the institutions were administered by individuals with personal ideologies and agendas. I prefer to use "institutionalization" because in the case of music the new cultural and music institutions were crucial to the centralization of power and knowledge production.

INSTITUTIONALIZATION AND FISSURES   149

on ideological bases. Antón Arrufat and Norberto Fuentes had also been awarded prizes in 1968 by Casa de las Américas, with similar reactions and disapproval from the UNEAC and *Verde Olivo* (the newspaper of the Armed Revolutionary Forces). Tensions escalated when Padilla was arrested and detained for thirty-eight days in March of 1971 after a poetry reading at the UNEAC. Padilla's arrest was well-publicized abroad and many international artists who had supported the Cuban Revolution wrote in defense of Padilla and artistic and intellectual freedom. It was a watershed moment in how the Cuban state handled dissidence from within the Cuban cultural elite. These events and the repression the state exerted over artists over the first half of the 1970s led to the formation of a younger generation of writers who matured during times of dogmatism; they felt pressure to avoid certain topics (even magical realism) out of fear of being misread and blacklisted (or worse, imprisoned or sent to a labor camp). With the exception of certain institutions, such as Casa de las Américas and the Ballet Nacional, the majority of the cultural organisms in Cuba became sterile and stagnant until 1976.

Between 1965 and 1968, many intellectuals and artists were blacklisted, their UNEAC memberships revoked and their works would not be published or exhibited or performed; some (most for committing the "sin" of homosexuality) were sent to "reeducation" camps, otherwise known as Unidades Militares de Apoyo a la Producción (UMAP, Military Units of Production Support). After the disbanding of UMAP and during the *quinquenio gris* artists who had served in the camps or who had been blacklisted had to seek employment outside of cultural institutions or artistic fields, some in construction or agricultural industries. Some died before they could be rehabilitated as artists. Many fled Cuba, settling in countries and cities where they could pursue their artistic careers without persecution. The artists most affected by the great purge of the *quinquenio gris* were writers and playwrights, with visual artists and singer-songwriters also being targeted. Classical music composers, however, were not as directly affected by the extreme censorship that characterized the *quinquenio gris*. Yet, there was increasing pressure from Moscow on Cuban officials to crack down on dissent. The *quinquenio gris* came to an end in 1976 with the creation of the Ministry of Culture (prior to this the Consejo Nacional de Cultura (CNC) operated under the purview of the Ministry of Education) and Armando Hart's appointment as its Minister.

This period of Stalinization in Cuban culture was marked by a call for socialist realism in the arts.[9] Notoriously difficult to prescribe and define in the realm of classical music (even in the Soviet Union during its height in the 1930s and

---

[9] Weppler-Grogan, "Cultural Policy, the Visual Arts, and the Advance of the Cuban Revolution in the Aftermath of the Gray Years," 147.

150　CUBAN MUSIC COUNTERPOINTS

1940s),[10] socialist realism for Cuban composers did not mean an abandonment of the avant-garde and experimental techniques they had begun utilizing in the 1960s. An examination of the titles and texts (such as Gramatges's use of Guillén's poem "Che comandante" in *La muerte del guerrillero*) Cuban composers used during these years, shows that they reframed their artistic output as overtly committed to Cuban socialist-revolutionary ideals. Although this could be read as a turn towards "socialist realism" in music composition in Cuba, the musical language and techniques they employed do not easily conform to these aesthetic and ideological categorizations. There was an increase in the overt use of titles, texts, and dedications that directly celebrated socialist and revolutionary themes, but, as we saw with Gramatges's and Valera's works, they were only one component of avant-garde and experimental compositions. Moreover, unlike examples of literary works that were either censored or promoted by the state because of their anti-socialist content or complex form (be it language, structure, or use of magical realism), in instrumental music content and form are not easy to disentangle; in many instances the content of a work arises from its form. Another aspect that distinguishes classical music from visual arts and literature is the temporal, aural, and ephemeral qualities of the experience; officials would have had more difficulty censoring a musical composition if they were not present at a performance or if they didn't have access to a manuscript or published music score in comparison to a novel or story, for which they would have had a physical copy. And even if they had a physical copy of a music score, most officials would have lacked the musical knowledge to find any particular passage or use of technique objectionable.

The most salient aspect that determined the use of more accessible musical language versus more avant-gardist techniques was function. The purpose of a work was the main factor that drove a composer's aesthetic decisions. In post-revolutionary Cuba, individual composers could not be categorized as purely conservative or traditionalist, experimental or avant-gardist. In one composer's oeuvre we find incredibly accessible compositions, such as Blanco's "Himno a la defensa popular," as well as more experimental works, such as his *Contrapunto Espacial III*. In the early 1970s composers were called to produce works that appealed to broader segments of the population. Thus, we find more compositions for amateur guitarists and the amateur choral movement, while at the same time a proliferation of compositions for solo piano, chamber settings, and electronic media that used new experimental techniques. The latter group of compositions were often performed by highly-skilled musicians who sought out and collaborated with composers on extended techniques and graphic scores

---

[10] David G. Tompkins, *Composing the Party Line: Music and Politics in Early Cold War Poland and East Germany* (Purdue University Press, 2013), 17–18.

INSTITUTIONALIZATION AND FISSURES   151

(such as pianist Ninowska Fernández-Brito and guitarist Jesús Ortega), and their performances took place in the more intimate setting of the Cuban intellectual elite institutions where musical experimentation was welcomed, such as the UNEAC headquarters. The 1970s ushered in a period of cementing socialist and revolutionary ideals, it marked a close to the first decade of the Revolution, which was characterized by social, political, economic, and artistic experimentation. Art and culture reflected and enacted the more conservative political and economic turn of the 1970s that was influenced by both internal Cuban affairs as well as by Cuba's relationship to foreign powers, especially the Soviet Union. This is a period and process that, as discussed in the introduction, is marked by intense *institutionalization*, a term the Cuban state itself used in reference to the process of consolidation of government agencies that lead to the 1976 Constitution. To understand the changing relationship between Cuba and the Soviet Union in the early 1970s, we must step back and also examine Fidel Castro's relationship to Soviet leadership throughout the 1960s.

Havana–Moscow Relationships and their Effects on Cuban Culture

In 1962, after the Soviet Union pulled their nuclear missiles from Cuba, a humiliated yet revengeful Castro "reacted by adopting policies and views that came to be known as the Castroite heresy."[11] For the next five years both liberals and Marxists in Cuba battled over the arts. In 1967, Castro openly criticized the Kremlin "for its foreign policy, its failure to support the Guevara expedition to Bolivia, and its interpretations of the doctrines of Marx and Lenin in general."[12] Additionally, two events in the cultural arena show Castro's departure from Soviet cultural policy. First was the 1967 display of ultra-avant-garde Western art by the *Salon de Mai* from Paris, considered much more "decadent" and "bourgeois" than the earlier Moscow art exhibits deemed inappropriate by Khrushchev.[13] The second incident took place at the beginning of the 1968 Cultural Congress held in Cuba, attended by foreign writers and artists, when Castro criticized Soviet foreign policy once again, voicing the same sentiments as in his 1967 statement. However, Castro's period of heresy came to a halt when Soviet tanks rolled into Czechoslovakia in 1968 to squelch the Prague Spring. In part to secure continued Soviet economic support, Castro publicly approved of the attack on Czechoslovakia, siding with the Soviet officials and gaining their

---

[11] Enrique A. Baloyra, "Political Control and Cuban Youth," in *Cuban Communism*, ed. Irving Louis Horowitz (New Brunswick, NJ: Transaction Publishers, 1989), 393.

[12] Ibid., 393.

[13] Ibid., 393.

152 CUBAN MUSIC COUNTERPOINTS

approval.[14] Georgina Dopico notes that the period between 1966 and 1968 was marked by a higher degree of tolerance, but this soon shifted in 1968 for a period that stretched into 1976 of increased censorship and repression of literary works.[15] After 1968, Castro and many high-ranking officials turned to attacking or "criticizing" literary works by Cuban writers that he deemed decadent. This was followed by a writing contest where, as critics pointed out, winners were selected based on the political content of their pieces and not on artistic merits.[16] 1968 was also marked by Castro's "Ofensiva Revolucionaria," which Lillian Guerra describes as "aimed at rectifying the ideological backsliding among loyal citizens that Fidel blamed for Cuba's long-standing economic stagnation, [and] would create a true command economy: it criminalized all remaining private commercial exchanges and declared smalltime entrepreneurs traitors to socialism."[17] Although Cuban historians point to the *quinquenio gris* as spanning from 1971–1975, these events of the late 1960s set the foundation for the increased censorship, repression, and institutionalization of the five-year gray period. At the first Congress on Education and Culture, in 1971, cultural policy veered into what many critics deemed more clearly Stalinist terrain, with the arrest and persecution of dissenting writers, as well as the dismissal of faculty members of the University of Havana because they did not conform to the socialist agenda.[18] In order to publish literary works within Cuba, writers had to supply a detailed description of their background, more specifically their political activities, and provide letters of support from their workplace that vouched for their political attitude.[19] Further involvement and pressure from the Soviet Union to comply with Soviet policies increased when Cuba joined the Consejo de Ayuda Mutua Económica (CAME) in 1972.

In addition to Fidel Castro's history of dissent from the Soviet Union, eventual approval of repressive Soviet actions, and subsequent repression and criticism of Cuban artists, we must take into account the history of Cuban cultural institutions and their leadership. Starting in 1959, cultural matters in Cuba were initially governed by the Dirección de Cultura of the Ministerio de Educación (Culture Division of the Ministry of Education); that body was dissolved on January 4, 1961, when the government established Consejo Nacional de Cultura (CNC, National Culture Council), intended to oversee all aspects of cultural production in Cuba. Between April 23 and 31, 1971, the government held the

---

[14] Ibid., 394–395.
[15] Georgina Dopico Black, "The Limits of Expression: Intellectual Freedom in Postrevolutionary Cuba," *Cuban Studies* 19 (1989): 109.
[16] Baloyra, "Political Control and Cuban Youth," 395.
[17] Lillian Guerra, *Visions of Power in Cuba: Revolution, Redemption, and Resistance, 1959–1971* (Chapel Hill: The University of North Carolina Press, 2012), 290.
[18] Baloyra, "Political Control and Cuban Youth," 396–397.
[19] Ibid., 398.

INSTITUTIONALIZATION AND FISSURES   153

First National Congress on Education and Culture, organized by the Ministry of Education. Among the many declarations, it reinforced the idea that culture and education could not be apolitical because they were "social historical phenomena conditioned by the needs of the social classes and their struggles and interests throughout the course of history."[20] The congress passed several resolutions in regard to education and cultural policies. These included the promotion of measures that reinforced ideological formation of young artists and of legitimate and spirited cultural expression in Latin America, Africa, and Asia in order "to assimilate critically the best from universal culture," foster the study of neocolonial cultural "penetration," and develop a plan of action to prevent its "harmful effects in the national field."[21] Education was considered not only a right, but also a social duty that all Cuban citizens had to fulfill. Education, which included artistic fields, was the primary tool for disseminating the values and ideology of the Revolution, creating the *hombre nuevo*, the ideal socially and politically committed "new man" who contributed to society through hard work and self-sacrifice. In regard to culture, the Congress declared:

> Culture in a *collectivist* society is an activity of the masses, not an elitist monopoly, the plaything of a few chosen ones or the label of a few misfits . . . In the heart of the masses true genius is to be found, and not in groups or isolated individuals. The classic culture profit has meant that until now only a few exceptional individuals excel. But this is only a symptom of society's prehistory, not a definitive cultural characteristic . . . Revolutionary art, will be *internationalist* at the same time as it is closely linked to our national roots. We will encourage the legitimate and combative cultural expressions in Latin America, Asia, and Africa, those which imperialism tries to destroy. Our cultural institutions will be vehicles for the true artists of those continents, those who have been ignored, persecuted, those who have not allowed themselves to be domesticated by cultural colonialism and who are militant in the ranks of their peoples in the anti-imperialist struggle . . . the congress cannot be the magical solution to all of our problems. It will contribute significantly to better our plans. Without doubt, it will aid us in obtaining positive results: but it will be the *hard work* of every day that will really make it possible for us to reap the fruits of this *collective* planning we are making with the help and creative initiative of our educators.[22]

---

[20] *Congresso Nacional de Educación y Cultura. Cuba '71* (Havana: Instituto Cubano del Libro Editorial Ambito, 1971), n.p. Original in English.

[21] Ibid.

[22] Ibid. My emphasis.

154 CUBAN MUSIC COUNTERPOINTS

The 1971 Congress of Education and Culture emphasized the ideals of collectivism, hard work, and egalitarianism.[23] This was the first time the Cuban state held an official national meeting on education and culture. Through the numerous meetings and declarations, the Congress reinforced the values of the Revolution and connected national efforts to the struggles of second and Third World countries in Latin America, Asia, and Africa, emphasizing the international scope of socialism. Political leaders defended national and local culture, but allowed for the critical assimilation of the best of universal culture. Cuban composers' writings on aesthetics and compositional practices, examined towards the end of this chapter, contain multiple instances of these same phrases and terms, not only after 1971, but since the beginning of the Revolution when they defended their use of compositional techniques adopted from European avant-garde and experimental music circles (as we saw in the previous chapter's discussion of Leo Brouwer and Juan Blanco's essays).

In addition, between 1971 and 1976, Luis Pavón Tamayo, the director of the CNC, led a campaign to purge and censor problematic artistic and intellectual figures. In fact, this period of artistic repression is also known as the *pavonato*, for Luiz Pavón's last name.[24] The beginning of the quinquenio gris, could be traced to "between November and December of 1968—when in the magazine *Verde Olivo* ("Olive Green") appeared five articles whose authorship is attributed to Luis Pavón Tamayo, an unprovable conjecture because the author used a pseudonym," that lambasted the works of Cabrera Infante, Heberto Padilla, and Antón Arrufat.[25] Journals and magazines that failed to promote a rigid, orthodox interpretation of Marxism and that were ecumenical in their interests were dissolved, most notably *Pensamiento crítico* ("Critical thinking"). Many writers and singer-songwriters were marginalized not only because of their opinions, but also because of their homosexuality. This led to a great deal of self-censorship on the part of writers and artists. This series of events came to a close with the ratification of a new Cuban Constitution on February 24, 1976, the first since the 1940 Constitution, officially declaring Cuba a socialist state.

By 1976, the situation in the cultural field had changed dramatically. Armando Hart was appointed head of the new Ministry of Culture, its own entity separate from the Ministry of Education, abolishing the previous CNC. The purpose of the new institution was to "direct, guide, control, and execute within its realm

---

[23] These traits have been emphasized by several other scholars as key factors in Cuban cultural politics, most notably Sujatha Fernandes, *Cuba Represent!: Cuban Arts, State Power, and the Making of New Revolutionary Cultures* (Duke University Press, 2006), 23.

[24] Weppler-Grogan, "Cultural Policy, the Visual Arts, and the Advance of the Cuban Revolution in the Aftermath of the Gray Years," 145.

[25] Ambrosio Fornet, "El quinquenio gris: revisitando el término," *Revista Criterios* (January 2007); translated by Alicia Barraqué Ellison and others in *Translating Cuba*, https://translatingcuba.com/the-five-grey-years-revisiting-the-term-ambrosio-fornet/

INSTITUTIONALIZATION AND FISSURES   155

of competency the application of the State's and Cuban Government's cultural policy, as well as to guarantee the defense, preservation, and enrichment of the cultural patrimony of the Cuban nation . . . promote freedom of artistic creation and the defense of the identity of Cuban culture, conservation of cultural patrimony and artistic and historic richness, and the protection of national monuments."[26] The establishment of the Ministry of Culture coincided with an overall move toward greater centralization in the mid-1970s, a process that had started with the failed *zafra* of 1970 and with heightened artistic and intellectual censorship of the first half of the decade, the *quinquenio gris*.[27] The Ministry of Culture's foundation signaled both the full realization, the epitome of these centralizing and institutionalizing efforts, and also the beginnings of a process of liberalization in the aftermath of the *quinquenio gris*. After 1976, the Ministry of Culture began to rectify some of the state's abuses on cultural figures rehabilitating some individuals in the areas of literature and visual arts. Although classical composers were able to maintain a greater degree of freedom and experienced less state repression than their counterparts in theater, visual arts, and literature, in general there was a turn away from the extreme experimental works in larger and more public contexts of the late 1960s, such as the OSN's concerts. And composers had to be particularly watchful over which other composers and musicians, within and outside of Cuba, they aligned themselves with, whether ideologically or aesthetically. If there was ever a time when professional and creative networks mattered, it was in the early years of the 1970s. And few composers took advantage of their global network as effectively as Leo Brouwer.

The Piano as a Laboratory for Musical Experimentation

The piano served as a key site for musical experimentation for Cuban composers. By writing for the piano they could try out techniques in ways that were not feasible in larger ensemble formats, such as the orchestral works discussed earlier in the chapter. Experimental works for the piano were fairly easy to publish, perform, and record, leading to wider dissemination than works for larger

---

[26] "Dirigir, orientar, controlar y ejecutar en el ámbito de su competencia la aplicación de la política cultural del Estado y del Gobierno cubano, así como garantizar la defensa, preservación y enriquecimiento del patrimonio cultural de la nación cubana . . . la libertad de creación artística y la defensa de la identidad de la cultura cubana, la conservación del patrimonio cultural y la riqueza artística e histórica de la nación y la protección de los monumentos nacionales." *Ministerio de Cultura de la República Cubana*, http://www.min.cult.cu/ (accessed May 19, 2015).

[27] *Zafra* is the sugar harvest. In 1970 the government set a goal of producing a record breaking 10 million tons of sugar to increase external revenue. The government launched a nationwide campaign encouraging all citizens to contribute to the national harvest goal. The 10 million ton goal was not met, resulting in a blow to the national economy. Nicola Miller, "A Revolutionary Modernity: The Cultural Policy of the Cuban Revolution," *Journal of Latin American Studies* 40, no. 4 (2008): 678.

156 CUBAN MUSIC COUNTERPOINTS

ensembles. Through experimentation in works for piano, Brouwer, Gramatges, and other Cuban composers engaged with techniques and aesthetic practices that aligned with Alejo Carpentier's concept of *lo real maravilloso* through the fantastical elements they brought to the printed page and performance event. Although their practices have been labeled by Cuban music critics as idio-syncratically Cuban, they also dialogued with an international network of avant-garde and experimental music composers and performers that further legitimized their works as not just Cuban, but also universal. These works for piano serve as one more node in the local and international networks Cuban composers fostered throughout their careers. Furthermore, the piano had a long legacy in Cuban music history as a vehicle for exploring *cubanía* within inter-national music trends, such as the nineteenth-century piano works of Manuel Saumell and Ignacio Cervantes (which engaged with Frédéric Chopin and Louis Moreau Gottschalk), and the neoclassical compositions of the Grupo de Renovación Musical in the 1940s (which engaged with Manuel de Falla, Maurice Ravel, and Aaron Copland). Here we'll examine Brouwer's *Sonata pian e forte* and Gramatges's *Móvil I* as exemplary models of Cuban pianism's fusion with experimental idioms.

Brouwer's *Sonata pian e forte*

In 1970, Brouwer completed his *Sonata pian e forte*, reproduced in Fig. 4.1, while residing in West Berlin,[28] where he was collaborating with Hans Werner Henze on the German composer's opera *El Cimarrón*.[29] The score for Brouwer's *Sonata* was published by Ars Viva Verlag in 1973, with instructions in Spanish, English, and German and a dedication to Roger Woodward. The *Sonata* reflects Brouwer's absorption of numerous avant-garde approaches to composition pop-ular among European composers during this period. He employed graphic nota-tion, indeterminacy, and extended techniques in this and several other works for the piano.[30] As in some of his most experimental works—such as *La tradición se*

[28] The work was published by Ars Viva Verlag, in Mainz in 1973. Brouwer dedicated the work to Australian pianist Roger Woodward, who, after studying in Poland, made a career of collaborating with some of the most prominent avant-garde composers, including Luciano Berio, Pierre Boulez, John Cage, Morton Feldman, and Olivier Messiaen among others. Brouwer probably met Woodward when the pianist toured Havana in 1969, or possibly earlier through their mutual connections in Poland. Brouwer spent 1970–1972 in West Berlin under a DAAD scholarship where he collaborated with Hans Werner Henze, met other influential Western composers, such as Morton Feldman, and made a series of important recordings of guitar performance for Deutsche Grammophon.

[29] Henze's project was based on Cuban writer Miguel Barnet's biography-novel of Esteban Montejo, a runaway slave (cimarrón), *Biografía de un cimarrón* (1966).

[30] As a guitar virtuoso Brouwer also composed similar works for his instrument. His interest in improvisation can be seen, not only in *Sonata pian e forte* but in many other works, in particular those for guitar.

INSTITUTIONALIZATION AND FISSURES   157

rompe . . . , discussed in the previous chapter—Brouwer also quoted fragments of compositions from several time periods and styles within the context of his own dissonant sonorities. The score of Brouwer's *Sonata* consists of nineteen boxes that surround a large circle, with a small circle indicating the final chord tucked in on the right side. Of the nineteen boxes, one has no notation and only reads "Improvisation," and four others indicate quotations from the "classics." Three of the quoted "classics" are indicated by composer and title in the score: Giovanni Gabrieli's Sonata "Pian e forte," Karol Szymanowski's opera *King Roger* and Violin Concerto, and an unspecified Piano Sonata by Scriabin. The fourth one is a quote from the recapitulation of the main theme in the first movement of Beethoven's Sonata op. 57 "Appassionata" written out in musical notation. By quoting the Gabrieli and Beethoven sonatas, Brouwer engaged with works that were important in the development of the sonata as a musical form and genre. However, Brouwer's reason for employing the Szymanowski and Scriabin quotes is less overt, but can be attributed to his admiration for Polish and Russian modernist composers, whose music he encountered when he attended the Warsaw Autumn Music Festival in the early 1960s. The center circle contains five passages that are to be played at soft dynamics; these five elements all feature fast atonal motives of two lines that move in parallel or contrary motion. The outer fourteen boxes each contain unique passages that employ dissonant, angular melodies, sometimes with very thick chordal textures, and at other times texturally very sparse but using the whole range of the piano; these passages are to be played at much louder dynamics and provide a contrast to the quieter and more sparse passages from the central circle. Each performance or recording of the *Sonata pian e forte* will result in a unique work stemming from the pianist's choice of order of sections, speed of each section, and length of choice of quotations.

The work is characterized by controlled indeterminacy, quotation, contrasting sections, and open form. As a whole, the *Sonata* bears resemblance to Morton Feldman's and John Cage's compositions in its use of indeterminacy, but also to Luciano Berio's approach in the use of quotations, Henry Cowell and Karlheinz Stockhausen in the use of extended techniques, and Bogusław Schaeffer in the employment of a graphic score.[31]

The same year as the *Sonata* was published, Brouwer's article "La improvisación aleatoria" was published in *Boletín Música*.[32] Following an introduction dealing with various topics—including the "interior world of the composer," scientific advancements, themes of childhood and magic, and the philosophical, social,

---

[31] *Sonata pian e forte* was performed by Nancy Casanova in 1985 at the Sixth Festival of Music from Socialist Countries on March 26, 1985, and in 1989 at the Fifth Festival de Contemporary Music in Havana, held at the Casa de la Música "Alejandro García Caturla" on 1989. Her performances were also broadcasted through the CMBF and recorded by the EGREM.

[32] Brouwer, "La improvisación aleatoria," *Boletín Música*, no. 38 (1973): 20–26.

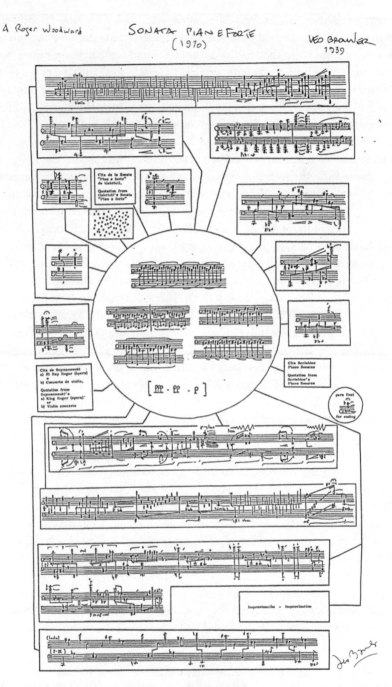

Figure 4.1. Leo Brouwer, *Sonata "pian e forte"* (1973) manuscript, reproduced with permission of Leo Brouwer from his personal archive.

INSTITUTIONALIZATION AND FISSURES   159

and political context of art music in Cuba—Brouwer delved into a discussion of improvisation in art music. He cited Chopin and Bach as examples of great improvisers of their times and he urged readers to locate improvisatory practices in contemporary music within a historical narrative of Western Art music. He argued that sound itself had become "something pure with its own identity, absolute, as an artistic message."[33] Brouwer also provided a table where he organized and categorized the "most elemental aleatoric parameters for the performance of contemporary music of our century, in which improvisation is a very essential factor."[34] Following the table, he listed "some elements from tradition that today neutralize the improvisatory capacity": "1) Rigorous elements from the past: affinity with the performer's taste; 2) Regular formal structures: long period, period, semi-period, phrase, semi-phrase, motive, cell, etc.; 3) Concept of subordination of diverse parameters to **one** fundamental parameter (for example: rhythm in music of African origin, melodic line in song genres or harmonic progressions in the jazz 'standard'); 4) The different precise metrics: repeated periodic rhythms."[35] Brouwer concluded by granting open forms, aleatoricism, and improvisation a privileged place within contemporary music.[36]

The article was published while Brouwer was still in West Berlin under a DAAD scholarship, a rare opportunity Brouwer must have secured thanks to Henze's support. While in Berlin he met US composer Morton Feldman—one of the leading figures of the New York experimental music and art scene and key figure in the development of the core principles of indeterminacy in music—whose influence on Brouwer is evident in this article.[37] The *Sonata pian e forte* combined controlled indeterminacy with quotations of compositions spanning from the Baroque period to the twentieth century. This was not the first time that Brouwer inserted quotations from the European classical tradition. By alternating musical quotations with passages that result from controlled indeterminacy Brouwer

---

[33] El sonido se ha convertido en algo puro con entidad propia, absoluta, como mensaje artístico." Ibid., 22.

[34] Ibid., 23. A translation and reproduction of this table can be found in Quevedo, "Cubanness, Innovation, and Politics in Art Music in Cuba, 1942–1979" (Ph.D. diss, Indiana University, 2016), 288.

[35] "algunos elementos de la tradición que neutralizan la capacidad improvisatorial en la actualidad:
1. Elementos rigurosos del pasado: afinidad con el gusto del intérprete
2. Estrucutras formales regulares: gran período, período, semiperíodo, frase, semifrase, motivo o célula, etc.
3. Concepto de supeditación de diversos parámetros a **uno** fundamental (como por ejemplo: el ritmo para la música de origen africana, la línea melódica para el género canción o el encadenamiento armónico para el jazz 'standard.'
4. Las diversas métricas exactas: ritmos periódicos reiterados." Ibid., 25. Emphasis in original.

[36] "La manera de aprender la 'vida' en un suceso momentáneo, le concede a la improvisación y a la 'forma abierta' el derecho de titularse 'el medio condensado de más intensa comunicación' en el arte de la música." Ibid., 25.

[37] Morton Feldman, *Morton Feldman Says: Selected Interviews and Lectures 1964–1987* (London: Hyphen Press, 2006).

160 CUBAN MUSIC COUNTERPOINTS

re-signifies the works he borrows. He challenges performers and audiences to hear the borrowed material in the context of disorder, an almost controlled chaos. That irreverence is central to the Cuban practice of *choteo*—a tongue-in-cheek sense of humor that destabilizes hierarchies and power dynamics—and an understanding of this practice nuances our reading of *Sonata pian e forte* not just as an experimental piece, but as an idiosyncratically Cuban way of engaging with experimental music approaches.

Gramatges's *Móvil I*

The piano became one of the preferred vehicles for experimentation among Cuban composers, and no other Cuban composer wrote as prodigiously and deliberately for the piano as Harold Gramatges. As a pianist, Gramatges had been composing for this instrument his entire career, evidenced in the works discussed in chapters 1 and 2. Although Gramatges was one of the most influential and recognized Cuban composers before and after the Revolution, in comparison with Brouwer and other Cuban composers of the younger generation, Gramatges's compositional output decreased in the early 1960s due to his diplomatic and administrative responsibilities. In spite of this shift in professional endeavors, during the 1960s, in order to internalize the "elements that were compatible with his own aesthetic," Gramatges embarked on a systematic study of avant-garde compositions and the various approaches that became popular among European and US composers.[38] This was facilitated in part by his appointment by the Cuban state to serve as Cuba's ambassador to France, where he had access to scores and recordings of the latest music compositions.[39] His employment of new compositional techniques first bore fruit in his 1968 work for narrator and orchestra discussed in the opening of this chapter, *La muerte del guerrillero*. A year later Gramatges composed *Móvil I* for piano, the first in a series of *Móviles* (Mobiles) in which Gramatges employed open forms, indeterminacy, and extended instrumental techniques—the hallmarks of Cuban experimental music of the late 1960s and early 1970s.

Móvil I was premiered in Cuba in 1971 by pianist Nancy Casanova and she continued to perform the piece in later recitals.[40] Casanova became known for specializing in repertory of new music for piano. She studied in Havana and

---

[38] "Gramatges se dedicó al studio sistemático de las nuevas corrientes y de selección de aquellos elementos compatibles con su propia estética musical . . ." Brouwer, "La improvisación aleatoria," 28.

[39] An appointment he initially questioned. Heriberto Feraudy Espino, *Yo vi la música: vida y obra de Harold Gramatges* (Havana, Cuba: Editorial de Ciencias Sociales, 2009), 40–41.

[40] Including her 1978 recital of piano music by Cuban and Latin American composers, at the Museo Nacional de Bellas Artes. The commercial recordings available of the work are also by Nancy Casanova, and the work was published in 1986 by the Editora Musical de Cuba.

Music Example 4.2. Gramatges, *Móvil I*, excerpt from page 6.
Note: Gramatges, *Móvil I* (Havana, Cuba: Editora Musical de Cuba, 1988), 6.

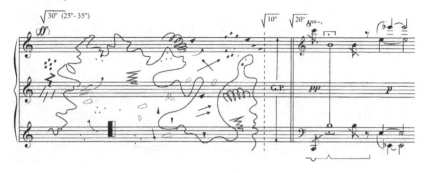

Warsaw and throughout the 1970s taught piano at the Conservatorio Amadeo Roldán; she represented Cuba at international piano competitions and toured Eastern Europe and Latin America. Performers such as Casanova, who moved in international music circles and were familiar with new music from Eastern Europe and Latin America, were crucial figures for disseminating the work of Gramatges and other avant-garde Cuban composers. Gramatges's *Móviles* were performed by her and other Cuban musicians in concerts abroad during the 1970s and 1980s. For example, in 1977 *Móvil I* was performed in a concert in Warsaw organized by the Composers Union of Poland and the UNEAC, while *Móvil III*, for flute and piano was premiered that same year in the Interpodium Music Festival in Bratislava, in former Czechoslovakia.[41]

In *Móvil I*, Gramatges utilizes extended instrumental techniques, including the use of fists, nails, and percussion sticks and mallets to strike the piano strings. Like Brouwer's *Sonata pian e forte,* every performance of the work will differ, as the performance indications allow for a great degree of improvisation and variation within a given set of parameters, such as register, dynamic range, and duration, resulting in controlled indeterminacy. Gramatges provides a guide for interpreting the special notation he uses throughout the work and employs graphic notation to specify free improvisation, improvisation with two or more sounds, *accelerando* and *rallentando*, and tone clusters. Sections are demarcated by duration of seconds instead of meter or traditional rhythmic notation, as shown in Music Example 4.2, which also displays the type of notation Gramatges used for sections of guided improvisation.

Gramatges found in the piano the ideal medium for experimentation with extended instrumental techniques and in pianists he found willing partners and performers in his search of new forms and ways to organize and structure his

---

[41] *Perfiles cultruales, 1977*, 18.

Music Example 4.3. Gramatges, *Móvil I*, opening.
Note: Ibid., 1.

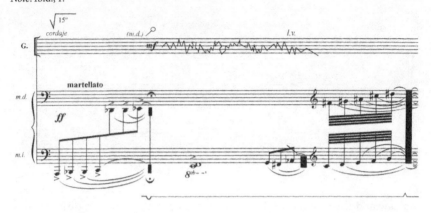

works. In *Móvil I* and other works for piano as well as a series of chamber works composed during the 1970s, Gramatges strove to provide structural cohesiveness through melodic-rhythmic relationships that allowed the contrast of dynamics, register, and timbre to become the focal features. For instance, in *Móvil I*, he uses the chromatic scale to give structure to the piece, which he divides into three groups: the first, an ascending diminished fifth from A to E-flat, the second, a harmonic E-F (minor second), and the third, the G-F-sharp-A-flat, shown in Music Example 4.3.[42] Through these works Gramatges developed his own style of graphic notation and symbols to visually convey the desired aural result. These works differed greatly from Gramatges's earlier compositions (discussed in chapters 1 and 2) in their lack of overt references to Cuban melodies, rhythms, and forms. In them, we see a full adoption of avant-garde and experimental techniques. Although Gramatges was already exploring the use of pitch cells in works from the 1950s, as discussed in the second chapter, in the late 1960s and early 1970s he ventured into more experimental approaches, similar to those explored by Brouwer and Blanco, including atonality, microtonality, indeterminacy, and open forms.[43] As previously mentioned, instrumental music's semantic ambiguity and polyvalent capacities helped most Cuban classical composers skirt questions regarding their compositions' political content or form. In Gramatges's case, these more experimental works connect to his compositional approach from the 1950s through Gramatges's pluralistic approach, one characterized by the incorporation of a wide range of techniques.

---

[42] Milvia Rodríguez, "Eclecticism in Modern Cuban Music as Reflected in Selected Piano Works by Harold Gramatges: An Investigative Analysis" (DMA document, University of Nebraska-Lincoln, 2006), 40–41.

[43] José Amer Rodríguez, *Harold Gramatges: Catálogo de Obras* (Madrid: SGAE, 1997), 17.

INSTITUTIONALIZATION AND FISSURES 163

Cuban music critic Leonardo Acosta hailed Gramatges as one of the most prominent figures in the Cuban art music scene of the 1960s and 1970s. As Acosta explains, Gramatges's *Móviles*, although clearly experimental, were also entrenched in a Cuban *vanguardista* tradition. Acosta noted that although Gramatges's use of rhythm may remind listeners of Bartók, Milhaud, and Varèse,[44] Gramatges was more directly influenced by Roldán and García Caturla, making his compositions "distinctly Cuban" because the rhythmic groupings and syncopations were drawn from Cuban vernacular music.[45] But this Cubanness, according to Acosta, is more rooted, more naked in its essence than that of Roldán and García Caturla, stepping away from colorful musical nationalism, and stripping the Cuban elements to their core in order to push Cuban music toward the future. In order to place Gramatges at the forefront of musical innovation and at the same time as a quintessentially Cuban artist, Acosta compares Gramatges's music to the paintings of Wifredo Lam. For Acosta, Gramatges's and Lam's work aligned with surrealism because both explored magical elements, which are present in "our America," labeled by Alejo Carpentier as *lo real maravilloso*.[46] As both a music and literary critic, Acosta went to great lengths to tie Gramatges's output to broader cultural trends and theories that circulated among the Cuban intellectual elite. By linking Gramatges's musical aesthetics to Carpentier's *lo real maravilloso* and Lam's work, Acosta legitimized Gramatges as heir to the art music traditions established by Roldán and García Caturla, as a musical innovator, and as quintessentially Cuban. Acosta's essay is another example of how local music critics connected avant-garde and experimental music to Carpentier's *lo real maravilloso*. I further contend that Gramatges's *Móvil I* is tied to *lo real maravilloso* at a deeper aesthetic level: Gramatges's use of extended techniques, the open-endedness of the work's structure through controlled indeterminacy, the focus on sound itself (rather than specific pitches) result in a composition that will be completely unique at each performance. Even if the same pianist performed *Móvil I* more than once, each iteration would never replicate the previous one. The newness and anticipation of the unexpected, afforded by the use of improvisation and controlled indeterminacy, was also a key trait of the compositional approach of other contemporary composers from various countries, providing a connecting thread between the Cuban composer and international musical networks. In this sense, the same aspects that made Gramatges's compositions Cuban, by engaging with *lo real maravilloso*, also made the works universal through experimentalism. Gramatges and his works are a particularly fruitful link or node within the Cuban classical music scene and the international

[44] By this Acosta probably meant Gramatges's use of 5/8 and 7/8 meters or no meters at all, syncopations, and unusual groupings and phrasing within meters.
[45] Leonardo Acosta, "Harold Gramatges y sus Móviles," *Boletín Música*, no. 106 (1985): 34.
[46] Ibid., 30.

164 CUBAN MUSIC COUNTERPOINTS

networks of new music. Although he engaged with practices that music critic Leonardo Acosta identified as idiosyncratically Cuban, these practices also resonated with international discourses over avant-garde and experimental art's capacity to challenge the classical music mainstream and to lead performers and audiences to question their roles (and art's role) as socially and politically engaged. And the Cuban cultural and musical elite saw itself as a leader among its Latin American brethren in fostering socialist and leftist artists and artistic production that also reflected and pushed the vanguard of musical aesthetics. One key event in securing the Cuban musical establishment's place as a leader in the region was the 1972 Encuentro de Música Latinoamericana.

1972: Encuentro de Musica Latinoamericana

The Cuban music establishment saw itself as particularly well-situated to lead composers and musicians from the Third World to create art that questioned what they viewed as a political and economic threat from foreign capitalist and commercial enterprises on local cultures and traditions. One of the many ways in which the Cuban music scene championed alternative Third World paths to music production was through specialized music festivals. In 1972, the Music Department of Casa de las Américas organized the Encuentro de Música Latinoamericana. One of the Encuentro's main objectives was to unite Latin American composers, fostering a sense of cohesion to a contemporary music scene that seemed scattered throughout the continent, a scene that was also closely connected to the rise of socialist and anti-imperialist movements in the region. The Encuentro, however, was also attended by non-Latin American composers, notably from Eastern European countries. It included the participation of individuals from Cuba, Chile, Mexico, Peru, Puerto Rico, Uruguay, and also from Bulgaria, Hungary, Italy, East Germany, and Rumania. The inclusion of participants from Europe hints at the event's organizers' intention to present Latin American music production within an international scope. The meeting also revealed Latin American composers' awareness of and engagement with international compositional trends, as evinced in the inclusion of Italian avant-garde composer (and avowed Marxist) Luigi Nono. The festival's programming was not limited to classical works and included popular and traditional music by Latin American composers and musicians. With multiple activities scheduled each day between September 24 and October 10, the festival programmed discussion panels, concerts and recitals of orchestral, chamber, choral, and electro-acoustic works, as well as music produced by the Grupo de Experimentación Sonora and performances by the Conjunto Folklórico Nacional and Afro-Peruvian ensembles. Some of the compositions that were performed at the

INSTITUTIONALIZATION AND FISSURES 165

festival were recorded and later released in an LP. As part of the Encuentro, Casa held a series of round tables in which the composers shared their thoughts on compositional matters. Casa de las Américas chronicled the discussions through photojournalistic pieces in *Boletín Música,* the Music Department's journal, as well as full-text reproductions of some of the lectures, speeches, and round tables. The issue of the journal also included several declarations regarding political issues; specifically, they condemned US imperialism and its involvement in Puerto Rico, Vietnam, and Chile.[47] They also published a broad statement that celebrated the general sense of awakening within Latin American countries against tyranny—the Cuban Revolution, the triumph of Velasco Alvarado's leftist military government Peru and of socialist Salvador Allende's presidency in Chile, and the unrest of pro-independence groups in Puerto Rico.[48] The Encuentro took place almost a year after a similar meeting in Uruguay, organized by Héctor Tosar, and many of the composers who participated in the event in Uruguay also attended the Cuban Encuentro.

At the time, the Music Department of Casa de las Américas was headed by Harold Gramatges, who was an avant-garde composer and had begun experimenting with graphic notation and controlled indeterminacy in his *Móviles,* and Argeliers León, whose music was strongly influenced by Afro-Cuban traditions and whose ethnographic research focused on these traditions. The 1972 Encuentro was a continuation of the precedents set by Casa de las Américas in earlier years. In its mission to unite the artists of the region, Casa held the Encuentro de la Canción Protesta (Protest Song Encounter) in 1967, a catalyst moment that unified the protest and political song movement of Latin America with participation of the most influential leftist singer-songwriters.[49]

The opening concert of the Encuentro was dedicated exclusively to works by Roldán and García Caturla. In his article in the *Boletín Música* issue, Jorge Berroa reproduces the same narrative Carpentier, Martín, and Ardévol presented in their accounts of Cuban music history (discussed in the previous chapters), extolling Roldán and García Caturla as the first Cuban nationalist composers who engaged with "large" genres (symphonies, ballets) by using the latest European techniques while incorporating Afro-Cuban elements.[50] Turning to one of the living Cuban composers, Berroa praised Roberto Valera's *Devenir* for

---

[47] For more on the participation of Puerto Rican composer Rafael Aponte-Ledée in the Encuentro, see Noel Torres Rivera, "The Making of an Avant-Gardist: A Study of Rafael Aponte-Ledée's Early Life and Works (1957–1966)" (Ph.D. diss, City University of New York, 2021).

[48] *Boletín Música* (1972), no issue number.

[49] Juan Alberto Salazar Rebolledo, "La rosa y la espina: expresiones musicales de solidaridad antiimperialista en Latinoamérica. El Primer Encuentro de la Canción Protesta en La Habana, Cuba, 1967," *Secuencia,* no. 108 (2020): 1–26.

[50] Jorge Berroa, "Encuentro de música latinoamericana septiembre de 1972," *Boletín Música,* no. 29 (1972): 10–19.

166   CUBAN MUSIC COUNTERPOINTS

"achieving an individual language that is at the same time universal."[51] Berroa's commentary reproduced the value that other Cuban music critics placed on both individuality through nationality and universality.

The LP released to commemorate the Encuentro de Música Latinoamericana Contemporánea included recordings of the live performances of Roberto Valera's *Devenir*, Enrique Pinilla's (Peru) *Concierto para piano y orquesta*, Fernando García's (Chile) *Sebastián Vázquez*, all for orchestra, Harold Gramatges's *Móvil II*, Celso Garrido-Lecca's (Peru) *Intihuatana*, Héctor Tosar's (Uruguay) *Espejos 1 y 2*, José Ardévol's, *Ninfra*, for chamber ensembles, and Serafín Pro's *Madrigal*, Nilo Rodríguez's *Ya no se mi dulce amiga*, Ardévol's *De enero a enero*, and Alejandro García Caturla's *Canto de los cafetales* (son), all choral pieces. The choral pieces, all by Cuban composers, presented repertory that relied on conventional harmonies and used elements from Cuban popular and traditional music. The rest of the works, however, all employed newer techniques. Ardévol's *Ninfra*, though more adventurous than some of the composer's earlier works, with its clusters and polyrhythmic contrapuntal writing, did not venture away from conventional notation, using meters and highly specific notation. By contrast, Gramatges's *Móvil II* featured graphic notation, open form, and controlled indeterminacy and left several of the musical parameters up to the performers' interpretation. There were some glaring omissions from the Encuentro's program: the experimental works of Brouwer, Blanco, and Fariñas. Perhaps the presence of folk and popular music genres from Cuba and other Latin American countries made the Encuentro appealing to a larger audience, leaving little room for highly experimental works. The exclusion of extreme experimental music may also have had something to do with the overall centralization and repression of artists and intellectuals already underway by 1972. This exclusion of experimental pieces could have also resulted from the debates over musical innovation that took place in the late 1960s and early 1970s, in particular surrounding the OSN premiere of works by Brouwer, Blanco, and Fariñas in the concert held on October 10, 1969, discussed in the previous chapter.

Although regional and international festivals had already been organized throughout the 1960s, efforts to host and organize festivals with different (yet sometimes overlapping) scope seem to have increased exponentially in the 1970s.[52] In January 1973, they held a Festival de Música Cubana; in 1974, they hosted the Primer Festival de Música Contemporánea de los Países Socialistas

---

[51] "El logro de un lenguaje propio que al mismo tiempo sea universal." Ibid., 12.

[52] This was not the first instance of Cuban participation in or convening classical music festivals. If we look back to the 1950s (as discussed in the second chapter) and the early 1960s, we can observe how Cuban composers had been involved in the Caracas Festivals of Latin American Music, the Inter-American Music Festivals in Washington D.C., and held their own Festival of Latin American Music in 1961.

INSTITUTIONALIZATION AND FISSURES   167

(First Festival of Contemporary Music of Socialist Countries); in 1977, the location was de-centered from Havana and we see a major festival in the City of Camagüey (the third largest city in Cuba) with the Festival Internacional de Música Contemporánea de Camagüey. And the Cuban cultural establishment also sent Cuban composers and performers to represent Cuba in international new music festivals.

1974, Primer Festival de Música Contemporánea de los Paises Socialistas

The Primer Festival de Música Contemporánea de los Paises Socialistas (First Festival of Contemporary Music from Socialist Countries) in 1974, held between October 12 and 20, consisted of seven chamber music concerts performed by musicians of the OSN, with works by composers from Cuba, Rumania, Bulgaria, Hungary, Czechoslovakia, Poland, East Germany, and the Soviet Union. The festival was also sponsored by UNEAC and the CNC, two cultural entities with different goals than Casa de las Américas. The program notes for the festival credited the Revolution and socialism with bringing in a new era for Cuban citizens and artists to enjoy cultural events and to foster relations with foreign countries on their own terms. What is most striking about the language of these notes is the direct mention of the proletariat and workers, which usually did not receive any mention in program notes for other OSN concerts:

> Thanks to the triumph of the Revolution in January 1959, fruit of the continuous struggles that our *mambises* began in the year 1868, a new horizon has opened in our nation, which frames a different landscape where the development of the nation and its relations with other countries of the world is in the hand of the workers.
>
> The hateful ties of subservience imposed by *yanqui* imperialism have been replaced by relations based on equality of rights, independence and respect of our sovereignty, presided not by the miserable mercantile sprit but rather by the wide concept of proletariat internationalism.
>
> There have been multiple laws, decrees, and activities created by our government in support of the cultural development of the people . . . [since] the sponsorship of the work of artists and intellectuals, our revolution has made very decisive strides to elevate the cultural level of our people.
>
> The existence of this process makes it possible for the UNEAC to take on the organization of recurring music festivals of socialist countries, as a way to

168 CUBAN MUSIC COUNTERPOINTS

broaden our mutual knowledge about the successes achieved in this field by Cuban creators.[53]

This passage presents the festival as a product of the Revolution, which supported the arts and music institutions because the government has the interests of the proletariat in mind, not imperialist and commercialist objectives imposed by the United States. These notes emphasized the socialist Revolution's role in elevating the cultural level of the common man, while also connecting the festival to the international achievements of socialist movements. One of the festival's goals was to promote the work of Cuban composers; by placing national artistic production side by side with compositions by composers from other socialist countries, the Festival showed that Cuban composers could share the same stage as their foreign counterparts.[54]

The concert programming and the accompanying notes connected the music to the revolutionary and socialist values of collectivism, hard work, and egalitarianism. They also emphasize aesthetic innovation and *vanguardismo* as both Cuban and revolutionary traits. Other values also emerge, among them Cuba's commitment to voicing struggles of Third World countries and the international proletariat; these events positioned Cuba as a leader among Latin American countries and defender of Latin American autonomy from capitalism and imperialism, and as promoter of art and culture as crucial elements of the everyday lives of the masses. The festivals and Encuentros are fruitful moments through which we can trace the local and global nodes of the artistic networks these composers, and the institutions they worked through, cultivated at a time of increasing centralization and institutionalization. These festivals form part of the same networks Cuban composers inhabited as national cultural figures, leaders

[53] "Gracias al triunfo de la Revolución en enero de 1959, fruto de las continuas luchas que inciaron nuestros mambises en el año 1868, se ha abierto para nuestra patria un nuevo horizonte que enmarca un paisaje diferente en el cual el desarrollo de la nación y sus relaciones con los demás países del orbe están en manos de los obreros. Se han sustituido los odiosos lazos de servilismo que nos imponía el impreialismo yanqui, por unas relaciones basadas en la igualdad de derechos, independencia y respeto a nuestra soberanía, presididas no por el mezquino espíritu mercantilista sino por el amplio concepto del internacionalismo proletario. Múltiples han sido las leyes, decretos y actividades creados por nuestro gobierno en pro del desarrollo cultural de la población, por lo tanto su sola enumeración resulta imposible en este espacio, pero desde la nacionalización de la enseñanza, pasando por la gigantseca labor de la campaña de alfabetización, hasta el patrocinamiento del trabajo de los artistas e intelectuales, nuestra revolución ha dado pasos muy decisivos para elevar el nivel cultural de nuestro pueblo. La existencia de este proceso hace posible que la Sección de Música de la UNEAC se haya propuesto llevar a cabo festivals periódicos de música de países socialistas, como forma de ampliar nuestros conocimientos mutuos sobre los éxitos obtenidos en este campo por los creadores cubanos." "Primer Festival de Música Contemporánea de los Países Socialistas," Program, October 1974.
[54] Most of the works by Cuban composers included in this Festival are not available through published editions or recordings, therefore my discussion of this Festival is limited to the description of the event as a whole provided in the Festival booklet. The booklet only provides the concert programming and has no program notes.

INSTITUTIONALIZATION AND FISSURES   169

of the Latin American new music scene, and participants in the international socialist arena.

From Artistic Repression to Cultural Fomentation: 1976

When Armando Hart was named Minister of the newly created Ministry of Culture in 1976, Cuban cultural activities dramatically increased in the number and scope of performances. This was achieved through several initiatives. One was the creation of the Instituto Superior de Arte (ISA, shown in Fig. 4.2), an arts university designed and built on the grounds of a former golf and country club, with departments in each artistic field and offering bachelors, masters, and doctoral degrees. The ISA was an extension of the arts university, the Escuela Nacional de Artes (ENA), that had already been established in Miramar in 1962. Through the creation of a music department at the ISA, we clearly see which individuals had gained authority over the previous fifteen years, as they were placed at the highest faculty positions in music composition in the island. These were: José Ardévol as the Dean of the Music Department but also the mastermind behind the planning, organization, and foundation of the ISA, and professor of composition and orchestration; Juan Elósegui taught basic music skills; Dolores Torres was in charge of courses in polyphony; José Loyola taught courses on musical forms; Roberto Valera taught contemporary techniques; Alfredo Diez Nieto taught contemporary harmony/counterpoint; and Sergio Fernández Barroso taught composition, among others who also included Harold Gramatges and Teresita Junco. Loyola and Valera had studied in Warsaw, Poland, and brought a particularly avant-garde point of view to their compositions and teaching; both are also the first black Cubans to obtain such high levels of musical training and teaching positions in Cuba. In an essay reflecting on her time studying at the ISA in those early years, composer Magaly Ruiz notes that she studied with Gonzalo Romeu and (unnamed, but qualified as "magnificent") professors from the Soviet Union. She also comments on the replacement of Ardévol as Dean by Carlos Fariñas, which, according to Ruiz, led to rumors about differences between professors who held professional degrees and titles (Fariñas) and those who didn't (Ardévol).[55] Ruiz mentions two Soviet professors, Vladimir Klopov and Leonid Di, who taught musical analysis and harmony (a term most often used in Spanish-speaking Latin America to refer to sixteenth-century counterpoint) through different conceptual and theoretical frameworks that challenged

---

[55] Magaly Ruiz, "El ISA, '45 Aniversario' . . . La Facultad de Música. Memorias como alumna de Composición y profesora," *Del canto y el tiempo* (blog), June 28, 2021. https://cidmucmusicacubana. wordpress.com/2021/06/28/el-isa-45-aniversario-la-facultad-de-musica-memorias-como-alumna-de-composicion-y-profesora/.

170   CUBAN MUSIC COUNTERPOINTS

the young Cuban composers. Along with Anunciata Calcavecchia and María Álvarez del Río, Magaly Ruiz was one of the first three women to graduate from the ISA with a composition degree at the "superior" level (the equivalent of a bachelors degree). Ruiz was eventually appointed professor of counterpoint, harmony, and musical forms at the ISA in 1996. The cases of Valera, Loyola, Ruiz, Calcavecchia, and Álvarez del Río attest to the shifts in the demographic makeup of composers in Cuba within the first two decades of the Revolution; the social, political, economic, and institutional changes, although not entirely positive for the whole population, did set more favorable conditions for black and women composers to further their careers.

The Ministry of Culture also publicized its achievements through the publication of *Perfiles Culturales*.[56] The publication's purpose was "to offer the most outstanding aspects of cultural work developed by the people, the artists and the intellectual workers."[57] The music section in *Perfiles Culturales* listed the participation of Cuban composers and performers in art music festivals in Europe, which included Bratislava Music Festival "Interpodium"; Ostrogski Palace, Warsaw and International Popular Song Contest in Sopot, Poland; Music and Theater Festival in Berlin; International Dance Festival in Paris; and Summer International Festivals in Spain, Belgium, Italy. The performances in Bratislava and Warsaw specifically featured new music by Cuban composers and included compositions by Gramatges, Ardévol, E. Martín, Héctor Angulo, Jesús Ortega, Jorge Berroa, and Brouwer. The concert performed in Warsaw in April of 1977, organized by the Composers Union of Poland and the UNEAC, included contemporary Cuban work as well as pre-revolutionary Cuban composers, most notably Amadeo Roldán. These compositions were representative of three aesthetic points of view that combined national and international approaches: Cuban nationalism (Amadeo Roldán), folkloric internationalism (Berroa and Brouwer), and contemporary international new music (Gramatges, Ardévol, Martín, and Angulo). Through this concert program, the Polish audience heard an overview of twentieth-century Cuban music that ranged from the modernist nationalism of Roldán to the more avant-garde contemporary works by Brouwer and Gramatges.

Perfiles Culturales's main objective was to publicize the success of the Ministry of Culture in coordinating Cuban artistic activity, not only within the island but also abroad. It specified the number of foreign artists who visited Cuba

---

[56] Only two editions of *Perfiles Culturales* were published: 1977 and 1978. It seems that it was an initiative of the newly founded Ministry of Culture, and may have been intended as a yearly publication, but it was not continued past 1978.

[57] "Consideramos que este, es sólo un primer intento del Miniterio de Cultura—creado a finales de 1976—por ofrecer los aspectos más destacados del trabajo cultural desarrollado por el pueblo, los artistas, y los trabajodres intelectuales." *Perfiles Culturales* (1977), 3.

Figure 4.2. Aerial view of the roofs of the Instituto Superior de Arte. Photo courtesy of the Cuban Heritage Collection at the University of Miami.

Note: "Aerial View of the Roofs of Cuba's National Art School—Guillermo 'Willy' González Collection—Digital Collections." CHC017 Guillermo "Willy" González Papers, Box. No. 4, Binder No. 1, Binder Name: Slide Book No. 1, Tab: Escuela Nacional de Artes. University of Miami Cuban Heritage Collection. https://digitalcollections.library.miami.edu/digital/collection/chc0170/id/4074/rec/1 (accessed August 30, 2021).

in the previous year and compared them to the number of Cuban artists and performances exported to other countries.[58] If a qualitative assessment of all the cultural events in which Cuba participated during 1977 was not enough, then a quantitative one was to assure readers that the new Ministry of Culture and its director, Armando Hart, were fulfilling their mission. The summary of activities provided in *Perfiles Culturales* served as proof that the Ministry of Culture was putting into action the official cultural policy of the state, and demonstrated that cultural institutions were capable of meeting their mandate. In one particular passage, the publication reiterated the goals established in the 1971 Education and Culture Congress discussed above, specifically elevating people through art, making art that reached the masses, and reinforcing socialist teachings.[59]

---

[58] It specified the numbers of the foreign artists who visited Cuba, 514 artists performing a total of ninety-one presentations, which they compared to the numbers of Cuban artists and performances exported to other countries, 333 artists in 492 performances. *Perfiles Culturales* (1977), 29.

[59] "El objetivo final de la educación artística, en tanto que parte de la educación comunista en su conjunto, es la formación del ámbito espiritual, ideológico y del propio sentido moral del hombre dentro de la concepción científica del mundo. En consecuencia, masividad, rigor técnico, desarrollo de las capacidades innatas y realización plena de los talentos—que ahora tienen la posibilidad de

172   CUBAN MUSIC COUNTERPOINTS

The narrative presented in *Perfiles Culturales* went further back in time by connecting recent events to the earliest initiatives on culture by the state, citing Castro's *Palabras a los intelectuales* (1961) and the foundation of the Escuela Nacional de Arte (1962, as a predecessor of the ISA). Yet, the publication's emphasis on the exported and imported acts points to an increasing concern on the part of the cultural establishment with placing Cuban artists on an international stage. It was no longer enough to make music for the Cuban people or even a Latin American audience: the world stage was the new frontier. Of course, as we saw through the work of Blanco, Brouwer, Gramatges, and Valera in the 1960s, composers had been engaging with the international music scene; but it seems that finally, after more than fifteen years, the official, national, Cuban cultural institutions were overtly promoting these international cultural exchanges. Sending Cuban acts aboard, however, had a limited impact, for only a small audience of the foreign artistic elite would have heard the Cuban composers' works. Cuban composers needed further means, and media, for promoting their work within and outside the island.

Empresa de Grabaciones y Ediciones Musicales (EGREM, Enterprise of Recordings and Musical Editions)

One of the most significant post-1959 Cuban cultural institutions for the dissemination and promotion of Cuban music nationally and internationally is the Empresa de Grabaciones y Ediciones Musical (EGREM, Enterprise of Recordings and Musical Editions). The EGREM was established in 1964, as part of the state's nationalizing efforts of all aspects of Cuban businesses and culture, which in this case constituted the former facilities of the Panart recording music studios, the first Cuban-owned sound recording studios established in 1944. Under the auspices of the Imprenta Nacional de Cuba, the EGREM was created to oversee all aspects of music publication and recording, a mission it still

---

desplegar todas sus facultades—así como la formación de las nuevas generaciones de artistas, profesores y técnicos promotores de la cultura dentro del espíritu de las concepciones marxistas-leninistas: a esto aspiran las escuelas de arte de nuestro país. Hoy el arte pertenece al pueblo. Pero para que el arte se acerque al pueblo, y el pueblo se acerque al arte, es indispensable elevar, tanto el nivel de instrucción y de cultura general del pueblo, como el de sus artistas. Esta preocupación por parte del gobierno revolucionario se evidencia desde los primeros momentos. Ya en 'palabras a los intelectuales,' Fidel se refería a la necesidad e importancia del trabajo que recién comenzaban los instructors de arte, así como a los planes de construcción y organización de escuelas para la enseñanza artística. De esta forma, en febrero de 1962, se funda la Escuela Nacional de Arte, y a partir de ese momento, la enseñanza de las artes se va extendiendo hasta contar, en la actualidad, con instalaciones en todo el país." *Perfiles Culturales* (1977), 65

INSTITUTIONALIZATION AND FISSURES   173

continues to serve today.[60] It functions as an umbrella recording enterprise that manages several labels—Areito, Siboney, Miramar, and Auténtico—each with its own recording facilities. Most of the published music editions and recordings of new music by Cuban composers throughout the 1960s, 1970s, and 1980s were produced under the auspices of the EGREM.

Unlike the previous national recording labels, which ignored contemporary Cuban classical music, EGREM resourses were allocated for Cuban composers to record and disseminate their music. The EGREM also gave composers access to technology that allowed them to experiment with electroacoustic composition. As the national recording studio, it had the responsibility of promoting the work of Cuban composers by recording and releasing their compositions as LPs not only in Cuba, but also abroad. Avant-garde works were the focus of an album series titled *Contemporáneos*, as shown in Table 4.1. The series was exportable audible-sonic proof of Cuban composers' artistic freedom to engage with avant-garde techniques and the institutional support the state provided to have their music performed and recorded as participants in the international music scene. If we examine the *Contemporáneos* series within the context of the Cold War cultural arms race, these albums launched the Cuban musical *vanguardia* into an international market, proving that the Revolution provided the political, economic, social, and *technological* conditions necessary for composers to thrive.

Released during the late 1970s and 1980s, almost all of the LPs in the *Contemporáneos* series consisted of works by Cuban composers, with the exception of one album. *Contemporáneos 2* included Brouwer's woodwind quintet *El reino de este mundo* (1968), Soviet composer Edison Denisov's *Ode* (1968), for clarinet, piano, and percussion, and Bulgarian composer Ivan Spassov's *Episodes for Four Timbral Groups* (1965).[61] The two non-Cuban composers in the series were known for their avant-garde compositional approaches, and these compositions had been performed in Cuba by members of the OSN in 1970 and 1971 respectively. Their inclusion in the album series reinforced the

---

[60] According to the EGREM's webpage its activities include the "production, promotion, distribution, and commercialization in Cuba as well as abroad of phonographic production; licensing; edition of specialized Cuban music publication; national and international artistic representation; presentation of Cuban and foreign artists in the circuit of Casas de la Música, and providing food and boarding services as part of the music industry." "Producción, promoción, distribución y comercialización tanto en Cuba como en el exterior de producciones fonográficas. Licencia de matrices. Edición de publicaciones especializadas en música cubana. Representación artística nacional e internacional. Presentación de espectáculos musicales de los artistas cubanos y extranjeros en el circuito de Casas de la Música y la oferta de servicios gastronómicos y de hospedaje como complemento al fin empresarial." "EGREM," http://www.ecured.cu/index.php/EGREM (accessed May 14, 2015).

[61] Later, Denisov dedicated his *Ode* to the memory of Che Guevara. Denisov's and Spassov's works were recorded in 1972, and Brouwer's Quintet was recorded in 1974. For a discussion of Denisov within the context of the Soviet music establishment, see Peter John Schmelz, *Such Freedom, If Only Musical: Unofficial Soviet Music during the Thaw* (Oxford; New York: Oxford University Press, 2009).

174   CUBAN MUSIC COUNTERPOINTS

Table 4.1. Repertory recorded in the *Contemporáneos* series of the EGREM.

Contemporáneos 1 (1976)	Leo Brouwer, Concerto para Guitarra y Pequeña Orquesta Harold Gramatges, *Móvil 2*
Contemporáneos 2	Leo Brouwer, *Quinteto "El reino de este mundo"* Edison Denisov, *Oda* Ivan Spasov, *Episodios para cuatro grupos de timbres*
Contemporáneos 3 (1979)	Leo Brouwer Concierto para Flauta y Orquesta de Cuerdas (1972) [premiered on January 28, 1973]: I. Movimiento, II. Movimiento, III. Movimiento Concierto para Violín y Orquesta (1973) [premiered on May 7, 1978]: I. Discursos, II. Toccata I, III. Música Nocturna, IV. Toccata II
Contemporáneos 4 (1979)	Juan Blanco *Música para un joven mártir* (Homenaje a Conrado Benítez) *Galaxia M-50* *Desde su voz amada* (Homenaje a V.I. Lenin) *Estructuras*
Contemporáneos 5	
Contemporáneos 6	
Contemporáneos 7 (1983)	Argeliers León *En homenaje a un amigo*—para un ejecutante y tres fuentes tímbricas *Hoy canto a mi patria sobre aquella sangre heroica vertida en el Moncada*—Concertante para Piano y Orquesta
Contemporáneos 8	
Contemporáneos 9	
Contemporáneos 10	Leo Brouwer *Sonata para cello solo*: Allegro, Adagio, Scherzo, Final *Variantes para un percusionista* *Per suonare a due*: Prólogo, Scherzo de bravura, Gran pas de deux, Intermezzo, Epílogo
Contemporáneos 11	Harold Gramatges *Oda Martiana* *In Memorian Frank Pais*

INSTITUTIONALIZATION AND FISSURES   175

Table 4.1. Continued

Contemporáneos 12	Héctor Angulo *Sonata para once instrumentos* *La estrella y la paloma*/Text By—José Martí *Tres Cantos* (Para Barítono y Orquesta): I. El poeta eres tu/Text By—Miguel Barnet II. Niños de Viet Nam/Text By— Héctor Angulo III. Homenaje a Victor Jara/Text By— Gerardo Fulledo León *Homenaje a Salvador Allende*/Text By— Pablo Neruda *Toque* (Para piano y percusión cubana)
Contemporáneos 13 (1984)	Carlos E. Malcolm *Eclosión* *Adagio para cuatro manos* *El remediano* *Articulaciones* *Quetzalcoatl* Canto 1 &Canto 2 *Beny Moré Redivivo*

ties between avant-garde composers from socialist countries and also placed the Cuban composers within the network of international new music. In addition to the composers we encountered already—Juan Blanco, Leo Brouwer, Harold Gramatges, Argeliers León—the series also featured Héctor Angulo (1932–2018) and Carlos Malcolm (b.1945), two relatively younger composers with connections to foreign music circles. In the 1980s Malcolm traveled to Ecuador and to Poland, where his work *Quetzalcóatl* (1985) was performed at the Warsaw Autumn Music Festival. The *Contemporáneos* series presented a 'who's who' of the Cuban contemporary music scene to listeners around the world.

Composers' Writings on Music Aesthetics and Ideology

In addition to continued participation in local and foreign festivals and concerts and the production of EGREM recordings, Cuban composers situated their work within an international context through their writings on their music, its function, and how their aesthetic choices were tied to political ideology. In the previous chapter, we already encountered writings by Juan Blanco and Leo Brouwer in which they justified the use of new avant-garde and experimental techniques in the service of the Revolution. Within the context of the *quinquenio gris*, it seemed even more pressing to justify aesthetic choices by defending their functionality in socialist society and their connection to a broader international

176 CUBAN MUSIC COUNTERPOINTS

network of revolutionary artists. In the early 1970s Casa de las Américas's *Boletín Múisca* published three essays by three major figures within the Cuban art music world: Roberto Valera's "Posibilidades de la técnica musical en la nueva sociedad" (Possibilities of music technique in the new society);[62] an interview with Juan Blanco "¿Hacia otra nueva música?" (Towards another new music?);[63] and Leo Brouwer's "La improvisación aleatoria," already discussed in relation to his piano work *Sonata pian e forte*.[64]

In the first of these essays, Valera defended his and other Latin American composers' use of new techniques in the service of the "new society" (i.e. socialist, revolutionary society). Valera penned the essay after attending a workshop on music composition in Latin America held in Uruguay in December 1971. By this point, he was no longer a young composer trying to establish himself among Cuba's cultural class, but an accredited member of the musical establishment; he had returned from studying composition in Poland, had a successful symphonic premiere with *Devenir*, and represented Cuba at the Latin American new music workshop held in Uruguay. His essay appeared alongside other writings on new music in Latin America by Luigi Nono and the Uruguayan violinist and composer Federico Britos, and in a periodical that was intended for dissemination through Latin America. These years were marked by military coups and insurgencies in the region, when leftist political movements were fighting for control of their respective countries, and Cuba supported (not just ideologically but in very real and material ways) leftist guerrilla movements in Bolivia and Nicaragua. Valera's defense of Latin American composers' freedom was influenced by this political context, as he asks "why consider some musical techniques forever marked by the original sin of their bourgeois origin, while others—originated in the same sin, more generalized, more useful for the ends of imperialist ideological penetration for being easier to comprehend by the large masses, since they respond to the sonic habits that for centuries have been commercially exploited—are considered inoffensive?"[65] He made one of the most compelling arguments for the use of avant-garde art in the revolutionary and socialist context by connecting 1960s and 1970s *vanguardismo* to the political commitment of avant-garde artists in early twentieth-century communist movements. He reminded his readers that the October Revolution was supportive of avant-garde art, and

---

[62] No. 20, *Boletín Música*. This issue of Boletín Música collected the writings of composers who attended a workshop on music composition in Latin America held in Uruguay in December 1971.

[63] Pedro Simón and Juan Blanco, "¿Hacia otra nueva música?," *Boletín Música*, no. 22 (1972).

[64] Brouwer, "La improvisación aleatoria," 20–26.

[65] "¿Por qué considerer algunas técnicas musicales marcadas para siempre con el pecado original de su procedencia burguesa, y a otras—originadas en el mismo pecado, más generalizadas, más útiles a los fines de la penetración ideológica imperialista por ser de más fácil comprensión por las grandes masas ya que responden a los hábitos sonoros que durante siglos han sido explotados mercantilmente—, considerarlas inofensivas?" Roberto Valera, "Posibilidades de la técnica musical en la nueva sociedad," *Boletín Música*, no. 20 (1972): n.p.

INSTITUTIONALIZATION AND FISSURES 177

it was not until later that avant-garde techniques came under scrutiny and became associated with bourgeois decadence. He also convincingly argued that composers in socialist countries had the advantage of an audience that was not alienated or marginalized as in capitalist societies.

The following year, in an interview with Pedro Simón, Blanco explicated how new music could fulfill the needs of revolutionary society. He defended the use of any music technique or style, as long as the composer considered it the most appropriate approach to deliver his or her message and as long as the work's function called for the use of the techniques employed. For Blanco, wrote Pedro Simón, "there can be no hurried rejections of techniques, methods, systems, etc., of any sort, adopting in each situation those that better serve the purpose—adapting them, modifying them, or inventing others—if it is essential."[66] As long as the composer considered a particular compositional technique the most appropriate approach to deliver their message and as long as the work's function called for the use of the techniques employed, they should enjoy complete aesthetic freedom; the work's function should determine their choice of techniques. As one of the leading Cuban composers of electroacoustic music, Blanco provided a detailed description of how this medium was better suited to reach the masses than works that must be performed in a concert hall, citing his own works and collaborations with visual artists for electronic media in large outdoor spaces.[67] Blanco proposed future applications of electroacoustic works in public spaces through the permanent "sonorization" of urban spaces, an aspect of this interview that is further discussed in the next chapter. Similarly, in Brouwer's 1973 article, discussed above in relation to his *Sonata pian e forte*, the younger composer echoed his contemporaries and his own writings from the late 1960s, defending the composer's freedom of choice in terms of compositional techniques, while exalting the conditions afforded to them by the socialist systems. But rather than focusing on electroacoustic media, like Blanco, Brouwer focused on how improvisatory procedures facilitated breaking from the confining strictures of composing while utilizing more "traditional" techniques. In all instances, these composers connect the use of new techniques to a process of awakening for the composers, performers, and audiences, a process through which they questioned their stance on and relation to sound, event, tradition, and society, leading to a renewal of social and political consciousness.

Yet, not all Cuban composers defended the use of avant-garde and experimental techniques with as much fervor as Brouwer, Blanco, and Valera. In his

[66] "En la búsqueda de esa función no puede haber rechazos apriorísticos de técnicas, métodos, sistemas, etc., de clase alguna, debiendo adoptarse en cada caso aquél o aquellos que mejor sirvan a ese propósito—adaptándolos, modificándolos o inventando otros—si fuere menester." Simón, "¿Hacia otra nueva música?," 12.

[67] Marysol Quevedo, "Cubanness, Innovation, and Politics in Art Music in Cuba, 1942–1979," 205.

178   CUBAN MUSIC COUNTERPOINTS

1971 book on Cuban music, *Panorama histórico de la música en Cuba*, Edgardo Martín questioned the Cuban (and Latin American) composers' fascination with

> Stravinsky, Hindemith, or Schoenberg; later, to the streams of the "Polish school," Stockhausen, or the latest Italian intellectual fad ... They have lost sight [of the fact] that in all of these cases, the European creators have worked from their own [national and historical] foundations . . . and the American . . . can only achieve universality of ITS art by achieving the highest esthetic hierarchy in its own artistic creation, with its own elements, with a confrontation of everything that the rest of the world conveniently takes from the actual reality of the American man.[68]

In a later passage, Martín grouped Juan Blanco, Carlos Fariñas, and Leo Brouwer and the conductor Manuel Duchesne Cuzán under the rubric of *La Vanguardia Cubana*, as a faction of artists united by the objectives of "assimilating, disseminating, and developing in Cuba" techniques known in Europe as "concrete music, electronic music, aleatorism [sic] and spatialism."[69] In Martín's estimation, this group of composers had gained a following because they "controlled, from the music section of UNEAC, diverse marketing media and spaces in newspapers . . ., mobilizing in their favor young and amateur musicians, and attracting the curiosity of intellectuals and people interested in some way in the new . . . at the same time that they made negative judgments against all Cuban musical art achieved in the three preceding decades, which they marked as 'nationalist' and 'limited.' "[70] Martín notes that the group had privileged access to various organizations and media through which they promoted experimental

---

[68] "Muchos compositores de América Latina—de Cuba, incluso—han creído escapar a las limitaciones nacionalistas adhiriendose, primero, al estilo de un Stravinski, un Hindemith o un Schoenberg; luego, a las corrientes de la 'escuela polaca,' de un Stockhausen o al último grito de la moda intelectual italiana. Han perdido de vista, que en todos esos casos, los creadores europeos han trabajado sobre bases propias, sobre su misma historia; y que América—la América 'mulata,' la 'aborigen,' la 'africana' o como se le quiera matizar más o menos parcialmente—solo puede alcanzar la universalidad de SU arte obteniendo un máximo de jerarquía estética en su propio quehacer artístico, con sus propios elementos, con una confrontación de todo lo que del resto del mundo le convenga tomar, desde la realidad misma del hombre americano." Edgardo Martín, *Panorama histórico de la música en Cuba* (Havana, Cuba: Universidad de La Habana, 1971), 7–8.

[69] Ibid., 156.

[70] "Este grupo controló de inmediato, desde la sección de música de la Unión Nacional de Escritores y Artistas, diversos medios publicitarios y espacios en periódicos -por ejemplo, la sección 'Artes y Letras,' de la revista 'Bohemia'-; controló asimismo parte de la programación de la Sinfónica Nacional y procuró influir en algunos sectores del estudiantado de música, logrando con todo ello, en poco tiempo, despertar una gran expectación pública, movilizar en su favor a sectores jovenes de músicos y aficionados, y atraer la curiosidad de los intelectuales y de gentes interesadas de alguna manera por lo nuevo. Para sacudir áun más al medio habanero, procedieron a dar conferencias y charlas explicativas, con ilustraciones sonoras, abundando en la apología de sus propias directrices experimentalistas -al mismo tiempo que vertian juicios negativos contra todo el arte musical cubano logrado en las tres decadas precedentes, al que tildaban de 'nacionalista' y 'limitado.' " Ibid., 156.

INSTITUTIONALIZATION AND FISSURES   179

music, and that this band of *compositores de vanguardia* criticized nationalist musical works, Martín's preferred compositional aesthetic. He describes the tension between two camps of Cuban composers: those of the *vanguardia* and those who continued working with what Martín categorized as "*medios tradicionales*" (traditional means).[71] Martín adds that the disagreements did not play out in public but "entre telones" (between the curtains), and that the arguments brought forth a healthy discussion among composers and musicians, challenging established definitions of music, and opening up the possibilities for exploring the creation of *sound* itself as a compositional endeavor. Martín concludes by acknowledging that even if the new techniques did not replace what he terms "traditional means of composition," these new techniques now could be incorporated within said "traditional" or "conventional" means.[72]

By the end of the decade, Harold Gramatges, provided a retrospective look at the past two decades of classical music production in Cuba that would serve as the foundation for later accounts of classical music developments in revolutionary Cuba in his 1979 essay "The Presence of the Revolution in Cuban Music."[73] After serving as the Cuban ambassador to France between 1961 and 1964, Gramatges understood, probably better than any of his fellow Cuban composers, the art of cultural diplomacy and compromise. Gramatges's writings echoed what had become Cuban composers' party line: their music was foremost Cuban because they were Cuban, in other words, the music did not have to sound Cuban to be Cuban; their music was also innovative and *vanguardista* because the Revolution had set the economic conditions that allowed composers the freedom of choice of compositional means; finally, their music was a reflection of the socialist conditions that were framed by an international context. Gramatges reiterated that Cuban composers regularly incorporated foreign musical styles and techniques, but always within their Cuban, revolutionary character, stating that "in the realm of art or elaborated [i.e. classical] music, the Cuban composer expresses himself through a technique, that stemming from European culture, adapts each time in a better way to his expressive needs, allowing his work to situate itself in the realm of the universal."[74] For Gramatges, serial technique and electronic music composition had been incorporated by Cuban composers' into their compositional language thanks to the freedom that resulted from the Revolution's triumph. In his view, "experimentation and the incorporation of new techniques in the majority of Cuban composers has allowed the development of the search for

[71] "El violín, el piano, la orquesta . . . el canto humano, la dodecafonía, el serialismo; la sonata, el cuarteto, la cantata . . ." Ibid., 157.

[72] Ibid., 158.

[73] Harold Gramatges, *Presencia de la Revolución en la música cubana* (Havana, Cuba: Editorial Letras Cubanas, 1983).

[74] Gramatges, "La presencia de la Revolución en la música cubana," reproduced in *Presencia de la Revolución en la música cubana*, 17–18.

180   CUBAN MUSIC COUNTERPOINTS

national identity through different paths, accounting for, dialectically, that tradition is always in movement, in a process of enrichment that can modify its traits without losing its most legitimate essences."[75] Gramatges evoked the process of transculturation that shaped Cuban intellectual thinking with regards to the process of identity formation: new elements could be incorporated into Cuban culture, because national identity was in a constant process of transformation and self-identification.

Twenty years into the Revolution, and even as leaders within state cultural institutions, this group of Cuban composers relentlessly defended their compositional and aesthetic choices as natural outcomes of the socialist-revolutionary process. As we examine the writings of Valera, Blanco, Brouwer, Martín, and Gramatges a more complicated picture of the new music scene in 1970s Cuba is revealed. Although not all Cuban composers engaged with experimental techniques, those who did had access to and influence on concert programming, advisory and editorial boards at Casa de las Américas, *Bohemia,* the ICAIC, the OSN, and several other institutions through which they widely circulated the idea that experimental music was a result of the Revolution. In other words, they were active nodes within a network that gave them privileged access to resources and scenes within and outside of Cuba. Although Ardévol and Martín were staunch revolutionaries, had access to institutional resources, and served the government in various capacities, their work was limited to administrative and teaching posts in educational institutions, unlike Brouwer and Blanco, who were involved in selecting concert programming for major ensembles and promoted their brand of new music as editors and contributors for magazines and journals. All of these writings, however, concurred on several points that reinforced the values of Cuban socialist-revolutionary ideology. They positioned their contemporary works as the most recent link in a historical chain, as part of a lineage, the result of all the nationalist and revolutionary struggles of past musical and political figures. They credited the Revolution with breaking with the old values that stifled local musical creation and with setting the ideal social, political, and economic circumstances that allowed composers to freely express themselves. Furthermore, writing about music composition and their works' role within socialist-revolutionary society was one of the key activities through which composers placed themselves and their peers within local and international music networks that would facilitate the circulation of their ideas and compositions.

---

[75] "La experimentación y la incorporación de nuevas técnicas en la mayoría de los compositores cubanos ha permitido desarrollar la búsqueda de la identidad nacional por diferentes caminos, teniendo en cuenta que, dialécticamente, la tradición siempre está en movimiento, en un proceso de enriquecimiento que puede modificar sus características sin perder sus más legítimas esencias." Ibid., 19.

INSTITUTIONALIZATION AND FISSURES   181

Throughout this chapter we have seen how musical networks were shaped by the circulation of composers through concerts, travel related to music festivals, tours, and workshops, or the circulation of their works or writings through recordings, radio broadcasts, publication of scores, recordings, and articles. These events, compositions, and writings show how Cuban artists in general had to respond to the pressures all artists faced during the *quinquenio gris* and the 1970s as a decade characterized by *institutionalization*, and how, composers in particular, dealt with calls for overt politization of their output through strategic use of titles and texts, while maintaining an avant-gardist musical language that engaged with the international music scene in which they participated. Thanks to the semantic ambiguity of instrumental music, most classical music composers continued to produce works utilizing avant-garde and experimental techniques throughout the 1970s, in spite of the repression and censorship their colleagues in other artistic fields faced during the *quinquenio gris*. With the shifts in political winds around 1976, which included the ratification of a new constitution and the establishment of a new Ministry of Culture, also came a renewed commitment to international affairs, one that manifested in the musical scene with more performances and participation abroad and ongoing interests to promote new music at an international level through recurring regional and international music festivals. As we will encounter in the next chapter, these efforts would be severely undermined by new political and economic crises of the 1980s, a decade marked by external pressures that included a rise in neoliberalism and an intensification of *globalization*.

5

"Hacia nuevos horizontes"

Electroacoustic Music and Globalization in 1980s Cuba

In his 1979 article, "La música electrónica hacia nuevos horizontes (sobre el primer período en el Panorama de la Múisca Electrónica)," published in *El Caimán Barbudo,* music critic Frank Padrón Nordase wrote:

> A dissimilar set of countries, trends, genres and composers of [electronic music], which almost always reached us through that magical resource that is the magnetic tape . . . if you are a well 'informed' reader, you may know that it is a difficult genre, extremely labored, which is based on a rigorous elaboration of the sound, but far from being devoid of concepts and ideas,—as many believe or can think—opens an unlimited horizon in the human being and in society because through its language it fights for this, for the gratitude of man and for their definitive freedom, in addition to expressing sorrows, feelings, joys and contradictions. A genre that develops from our contemporaneity, because it is extremely young and speaks more precisely to man,[1]

In this article Padrón Nordase chronicled the 1979 electroacoustic concert series, held at the Biblioteca Nacional José Martí (BNJM). Anyone arriving at the BNJM would not be able to miss the Plaza de la Revolución and the Monumento a José Martí, located less than 300 meters from the library. The symbolic power emanating from these two landmarks in such proximity to one another, the Plaza de la Revolución and National Library, is further accentuated by the large portrait of Ernesto Che Guevara adorning the facade of the Ministry of the Interior's building that stands opposite to the Monumento a José Martí.

---

[1] "Un disímil conjunto de países, tendencias, géneros y compositores de la misma, que nos llegó casi siempre a través de ese mágico recurso que es la cinta magnetofónica . . . Si usted es un lector tanto 'avisado,' quizás sepa que se trata de un género difícil, sumamente trabajado, que se basa en una rigurosa elaboración del sonido, pero lejos de estar desprovisto de conceptos e ideas, —como muchos creen o pueden pensar—abre un ilimitado horizonte en el ser humano y en la sociedad porque a través de su lenguaje lucha por esto, por el agradecimiento del hombre y por su definitiva libertad, además de expresar penas, sentimientos, alegrías y contradicciones. Un género que se desarrolla a partir de nuestra contemporaneidad, por lo que es sumamente joven y habla con más precisión al hombre." Frank Padrón Nordase, "La música electrónica hacia nuevos horizontes (sobre el primer período en el Panorama de la Múisca Electrónica)," *El Caimán Barbudo*, no. 142 (October, 1979): 28–29, 31.

Cuban Music Counterpoints. Marysol Quevedo, Oxford University Press. © Oxford University Press 2023.
DOI: 10.1093/oso/9780197552230.003.0006

Padrón Nordase's comments anticipated the readership's resistance or antagonism towards electronic music, as he echoed what Brouwer and Blanco had been articulating throughout the 1960s and 1970s: that new music techniques that were of "our time" were best suited to reflect contemporaneous sentiments, issues, and aesthetics. He also noted the makeup of the attending audience, "it is not only the specialized public that is interested in these issues; we saw new faces there, students, workers, and housewives who, for the first time, encountered an event of this kind. And this is already, in itself, a success that must continue to be nurtured."[2] In the two previous decades, Juan Blanco had been creating electroacoustic works that reached the masses, but this series differed from other presentations of electronic music (discussed further below) in that compositions by Cuban composers were part of programs that also included works by foreign composers, and in doing so, the series placed local artistic works within a broader, more global framework and for a non-specialist audience.[3]

Throughout this chapter I will explore a series of developments in Cuban electroacoustic music production beginning in 1979, although I provide a brief retrospective account of the history of this compositional approach in the island dating back to the early 1960s. Electroacoustic music (as well as classical music in general in Cuba), like in many other new music scenes in cosmopolitan centers throughout the Western world, was presented by concert organizers to audiences within increasingly globalized conceptual frameworks. The effects of globalization and emerging postmodernist theories from Europe (theories that validated aesthetic practices Cuban artists had been employing for decades prior to European theorizations of postmodernism) impacted how Cuban composers approached their craft, how audiences listened to classical music, and how composers engaged with audiences through their compositions. These developments in shifting aesthetics and worldviews took place during a period of relative economic stability for the island and growing access to the

---

[2] "no es solo el público especializado el que se interesa por estas cuestiones; vimos allí caras nuevas, estudiantes, obreros y amas de casa que por primera vez se enfrentaban a una actividad de esta índole. Y esto es ya, de por sí, un éxito qué hay que seguir alimentando." Ibid.

[3] The first concert in March of 1979 included the premiere of Juan Blanco's *Galaxia M-50*, along with *La discordatura*, by Christian Clozier (France), *Corales* (1971) by F. Barroso-C. Fariñas (Cuba), *Androginia* (1978) Barry Truax (Canada), *Isla de juguetes* (1968) by Miloslav Istvan (RSCH), *Ecos* (1979) by Beatriz Ferreyra (Argentina). Second concert in April, *Siesta Blanca* (1972) by Beatriz Ferreyra, *Elegía para contrabajo y banda magnetofónica* (1969) by David Keane (Canada), *Il Duce* (1973) by Louis Andriesen (Netherlands), *Yantra IV* (también Chile tiene su Apocalipsis) (1975), by Fernández Barroso (Cuba), *El mar en la aborada* (1975) by John Piché (Canadá), and *Música socialista para cémbalo y banda magnetofónica*, by Luc Ferrari (Italy). Third concert in May, *Pajáro Rojo* (1977) by Trevor Wishart (England), (1964) [the other works were not listed]. Fourth concert (date not specified) *Cordes ci, cordes ca* (1975), by Francoise Barrier (France), *Lo viviente, lo no viviente* (1970), by Sofía Gubaidulina (Soviet Union), *Gradual* (1974), by Denis Smalley (New Zealand), *El arcoiris en el aire curvo* (1968), by Terry Riely (USA), and the world premiere of *Desde su voz amada* (Homenaje a Lenin, 1979), by Juan Blanco.

184   CUBAN MUSIC COUNTERPOINTS

outside world, while also coinciding with album releases and the establishment of institutions and festivals that promoted new and electroacoustic music in national and international audiences. In this final chapter I examine the Festival de Música Electrónica Primavera en Varadero, the LPs of electroacoustic music by Cuban composers released by the EGREM, and the establishment of institutions designed to meet the needs of composers, researchers, and artists, Asociación Hermanos Saíz and the Taller ICAP de Música Electroacústica (TIME). As these events, institutions, and objects demonstrate, the composers and works represented in these spaces both reflected and enacted the economic, social, political, and aesthetic shifts that took place in Cuba during the last decade of its diplomatic and economic ties to the Soviet Union. The case studies explored in this final chapter show how one particular genre, electroacoustic music, facilitated compositional innovation and artistic networking for Cuban composers who increasingly viewed their work as both Cuban and global.

Over the course of the 1980s there was a proliferation of compositional approaches and techniques among Cuban composers of a younger generation. This generation reached maturity in the 1970s under the tutelage of Argeliers León, Gramatges, Juan Blanco, Fariñas, Edgardo Martín, and Ardévol. Yet, Brouwer, Blanco, Valera, and Fariñas still maintained their prominent positions within the cultural establishment. This older generation of composers had been so successful at promoting their work and at recruiting and retaining composition students in the first two decades of the Revolution that once a younger generation came of age in the late 1970s and early 1980s the field was brimming with new talent. This younger generation also faced dramatic changes in foreign policy not seen since the triumph of the Revolution nearly twenty years prior. The onset of visits of Cuban exiles living in the United States in 1979, the subsequent Mariel Boatlift crisis, a saturated and competitive new music scene, and the challenging material conditions specific to the music industry in the island—such as the lack of new instruments and technological equipment necessary for the composition of new music—led some of these younger composers to leave Cuba not only to further their music education and pursue new opportunities but also to settle permanently in other countries where artistic life in general wasn't as precarious.

Yet those who stayed continued to cultivate a seemingly thriving music scene in spite of considerable material deficits on the island. Instrumentalists' needs ranged from reeds, mouthpieces, strings, and other basic equipment to full sets of new instruments, music stands, and new editions of standard repertory. In spite of the lack of materials and financial means, new music activities in Cuba during the 1980s centered around several festivals and recording series that helped disseminate new music not only by Cuban composers, but also by their contemporaries from other socialist countries: "Jornadas de Música

Contemporánea de La Habana (from 1978 to 1986), the Festival de Música Contemporánea de los Países Socialistas (from 1974 to 1985), the first versions of the Festival Internacional de Música Contemporánea de La Habana (starting in 1984),"[4] the Festival de Música Electroacústica Primavera in Varadero (starting in 1981, now Primavera en La Habana). The increase of festivals and exchanges with foreign music circles reflected Cuba's rise in the international arena, from its involvement in African liberation struggles to becoming a leader in the Non-Aligned Movement (NAM).[5]

Most composers, even the older ones (particularly Brouwer), explored a wide range of compositional approaches, techniques, and styles that defied categorization. Most returned to (or continued) composing in a tonal language. All (at some point) explored electronic music composition but not exclusively. Many employed musical devices associated with minimalist and postminimalist practices while solo piano and chamber ensembles continued to be the preferred vehicles for new compositions (not that orchestral music and solo pieces were uncommon). Some composers (like Edesio Alejandro) explored new hybrid genres, such as rock opera, that crossed categorical boundaries, while others found in Cuban folk and popular music inspiration for their compositions, even if those sources were transformed to such a degree that the original sources remained unidentifiable. In short, in an increasingly globalized postmodern world, Cuban composers, in spite of the effects of the US-imposed embargo on culture, drew from a wide range of techniques and influences, some local and many foreign, that they grafted onto their individual artistic rootstock. Some branches bore more fruits than others for certain composers, but all produced an eclectic oeuvre that challenged classification. The new festivals and recording series explored in this chapter facilitated the circulation of Cuban composers' works and ideas, broadening their local and global artistic networks during a decade marked by drastic social and political changes.

Political, Economic, and Social Conditions in 1980s Cuba

Much like the preceding two decades, the island's political and economic circumstances in the 1980s were in large part affected by its relationship to the Soviet Union, while the Cuban government attempted to maintain a certain

---

[4] Iván César Morales Flores, "Leo Brouwer y la re-territorialización de un modelo de dirección artística habanero en la Orquesta de Córdoba (1992–2001)," in *En, desde y hacia las Américas: músicas y migraciones transoceánicas*, ed. Belén Vega Pichaco, Javier Marín-Lòpez, and Victoria Eli Rodríguez (Dykinson, 2021), 309.

[5] Luis Martínez-Fernández, *Revolutionary Cuba: A History* (Gainesville, FL: University Press of Florida, 2014), 129.

186 CUBAN MUSIC COUNTERPOINTS

degree of autonomy and a preeminent place as a leader among third-world countries. State-sponsored cultural agendas reflected and enacted these same power dynamics, with festivals, recordings, and tours that served to broadcast Cuban music to the world and that in turn facilitated Cuban composers', musicians', and listeners' access to international musical trends. In the later 1970s and early 1980s Cuban citizens encountered new political and economic contexts as Cuba became a leader among Third World nations, a further opening to tourism (which had started in the 1970s and would increase dramatically after 1991), and the return of Cuban exiles visiting their families for the first time since the early years of the Revolution. Improved relations between Cuba and the United States were in great part due to US President Jimmy Carter's lifting of travel bans to Cuba in 1977. The Cuban state had also eased restrictions that allowed US visitors and Cuban-Americans residing in the United States to travel to Cuba beginning in 1979.[6] Through this process, Cubans residing on the island were exposed to the luxuries and commodities their US counterparts took for granted as everyday necessities. This contributed to the discontent among a sector of the population that desired to leave the island, culminating in the occupation of the Peruvian embassy on April 1, 1980, and the Mariel Boatlift between April 15 and October 30.[7] Instead of severely punishing citizens who had occupied the Peruvian embassy, Castro announced that all Cubans who wanted to leave would be allowed to do so by boat departing from the Port of Mariel. Cuban exiles in Miami rented fishing vessels to travel from Florida to Mariel. The boats were precariously overloaded with men, women, and children. The Cuban administration took advantage of this crisis to strengthen its core values by depicting these defectors as "lumpen" (individuals not committed to the revolutionary and socialist cause) and as mentally unstable and/or criminals.[8] Some political commentators point to this moment as one of the factors that led to Ronald Reagan's victory in the presidential election of 1980.

After the failed *zafra de los 10 millones* of 1970, the state undertook a series of reforms that relied on "Soviet-inspired material incentives reminiscent of the capitalist, individualistic vestiges the Cuban leadership had vehemently denounced during the 1960s"; a new system of *normas* set standards for production bonuses for workers or *primas* and *premios*, a system for distributing profits among works or reinvesting profits into social projects or back into the

---

[6] Tony L. Henthorne, *Tourism in Cuba: Casinos, Castros, and Challenges* (Bingley: Emerald Publishing Limited, 2018), 48–50. Iraida H. Lopez, *Impossible Returns: Narratives of the Cuban Diaspora* (Gainesville, FL: University Press of Florida, 2015), 48.

[7] Victor Andres Triay, *The Mariel Boatlift: A Cuban-American Journey* (Gainesville, FL: University Press of Florida, 2019), 30.

[8] The US press reproduced this portrayal of Cuban migrants as bad citizens, leading to backlash among the general US population against this particular wave of Cuban immigration. Ibid.

"HACIA NUEVOS HORIZONTES" 187

businesses.[9] The system made the late 1970s and early 1980s a period of relative economic stability for the state and its citizens. Another major change in Cuban state policy was its newfound interest in the tourism industry. As Tony Henthorne has suggested, the Cuban state's renewed investment in tourism was partly in response to the failed *zafra* of 1970.[10] The slow but steady growth in the Cuban tourist industry that began around 1970 was meant to counteract the economic effects of Soviet reductions of Cuban sugar imports and plummeting sugar prices. The Cuban state invested in tourism infrastructure to attract desperately needed international foreign currency that could ameliorate the island's economic crisis. In spite of the increasingly apparent cracks in the Soviet socialist model and in order to continue legitimizing their socialist regime, the Cuban government continued to promote Cuban brand socialism with an emphasis on the Marxist-Leninist socialist system, pre-1959 Cuban nationalist symbols and history, and the United States as the enemy and cause of Cuban economic strife. But the labor reforms that used material incentives to promote worker engagement and production and the reinvestment in the tourist industry began to point to a more flexible economic policy that also began to open up Cuba to more foreign visitors and capital.

As part of the changing economic, political, and cultural landscape, one key aspect of the 1980s Cuban classical music field was the cementing of an institutional elite constituted by the older composers, conductors, and musicians who had represented the rebellious spirit of the early Revolution in their youth. The networks and circles of influence I traced in earlier chapters were extremely successful in securing these individuals[11] the cultural capital necessary to control much of the (limited) means of cultural production within the island. The very pragmatic and material decisions regarding access to institutional resources, ensembles, publications (print scores and recordings), travel permits and funding to attend international festivals and other events were determined by these older, more ensconced individuals who leveraged their reputations and standing in the national and international musical scene to maintain their positions. Influence begot more influence.

The 1980s was also the decade of the coming-of-age of the first generation of Cubans born and raised under socialism: they had not fought in the revolutionary struggles of the 1950s and early 1960s, and were more vocal in their criticisms of the state. Consequently, younger generations of composers and musicians had to fight over scant available resources, some through newly created organizations geared toward promoting the work of younger artists, such

[9] Martínez-Fernández, *Revolutionary Cuba: A History*, 130.
[10] Henthorne, *Tourism in Cuba*, 48.
[11] Argeliers León, Harold Gramatges, Juan Blanco, Leo Brouwer, Roberto Valera, Manuel Duchesne Cuzán.

188 CUBAN MUSIC COUNTERPOINTS

as the Asociación Hermanos Saíz. This arrangement kept the established intellectual elite protected at the top (mainly in the UNEAC offices) from competing for resources with younger artists and intellectuals who were hungry for more institutional and financial support and exposure as they came into more frequent contact with the outside world.

Musical Aesthetics during the Rise of Globalization and Neoliberalism

Towards the end of the 1970s and into the 1980s, Cuban composers, like many composers throughout the world, were deeply affected by globalization, the development of compositional styles that both performers and listeners found more accessible than the highly experimental and avant-garde idioms of the preceding two decades. They also returned to a less dissonant language that employed Cuban vernacular music elements more overtly, such as Fariñas's string ensemble work *Punto y Tonadas* (1980–1981), Brouwer's trio for piano, violin, and cello *Manuscrito antiguo encontrado en una botella* (1983), and Blanco's work for magnetic tape and Cuban percussion *Cirkus Toccata* (1984). Some composers had never abandoned the use of Cuban vernacular music in their compositions, such as Edgardo Martín and Argeliers León. However, this more widespread return to more accessible idioms coincided with the global turn toward postmodernism and, in Cuba, a particular perspective on these developments resulted in an expanded musical vocabulary and network of collaborators and influences beyond what transpired throughout the 1960s and 1970s. Later in the chapter I will examine Brouwer's writings on postmodernism and what this meant for Cuban composers. In Western Europe and the United States, postmodernism in music, more than a specific musical style or technique, came to be associated with a breakdown of hierarchies between classical, popular, and folk musics as composers drew from various traditions and many strove to write in a more accessible style. Some of these postmodernist approaches to composition could be described as hybrid, eclectic, and polystylistic; it is important to note, however, that these traits already were, and still are, a hallmark feature of Cuban and, more broadly, Latin American classical music. The return to vernacular sources that I note within the output of Cuban composers like Brouwer dialogued *both* with the past practices in Cuban classical music history of engaging with vernacular elements *and* with the Western classical music scene's return to accessible and vernacular idioms through a postmodern stance. Within these broader trends, the Cuban electroacoustic music scene in particular saw drastic growth in the number of composers who regularly worked in this medium, especially those of the younger generation. In the remainder of this chapter, I will examine

"HACIA NUEVOS HORIZONTES" 189

particular developments in the Cuban electroacoustic music scene—the release of LPs, the organization of festivals, and the establishment of dedicated facilities all devoted to electroacoustic music—as fertile ground for exploring the intersection of changing political climates, technological advancements, and shifts in aesthetic predilections.

Juan Blanco's Electroacoustic Music Galaxy (Constellation)

In 1979 the EGREM released the fourth LP in its *Contemporáneos* series (discussed in the previous chapter), an entire album dedicated to the compositions of Cuba's electronic music founding father, Juan Blanco. *Contemporáneos 4* (1979), was a bit of an outlier within the album series, for it heavily featured electroacoustic compositions and the album's graphic design departed dramatically from the rest of the LPs' covers in the series. Until 1979 these had been the only state venues where composers could experiment with electronic compositional techniques. The two LP covers demonstrate the contrast between the black and grey abstract design of the LP cover that unified the look of *Contemporáneos* as a series and Blanco's LP. Blanco's name, in all caps, is printed in neon blue, pink, and white three-dimensional typeset over a black background peppered with bright blue and pink specks; the cover art evoked outer space through a graphic design more fitting for a pop artist than for an experimental music composer; the design also reflected Blanco's status as pioneer of electronic music.

The album was released the same year that Blanco's brainchild, the Taller ICAP de Música Electroacústica (TIME), was founded. TIME was the first Cuban national electronic music laboratory that was not tied to any national radio or television studios or the recording studios at the EGREM or the ICAIC. The LP presented Blanco as musical innovator and revolutionary artist, offering a sample of Blanco's creative output. The A-side included two works from 1975, one electroacoustic, *Galaxia M-50* (1975), and the other for symphonic orchestra and a *trovador* accompanying himself on the guitar, *Música para un joven mártir—Homenaje a Conrado Benítez* ("Music for a young martyr—Homage to Conrado Benítez," 1975).[12] These two works showcased Blanco's range as a composer who worked on both electronic and more traditional media. The B-side of the album

---

[12] *Música para un joven mártir*'s dedicatee was a teacher who was murdered in 1961 by counterrevolutionary forces when he was working in the rural area of the Escambray as part of the literacy campaign. In this work, Blanco provides a sparse, atonal orchestration of sustained dissonances, punctuated by percussive intrusions that eventually lead to a traditional tonal song in the *nueva trova* style that occupies the last brief segment of the piece. By using a *trovador* singing in a vernacular style, Blanco marked the work as distinctively Cuban. The dedication to the memory of a revolutionary martyr made the work overtly political. This combination of elements fulfilled all of the requirements of *vanguardista* music by an *artista comprometido*: it was innovative, revolutionary, and Cuban.

190 CUBAN MUSIC COUNTERPOINTS

featured two electroacoustic pieces that bookended Blanco's electroacoustic output: first, one of his most recent (at the time) works, *Desde su voz amada* ("From his beloved voice," 1979), and finally one of his earliest electroacoustic compositions, *Estructuras* ("Structures," 1963). The juxtaposition of newer and older works evinced Blanco's twenty-plus years of activity as both a pioneer of electroacoustic music and an *artista comprometido* in socialist-revolutionary Cuba. Both works engaged with socialist-revolutionary ideals, albeit one more overtly than the other.

In *Desde su voz amada* ("From his beloved voice") Blanco manipulated recordings of various speeches by Vladimir Lenin through echo effects and then overlapped the manipulated recordings on several tracks, creating a dense texture with a crescendo and decrescendo. Blanco described the resulting effect "a 'quasi coral' sonic climate that evokes the ancestral Russian choral tradition."[13] By multiplying the voice through multi-tracking, Blanco created the effect of a growing mass of people, which eventually "decrescendo[es] as though it is [moving] forward, toward the horizon, toward the future."[14] Through the title, source materials, and his description of the work, all of which paid homage to Lenin, Blanco imbued *Desde su voz amada* with overt political associations that connected the Cuban musical *vanguardia* to the international socialist cause. Additionally, by employing electroacoustic techniques of pre-recorded sound manipulation, Blanco engaged with the musical language of the international avant-garde. Through the manipulation of Lenin's voice Blanco evoked his version of a traditional Russian past (choral music), but the work's ending pointed towards the future. The use and transformation of borrowed materials reflect an idiosyncratic tendency among Cuban artists to reinterpret elements from other cultures and traditions and make them part of their vocabulary and voice. Through Blanco's transformation Lenin's original speech is barely detectable; it becomes something else, something new, but audibly made up of something borrowed—not unlike Brouwer's treatment of borrowed materials in *La tradición se rompe . . .* (discussed in the third chapter).[15]

The other two electroacoustic compositions included in Blanco's LP, however, lacked overtly political texts or titles. *Galaxia M-50* was meant to evoke the feeling of a space shuttle taking off, providing contrasting moments or "layers"—as Blanco described it in the LP notes—of violence and calm, until "arriving to an environment of poetic serenity."[16] Blanco delivered a short

---

[13] Liner notes, *Contemporáneos 4* (Cuba, EGREM, Areito, LD: 3809, 1979).

[14] Ibid.

[15] The Soviet Union released in LP format many of these Lenin speeches. But, unlike Blanco's treatment of the recordings, Soviet composers would have never used them as primary material to be manipulated, as this was seen as a violation of the sacrosanct voice of their deceased leader. Gabrielle Cornish, "Sounding Socialist, Sounding Modern: Music, Technology, and Everyday Life in the Soviet Union, 1956–1975." (Ph.D. diss., University of Rochester, 2020), 194.

[16] Liner notes, *Contemporáneos 4.*

explanation of *Galaxia M-50*, at its public premiere in March 1979, the first concert of a four-part series dedicated solely to electroacoustic music (discussed in the chapter's opening), noting that beyond the electronic elements, there were some effects from ordinary sounds (such as hitting objects against a plate placed vertically). Writing for *El caimán barbudo,* critic Padrón Nordase remarked that *Galaxia M-50* was "always a process of rigorous work, to perfectly achieve the message: a cosmonaut crossing space reaches areas of greater and lesser calm; the end of the voyage is a female voice that announces in echoes and in 'off' a grand slogan: LOVE. Between applause, long ovations and the congratulations to the author, this work received a deserved reception among the listeners,"[17] adding, Blanco creates "a subtle, atmospheric composition with low amplitude sounds" by using "white noise, low frequency sine waves, flanging, and reverb."[18] In Padrón Nordase's evocative commentary the music critic attempted to capture the ethereal qualities of Blanco's work while also educating readers on the technical processes the composer used to achieve such effects. The first word we hear the female voice softly utter is "amor" (love) (6:51/9:02), which ties the recited text to the title of the piece as M-50 is a cluster of stars (not actually a galaxy, as the title suggests) found in the constellation Monoceros that forms a heart-shaped figure.[19] The combination of the electronically produced sounds and female voice evokes both outer space and carnal sensuality, creating a sonic representation of the heart-shaped M-50. Yet, even if on its surface the work doesn't contain overt political references, throughout the Cold War space exploration was a highly politicized arena, as evinced by the competitive scientific developments in the Soviet Union and the United States that led to the Soviet satellite Sputnik, cosmo-canine Laika, and cosmonaut Yuri Gagarin to orbit the earth for the Soviets and the Apollo 11 Moon landing for the United States. The LP's cover served as a visual metaphor for Blanco's role as Cuba's pioneer of electroacoustic music: it launched Blanco's name into space, or at least into the orbit of the international musical avant-garde. The album made a concrete connection to outer space through its graphic design and the inclusion of *Galaxia M-50*. This reference to space through musical innovation could have been Blanco's allusion to both the Cold War's space race and the cultural arms race. In the late 1970s Cubans were heavily invested in space exploration, as their own Arnaldo Tamayo

---

[17] "pero siempre proceso de un riguroso trabajo, para lograr perfectamente el mensaje: un cosmonauta que atraviesa el espacio llega a zonas de mayor y menor calma; el final del viaje es una voz femenina que anuncia en ecos y en 'off' una gran consigna: AMOR. Entre aplausos, largas ovaciones y la felicitación del autor, recibió esta obra la merecida acogida entre los oyentes." Padrón Nordase, "La música electrónica hacia nuevos horizontes," 28–29, 31.

[18] Ross Feller, "Juan Blanco: Nuestro Tiempo (album review)," *Computer Music Journal* 38, no. 2 (Summer 2004) http://www.computermusicjournal.org/reviews/38-2/feller-blanco.html (accessed April 4, 2016).

[19] "Messier 50," http://messier.seds.org/m/m050.html (accessed April 4, 2016).

192 CUBAN MUSIC COUNTERPOINTS

Méndez (b. 1942) trained in the Soviet Intercosmos program beginning in 1978. Launching on September 18, 1980, the Soyuz 38 spacecraft took Tamayo on a nearly eight-day orbit around the Earth, making Tamayo the first Cuban, Latin American, and Afro-descendant cosmonaut in space. Given Cuba's participation in the Intercosmos program and the Cold War space race context, *Galaxia M-50* gains a further layer of significance. However, by claiming that a work inspired by space exploration culminates with "arriving to an environment of poetic serenity," Blanco projected a vision of space that transcended political and ideological divides through emotions that cut across all human experience: love, ecstasy, serenity.

The fourth work in the LP, *Estructuras,* was one of Blanco's first electroacoustic compositions. He composed *Estructuras* to accompany a gymnastics choreography in a national sports showcase in 1964, not surprising considering Blanco's life-long involvement in national sports (he was a national diving champion in his youth). Like *Galaxia M-50, Estructuras* seems to be devoid of political meaning. Yet, by writing a piece to accompany a gymnastics routine, a sport that increasingly became a vehicle for demonstrating artistic and athletic superiority during the Cold War and that served as a way for Cuba to strengthen ties with the Soviet Union, Blanco was participating in both cultural and athletic diplomacy. This piece also demonstrates how individuals from diverse backgrounds—music and sports—collaborated in projects that promoted socialist and revolutionary values and ideals. In *Estructuras,* Blanco uses recorded sounds produced by a piano, or sound "structures" as Blanco referred to them, and then alters these structures through the use of echo, reverb, and panning resulting in a spatial effect.

The three electroacoustic works included in the LP all play with the listeners' sense of space and time, whether it is the beloved voice of a historical figure that is transformed to point to a serene future, the explicit evocation of space and space travel in *Galaxia M-50,* or the general sense of bodies moving through space in *Estructuras.* Even *Música para un joven mártir* evokes a sense of space, the space into which the *trovador* enters, or perhaps the space of the countryside where Conrado Benítez was murdered. *Música para un joven mártir* and *Desde su voz amada* were both overtly political works that paid homage to a revolutionary martyr and a socialist icon respectively. While *Estructuras* and *Galaxia M-50* were less overtly political, they exemplify Blanco's penchant for experimentation and commitment to advancing art and culture in the name of the Revolution and the utopic goal of shaping the *hombre nuevo.*

While this LP launched Blanco into the international electronic music scene, the composer would also work towards bringing electronic music from around the world to Cuba. At first this was achieved through electronic music concerts at the Unión de Escritores y Artistas de Cuba (UNEAC) and the BNJM, briefly

"HACIA NUEVOS HORIZONTES" 193

discussed at the opening of this chapter. Eventually, however, Blanco and TIME members organized and hosted the First International Electroacoustic Music Festival "Primavera en Varadero" (Spring in Varadero) in 1981. Before exploring the composers, works, and countries who participated in the Primavera en Varadero festivals, I will trace the developments of electronic music in Cuba leading up to these culminating events.

Electroacoustic Music in Cuba before 1979

Although most accounts of electronic music in Cuba mark 1964 as the year of foundation of electroacoustic music on the island, with Blanco's first concert of electroacoustic music at the UNEAC, Rodríguez Alpízar notes that, in 1942, Blanco submitted a description and graphic design of an electronic instrument he named *multiórgano* to the Registro de Marcas y Patentes (Registry of Brands and Patents) in Havana.[20] According to Blanco, he didn't register the design with the Cuban patents office because he didn't have the funds to submit the official application.[21] It wasn't until the early 1960s that, with the purchase of two tape recorders at a local Sears department store (before they closed their Cuba locations) that Blanco began to explore the possibilities of composing using *musique concrète* techniques.

As Ileana Güeche notes, if the 1960s marked the beginning of electroacoustic music in Cuba, then by the 1980s, the scene had reached a period of maturation. She points to the political "opening" in the 1980s—facilitated by Jimmy Carter's short-lived diplomatic efforts—as setting the stage and giving composers the motivating momentum to broaden the scope of compositional tools, leading to an increase in the number of composers involved in electroacoustic music, as well as a diversification of stylistic approaches by this growing number of composers.[22] In the early years, electroacoustic music in Cuba was composed in the facilities of the Estudios de la Empresa de Grabaciones y Ediciones Musicales

---

[20] Fernando A. Rodríguez Alpízar, "Juan Blanco y la profecía del sonido futuro," *Boletín Música*, no. 39 (2015): 45. For a more detailed description of the instrument and its functions see Rodríguez Alpízar's article. In 1991 at the Musical Inventions and Creations: Denial of Utopia symposium in Bourges, France, Blanco presented his design from 1942. The symposium also had in attendance Donald Buchla, Christian Clozier, Otto Luening, Max Mathews, Robert Moog, Pierre Schaeffer, Léon Theremin, and Iannis Xenakis. At the end of the symposium, organizers agreed to include Blanco's multiorgan in the International Memory Archives of the Science and Art of Electronic Music, sponsored by the UNESCO. This was the same year he graduated as a Civil Lawyer from the University of Havana.

[21] Marta Ramírez, "Juan Blanco: Aún a la vanguardia," *Clave—Revista Cubana de Música* 4, no. 3 (2002): 35.

[22] Ileana Güeche, "Breve caracterización de la música electroacústica en Cuba," *Pauta: Cuadernos de Teoría y Crítica Musical* 14, no. 53–54 (1995): 151.

194   CUBAN MUSIC COUNTERPOINTS

(EGREM) and the Instituto Cubano de Arte e Industria Cinematográficos (ICAIC).[23] Eli and Güeche emphasize the "plurifunctionality" of electroacoustic music in Cuba from its earliest instances, when composers employed electroacoustic composition for works for the concert hall, sonorization of spaces, and background music for film, television, dance, and theater.[24] In fact, most of the early electroacoustic works from the 1960s are more "easily" found in the film scores for ICAIC-produced documentaries, short films, and feature films than in LPs of electronic or experimental music. Brouwer, Valera, Fariñas, and Blanco all worked on music for film at some point in the 1960s and 1970s. In 1999 Fariñas emphasized the importance of the ICAIC projects, noting that "these [electroacoustic] procedures began to be worked on and completed for film, which was a very important laboratory for contemporary Cuban music."[25] The ICAIC recording studios are famously known for hosting the GESI, the Grupo de Experimentación Sonora del ICAIC, which, under Brouwer's direction, allowed young singer-songwriters to experiment with musical styles and themes that had been blacklisted in the Cuban state's radio, television, and sound recording projects, and also to experiment with new production techniques in the film recording studios. But beyond this group that famously led to the *nueva trova* movement and the solo careers of Silvio Rodríguez and Pablo Milanés, the ICAIC allowed Cuban composers to experiment with electronic composition techniques in music scores for film projects. Electroacoustic music in Cuba, from its earliest instances, was deeply imbricated with visual components and multimedia.

The previously mentioned 1964 concert took place on February 5 at the UNEAC, with the presentations of *Estudios I* and *II* and *Ensamble V* (magnetic tape works), and was preceded by a lecture, "La revolución técnica de la música" ("Music's technical revolution"), delivered by Blanco. The newspaper *Revolución* advertised the concert with the headline "Primera audición en Cuba de música concreta esta noche" ("First listening of concrete music in Cuba tonight"), and included the following statement:

> The development of contemporary science and technique in the field of sounds creates a true revolution in the musical order, and makes it possible for composers who have decided to apply it in their works to obtain unusual

---

[23] Victoria Eli Rodríguez and Ileana Güeche, "Caminos de la electroacústica en Cuba," *Clave—Revista Cubana de Música* 4, no. 3 (2002): 25.

[24] Ibid.

[25] "la realización de estos procedimientos se comenzaron a hacer en el cine, que fue un laboratorio muy importante para la música contemporánea cubana." Carlos Fariñas, *Clave*, no. 2 (1999), 6.

"HACIA NUEVOS HORIZONTES"   195

sounds until now not achieved even in the most daring works composed for symphony orchestra or any other conventional sound medium.[26]

Rodríguez Alpizar notes that Blanco's approach to combining a lecture and a concert became his standard procedure for presenting and promoting electronic and experimental music in Cuba. Along with other musicians and composers, they became "the pillars of the most transgressive [figures] in the music scene."[27] Two weeks later at the UNEAC Brouwer premiered *Sonograma I*, the first work by a Cuban composer for prepared piano combined with indeterminacy. As mentioned in chapter 3, these two concerts in 1964 marked the beginning of the 1960s Cuban *vanguardia*, characterized by its two salient traits: electroacoustic composition and indeterminacy.[28] The leaders of this movement were initially Brouwer, Blanco, and conductor Manuel Duchesne Cuzán, with Fariñas and Angulo eventually joining them.[29] However, as Blanco noted, initially his experimental works in electroacoustic music were not well-received by all members of the musical establishment:

Immediately after I offered the first electroacoustic concert in 1964, almost all old composers and most of them of the former Grupo de Renovación Musical, out of ignorance or reactionary immobility, unleashed a war against musical experimentation and against me personally. Given the lack of solid aesthetic and artistic arguments, they opted—some more directly and others more covertly—to give the matter a political and ideological character and opened a campaign that confused some well-meaning but unintelligent officials. Obviously this created difficulties for me that were attenuated by the attitude of more intelligent officials with the help of whom, and the support of intellectuals of the prestige of Alejo Carpentier, I was able to overcome the obstacles that came my way and, little by little, carry out electroacoustic music practice to the degree of irreversibility that it presents today.[30]

---

[26] "El desarrollo de la ciencia y la técnica contemporáneas en el campo de los sonidos, crea una verdadera revolución en el orden musical, y hace posible que los compositores que se han decidido a aplicarla en sus obras obtengan sonoridades inusitadas, no logradas hasta ahora ni siquiera en las obras más atrevidas compuestas para orquesta sinfónica o cualquier otro medio sonoro convencional." *Revolución*, February 5, 1964, reproduced in Rodríguez Alpízar, "Juan Blanco y la profecía del sonido futuro," 46.

[27] "los pilares de lo más transgresor en materia musical," Ibid., 46.

[28] Ibid., 46.

[29] Ibid., 47.

[30] "Inmediatamente después de que ofrecí el primer concierto electroacústico en 1964, casi todos los compositores viejos y la mayor parte de los del antiguo Grupo de Renovación Musical, por ignorancia o por inmovilismo reaccionario, desataron una guerra contra la experimentación musical y contra mí personalmente. Ante la carencia de argumentos sólidos en el orden estético y artístico, optaron—unos más directa y otros más solapadamente—por darle carácter político e ideológico al asunto y abrieron una campaña que confundió a algunos funcionarios de buena fe pero poco inteligentes. Obviamente esto me creó dificultades que fueron atenuadas por la actitud

196 CUBAN MUSIC COUNTERPOINTS

Speaking about the classical music scene in Cuba after 1959, Blanco noted that the dominating trend among the most modern Cuban composers was neoclassicism with Cuban music elements, remarking "I never went through that stage,"[31] although my analysis of his *Quinteto No. 1* in chapter 2 suggests otherwise. He had grown tired of the same approaches and confided in Alejo Carpentier, who shared his frustration. Every Thursday, Blanco and other like-minded musicians would gather at Carpentier's house for listening and discussion sessions of new music, in particular the latest developments in Central Europe, such as *Kontakte* (1960) by Stockhausen, and *Le voile d'Orphee* (1953) by Pierre Henry. Carpentier also turned Blanco to Pierre Schaffer's *In Search of a Concrete Music* (1952), which was incredibly influential on the Cuban composer.[32] In several interviews and writings Blanco emphasized the importance of Pierre Shaffer and Luigi Nono to his aesthetic and compositional development during these years. Along with Brouwer, who had similar interests after attending the Warsaw Autumn Music Festival, and conductor Manuel Duchesne Cuzán, the three began promoting new music through the Orquesta Sinfónica Nacional de Cuba (OSN). Initially, composers who had been members of the Grupo de Renovación Musical opposed the daring avant-garde and experimental approaches that Blanco and his close colleagues promoted, but this opposition did not last long: nearly every composer from the GRM later dabbled in electroacoustic, serial, indeterminate, or graphic score composition. In a 2005 interview Blanco went as far as to state "I think that if this [the new music concerts in the early 1960s] hadn't happened, we would still be composing habaneras," implicitly criticizing the overtly nationalist and neoclassical approaches of the GRM.[33] Unfortunately most of the early electroacoustic works that were recorded in the 1960s on magnetic tapes were lost in the 1970s, when they were reused due to a scarcity of materials resulting from the country's economic crisis.[34]

In the 1980s we see a flourishing of activity in electroacoustic music composition, as evidenced in the surge of EGREM-produced LP releases of original electroacoustic works by Cuban composers and the proliferation of concerts and festivals of electroacoustic music. With the establishment of the Estudio

---

de funcionarios más inteligentes con la ayuda de quienes y el apoyo de intelectuales del prestigio de Alejo Carpentier, pude ir venciendo los escollos que me salían al paso y, poco a poco, llevar la práctica musical electroacústica al grado de irreversibilidad que hoy presenta." Layda Ferrando, "Separata: Juan Blanco," *Boletín Música* 51 (2019): 6.

[31] "yo nunca pasé por esa etapa," Marta Ramírez, "Juan Blanco: Aún a la vanguardia," *Clave—Revista Cubana de Música* 4, no. 3 (2002): 35.

[32] José Manuel García and Juan Blanco, "Monólogo de cumpleaños," *Clave—Revista Cubana de Música*, no. 13 (1989): 3–5.

[33] "Creo que si esto no hubiera ocurrido todavía estaríamos haciendo habaneras." Ramírez, "Juan Blanco: Aún a la vanguardia," 35.

[34] Güeche, "Breve Caracterización de La Música Electroacústica En Cuba," 151.

Electroacústico sponsored by the Instituto Cubano de Amistad con los Pueblos (ICAP), (eventually known as Taller ICAP de Música Electroacústica (TIME) and later renamed Laboratorio Nacional de Música Electroacústica (LNME)), a younger generation of composers had a space with newer equipment and Blanco as a teacher and mentor who led lectures and workshops on "[the] history of electroacoustic music [and] classical composition techniques, based on works for concrete sources and analog electronic equipment."[35] This new generation of Cuban composers trained by Blanco at TIME included Miguel Bonachea, Mirtha de la Torre, Fernando Rodríguez, Marieta Veulens, Edesio Alejandro, José M. García, Jorge Maletá, and Juan Piñera, along with Jesús Ortega, Calixto Álvarez, and Héctor Angulo, older composers who had already been active in this area.[36] One of the most notable composers of this younger generation was Juna Piñera, who has now served as composition professor for decades. In 1984 he was awarded the First Prize in the Experimental Music International Competition of Bourges. In 1988, two of the five first prizes in music composition awarded by the UNEAC went to Piñera for *Como naufragio* and *Germinal* (for symphony orchestra and for electroacoustic composition, respectively). Julio Roloff received the first prize in the wind ensemble category for *Leyenda No. 1*, and Magaly Ruiz received the first prize in the solo instrument category for *Estudios* for piano. Both Roloff and Ruiz were active throughout the late 1970s and 1980s, receiving prizes and premieres of their works by major national ensembles. Roloff relocated to South Florida in 1993, and Ruiz, who has remained on the island, has taught music theory and composition at the ISA, the Instituto Superior Pedagógico Enrique José Varona, and the Conservatorio Alejandro García Caturla.

At the close of the decade, the Instituto Superior de Arte (ISA) could finally count with a dedicated space and equipment for electroacoustic music composition instruction in its Miramar facilities. The ISA established the Estudio de Música Electroacústica y por Computadoras (EMEC, Electronic Music Studios) in 1989 under the direction of Carlos Fariñas (the studio is now named after Fariñas). At ISA's EMEC another generation of distinguished composers has since trained, including Julio García Ruda, Ileana Pérez Velázquez, Jorge Maletá, Carlos Puig, Eduardo Morales, Elio Villafranca, Ailem Carvajal, Orestes Águila, Janet Rodríguez, Irina Escalante Chernova, Teresa Núñez, Mónica O'Reilly, and Jesús Morales.[37] A salient aspect is the increased participation of women in the composition programs, in particular in the electronic music courses.

---

[35] "historia de música electroacústica, técnicas de realización clásicas, basadas en creaciones para fuentes concretas y equipos electrónicos analógicos." Eli Rodríguez and Güeche, "Caminos de la Electroacústica en Cuba," 27.

[36] Ibid., 27.

[37] Ibid., 27.

198   CUBAN MUSIC COUNTERPOINTS

Due to the scarcity of electronic instruments, most of the works created in the 1960s were composed using *musique concrète* techniques. The most common sources for *musique concrète* in the 1960s were acoustic instruments (mostly guitar, piano, and percussion), voice (singing or declaimed), and "other sources such as machines or ambient sounds."[38] The oscillator dominated electronic compositions in the 1970s, while synthesizers entered the scene in 1980s,[39] most especially the Mini Moog, Roland Jupiter 8, Moog Sonic Six, and Yamaha CS 70 M synthesizers.[40] The NeXT computer was introduced at the LNME in 1992. Sampling technique was introduced in 1990–1991, with *Palmas* (voice sampling) by Roberto Valera and *Efí-efó* (abakuá drums sampling) by Julio García Ruda.[41] All three stages share what Güeche notes as an economy of means or media: the equipment, the sources of sounds, and syntheses and processes of elaboration of these sources are all reduced or limited.[42] She also notes a series of compositional principles to which most composers adhere: cellular principle (using a small cell as the point of departure for composing the works); principle of recurrence (repetition); ternary principle (form); principle of alternation; principle of elaboration (variation); principle of fusion with images as dramaturgical elements; and principle of fusion of languages (use of traditional or conventional compositional devices with more experimental ones).[43] Güeche also notes that classical composers in Cuba use similar structural procedures (development, variation, tripartite structure) regardless of their choice of media or sonic source, equipment, or technology: most Cuban composers who specialize in electroacoustic music also write for acoustic instruments and ensembles.[44] These structural procedures, also common in non-electronic works, usually begin with a cell (a melodic motive, a timbre or pitch) that is transformed in the development section through procedures chosen by the composer, such as Fariña's *Aguas Territoriales* (discussed below).

In spite of a continuity in the use of technology and techniques and the principles she outlines, Güeche highlights key differences from the early years of electronic music composition in Cuba and subsequent decades, specifically in terms of aesthetics and conceptualization. While composers in the 1960s strove to break from previous theories and "impose a totally renewing [language]," aided by the incorporation of indeterminacy, serialism, stochasticism—which correlates

---

[38] Güeche, "Breve caracterización de la música electroacústica en Cuba," 153.

[39] Ibid., 152.

[40] Ibid., 154.

[41] Based on these shifts in electronic music production, Güeche periodizes electronic music in Cuba into three stages: the 1960s characterized by music concrete; the 1970s as a mixed period where composers combined concrete and electronically produced sounds; and the 1980s and early 1990s as a fully electronic period. Ibid., 154.

[42] Ibid., 155–156.

[43] Ibid., 156–157.

[44] Eli Rodríguez and Güeche, "Caminos de la electroacústica en Cuba," 27.

with my analyses of non-electronic musics in chapter 3—the composers of the 1980s and early 1990s employed a more traditional language that appealed to listeners, a shift in electronic music that I identify as overlapping with the post-modern turn in Western Europe and the United States.[45] By including recognizable citations of known works from popular, folk, and classical music with other more experimental techniques, composers engaged in more overtly "postmodern" aesthetics, that have since ruled Cuban classical composition.[46] This is not to say that in the 1960s composers didn't care about connecting or reaching their audiences or that after 1980 composers didn't continue on the experimental path forged by earlier composers. On the contrary, as we saw earlier, in the 1960s and 1970s Blanco showed a deep interest in connecting with his audience and explaining to listeners the meaning behind his works, as he did in his pre- and post-concert talks. Both *vanguardista* and postmodernist tendencies continue in electronic composition in Cuba to this day, and this includes the use of Cuban folk instruments either as sampled material or as live acoustic instruments played along an electronic track (be it tape or digital track), such as Juan Blanco's *Cirkus Toccata*.

TIME (Taller ICAP de Música Electroacústica) and the EGREM Albums

The same year that his album was released (1979) Blanco founded the Taller ICAP de Música Electroacústica (TIME) under the sponsorship of the Instituto Cubano de Amistad con los Pueblos (ICAP) and the auspices of the Instituto Cubano de la Música. In a 2015 article composer Fernando A. Rodríguez Alpízar recalled how in the late 1970s he and other young composition students who had graduated from the Escuela Nacional de Arte and the Conservatorio Amadeo Roldán approached Juan Blanco to learn more about electroacoustic composition. As mentioned above, sound recording facilities were only found at the state-run television, film, and radio studios, much like the European models, and served as institutional spaces where composers could work on electroacoustic works. Rodríguez Alpízar noted that he and his colleagues went to the radio studios and eventually received formal training from Blanco at the Electronic Music Studios of the ICAP (TIME).[47] One of the main functions of the TIME/LNME has been to organize and host an international electronic music festival in Varadero, known as *Primavera en Varadero*, first held in 1981. In 1998 the festival

---

[45] Güeche, "Breve caracterización de la música electroacústica en Cuba," 157.
[46] Ibid., 159.
[47] Rodríguez Alpízar, "Juan Blanco y la profecía del sonido futuro," 43.

200   CUBAN MUSIC COUNTERPOINTS

was permanently transferred to Havana, and since then it has been known as *Primavera en La Habana*. The LNME's main objective was to promote the creation and dissemination of electronic music by Cuban composers. In more recent years the LNME has broadened its scope to also include the promotion of electronic music by local and international EDM DJs and producers. The LNME makes available its recording and producing facilities to local composers and DJs and to composition professors and their students for educational purposes. The LNME also fosters collaborations between electronic music composers and artists in other artistic disciplines, including theater, ballet, modern dance, and visual arts. Both the Festival Primavera en Varadero and a handful of EGREM LPs of electronic music by Cuban composers released throughout the 1980s served to showcase the flourishing electronic music scene in Cuba during this period.

Festival Primavera en Varadero

In April 15–21, 1981, Juan Blanco and the TIME members hosted the first International Festival of Electroacoustic Music "Primavera in Varadero" ("Spring in Varadero"). Organized by Ministerio de Cultura, Comité Cubano del Consejo Internacional de la Música de la UNESCO (CIM), Estudio Electroacústico del Instituto Cubano de Amistad con los Pueblos (ICAP), the UNEAC, and the Instituto Cubano de Radio y Televisión (ICRT), the festival included participants from Mexico, Canada, Denmark, the United States, Spain, Italy, Federal Republic of Germany, and Cuba. Attendees included not only composers and performers, but also musicologists, music critics, and journalists. Guests stayed at the Hotel Internacional of Varadero beach, where festival organizers set up a concert hall with quadrophonic sound reproduction equipment. The promotional materials for the 1983 edition of the Festival included the following description:

> Besides concerts, lectures and discussion sessions, this Festival will feature sonorization of extensive areas near the beach, through sound-light performances of a high artistic level for a massive enjoyment by the public. Participants in this festival may individually or collectively work in sonorization of a section of the abovementioned area. Throughout the Festival, this area will become a great international exhibition of this art form, a true holiday of color and sound.[48]

---

[48] Festival Primavera en Varadero 1981 Brochure.

Table 5.1. Programming of Primavera en Varadero Electronic Music Festival 1981.

Compositions:
Alas, by Wlodzimier Ktonski (Poland)
Rondo, by Jesús Ortega (Cuba)
For John, by Lars Gunnar Bodin (Sweden)
Viols, by Manuel Enríquez (Mexico)
Electronic Sonata, by Lejaren Hiller (USA)
Psaume pour abri, by Pier Mercure (Canada)
Mol, by Mercelle Derchenes (Canada)
Visione, by Bent Lorentzen (Denmark)
Da Niente, by Gunner Moller Pedersen (Denmark)
Galaxia M-50, by Juan Blanco (Cuba)
Conjuro, by Manuel Enríquez (Mexico)
Progetto Secondo, by Fausto Razzi (Italy)
Winter Leaves, by Lauro Graziani (Italy)
Grochi di velocite, by Roberto Doati (Italy)
Conditional Assemblies, by Jares Dashow (Italy)
La tierra que nos vio nacer, by Fernando Rodríguez (Cuba)
Paz, meditación y metáfora, by Marietta Veulens (Cuba)

La extraña balada del juego inconcluso, by Juan Marcos Blanco (Cuba)
Conceirto-espectáculo, by Carles Santos (Spain)
Furia-calma, multimedia by Juan Blanco (Cuba)
Música de papel, multimedia by Leo Brouwer (Cuba)
Madrigal, multimedia by Carlos Fariñas (Cuba)

Lectures:
—Sonorizaciones de exteriors urbanos y rurales, by Juan Blanco (Cuba)
—Las computadoras en la música, by Lejaren Hiller (USA)
—La música electroacústica en Dinamarca, by Gunner Moller Pedersen (Denmark)
—Música y computadoras en Italia, by Alvise Vidolin (Italy)

Discussion session:
"Música electroacústica: lenguaje y comunicación"

The festival's name was a play on the Warsaw Autumn Music Festival through which, as discussed in chapter 3, Cuban composers became familiar with the international avant-garde scene in the early 1960s. This was one more way in which Blanco promoted revolutionary Cuba as a fertile ground for aesthetic innovation, a meeting place for electroacoustic music composers from around the world, listed in Table 5.1.

The selection of the location was strategic; Varadero's beaches had already been used to draw audiences for other International Music festivals, such as the Festival de la Canción.[49] Not ones to shy away from mixing work with pleasure, in the 1983 promotional booklet Festival organizers noted that the festival's location allowed "participants and attendees to combine the event's official activities with the enjoyment of one of the best beaches in the world,"[50] enticing potential visitors through the lure of one of the most pristine beaches in the world. Over the years, the festival and the LNME hosted foreign composers who delivered

[49] Moore, *Music and Revolution,* 71.
[50] "La celebración del Encuentro en la playa de Varadero propició que los participantes y visitantes pudieran conjugar las actividades propias del evento con el disfrute de un de las mejores playas del mundo," Festival Primavera en Varadero 1981 Brochure.

202   CUBAN MUSIC COUNTERPOINTS

lectures and workshops, including Luigi Nono, Jon Appleton, Tomas Kessler, Gabriel Brnčić, Andrew Schloss, Luigi Abbate, and Leo Kupper.[51] Primavera en Varadero was a truly international music festival with participation of composers not only from countries that had been Cuban allies since 1959—such as Mexico and Poland—but also Lejaren Hiller from the United States. This inclusion, not only of a performance of an electroacoustic work by Hiller but also his lecture on the use of computers in music composition, hinted at a relative improvement in US–Cuban relations—a short window of diplomatic normalization during Jimmy Carter's administration that was quickly closed with Ronald Reagan's reversal of Carter's policies on Cuba and the Mariel Boatlift crisis. Furthermore, in 1986, US musicologist Neil Leonard III visited Cuba for the Festival Primavera en Varadero, along with a few other US musicologists who were hosted by the ICAP.[52] Leonard would go on to visit Cuba repeatedly in connection to the electronic music festival, writing about the festival and the Cuban electroacoustic music scene for US-based journals and magazines, emphasizing for US readers—and sometimes admitting his own amazement—this genre's development in Cuba and the Cuban composers' achievements in spite of the economic and material challenges imposed by the US embargo. When asked in 2002 about the significance of the electronic music festivals, Blanco responded that "they've meant that there is a worldwide positive awareness and opinion of contemporary musical art in Cuba."[53] The Festival Primavera en Varadero allowed Cuban composers, even well-established ones like Blanco, to expand their artistic networks; they forged connections with composers from around the world through a shared interest in a compositional approach that was becoming increasingly accessible thanks to technological advancements. Furthermore, by combining some of the performances with light displays, Blanco continued the collaborative and collective (two pillars of Cuba's socialist-revolutionary ideology) artistic work he had carried out since the 1950s, when he provided the film score for *El Mégano* (1956), discussed in chapter 2.

Electronic Music Releases by the EGREM

In addition to the Primavera en Varadero Festival, the EGREM's release of several albums of electroacoustic music by Cuban composers, listed in Table 5.2, circulated Cuban electroacoustic music to a much wider audience than concerts

---

[51] Eli Rodríguez and Güeche, "Caminos de la electroacústica en Cuba," 27.

[52] Neil Leonard III, "Juan Blanco: Cuba's Pioneer of Electroacoustic Music," *Computer Music Journal* 21, no. 2 (1997): 10.

[53] "Los festivales han significado que exista mundialmente un conocimiento y una opinión positiva sobre el arte musical contemporáneo de Cuba." Ramírez, "Juan Blanco: Aún a la vanguardia," 36.

"HACIA NUEVOS HORIZONTES" 203

Table 5.2. LPs of electroacoustic music by Cuban composers released by the EGREM between 1979 and 1989.

1979: Juan Blanco, *Contemporáneos 4*	*Música para un joven mártir* (Homenaje a Conrado Benítez); *Galaxia M-50; Desde su voz amada* (Homenaje a V.I. Lenin); *Estructuras*
1981: Carlos Fariñas, *Aguas territoriales*	*Madrigal; Aguas territoriales*
1984: Juan Marcos Blanco, *Caballos Música Electroacústica*	*Trotes, Canción equina, Sueños, Amanecer, La doma, Nostalgia, La fuga, La manada*
1984: *Música Electroacústica*	Juan Piñera and Edesio Alejandro, *Tres de Dos;* Julio Roloff, *Halley 86;* Juan Marcos Blanco, *Ritual.*
1986: Juan Blanco—*Música Electroacústica*	*Cirkus Toccata, Tañidos, Espacios II*
1987: *Música Electroacústica (TIME)—Jóvenes Compositores Cubanos*	Fernando Rodríguez, *El otro huevo de la serpiente;* José Manuel García Suárez, *Nidia;* Miguel Bonachea, *El peldaño omitido, El primer abrazo.*
1987: *Juan Blanco—Música Electroacústica*	*Suite de los niños* composed at the GMEB of Bourges in 1984. Dedicated to Françoise Barrière; *Suite erótica* composed between 1979 and 1986.

and festivals could reach. In addition to disseminating the music, the albums also preserved these works in an unprecedented manner. These releases included not only the works of the older mentors of TIME, Juan Blanco and Carlos Fariñas, but also more recent compositions by the younger generation of composers. One of Blanco's sons, Juan Marcos Blanco, released a full solo album, while most of the other albums consisted of compilations of works by several composers. The other composers included in this series were Juan Piñera, Julio Roloff, Edesio Alejandro, Mirtha de la Torre, and Fernando Rodríguez. In spite of ongoing activities in electroacoustic music compositions since the mid-1960s, the first commercial albums of electronic music by Cuban composers weren't released until 1979, with Blanco's debut album discussed above, soon followed by Fariñas's *Aguas territoriales* and subsequent releases throughout the 1980s.

Although a full analysis of each of the albums and works listed in the Table 5.2 is beyond the scope of this chapter, some key aspects are worth noting. The composers and works included in these LPs showcased both the older, first generation of composers who worked in this medium, as well as the new generation who trained with them throughout the 1970s and congregated at the TIME studios. Some of the works

204   CUBAN MUSIC COUNTERPOINTS

engaged with similar topics to the ones Blanco had explored in his album, such as Roloff's *Halley 86*, written in 1984 in anticipation of Halley Comet's near orbit to earth in 1986. In the more political work *El otro huevo de la serpiente* ("The Serpent's Other Egg"), Fernando Rodríguez transformed excerpts of recordings of Schoenberg's *A Survivor from Warsaw*. In the title, Rodríguez alluded to Ingmar Bergman's 1977 film *The Serpent's Egg*, where the Jewish genocide at the hands of the Nazis is criticized, but Rodríguez's intention was to highlight the irony in that the victims now were the people of Palestine at the hands of the state of Israel.[54] Rodríguez's and Roloff's compositions were also presented in the 1984 Mexico–Cuba Electronic Music Festival, another instance of electronic music exchanges with composers from countries who had been strong allies of the Cuban socialist-revolutionary state.

Carlos Fariñas and *Aguas Territoriales* (1980)

Well before the release of his first fully electroacoustic solo album, *Aguas Territoriales* (1980), Carlos Fariñas had been experimenting with electroacoustic composition through various projects since the 1960s. Initially, writing for films, including, *La canción del turista* from 1968 and *Posición uno* (documentary by Rogelio París), Fariñas eventually followed in Blanco's footsteps by compositing his first multimedia work in 1973, *Diálogos*, for magnetic tape, visual projections and audience participation, followed by *Corales* (1973) and the film score for *Mella* (1975), where he electronically transforms the sounds of batá drums.[55] He was among the few Cuban composers who would spend extended periods of time studying or doing artistic residencies abroad, including a residency at the Berliner Künstlerprogramm between 1975 and 1977, a privilege that attests to his artistic talent and his political commitment to the Revolution. In a 1986 interview, reflecting on his work as a film music composer, Fariñas explained that when preparing to write a film score, he would "at the same time investigate, soak up the genres and styles of the times, folklore of Cuba and other countries, 'fashionable' music, military marches, street congas, and compose music for such environments, and dabble in jazz, rock and roll, compose boleros, songs, *sones*, and, of course, the central musical ideas that characterize the conflict, whether expressed in the objective images of the plot or at a sociological level."[56] Fariñas's

---

[54]   Concert program for the II Encuentro Mexico-Cubano de Música Electrónica, Mayo 1984.

[55]   Eli Rodríguez and Güeche, "Caminos de la electroacústica en Cuba," 25.

[56]   "A la vez indagar empaparme de géneros y estilos de épocas, del folclor cubano y de otros países, músicas de 'moda,' marchas militares, congas callejeras, y componer música para tales ambientes, e incursionar en el jazz, el rock and roll, componer boleros, canciones, sones, y, desde luego, las ideas musicales centrales caracterizadoras del conflicto, ya sea expresado en las imágenes objetivas del mismo, ya en su plano sociológico." Carlos Fariñas, "Reflexiones a un cuarto de siglo," *Clave—Revista Cubana de Música*, no. 1 (1986): 29.

"HACIA NUEVOS HORIZONTES" 205

comment echoes the discourse Brouwer and Blanco deployed throughout the 1960s and 1970s—as discussed in chapters 3 and 4—wherein they defended Cuban composers' absorption and manipulation of diverse sources and music traditions in service of a given composition's function, in this case film music.

In a 1999 interview, Fariñas expressed a particularly postmodern attitude towards composition and nationalist music, where he quoted fellow Cuban composer Roberto Valera:

> Roberto Valera says—I always quote him because he says very true things with a great sense of humor—"I don't wear a *guayabera* when I sit down to compose; I wear a shirt, or I do it without it [a shirt]." The same thing happens to me, I don't dress as a Cuban to write music. That is one of the features that differentiate "nationalism" from the man who uses the language of a given time period.[57]

He later added, "in my work there are elements that can be identified as belonging to Cuban traditions; there are others that are more distant; and I have others that if they were passed through a nationality humidor, according to what some consider 'Cuban,' it would be concluded that I am very far from our nationality, and some would accuse me of [having been] 'Germanized.'"[58] These statements coincide with Brouwer's omnivorous aesthetic predilections, while also rejecting the notion that to be considered a Cuban composer his work had to include overt references to Cuban musical traditions. Fariñas also drew comparisons to works in visual art that, even though they do not depict "a palm tree or hut," are clearly by a Cuban artist because of how they are constructed.[59] Through their writings from the 1960s, 1970s, 1980s, and even late 1990s, Brouwer, Blanco, and Fariñas constantly justified their compositional practices by defending the composer's freedom to employ whichever compositional techniques they considered most appropriate in a given work. They all claimed their music to be inherently Cuban by virtue of being written by a Cuban composer; for them, their works didn't need to sound Cuban in a nationalist vein to prove the Cubanness of their creators.

---

[57] "Dice Roberto Valera—siempre lo cito porque dice cosas muy ciertas con un tremendo sentido del humor: 'Yo no me pongo guayabera cuando me siento a componer; me pongo camisa, o lo hago sin ella.' Me sucede lo mismo, no me visto de cubano para escribir música. Ese es uno de los rasgos que diferencian al 'nacionalismo' del hombre que utiliza el lenguaje de una epoca." Yarelis Domínguez Benejam, "Carlos Fariñas: No me visto de Cubano para componer," *Clave—Revista Cubana de Música* 1, no. 2 (1999): 4.

[58] "En mi obra hay elementos que se pueden identificar como pertenecientes a tradiciones cubanas, hay otras que estan más distantes, y tengo otras que si las pasaran por un humidor de nacionalidad, según lo que algunos consideran como 'lo cubano,' se concluiría que estoy muy alejado de nuestra nacionalidad, y me acusarían de 'germanizado.'" Domínguez Benejam, "Carlos Fariñas: No me visto de Cubano para componer," 4.

[59] Ibid.

206 CUBAN MUSIC COUNTERPOINTS

Their viewpoint was one of Cuban composers who strived to be in dialog with the outside world, to be part of a global network of composers, and to be respected as both Cuban and universal. These views, along with an understanding that the *function* of a given piece of music dictates which styles, techniques, and genres need to be employed—as he explains in his piece on film music composition—reinforce Cuban composers' practices spanning several decades as I have outlined throughout this book, mainly the multiple and varied sources of musical and artistic inspiration and a denial of a need to sound "Cuban." This attitude is exemplified in the electroacoustic work *Aguas territoriales*.

In *Aguas territoriales* (1981) for magnetic tape, Fariñas takes the sound of a drop of water as the source of the entire work. Fariñas then manipulates the drop of water's recording's timbre through six speed variables, filtering of high, medium and low frequency partials, reverb, filtering through gates, and delay, all mixed through sixteen tracks.[60] Through the re-exposition of timbral/thematic cells, the listener can perceive a quasi-ternary form.[61] The work begins with a nearly imperceptible series of drops of water that grow louder and multiply. When one listens using stereophonic playback, the spatiality of the drops takes over, immersing the listener in the liquid sonority. The drops are manipulated, their reverb filtered, becoming less liquid and more electronic, as though the drops are charged with an electric current, panning from right to left. The reverb grows, suggesting a large echo chamber. After a climax of textural saturation, Fariñas works his way back through the process, ending with the single drop of water with which the work started. The circular aspect of the work, an audible process of transformation of the original sonic sources and a return to the original, recalls both minimalist and postminimalist procedures, and also the cyclical structures of Afro-Cuban religious percussive practices, such as toques de batá, which he had recorded and altered in previous electroacoustic works. Fariñas drew inspiration from Luis Martínez Pedro's painting series titled *Aguas Territoriales* (1963–1973, which was used for Fariñas's LP cover art) and *Ojos y desnudos del mar* (1970), dedicating this composition to the Cuban painter. Martínez Pedro's paintings feature several shades of blue forming round shapes and lines that lead the viewer to focus on circular movement. The liner notes included in the LP jacket further explain:

> The work starts from the real sound, evocative of the soft beat of the water against the coast, towards a culminating center of maximum timbral transformation and dramatic concentration, evocative of the deep tension of the

---

[60] Carlos Fariñas, *Aguas Territoriales / Musica Electroacustica*. Vol. LD-4230. Havana: Areito, 1981. Liner notes by Hiario González.

[61] Eli Rodríguez and Güeche, "Caminos de la electroacústica en Cuba," 28.

great marine abysses "in which, in the most solemn silence, life germinates and boils ... The use of a single sound source registered in only one of its possibilities was an a priori self-imposed challenge, with the purpose of obtaining the most diverse results in the processing of timbre and expression, through a complex work of electronic elaboration of a purely concrete source."[62]

This description of *Aguas territoriales* echoes how Martínez Pedro's paintings have been described as also immersing the spectator through a whirlpool effect.[63] Just like viewers may experience anxiety or tranquility while observing Martínez Pedro's painting, so too can listeners expeirence a variety of he feelings when encountering Fariña's composition. Water can satiate, give life, heal, nurture, and soothe, as much as it can flood, drown, pull, beat, and destroy everything in its path. Fariñas's album, along with Blanco's *Contemporáneos*, opened the flood gates for electronic music composition in Cuba. Like a constant drop of water carving a stone, the incessant activities of these older composers in the realm of electroacoustic composition eventually led to carving spaces, festivals, and LP releases solely dedicated to electronic music composition and dissemination.

Conclusion

The specifically Cuban approach to experimentation we saw in Brouwer's earlier works and Juan Blanco's electroacoustic pieces, one marked by quotation, collage, eclecticism, and a disregard for hierarchies and divisions between "classical" and "popular" lent itself to useful reinterpretation and incorporation into the broad umbrella term *postmodernism*. By the end of the decade Brouwer would go on to reconcile these Cuban artistic and compositional practices with the newly emerging theories on postmodernism among the European and US intellectual and artistic elite through his lectures and publications. In his seminal 1989 article Brouwer claimed to use the term postmodernism because it allowed him to deal with the "absolute freedom that pluralism gives in terms of artistic culture."[64]

---

[62] "La obra parte del sonido real, evocador del suave batir del agua contra la costa, hacia un centro culminatorio de máxima transformación tímbrica y concentración dramática, evocador de la profunda tensión de los grandes abismos marinos 'en los cuales, en el más solemne silencio, germina y hierve la vida," nos dice el autor, quien añade: "La utilización de una fuente sonora única registrada en una sola de sus posibilidades, fue un reto autoimpuesto a prioir, con el propósito de obtener los más diversos resultados en el proceso del timbre y la expresión, mediante un complejo trabajo de elaboración electrónica de una fuente puramente conreta." Fariñas, *Aguas Territoriales / Musica Electroacustica*.

[63] "Pedro, Luís Martínez (1910–1989): Territorial Waters, 1967: The UNESCO Works of Art Collection." http://www.unesco.org/artcollection/NavigationAction.do?idOeuvre=3074 (accessed June 14, 2021).

[64] "lo cual me permite tartar este momento lleno de absoluta libertad que da el prulasimo en términos de cultura artística." He expanded on this topic in an article for the Cuban music magazine

208   CUBAN MUSIC COUNTERPOINTS

In explaining the title of his article, "Música, folclor, contemporaneidad y postmodernismo" ("Music, folklore, contemporaneity, and postmodernism"),[65] Brouwer admitted that he meant to be provocative, to raise questions and instigate a discussion. The 1989 article was an expanded version of a lecture Brouwer presented in 1988 at the Akademie der Kunst in East Berlin, which was noted in the essay's publication; therefore, although published in Spanish in a Cuban music journal, the original context of the lecture was an influential foreign artistic and intellectual institution, imbuing Brouwer's essay with weight and legitimacy. In Brouwer's assessment Latin American composers employed stylistic elements that were not accepted or adopted by the Central European classical music tradition because the roots of the musical language employed by Latin American composers were foreign to European and US composers.[66] Brouwer then defined postmodernism, not as what follows modernism, but as a "critique of modernism *within* modernism."[67] He quoted Mexican poet Octavio Paz (1914–1998) to illustrate this point: "acceleration is fusion; all the times and all the spaces coincide in the here and the now."[68] By citing this passage, Brouwer argued that the fast pace of the modern world led to an artistic and cultural fusion in which multiple and disparate aesthetic and cultural approaches can coexist in one single artwork.[69]

Brouwer pointed to one of his own compositions as a musical example of postmodernism: *La tradición se rompe . . .* (discussed in chapter 3), explaining that "it corresponds to the previously referred to notion, to the simultaneous, to the contraposition of forms that are culturally diverse, even opposites, in a certain way."[70] Brouwer then referred to Cuban novelist and musicologist Alejo Carpentier's description of *lo criollo*—that which is born in the New World, whether of Spanish or African ancestry—to explain how Cuban art is inextricably postmodern. Specifically, Brouwer summarizes *lo criollo* "as sum, as integration, plurality, mix—and, therefore *richness* . . . It is about reducing them [the factors] to common factors [of postmodernism and the *criollo*]: the mix, the link, opposition, different simultaneous languages, plurality of styles, the use of *kitsch*

Clave based on a lecture he delivered in 1988 at the Akademie der Kunst in East Berlin. Brouwer, "Música, folclor, contemporaneidad y postmodernismo," *Clave—Revista Cubana de Música*, no. 13 (1989): 53.

[65]   Ibid., 53–55.
[66]   Ibid., 53–55.
[67]   "es una crítca del modernismo *dentro* del modernismo." Ibid., 54.
[68]   "Aceleración y fusión; todos los tiempose y todos los espacios confluyen en un aquí y un ahora." Ibid., 54.
[69]   This kind of cyclical cosmology is exemplified by Fariñas's *Aguas Territoriales*.
[70]   "Una obra sinfónica que corresponde a la noción antes referrida, a lo simultáneo, a la contraposición de formas culturalmente diversas y hasta opuestas, en cierto modo." Se titula *La tradición se rompe . . . pero cuesta trabajo* (1967–1969)." Ibid., 54.

"HACIA NUEVOS HORIZONTES" 209

as possibly transcending aesthetic value, etcetera."[71] Brouwer links Carpentier's conceptualization of *lo criollo*, which builds upon Carpentier's definition and description of *lo barroco americano*, to postmodernism through the common traits of hybridity, plurality of styles and languages, and even *kitsch* (which I consider one possible element of Cuban *choteo*). While admitting that he didn't know how to categorize *La tradición se rompe*... at the time he composed it, by the end of the 1980s, however, Brouwer was finally able to classify it by connecting definitions of postmodernism to Carpentier's theories and observations on Latin American culture and its idiosyncrasies. Brouwer concluded the article by citing José Martí, the most famous and preeminent revolutionary figure of the first revolutionary struggle for independence, a figure that had been beatified by the Cuban socialist-revolutionary regime, quoting "Injértese en nuestras repúblicas el mundo; pero el tronco ha de ser de nuestras repúblicas" (Graft the world into our republics, but the trunk/rootsock must be of our republics). This botanical metaphor, which I quote as the introduction's epigraph, was apt for Cuban composers such as Brouwer, who conceived of their work as idiosyncratically Cuban at their rootstock, yet flexible and adaptable enough to graft onto it quotations, techniques, and styles created by composers from all cultural backgrounds and time periods. In keeping with his newly found postmodernist attitude—characterized by blurring and erasing hierarchical boundaries between classical, popular, and folk music, the use of folk, irony, and kitsch, and an eclectic musical style—Brouwer turned to a more accessible musical language that, while maintaining some of his irreverential borrowing of well-known excerpts from the Western Classical music tradition, appealed to diverse listeners and performers through his incorporation of varied musical styles and techniques. This new style is exemplified in works such as *Canción de Gesta* (1980–1981) and *Manuscrito antiguo encontrado en una botella* (1983).

Through the concepts and theories of postmodernism that were developed by intellectuals in Western Europe and the United States, Brouwer was able to articulate for a foreign audience and readership key aspects about Cuban artistic production and aesthetics that had characterized his (and other Cuban composers') works in prior decades. It's not that the development of postmodernist theories made Cuban art all of a sudden postmodern, but rather that Cuban (and much of Latin American) art was already postmodern due to its colonial history and condition, in which an amalgam of cultures defied Western European modes of thinking and making sense of the world. Cuban and Latin American art were (and are) characterized by a bricolage of time periods, religious practices, ethnic

---

[71] "Lo –criollo– como suma, es integración, pluralidad, mezcla—y por tanto, *riqueza*—en fin... Se trata solo de una reducción de factores communes: la mezcla, el enlace, la oposición, distintas lenguas simultáneas, pluralidad de estilos, uso de *kitsch* como valor estético posiblemente trascendente, etcétera." Ibid., 55.

210   CUBAN MUSIC COUNTERPOINTS

and racial intermingling that give birth to a new culture that is always in the making, never a finished product. Through the theorization of the postmodern condition, a coming to terms with drastic shifts in the relationship between subjects and art, Western European and Anglo-centric thought caught up with the disjointed existence of the majority of the Western Hemisphere. Brouwer simply deployed the newly developed term to help himself and other Cuban composers relate their creative output to composers, musicians, and critics outside Cuba, an effort to translate Cuban aesthetic practices into non-Cuban terms in order to extend intellectual dialogue as well as their own artistic networks.

The history of electroacoustic music composition in Cuba reveals how a technologically conscribed genre, highly dependent on equipment, raw materials, and skilled knowledge of the capabilities and limits of said equipment and materials, allowed Cuban composers to dialogue with like-minded composers abroad. The changing economic and political circumstances that "opened up" Cuba to foreign visitors in the 1980s also facilitated the exchange of works and ideas between Cuban composers and their international interlocutors. The EGREM LP releases, the foundation of TIME, and the Primavera en Varadero Festivals all attest to electronic music's appeal and efficacy as a site for exchange and artistic networking. Given the nascent global and postmodern perspectives of the 1980s, Cuban composers creating avant-garde and experimental music in a socialist-revolutionary context didn't seem as paradoxical to composers, musicians, and audiences outside of Cuba. The eclecticism, hybridity, social-political engagement, humor, and kitsch (among many other traits) that had characterized Cuban classical music for decades could finally be understood by global audiences because Western theories of postmodernism helped explicate non-Western epistemologies. The expansion of their global artistic network throughout the 1980s would serve most of these composers in the ensuing post-Soviet crisis. After the dissolution of the Soviet Union in 1991 many of the younger composers who were not as firmly established left Cuba in search of more promising careers and economic conditions. Even those who had become fixtures of the Cuban artistic elite would seek temporary career opportunities abroad. These permanent and temporary departures have only expanded Cuban composers' global networks, with the individuals who live abroad serving as active nodes that maintain constant contact with Cuban composers on the island and throughout the global Cuban diaspora. Many of the EGREM LP releases listed throughout this chapter have been digitized and are available through various official and unofficial channels. TIME is still a hub for electroacoustic music composition, now renamed Laboratorio Nacional de Música Electroacústica (LNME). The Primavera en Varadero Festivals have moved to Havana and continues to attract electroacoustic composers and EDM DJs from abroad. These projects have endured in spite of dire political and economic conditions in post-Soviet Cuba because of the artistic vision and indefatigable networking of a collective of composers who accrued the cultural capital necessary to promote their view of what Cuban contemporary classical music could sound like.

Epilogue

Unending and Repeating Coda—El "período especial" que nunca termina/The Never-Ending Special Period

In October 2011, as a PhD student working at the Latin American Music Center (LAMC) at Indiana University, I had the privilege of meeting three Cuban composers who live in the United States and who were visiting Bloomington Indiana as part of the LAMC's Fiftieth Anniversary Conference. In addition to helping organize the conference I presented a paper on Cuban-US classical music exchanges in which I referred to Cuban composers living in the United States as "exiles." The three Cuban composers in attendance—Tania León, Ileana Pérez Velázquez, and Orlando Jacinto García—objected to my use of the term. This was my first time presenting the research that would lead to my doctoral dissertation and this book to an audience that included Cuban composers. I had grown up in Puerto Rico with the children and grandchildren of Cubans who had left the island in the 1960s and proudly referred to themselves as "exiliados" (exiled). But León, Pérez Velázquez, and García viewed themselves in rather different terms: "exiled" carried a heavy connotation of political dissension with which they did not wish to be associated. It was an eye-opening experience that taught me about the nuanced, generational and individual differences of Cuban migration. Since then, I've been hyper-aware of how Cubans who live outside of the island wish to be represented, while also taking into account that discourses about Cubans in the diaspora are highly dependent on when the individual left the island and when the discourse is articulated. This discourse shifted dramatically after 1991, following the dissolution of the Soviet Union, during the so-called "Special Period in Times of Peace." The term "Cuban diaspora" gained wider acceptance and use than the term "exile," especially for those who had left after 1991, or who, before 1991 had left as children.[1] The last thirty-plus years have been marked by greater—albeit in relative terms given recent events discussed below—ease of circulation for Cubans (and foreigners) from and to the island. This increased mobility is the result of drastic changes in political and economic circumstances, with significant effects on all local Cuban music scenes.

---

[1] Rafael Rojas, *Tumbas sin sosiego: revolución, disidencia y exilio del intelectual cubano* (Mexico City, Mexico; Barcelona: Editorial Anagrama, 2006).

Cuban Music Counterpoints. Marysol Quevedo, Oxford University Press. © Oxford University Press 2023.
DOI: 10.1093/oso/9780197552230.003.0007

EPILOGUE 213

The (Not So) Special Period

After the fall of the Berlin Wall in 1989 and the dissolution of the Soviet Union in 1991, Cuba faced one of its worst economic and social crises since the 1959 Revolution. The end of the Soviet Union also led to the disbanding of the COMECON or CMEA (Council for Mutual Economic Aid, 1949–1991), the Soviet-centered economic aid organization that Cuba joined in 1972. Without the economic aid and imports from the Soviet Union or COMECON members, Cuba was left with no major trade partners or allies. Furthermore, the United States hardened its policies and sanctions against Cuba, through the Cuban Democracy Act (also known as the Torricelli Act, 1992) and Helms-Burton Act (1996), exacerbating the humanitarian crisis. These initial post-Soviet years were called by Fidel Castro as the "período especial en tiempos de paz" ("special period in times of peace"). Due to a shortage of petrol imports (which Cuba obtained nearly exclusively from the Soviet Union until 1991) the Cuban government implemented severe austerity measures, especially in rationing of gasoline, automobile use, food, medical supplies, water and electricity services. Cuba's agricultural industry that relied solely on sugar exports also faced drastic reforms since it couldn't compete with world market prices. Cuba's gross national product (GDP) steeply declined between 1990 and 1993 by 36%. Slowly the government had to identify alternative industries that would generate income, most especially tourism along with external investments. For everyday Cubans the conditions led to unemployment, malnutrition, severe illness, and higher mortality rates. Many sought asylum in the United States with thousands of Cubans arriving at the shores of South Florida in precariously built rafts. The Cuban Rafter Crisis reached its peak in 1994 and it marked one of the largest mass exoduses in recent Cuban history, leading the Clinton administration to instate the now defunct wet-foot/dry-foot policy.[2] Those who stayed and had family abroad began receiving more remittances from family and friends to make ends meet. Many other Cubans circumvented official state suppliers and found alternative avenues for finding basic food and medical supplies, some of which are locally referred to "por la izquierda" or "bolsa negra."

Eventually, the government responded with administrative and legal changes that allowed small private businesses to operate alongside State ones, leading to a small emergent entrepreneurial class. First, the local government depenalized carrying US dollars in 1993. This led to the simultaneous circulation of the Cuban moneda nacional and US dollars. Consequently, the state devised a two-currency system through which one local currency, the moneda nacional, would

---

[2] One of the most famous cases of a rafter incident years later in 1999 was the case of Elián González.

214 CUBAN MUSIC COUNTERPOINTS

be used by Cubans internally, and another one, the peso Cubano convertible (CUC, now retired), would be used for exchange with foreign currency to participate in the international market and supplant the use of US dollars in official transactions. Economic planning went from a central socialist planning model to a socialist market model that is slightly less centralized than previous Cuban models, but far more centralized than say China or Vietnam in recent decades. All of these political and economic changes affected the cultural sector in significant ways.

As Jorge Luis Arcana has commented, Cuban society in the 1990s went through a process of what he terms *"desatanización"* ("desatanizing") and *"desacralización"* ("desacralizing"). By *desatanización* he meant the process of accepting that which had been decried as incommensurate with socialist ideology: the US dollar, exiles, religion, and the past. This *desatanización* is by no means absolute or equal in all sectors of Cuban life, as can be seen in the continued erasure or censorship of musicians who leave the island or who collaborate with foreign multinational companies and producers. By *desacralización* he meant questioning and rejecting the cultural and material products from the Soviet Union, from socialist realism and children's cartoons to Soviet-made technology and equipment.[3] This process led to a revisiting of cultural manifestations that had been deemed capitalist, imperialist, and "yanqui," including hip hop and jazz. In addition the official discourse surrounding Cubans who had left the island shifted, from portraying their efforts as "counterrevolutionary" to a more nuanced view that understood that for many their decision to leave had been prompted by the economic situation and personal family dynamics.[4] In contrast to those who left Cuba in the 1980s beginning with the Mariel Boatlift (a situation marked by trauma discussed in chapter 5), most of the artists who left in the 1990s had a relatively positive attitude towards the Cuban State; when compared to earlier waves of migration, these individuals maintain more contact with their friends and family in Cuba and travel between Cuba and their new adoptive home countries with more frequency.[5] This has also led to more acceptance within Cuba of intellectuals who reside outside the island. Whereas before 1991 intellectuals who left were quickly erased from official accounts—and in the realm of music composers who left were omitted from concert programming and recording projects—since 1991 there has been an effort to reintroduce some of these individuals into the narratives of Cuban cultural history.[6] Such has

---

[3] Jorge Luis Acanda, cited in Joaquín Borges Triana, "Música cubana alternativa: Del margen al epicentro" (IASPM-AL, 2012). 13.

[4] Iván César Morales Flores, *Identidades en proceso. Cinco compositores cubanos de la diáspora (1990–2013)* (Fondo Editorial Casa de las Américas, 2018), 27.

[5] Ibid., 28.

[6] Ibid., 29.

EPILOGUE   215

been the case with composers Julián Orbón, Tania León, and even more recently Aurelio de la Vega.

The crisis of the *período especial* led to a slow down, if not a complete halt, of many cultural institutions' programming and publication activities. Those cultural industries that served venues and areas frequented by tourists (hotels, Casas de la cultura) continued to function, but most others had to cut down on all of their operational expenses. Budgets for cultural institutions and activities were cut in half.[7] We see this most clearly in the periodization of the publications of two of the most circulated and important music journals in Cuba—*Boletín Música* and *Clave*—into two phases: one that predates the período especial (Phase I or Primera Fase) and a second phase of resumed publication activities in the late 1990s and early 2000s. Similarly, performances of the Orquesta Sinfónica Nacional de Cuba (OSN) became less frequent in the early 1990s, as did the visits and collaborations with guest soloists and conductors. As Iván César Morales Flores has meticulously accounted in his publications on this period, the fall of the Soviet Union led to a complete disappearance of all artistic exchange programs between Cuban composers, musicians, and ensembles and their counterparts in Eastern Europe as I've discussed in chapters 3 and 4 of this volume.[8] The Cuban festivals mentioned in chapters 4 and 5 ceased or paused activities, while Cuban engagement in festivals and competitions in the former Socialist Bloc were also discontinued.[9] Several artists and intellectuals, including a high number of composers and musicians, relocated abroad, some temporarily while others permanently.[10] Out of fifty-three composers who graduated from the composition program at the Instituto Superior de Arte (ISA) between 1990 and 2010, only twenty-four still live in Cuba. Out of those who graduated between 1990 and 1999 only five remain in Cuba.[11] Morales Flores notes that generational differences were a leading factor in determining whether or not a composer settled aboard temporarily or permanently. For example, a younger composer who hadn't established themselves in the local Cuban classical music scene before leaving the island was more likely to remain abroad and pursue a professional career outside of Cuba than an older and more established composer.[12]

[7] Ibid., 25.

[8] Iván César Morales Flores, "Leo Brouwer y la re-territorialización de un modelo de dirección artística habanero en la Orquesta de Córdoba (1992–2001)," in *En, desde y hacia las Américas: músicas y migraciones transoceánicas*, eds. Belén Vega Pichaco, Javier López-Marín, and Victoria Eli Rodríguez (Dykinson, 2021), 309.

[9] These included the Warsaw Autumn Music Festival, the Prague Spring Music Festival and the Tchaikivsky Competition. Ibid., 309.

[10] Ibid., 310.

[11] Morales Flores, *Identidades en proceso*, 22–23.

[12] Morales Flores, "Leo Brouwer y la re-territorialización de un modelo de dirección artística habanero en la Orquesta de Córdoba (1992–2001)," 310.

216 CUBAN MUSIC COUNTERPOINTS

Leo Brouwer was among those more established composers to temporarily settle abroad during this period, albeit with the flexibility of returning to Cuba.[13] Through a joint effort between the administrations of Andalucía and Córdoba, Brouwer was contracted to establish and direct what became the Orquesta de Córdoba. The orchestra's founding was the result of an ambitious initiative that began in the mid-1980s in Spain to establish new symphonic ensembles throughout the country.[14] Between 1975 and 2019, the autonomous region of Andalucía was a beacon of socialist and communist activities; therefore, the state-sponsored establishment of symphonic ensembles aligned with similar state-sponsored cultural initiatives Brouwer had been engaged with in Cuba since the 1960s.[15] Brouwer worked with the Orquesta de Córdoba for six months out of the year, while the remaining six months were spent in Cuba where he continued his work as director of the OSN. This arrangement allowed Brouwer to meet all the official requirements to be able to work abroad and maintain his Cuban residency.[16] As Morales Flores notes, Brouwer's work in Córdoba led several Cuban OSN musicians to follow him to Spain to work in the newly established ensemble, which contributed to the circulation of Cuban musicians abroad.[17] Additionally, Brouwer invited Cuban soloists and conductors to perform with the ensemble and he toured with the orchestra through Southern Spain, Greece, Portugal, and France.[18] Finally, and quite significantly, Brouwer's programming highlighted the symphonic repertoire of composers from the Americas, an unprecedented initiative in the dissemination of symphonic music of the Western Hemisphere in Spain.[19] Brouwer also systematically programmed works by living Spanish composers (in particular Andalusian composers), also outliers in comparison to the more conservative symphonic ensembles' programming throughout Spain.[20] As Morales Flores concludes, Brouwer's most significant contribution in his role as director of the Orquesta de Córdoba was to bring the orchestra to the local community, to connect the ensemble to its audience, which he achieved also in part through the inclusion of local dance and flamenco music artists in the orchestra's performances, educational concerts geared towards children, religious music concerts in churches, pops music concerts, and programming concerts in large outdoor spaces for massive audience attendance.[21] In these last types of concerts he programmed a great deal of film music,

[13] Ibid., 311.
[14] Ibid., 312.
[15] Ibid., 312–313.
[16] Ibid., 313.
[17] Ibid., 313.
[18] Ibid., 313–314.
[19] For a detailed chart of the programming of works by American composers by the Orquesta de Córdoba during Brouwer's term (1992–1998), see pages 320–322.
[20] Ibid., 315.
[21] Ibid., 315–316.

EPILOGUE   217

from Max Steiner to John Williams.[22] I provide this summary of observations and findings from Morales Flores's work not only because they reflect a continuation of the programming efforts Brouwer championed in the Cuban OSN and propagated in Córdoba, but also because they provide an account of Brouwer's career after 1991, and how his privileged position within the Cuban artistic and intellectual elite afforded him favorable and unique opportunities not granted to many other Cuban composers during the *período especial*.

Departure of a Generation of Composers: Extending a Cuban Approach to Composition Beyond the Island

Due to the ensuing economic crisis, many composers who studied at the Instituto Superior de Arte during the 1980s and 1990s under the tutelage of Carlos Fariñas, Harold Gramatges, and Roberto Valera left Cuba to further their compositional studies and pursue professional career opportunities abroad. Iván César Morales Flores has written extensively on some of the most salient and successful Cuban composers of the diaspora. Through five case studies—Ileana Pérez Velázquez, Eduardo Morales-Caso, Keyla Orozco, Ailem Carvajal, and Louis Aguirre—he notes that these composers work from the margins, through fragmented and hybrid identities that are embodied in their works. Through their careers and compositions, they maintain a sense of Cubanness while adapting to the new cultural context in which they operate.[23] Morales Flores notes that their status as migrants led them to question their identities and reflect on them from a new cultural and geographical context, adding

> each one of these creators will revise, in their new environment, their formative heritage to reaffirm, adapt, assimilate and even leave behind some of the teachings received from their teachers. With this, evidently, they fulfill an individual need, but at the same time they contribute substantially, from other latitudes, to the Cuban cultural identity, while giving it a new visibility abroad. This makes each of these creators a representative node in the wide network that is currently known as the "Cuban diaspora."[24]

[22] Ibid., 316.

[23] For those readers interested in a detailed account of the economic and political context of 1990s Cuba and the composition department at the ISA in the 1980s and 1990s, see Morales Flores's book *Identidades en proceso: Cinco compositores cubanos de la diáspora (1990–2013)*, winner of the 2016 Premio de Musicología Casa de las Américas.

[24] "cada uno de estos creadores revisará, en su nuevo entorno, su herencia formativa para reafirmar, adaptar, asimilar e, incluso, dejar atrás algunas de las enseñanzas recibidas de sus maestros. Con ello, cumplen, evidentemente, con una necesidad individual, pero a su vez aportan de manera sustancial, desde otras latitudes, a la identidad cultural cubana, al tiempo que le dan una nueva visibilidad en el

218 CUBAN MUSIC COUNTERPOINTS

Morales Flores notes the difference in using the term "Cuban diaspora" rather than "Cuban exiles" in reference to this group of composers, as they fall in a generation that came of age and left Cuba in the 1990s and, that in contrast with the earlier waves of Cubans who left the island in the 1960s and consider themselves exiles, the 1990s Cuban diaspora is not necessarily driven by political opposition to the Cuban socialist state to the same extent.[25] Morales Flores contends that, even if Brouwer continues to be the most influential Cuban composer on an international scale, that these composers and their works offer a more diverse view on what constitutes a Cuban approach to composition.[26] Through an intertextual reading of their compositions, Morales Flores adds that the most common techniques in creating these intertextual connections are quotation, allusion, joke, and parody.[27] When placed in dialogue with the case studies and trends analyzed throughout this book, we can see that the composers of the Cuban diaspora whom Morales Flores examines employ the same strategies as their Cuban predecessors did in prior decades, albeit from their condition as Cubans living abroad.

Citing the writings of José Lezama Lima in the 1940s and Cristóbal Díaz Ayala in the 1990s, Morales Flores adds Cuban cultural production has always been marked by migration, by Cubans who leave the island and conduct most or part of their careers in other cosmopolitan centers. Since the late eighteenth century, migration and exile have been constant conditions for Cuban artists and intellectuals. Morales Flores adds "their massive departures abroad cannot be limited exclusively, under an a priori or narrow criterion, to an extenuating critical socio-political and cultural crisis, but also to the prodigal heritage of an entire insular culture that identifies from its foundations with the need to know and project beyond its borders."[28] The narratives of migration and travel outside of Cuba acquire additional symbolic and philosophical dimensions.[29] Rufo Caballero describes the travel experiences through a Bakthinian theory of the carnivalesque,

> space of redemption, suspension of bondage, wish eventually fulfilled, mutation in life, portrayed transience, proven transterritoriality; I am not at the

extranjero. Esto convierte a cada uno de dichos creadores en nudo representativo de la amplia red que se conoce en la actualidad como «diáspora cubana»." Ibid., 11.

[25] Ibid., 12.
[26] Ibid., 13.
[27] Ibid., 14.
[28] "sus salidas masivas al exterior no pueden ser limitadas exclusivamente, bajo un criterio a priori o estrecho, al atenuante de una coyuntura sociopolítica y cultural crítica, sino, también, a la herencia pródiga de toda una cultura insular identificada desde sus bases con la necesidad de conocer y proyectarse más allá de sus fronteras." Ibid., 34.
[29] Ibid., 34.

EPILOGUE   219

destination, nor at the departure, I am not at this point anymore, I am on the journey, another dimension, an exception of life that seems like an invention of culture, the journey is the variable that separates me from order without having to physically or totally violate it; that helps me to slip away, at least for a while, from History.[30]

Gerardo Mosquera provides a poignant taxonomy of visual artists (easily applied to musicians and composers) to categorize their residential status: "those who are [here] (islanded), those who left (de-islanded), those who are [here] but are dying to leave (involuntary islanded), those who left, pay their taxes and return on vacation (low-intensity exile), and those who come and go (papinization), in reference to Los Papines, a group of globe trotter drummers."[31] Mosquera's categories provide a colorful and complex picture of artists' different attitudes regarding the complicated relationship between those who stay and those who leave, but also internally among the ones who stay, where some may wish to leave, but can't. Although it is challenging to make generalizations regarding the reasons or motivations for entire groups and generations of artists' decisions or desires to leave their home country, examining composers' shared economic, political, and social context as well as overlapping aesthetic and compositional practices provide helpful points for analysis and comparison. As Joaquín Borges Triana notes in his book on Cuban popular music artists outside of Cuba, it is futile to attempt to draw lines between exile and diaspora, as both terms are deeply imbricated.[32]

The Passing of the Generation of the Grupo de Renovación Musical

By 2002, Juan Blanco was one of the few composers from his generation—the generation that had begun maturing before the Revolution and achieved international recognition after 1959—who were still alive. In a 2002 interview Blanco

[30] "espacio de la redención, suspensión de la atadura, deseo eventualmente realizado, mutación en vida, transitoriedad retratada, transterritorialidad probada; no estoy en el destino, tampoco en la partida, no estoy en este punto ya, estoy en el viaje, dimensión otra, excepción de la vida que parece invención de la cultura, el viaje es la variable que me aparta del orden sin tener que violentarlo física o totalmente; que lleva a escabullirme, un rato al menos, de la Historia." Rufo Caballero quoted in ibid., 35.

[31] "los que están (islados), los que se fueron (desislados), los que están pero están locos por irse (islados involuntarios), los que se fueron, pagan sus impuestos y vuelven de vacaciones (exilio de baja intensidad), y los que van y vienen (papinización), por referencia a Los Papines, un grupo de tamboreros globe trotters." Gerardo Mosquera quoted in ibid., 37.

[32] Joaquín Borges Triana, *Músicos de Cuba y del mundo: Nadie se va del todo* (Cuba: Ediciones ConCierto Cubano, 2013), 33.

220 CUBAN MUSIC COUNTERPOINTS

frankly shared his concerns or disappointment over what he observed in the younger generation of composers, "that whole movement [avant-garde music] has gone a bit backwards. Perhaps it is due to an exacerbation of Cubanness or the economic crisis that has led cultural institutions to collect foreign currency. Of course, that's easier with salsa. Although as Carpentier said in his book *Tientos y diferencias*, our music is also a reflection of Cuban identity, just as that of a Czech is a reflection of his country."[33] Blanco further elaborated when asked to evaluate the current state of new music:

> After the push that the avant-garde of the 1960s gave to Cuban music, the country caught up with universal sounds, without abandoning our Cubanness. Later there were composers who, due to their longing for the previous modes of composition, fluctuated. But today the atmosphere that prevails among the majority of young people in higher education conservatories is that of levels of contemporaneity [that is] in tune with these times.[34]

We can see in these remarks that, although he was disappointed with what he perceived to be a backwards turn in music composition and a predominance of commercial music genres, young composers were in step with current trends.

Over the course of the 1990s and 2000s the composers of generation of the Grupo de Renovación Musical—those who had gathered at the Conservatorio Municipal de La Habana in the 1940s—were reaching their eighties and nineties. Throughout these last three decades these composers have passed away, first Argeliers León in 1991, then Hilario González in 1999, Carlos Fariñas in 2002, and Edgardo Martín in 2004, followed by Gramatges and Juan Blanco in 2008, and even the younger composer Héctor Angulo in 2018. Although he was never a member of the GRM, the last remaining composer of that generation, Alfredo Diez Nieto, passed away in October 2021, just two days shy of his 103rd birthday. These individuals left indelible marks on the Cuban classical music scene, not only through their compositions and the knowledge they imparted on younger generations of Cuban composers, but also through their writings, music criticism, their work as "gestores culturales" or cultural producers, and by forging

---

[33] "todo ese movimiento ha retrocedido un poco. Quizás se deba a una exacerbación de la cubanía o a la crisis económica que ha llevado a las instituciones culturales a recaudar divisas. Por supuesto, eso es más fácil con la salsa. Aunque como dijera Carpentier en su libro *Tientos y diferencias*, nuestra música es también un reflejo de cubanía, como la de un checo es reflejo de su país." Marta Ramírez, "Juan Blanco: Aún a la vanguardia," *Clave—Revista Cubana de Música* 4, no. 3 (2002): 35, 36.

[34] "*¿Cómo evalúa el contexto actual para la llamada música nueva?* Después del empujón que la vanguardia de los 60 le dio a la música cubana, el país se puso al día de las sonoridades universales, sin dejar de beber de la cubanía. Posteriormente hubo compositores que, por su añoranza por los modos de composición anteriores, fluctuaron. Pero hoy el ambiente que impera entre la mayoría de los jóvenes de los conservatorios de la enseñanza superior es el de niveles de contemporaneidad a tono con estos tiempos." Ibid., 36.

connections with composers, musicians, and intellectuals in Cuba and abroad resulting in a vast artistic network that spans the globe. Their writings continue to be studied (for example the Centro de Investigación y Desarrollo de la Música Cubana (CIDMUC) is in the process of editing for publication the collected writings of Argeliers León in more than seven volumes), their compositions performed, the institutions they founded and administered are still standing, even if in a different iteration or under a new name. Yet, these institutions continue to face new challenges as the political, economic, and social conditions that supported their establishment drastically change.

One of these institutions founded by Harold Gramatges and Argeliers León, the Dirección de Música of Casa de las Américas has fervently continued to promote both musicological and compositional activities within Cuba and in dialog with Latin America. Since 2004 (although there was an initial edition in 1966–1967), they have organized the Premio de Composición (Composition Prize) on a biennial basis. Composers from any Latin American country or background may submit an original composition in that year's category (for example, symphonic work, chamber music, piano solo); a panel of judges that includes distinguished composers from Cuba and other Latin American countries convenes in Havana to evaluate the submissions and select a winner. The winner's work is professionally edited by the Dirección de Música team, published by Casa de las Américas' Press, and released with much pomp and circumstance in the following edition of the competition. Beginning in 2009 the Premio de Composición has been held in conjunction with the Taller de Composición e Interpretación, in which younger composers attend composition workshops, receive feedback and mentoring from the panel of judges as well as other invited guests, and have their works performed at the end of the week. Similarly, the Dirección de Música has held a Premio de Musicología (Musicology Prize) biennially (on alternating years with the Premio de Composición) since 1979, for which music scholars from Cuba, Latin America, and Spain submit unpublished monographs. Since 1999, the Premio de Musicología has been combined with the Coloquio Internacional de Musicología, a week-long musicology conference with presenters from Cuba, Latin America, the United States, and Spain in attendance. These two prizes and conferences/workshops foster a sense of community among scholars of Latin American music from all of the Americas and Spain. Recceiving one of the Premios from Casa de las Américas confers legitimacy and prestige to both the winners and the awarding institution. Casa de las Américas continues to be a powerful node in the local, regional, and global music networks.

222   CUBAN MUSIC COUNTERPOINTS

The Year 1996: Centro de Estudios Americanos (CEA Affair) and a New Minister of Culture

Internal riffs between the State and Cuban intellectuals led to one of the most polemical incidents in post-1991 Cuba, the CEA Affair (El Caso CEA) in 1996. The Centro de Estudios sobre América, founded in 1977, gathered a team of social scientists whose research and publications focused on matters of public policy affecting the Americas, adding to their interests internal Cuban matters as pressure mounted to rethink and redefine socialism and the local economy after 1989. In the early 1990s a group of intellectuals working at the CEA began disseminating views that ran in opposition to official State attitudes. The Cuban state conducted a massive purge of the CEA, reassigning individuals to other agencies, and even revoking the Partido Cubano Comunista (Cuban Communist Party, PCC) membership of some of these individuals. Although the purge was not publicized in Cuba, in 1998 Italian journalist Maurizio Giuliano published *El Caso CEA: Intelectuales e Inquisidores en Cuba. ¿Perestroika en la Isla?*, shedding light for the first time on a major schism between the state and Cuban intellectuals. Although the effects of this purge on Cuban composers and the classical music scene have yet to be explored, one cannot ignore the ripple effect such an incident must have had throughout cultural and intellectual circles in the island.

Another major event in the cultural realm since 1991 was the appointment of a new Minister of Culture in 1997, Abel Prieto (b. 1950). Unlike his predecessor Armando Hart Dávalos, who was a lawyer and political leader and not an artist, Prieto is a writer and intellectual, incredibly invested and involved in the development of Cuban culture. His appointment led to a liberalization in Cuban cultural institutions, unlike any seen in the first thirty-plus years since the Revolution. He served as Minister of Culture between 1997 and 2012, and again from 2016 to 2018.[35] Prieto currently serves as president of Casa de las Américas. In 1994 Prieto delivered a conference presentation on "Cultura, cubanidad y cubanía" for the cycle "La nación y la emigración," wherein he drew upon Fernando Ortiz's distinction between "cubanidad" (a caustic sense of belonging within Cuba culture) and "cubanía" (the individual's conscious and voluntary sense of being Cuban). Prieto expanded upon Ortiz by arguing that Cubans living abroad contributed to Cuban culture through an implicit sense of "cubanidad"; by extension, Prieto opened the doors for Cuban artists and intellectuals living abroad to be reinserted into the local discourse on national culture.[36] Since his first term as Minister of Culture (1997–2012), intellectuals and artists have been able to

---

[35] Moore, *Music and Revolution*, 85.
[36] Morales Flores, *Identidades en proceso*, 30.

EPILOGUE   223

travel for professional engagements (tours, conferences, competitions) with relatively more freedom than in previous decades. Also, changes in State policy over what constitutes Cuban residency have allowed artists to spend considerable time spans out of the year (months) working abroad, while being able to return to Cuba and keep their Cuban residency and passport. Prieto, however, also oversaw passing of the Decreto 349 as Minister of Culture, a highly controversial set of cultural policies currently in place, discussed in more detail below.

Music Dissemination and a Period of "Normalization"

Since 1879 Cuba has had some sort of regulation or law regarding copyright and the protection of authors' rights, "but the nationalization of the cultural apparatus [in the 1960s], along with the U.S. embargo against the island, rendered it ineffective."[37] Over the past century and a half, Cuba's legislature has passed various laws and has signed regional and international copyright agreements. In 1974, Cuba joined the United Nations World Intellectual Property Organization (WIPO), and later created Law 14 "Ley de Derecho de Autor," signed on December 28, 1977. However, since 1959 the management of royalties and copyright in Cuba has shifted through various entities: from the Instituto Cubano de Derechos Musicales (ICDM) in 1960 to the Consejo Nacional de Cultura in 1966, and eventually the Centro Nacional de Derecho de Autor (CENDA) in 1975. In 1987 the Asociación Cubana de Derechos de Autores Musicales (ACDAM), under the purview of the Instituto Cubano de la Música, was created to oversee all music copyright and royalties matters and it continues to serve this function. Based on the archival records from the 1960s and 1970s that I've examined, individuals who were employed as composers by the State would receive an annual salary with the expectation that they would complete a given amount of works for specified ensembles or functions. The records I've encountered do not outline the remuneration based on subsequent performances, recordings, or edited publications of a music score, and we can assume that classical music salaries followed the models of popular music artists in the absence of royalties.[38] A major shift began in 1988 when the Berman Amendment to the US Embargo on Cuba "lifted restrictions on the U.S. distribution of Cuban cultural materials. This reestablished copyright payments to Cuban authors for the use of their works in the United States."[39] Most significantly, "in 1997 Cuba signed the Berne Convention and agreed to update its intellectual property law to international

---

[37] Ariana Hernández-Reguant, "Copyrighting Che: Art and Authorship under Cuban Late Socialism," *Public Culture* 16, no. 1 (2004): 15.

[38] Ibid., 15.

[39] Ibid., 16.

224 CUBAN MUSIC COUNTERPOINTS

standards, which allowed it to sign reciprocal agreements with foreign countries, thus enabling authors to collect hard-currency royalties."[40] As Ariana Hernández-Reguant has noted, "as Cuba moved to salvage its economy from the deep crisis caused by the loss of its socialist trading partners, much of the state infrastructure of cultural production and distribution was turned into a network of for-profit semiautonomous enterprises."[41] In the context of "late socialism," Hernández-Reguant continues, "capitalist mechanisms of control over cultural products extended the reach of patrimonial rights well beyond national jurisdiction . . . the control over such images was exerted through a seemingly neutral, internationally binding juridical resolution made on the basis of authorship."[42] As Hernández-Reguant aptly problematizes, recent issues regarding culture and copyright in Cuba, state and private, socialist and neoliberal capitalist, as well as local and international interests all intersect and compete in the new cultural and economic landscape of the last thirty-plus years, generating a complex network of artists, institutions, and artistic products forced to negotiate the interests of various parties. In the case of classical music composition, Cuban composers began to collect international royalties through the Sociedad General de Autores y Editores (SGAE, Spanish General Society of Authors and Editors) since it set up a branch in Havana in 1997 to serve Cuban artists.[43] As the culture industries turn into copyright industries, they constitute "border zones" or "contact zones," which, according to Hernández-Reguant, "develop at the interface of a national state with a particular historical logic and neoliberal transnational capitalism, [and] often offer conditions for national discourses of identity and community to be challenged."[44] Music in particular, has proven a fertile ground for negotiations of national identity as the state allows the private cultural sector to fluoresce because through its work it legitimizes the state; but this strategy can also backfire, as artists who now participate in a transnational culture/copyright industry can also undermine the state's political legitimacy and authority. The result, as Hernández-Reguant has noted, is the emergence of an elite, or *farándula*, of cultural producers who lead a lavish lifestyle by comparison, leading to resentment among other cultural workers who only receive wages.[45] Although the state has introduced a taxation scale for cultural producers, these measures have done little to curtail the economic inequalities created by the influx of royalties for this creative elite.[46]

[40] Ibid., 16.
[41] Ibid., 2.
[42] Ibid., 2.
[43] Ibid., 18.
[44] Ibid., 8.
[45] Ibid., 6–7, 19.
[46] Ibid., 24.

EPILOGUE 225

The publication of scores, as mentioned in earlier chapters, was initially undertaken by the EGREM, through which the Editora Musical de Cuba (EMC) eventually arose. However, in 1988 the EMC began procedures to become an independent entity, which was finalized in 1993. Because of the scarcity of resources during the *período especial*, the EMC's activities were severely limited in the early 1990s. For example, between 1988 and 1989 they published more than 140 works, while publishing less than forty between 1993 and 2002. Since 1991, most of the EMC's efforts have been devoted to completing new editions of pre-existing works by well-known composers, in particular repertory for choral ensembles by Leo Brouwer, Roberto Valera, Silvio Rodríguez, Electo Silva, Beatriz Corona, and Conrado Monier. Over the last three decades, some composers have sought the publication of their works through foreign music publishers, making their works accessible to performers abroad and allowing composers to collect royalties on the sales and reproduction (through recordings) of their music. On January 22, 2022, the Museo Nacional de la Música Cubana (MNM) announced an agreement of cooperation with the EGREM, in which the EGREM will edit, publish, and sell Cuban music scores while the Museo will house a new "Fonoteca Nacional," a national archive and repository of sound recordings for the non-commercial use of music researchers and any other patrons.[47] The recent announcement demonstrates that the preservation and dissemination of Cuban music in print for performance and as sound archives for posterity and researchers is a current preoccupation of the administrators of the EGREM and the MNM.

In the past fifteen to twenty years the combination of new technology, socialism's value of the democratization of accessibility to information, and the particularly Cuban attitude of *resolver* (to figure things out) has led to a unique phenomenon of content sharing through swapping external hard drives and USB memory sticks. In the 1990s, especially after the worst years of the *período especial*, one could purchase popular music (both Cuban and foreign) through pirated cassettes and CDs. But since the advent of smaller, less expensive computers and the more frequent travel abroad of Cubans and their friends and family (who purchase laptops and electronic equipment to bring back to the island), more individuals now have access to laptops and, most importantly, external hard drives and memory sticks. This mode of electronic file circulation is Cubans' way to *resolver* the lack of internet access they have experienced until fairly recently. Through these physical objects (hard drives and memory sticks) music (PDFs of scores and MP3 and MP4 files of recordings) circulates through an "off-line"

---

[47] Museo Nacional de la Música, "La EGREM y El Museo Nacional de La Música Estrechan Lazos Históricos," *Museo Nacional de la Música* (blog), January 24, 2022. https://medium.com/museomus icacuba/la-egrem-y-el-museo-nacional-de-la-m%C3%BAsica-estrechan-lazos-hist%C3%B3ricos-c7332b5d200b.

226 CUBAN MUSIC COUNTERPOINTS

informal network. This proclivity for electronic file transfers has led to the phenomenon of the *paquete semanal,* a weekly package put together by individuals with illegal internet satellite connections. The curators and distributors of the *paquete* download all kinds of content—films, episodes of television series, mobile applications, video games, magazines, music tracks, and videos—created both abroad and in Cuba; and every week they offer a new "package" for purchase at different price points depending on which content users are interested in. Users then receive the files by bringing their external hard drives to one of the *paquete semanal* distributors. Through his research on and analysis of the dissemination of *reparto* (a subgenre of Cubatón—a Cuban off-shoot of reggaetón) Mike Levine has shown how the individuals in charge of the selection of music to be included in any given week's package respond to both users' (subscribers') taste and feedback and State censorship.[48] Although the *paquete semanal* collects and distributes mostly popular music, classical music circulates through the same process of electronic file sharing through external hard drives, albeit not through the *paquete,* as classical music doesn't have the same commercial appeal as reggaetón or Cubatón. In fact, because of the shortage of paper products in Cuba, most musicians prefer to exchange electronic files of scores than copying a physical paper version.

In the 1990s the sound recording industry, much like other industries in Cuba, also witnessed the appearance of studios outside the purview of the EGREM, until then the only official recording studios and label in Cuba. This transpired in part because of the cultural capital certain individuals had accrued in the previous decades, giving them legitimacy to travel outside of Cuba to acquire the equipment to set up independent recording studios and to set up the studios as a complement to (and not in competition with) the official State-run EGREM. The best-known case is Estudios Abdala (1998), established by Nueva Trova artist Silvio Rodríguez and now under the auspices of the Cuban Ministry of Culture. Other independent recording studios and labels have emerged through the last thirty years, including Producciones Colibrí (2003), which has a series titled "Roldán" dedicated to recording and promoting classical music by Cuban composers and performers.

In 1997 the the national music award *Cubadisco* was established to celebrate and acknowledge music production by Cuban recording studios and artists. The event not only includes an awards ceremony with prizes in twenty-five categories, but also concerts, workshops, and press conferences. One of the most surprising aspects of this event—from the point of view of this US-trained and based musicologist—is the involvement of musicologists as judges and "gestores

---

[48] Mike Levine, "Sounding El Paquete: The Local and Transnational Routes of an Afro-Cuban Repartero," *Cuban Studies* 50, no. 1 (2021): 139.

EPILOGUE 227

culturales," a term used throughout Latin America for professional cultural producers. The majority of musicologists in Cuba are not employed as professors or lecturers in higher education academic institutions. Many do teach at preparatory levels (elementary through high school music programs), but many others work as researchers and "gestores culturales" in any one of the many State-run cultural organizations. Musicologists are heavily involved in many aspects of Cubadisco, writing press releases, talking on mass media outlets (radio and television programs), and coordinating and facilitating workshops. Because of the emergence of an "alternative Cuban music" industry since the late 1980s, in which the means of cultural production have been de-centralized and opened to the private sector, an event like Cubadisco is not solely dominated by EGREM-produced albums and artists.[49]

When I began conducting research on Cuban classical music, few sound recordings of the works I read about or encountered as music scores were available. But over the course of just a few years this situation changed with Producciones Colibrí recording and releasing a series of albums featuring the most salient composers of the GRM, including Hilario González, Argeliers León, and Harold Gramatges, as well as other younger composers, such as Juan Piñera and Roberto Valera. The most significant event for the dissemination of Cuban music, however, was a deal struck in 2015 between the EGREM and Sony Music Entertainment, through which the two companies entered a licensing agreement that allows Sony to distribute internationally the EGREM's catalog of Cuban music.[50] Since then Sony has digitized, remastered, and released thousands of EGREM recordings, many of which are now available for streaming through various platforms. Although most of the publicity surrounding this agreement has focused on the recordings of legendary jazz and popular music artists, what few Cuban music audiophiles are aware of is that the EGREM-Sony deal includes dozens of albums of classical music. Some of the EGREM albums discussed in the last chapter have not been digitized and released by Sony yet, but they have been digitized by electronic music fans and uploaded to YouTube. Whether

[49] Joaquín Borges Triana, *Concierto cubano: la vida es un divino guión.* (Barcelona: Linkgua Ediciones, 2009).

[50] "Sony Music Entertainment Announces International Licensing Agreement with EGREM for Most Extensive Catalog Of Cuban Music," https://www.sony.com/content/sony/en/en_us/SCA/company-news/press-releases/sony-corporation-of-america/2015/sony-music-entertainment-announces-international-licensing-agreement-with-egrem-for-most-extensive-catalog-of-cuban-music.html (accessed January 12, 2022). This agreement is possible because of the "Berman Amendment," the "informational materials exemption" found in § 2502(a) of the Omnibus Trade and Competitiveness Act, Pub. L. No. 100–418, 102 Stat. 1107 (1988), and § 525 of the Foreign Relations Authorization Act, Fiscal Years 1994 and 1995, Pub. L. No. 103–236, 108 Stat. 382 (1994). These exemptions allow for informational transactions between Cuba and the United States without prior authorization or license from the US government, State Department, Treasury, or Office of Foreign Assets Control. Informational materials include books, magazines, videos, music, electronic information, photos, paintings, sculptures, and other works of art.

228   CUBAN MUSIC COUNTERPOINTS

or not they will remain there once Sony digitizes them and makes them commercially available remains to be seen. This deal between EGREM and Sony in 2015 took place during a period of political and economic "normalization" between the United States and Cuba during President Barack Obama's presidency. The Obama administration eased many of the hardline policies regarding US collaborations with and travel to Cuba, simplifying the process for those who wished to travel to Cuba under one of the twelve categories for travel outlined in a provision of the Cuban Assets Control Regulations, which are the federal regulations that govern implementation of US sanctions on Cuba, by eliminating the need to apply for a travel license through the Department of Treasury's Office of Foreign Assets Control (OFAC).

The ease in travel during the Obama administration went both ways as the process of obtaining visas to travel to the United States became easier when the US Embassy in Cuba expanded its operations—previously operating as an interest section—following the agreement on July 20, 2015, between Raul Castro and President Obama to restore all diplomatic relations between the two countries. However, since the alleged sonic attacks on foreign diplomats of 2016, the Embassy is minimally staffed and many Cubans who want to apply for a US visa see themselves forced to travel to a third country, most commonly Mexico or Ecuador, and make an appointment at their US Embassies, a process that is costly and time-consuming. In my personal communications and conversations with Cuban artists and scholars I've learned that many Cuban individuals have been granted five-year visas that allow them to travel between the United States and Cuba for short stays in the United States; many other shorter-term visas have been granted. It is no surprise that most of the individuals who obtain these visas are officially employed by some type of cultural organization or institution in Cuba and have official "letters of invitation" from US academic or cultural institutions, making them less likely to seek asylum once in the United States.

One of the most surprising and impressive activities in the realm of cultural diplomacy during these years was the 2012 US tour of the OSN. Although the orchestra had traveled through Europe and Latin America over the years, it had never toured the United States. I had the opportunity to attend their concert in West Palm Beach; their programming consisted of well-known works from the Western European classical tradition (Mendelssohn's *Italian Symphony* and Schubert's Symphony No. 8), works by US composers that heavily featured Cuban musical elements (Gershwin's *Cuban Overture*), and Cuban works that similarly employed musical elements drawn from Cuban popular and folk music traditions (such as Guido López Gavilán's *Guaguancó*). Absent from their tour programs were works from the 1960s and 1970s that would have challenged US audiences' preconceived notions of what Cuban classical music should or could sound like. Personally, it is difficult for me not to pass judgement on this

EPILOGUE 229

particular selection of repertory. Anyone attending an OSN 2012 US tour concert would have listened to what in my estimation is a rather limited view of Cuban classical music of the twentieth and twenty-first centuries, not least because it reinforced narratives of a Cuba frozen in time or "postcard musical nationalism" that Cuban composers and artists in the 1960s, 1970s, and even today, continuously attempt to challenge, overcome, and dismantle.

LNME-EDM

After the *período especial* a local EDM scene emerged, a rather surprising development given that EDM scenes in other urban centers in Europe and the United States have been tied to particularly costly events and venues, which makes this phenomenon in socialist Cuba a bit of a paradox. Additionally, the EDM scene in Cuba has developed under the auspices of the Laboratorio Nacional de Música Electroacústica (LNME), established by Juan Blanco in 1979 and discussed in chapter 5. The LNME organizes and promotes EDM events in public spaces, free of charge to audiences, featuring EDM DJs and producers from Cuba and abroad. The LNME continues to host the Primavera en La Habana Electronic Music Festival, but, unlike its earliest editions, many of the artists and events featured focus on EDM, while concerts of more "traditional" classical electronic music make up a smaller portion of the festival's programming. The 2020 edition, which was postponed due to the ensuing COVID-19 pandemic, was dedicated to the 100th birthday of its founder, Juan Blanco. The LNME continues to serve Cuban composers and composition students. Although the ISA has its own electronic music lab, established by Carlos Fariñas, its most recent director, composition professor Sigried Macías, still brings students to the LNME facilities in Vedado to work in its recording studios and with more updated equipment. Because of new technologies that allow composers to work on electronic tracks with their own computers and software, there is an increasing number of young Cuban composers (of both more "traditional" electronic music and EDM) working in this medium outside of the official music composition programs. The ISA, however, has engaged in academic exchange programs with the Berklee College of Music, facilitating some young Cuban composition students' visits to Boston to further their training.

La Fábrica de Arte Cubano (FAC)

Another more recent development—as the Cuban state relaxes its economic policies and allows for more small private businesses to operate legally—that has

230 CUBAN MUSIC COUNTERPOINTS

had a positive impact on the Cuban classical music scene is the establishment of new performance spaces outside of the direct supervision and management of state agencies. One of the most successful of these venues is the Fábrica de Arte Cubano (FAC, Cuban Art Factory), a converted soy, peanut, and cotton-seed oil refinery in the Vedado neighborhood of Havana. The conversion of the old factory into a performing and visual arts space was led by architect Ernesto Jiménez García. According to the FAC's website they describe themselves as "a large laboratory of interdisciplinary creation that features the best of Cuban contemporary art, with a marked social and community focus . . . FAC is an artistic project driven by the need to rescue, support, and promote the work of artists from all artistic branches: cinema, music, dance, theater, visual arts, photography, fashion, graphic design, and architecture. Through art/artist integration, it promotes the direct exchange and contact between the public and the creator at a massive level."[51] Thiago Soares has best described the FAC's relationship to Havana's tourism and culture sector:

> Since 2014, however, all the nostalgic ideal present in Havana's "tourism catalog" (driving classic cars, visiting rum and cigar factories, seeing the spaces where the facts of the Cuban Revolution happened) have been enhanced by a space that presents cultural attractions, contemporary art exhibitions, artistic performances, theater plays, and shows by DJs and Cuban rappers: the Fábrica de Arte Cubano (Cuban Art Factory). The building was a closed oil factory that in 2014 was converted into a space that welcomes a wide range of musical expressions of Cuban rap, rock, and electronic music and questions the institutional image of Havana as a "nostalgic city."[52]

The FAC is the brainchild of a group of Cuban artists, in particular X Alfonso, a hip hop and rock singer and musician, son of Carlos Alfonso and Ele Valdés, the founders of the fusion group Síntesis. The FAC opened its doors with an inaugural concert by singer-song writer Silvio Rodríguez on February 13, 2014. It has several performing spaces, with artwork by young Cuban visual artists constantly revolving on its walls. The largest performance space can be transformed from a fashion show runway to a black box-like concert hall to a film screening

---

[51] "es un gran laboratorio de creación interdisciplinario que expone lo mejor del arte contemporáneo de Cuba, con un marcado enfoque social y comunitario . . . FAC es un proyecto artístico impulsado por la necesidad de rescatar, apoyar y promocionar la obra de artistas de todas las ramas del arte: cine, música, danza, teatro, artes plásticas, fotografía, moda, diseño gráfico y arquitectura. A través de la integración arte/artista promueve el intercambio y acercamiento directo entre el público y el creador a nivel masivo." Fábrica de Arte Cubano. "Fábrica de Arte Cubano." http://www.fac.cu/ (accessed January 19, 2022).

[52] Thiago Soares, "Beyond Nostalgic Havana: Music and Identity in the Fábrica de Arte Cubano," in *Music Cities: Evaluating a Global Cultural Policy Concept*, eds. Christina Ballico and Allan Watson (Cham: Springer International Publishing, 2020), 64.

EPILOGUE 231

theater. The FAC also organizes workshops for children and has a VIP space for performers, special guests, and FAC patrons who pay the "black card" membership. The VIP area has comfortable seating and access to a bar/lounge where you can purchase restaurant quality food and premium alcoholic beverages. In a 2017 interview, X Alfonso defended the FAC against criticisms of "elitism" by noting that the cost of admission (which started at 20 MN) was about 50 MN (less than $2USD), giving patrons access to all of the spaces (except for the VIP area, which he doesn't mention in the interview).[53] He later adds "FAC is a symphony in constant creation and reflection where I share experiences similar to those I have when I compose a song, film or take a good photo. I consider it a work of art, a painting that you never finish."[54] The FAC has attracted the attention of not only local young Cubans, but also foreign visitors. The publicized visits by Lady Gaga, Mick Jagger, and Michelle Obama have made the FAC a "must see" venue for tourists. The project has garnered the attention of design and architecture firms and organizations, and of scholars who research and write about the emerging entrepreneurial scene in Cuba. The FAC has been praised as a model project/ space that balances new economic paradigms, local artistic and cultural production, and a commitment to serve the people through social programs, and as epitomizing the Triple Balance Empresarial model, one for businesses that strive to achieve balance between consumer satisfaction-economic success, social impact, and environmentally responsible practices.[55]

Although most of the press coverage of FAC events has focused on popular music artists, the larger performance space (or Naves as they call them) often holds classical music concerts. Because of the fluid nature of the FAC's space, patrons can enter and exit performance spaces without restriction. Someone going to the FAC for an EDM concert late in the evening could find themselves in a string orchestra concert of music by Guido López-Gavilán, Piazzolla, and Vivaldi if they arrived earlier and stopped by the larger Nave where the Orquesta de Música Eterna has performed. The FAC promotes not only multidisciplinary presentations of visual art and music, but also multi-generic experiences for patrons as they navigate the maze-like spaces of the FAC. This juxtaposition of artistic disciplines and varied musical styles and genres in a privatized space run by artists themselves points to the direction in which cultural production in

[53] Milena Recio, "X Alfonso: La Fábrica de Arte Cubano, una sinfonía en constante creación," *OnCubaNews* (blog), September 4, 2017. https://oncubanews.com/cultura/musica/x-alfonso-la-fabrica-arte-cubano-una-sinfonia-constante-creacion/.

[54] "FAC es una sinfonía en constante creación y reflexión donde comparto experiencias similares a las que tengo para componer una canción, filmar o hacer una buena foto. Yo la considero una obra de arte, un cuadro que nunca terminas." X Alfonso in ibid.

[55] Maya Quiroga, "Fábrica de Arte Cubano: industria de creación," *OnCubaNews* (blog), August 4, 2016, https://oncubanews.com/cultura/artes-visuales/fabrica-de-arte-cubano-industria-de-creacion/.

232 CUBAN MUSIC COUNTERPOINTS

Cuba is headed as the twenty-first century progresses: more independence from state control, more entrepreneurial efforts from independent artists and small business, more blurring between genres and styles, more cooperation based on a commitment to social impact (one based in socialist ideals and models). The FAC and classical musicians' engagement within its space and mission encapsulate that quintessentially Cuban spirit of *resolver*. X Alfonso saw a need for artists to explore and present their projects outside of the boundaries of State cultural institutions. He and his collaborators found a viable space in a desirable location, and transformed it into a cool, hipster venue not unlike the loft-scene in NYC in the 1960s, or the gentrified warehouse neighborhoods in Berlin, Brooklyn, and Wynwood in Miami in more recent years. The FAC has both met a need and created a demand (among the local Cuban artists and youth as well as foreign visitors) for a cosmopolitan urban space, that, although local in its conception, is also global in its projection. Its creators and managers operate through an understanding that there are similar spaces like it in major cosmopolitan centers throughout Europe and the Americas. This negotiation between the local and the global, as well as the insertion of the local into the global has been and continues to be a hallmark of the Cuban classical music scene that I have explored throughout this book.

Decreto 349, MSI and COVID-19

On April 20, 2018, the Council of Ministers of Cuba, with Abel Prieto serving as Minister of Culture, adopted the now infamous "Decreto 349" ("Decree 349"), which was publicly instituted on December 7 that same year. The Decreto 349 set off a wave of protests and outcries from artists within and outside of Cuba for the potential threats on artistic freedom that it presented. In 1997, the Decreto 226 set specific rules for artists contracted by any of the State cultural agencies under the umbrella of the Ministry of Culture, along with setting basic procedures and sanctions for those who were to be found in violation of the established rules. But Decreto 349 doesn't limit its jurisdiction to artists with state contracts: it expands its purview to all artists in Cuba, whether they work for a state organization, independently from the state, or through small private businesses. The most potentially threatening aspects of Decreto 349 include: the compulsory registration of all artists through the Ministry of Culture, state agencies' oversight of contract and payment negotiations, prohibition of a wide set of categories of audiovisual content, unilateral decision-making power for determining whether or not a work or artist follows the rules established in the decree, excessive punitive

EPILOGUE 233

measures for offenders, and lack of an adequate mechanism for appeals.[56] Artists can be removed from the registry (and therefore find themselves unable to work in Cuba) if their works contain "sexist, vulgar and obscene language" or go against the cultural politics of the Ministry of Culture.[57] Some artists have expressed concerns that the state will repeat the censorship and purges of the *quinquenio gris* (discussed in chapter 4). Citing the poor management and disorganized procedures of the state apparatus and its failure to register and keep track of artists, established Nueva Trova singer-songwriter Silvio Rodríguez called for the suspension of Decreto 349 until the necessary amendments could be set in place.

In September 2018 a group of Cuban artists, intellectuals, and journalists formed a coalition they called Movimiento San Isidro (MSI, named after the Havana neighborhood where it was founded) to protest the measures outlined in the Decreto 349. Because of their staged protests, many have been arrested, censured, and blacklisted by the State. On November 27, 2020, several Cuban artists staged a protest in support of the members of MSI in front of the Ministry of Culture offices, with Vice-Minister Fernando Rojas serving as liaison between the protestors and the ministry, leading to the creation of the N27 Movement. In February 2021 Descemer Bueno, Gente de Zona, Maykel Osorbo, El Funky, and Yotuel released the rap hit *Patria y vida,* in which they referenced the MSI and government censorship. The title is a twist on the Cuban revolutionary slogan "patria o muerte" (fatherland or death), through the lyrics insisting that they want both their fatherland *and* life. In April 2021, Cuban police attempted to arrest Maykel Osorbo, but protesters blocked the raid; Osorbo was eventually detained and sent to prison a month later. Visual and performance artist Luis Manuel Otero Alcántara, a leader of the MSI, was arrested on July 11, 2021. On June 24, 2022, Otero Alcántara was sentenced to five years in prison for contempt, public disorder, and "insulting symbols of the homeland," and Osorbo to nine years for contempt, public disorder, and "defamation of institutions and organizations, heroes and martyrs." Since then, several international human rights organizations, such as Amnesty International, have condemned the Cuban state's decision against the two artists as "examples of how Miguel Díaz-Canel's government uses the judicial system to criminalize critical voices, including through charges of alleged crimes that are incompatible with international law."[58]

---

[56] "El-Arte-Bajo-Presion_online.pdf." Artists at Risk Connection, 2019 40AD, https://pen.org/wp-content/uploads/2019/09/El-Arte-Bajo-Presion_online.pdf, 10–11.

[57] Rubén Gallo, "Opinion | Is This the End of Cuba's Astonishing Artistic Freedom?," *The New York Times,* February 18, 2019, https://www.nytimes.com/2019/02/18/opinion/cuba-censorship-arru fat.html.

[58] Amnesty International, "Amnesty International Condemns the Sentences of Luis Manuel Otero Alcántara and Maykel 'Osorbo' Castillo," June 24, 2022, https://www.amnesty.org/en/latest/news/2022/06/cuba-amnesty-condemns-sentences-luis-manuel-otero-alcantara-maykel-osorbo-castillo/.

234 CUBAN MUSIC COUNTERPOINTS

The State's repressive measures have overlapped with deteriorating economic conditions, a crisis exacerbated by the COVID-19 pandemic. With tourism as one of their leading industries and the island closing itself from visitors in order to abate the effects of the pandemic, the Cuban state and people have suffered dire economic consequences. Shortages in fuel, food supplies, and medicine—and their consequent rationing by the State—have led to increasing tensions between State officials and Cuban citizens, culminating in the protests of July 11, 2021, where the slogans "SOS Cuba" and "Patria y vida" were chanted and bandied on picket signs and banners. The state police met the demonstrations with arrests and violence, which led to subsequent protests in support of Cuban anti-government protesters in US and South American cities with strong Cuban-American presences, mainly Tampa and Miami in Florida and La Paz, Bolivia, and Santiago, Chile. Following the protests of July 11, 2021, Cuban composer Leo Brouwer wrote a note in response, which was shared (presumably by his managerial team, since they typed the comment while sharing a photo of his handwritten note with his signature) on social media: "What pain, what sadness that we've reached this abuse of power! . . . I never imagined that the forces of order in Cuba would attack common and peaceful people as us Cubans are. When the Cuban (person) protests, there is no doubt that politics, or better said, the political and military power has overreached! How can you live peacefully? . . ."[59] This note of support for the protesters and condemnation of the Cuban military's abuse of power is rare coming from a classical music composer, and even more surprising in that it was written and shared publicly by one of the most (if not *the most*) well-supported composer since the 1959 Revolution.

The protests have been headed mainly by visual artists and popular music figures, with the classical music world largely insulated from these developments, as with the *quinquenio gris* of the 1970s. For example the Festival de Música Contemporánea de La Habana, which, in spite of ongoing arrests and protests of political dissidents in the artistic field, carried on with their activities in November 2021. Journalistic coverage of the Festival doesn't acknowledge the ongoing crisis in the arts through the Decreto 349 or the MSI, demonstrating that the classical music scene can continue to operate relatively unencumbered by the highly repressive measures that affect artists in other fields. These latest developments point to an uncertain future for the Cuban cultural and artistic scenes. How the State responds to the protests and calls for just and fair treatment of artists will mark this as a possible second gray period in Cuban revolutionary history. These tensions and clashes between the State and the artistic class

---

[59] "Que dolor, que tristeza que se llegue al abuso del poder! . . . Nunca imaginé que las fuerzas del orden en Cuba fuesen a agredir a gente común y pacífica como somos los cubanos. Cuando el cubano protesta, no cabe duda de que la política o mejor dicho, el poder político y militar se ha extralimitado! Cómo pueden vivir tranquilos? . . ." Facebook post, July 13, 2021.

EPILOGUE   235

are ongoing, making it difficult for me to conclude this epilogue, not least because throughout my more than ten years of conducting research in Cuba I have developed close relationships (friendships and familial kinships) with Cuban musicians and composers within and outside of Cuba who have varying degrees of agreement and disagreement with state cultural policies and politics. But, if doing the research for and writing this book has taught me anything, it's that the Cuban spirit of *resolver* carries on through political and economic challenges. Regardless of the political and economic circumstances, Cuban musicians and composers always figure out ways to enact their identities through art that dialogues with local and global artistic networks.

For many journalists and critics the Decreto 349 is a "step backwards." One often hears comments of incredulity, "how can this still be happening?" Yet, this posture assumes a teleological and linear development of history. As Antonio Benítez Rojo notes in *The Repeating Island*, the Caribbean poses challenges to historians who come to study the region with methodological tools developed and taught to them through the study of other world histories and regions. The Caribbean, and Cuba in particular, pose obstacles due to patterns and conditions of fragmentation, instability, reciprocal isolation, uprootedness, cultural heterogeneity, lack of historical continuity, contingency, impermanence, and syncretism.[60] The region's historiography resists conventional methodologies. "The spectrum of Caribbean codes is so varied and dense that it holds the region suspended in a soup of signs."[61] Benítez Rojo uses Chaos (with a capital 'c') to describe the region in reference to mathematical and scientific Chaos theories, in which, to put it simply, order and patterns can be found in seemingly disorganized phenomena. Benítez Rojo adds:

> Chaos looks toward everything that repeats, reproduces, grows, decays, unfolds, flows, spins, vibrates, seethes; it is as interested in the evolution of the solar system as in the stock market's crashes, as involved in cardiac arrhythmia as in the novel or in myth. Thus Chaos provides a space in which the pure sciences connect with the social sciences, and both of them connect with art and the cultural tradition.[62]

Benítez Rojo's approach does not attempt to find an end goal or result, but rather it focuses on "processes, dynamics, and rhythms that show themselves within the marginal, the regional, the incoherent, the heterogeneous, or, if you like, the unpredictable that coexists with us in our everyday world."[63] In employing the term

---

[60] Antonio Benítez Rojo, *The Repeating Island: The Caribbean and the Postmodern Perspective*, Second edition. Post-Contemporary Interventions. (Durham, NC: Duke University Press, 1996), 1.
[61] Ibid., 2.
[62] Ibid., 3.
[63] Ibid., 3.

236   CUBAN MUSIC COUNTERPOINTS

repeating, Benítez Rojo relies on its inherent paradox, that with each repetition there will be difference. It is in this sense that hearing and reading about the latest clashes between the Cuban State and artists and intellectuals seems both a repetition of old events, of patterns, and different due to new circumstances and new players. If there are repeating patterns to note throughout the several decades, chapters, and case studies presented in this book, I would point to the heterogeneity in musical approaches; the tensions between tradition and innovation; the desires of composers to connect with their local audience *and* an international network of composers, musicians, and audiences; a tension between the local and the so-called universal. To be a Cuban composer is to inhabit this world of seeming contradictions, a constant counterpoint between Cuban and universal identities and musical traits.

Select Bibliography

10 [i.e. diez] años de cine cubano: publicado por el Departamento de Cine de "Marcha" en homenaje al Instituto Cubano del Arte e Industria Cinematográficos (ICAIC) en su X aniversario. Montevideo: Marcha, 1969.

"A Fidel Castro: Canción de gesta de Pablo Neruda, 1960." *Bayano digital* (blog), November 30, 2017. https://bayanodigital.com/a-fidel-castro-cancion-de-gesta-de-pablo-neruda-1960/.

Acosta, Leonardo. *Entre claves y notas: rutas para el pensamiento musical cubano.* Havana: CIDMUC, 2014.

Acosta, Leonardo. *From the Drum to the Synthesizer.* Havana, Cuba: José Martí PubHouse, 1987.

Acosta, Leonardo. "Harold Gramatges y sus 'móviles.'" *Boletín Música,* no. 106 (1985): 27–34.

Acosta, Leonardo. "Testimonio de Fe." *Clave—Revista Cubana de Música* 6, no. 1–3 (2004): 75–76.

Adlington, Robert. *Sound Commitments: Avant-Garde Music and the Sixties.* Oxford; New York: Oxford University Press, 2009.

"Aerial Image of Instituto Superior de Arte, Cuba, Google Earth." Accessed August 30, 2021.

"Aerial View of the Roofs of Cuba's National Art School - Guillermo 'Willy' González Collection - Digital Collections. CHC017 Guillermo "Willy" González Papers, Box. No. 4, Binder No. 1, Binder Name: Slide Book No. 1, Tab: Escuela Nacional de Artes. University of Miami Cuban Heritage Collection. Accessed August 30, 2021. https://digitalcollections.library.miami.edu/digital/collection/chc0170/id/4074/rec/1.

AfroCubaWeb. "Movimiento San Isidro – N27." Accessed February 8, 2022. https://www.afrocubaweb.com/san-isidro-n27.html.

AfroCubaWeb. "The Berman Amendment." Accessed September 21, 2022. https://www.afrocubaweb.com/bermanamendment.htm.

Alén Rodríguez, Olavo. "The Music Archives at the CIDMUC and Their Influence on the Musical Culture of Cuba." In *Archives for the Future: Global Perspectives on Audiovisual Archives in the 21st Century,* edited by Anthony Seeger and Shubha Chaudhuri, 130–142. Calcutta: Seagull Books, 2004.

Alonso Minutti, Ana Ruth. "Resonances of Sound, Text, and Image in the Music of Mario Lavista." Ph.D. diss, University of California, Davis, 2008.

Alonso Minutti, Ana Ruth. "Forging a Cosmopolitan Ideal: Mario Lavista's Early Music." *Latin American Music Review / Revista de Música Latinoamericana* 35, no. 2 (2014): 169–196.

Álvarez García, Alberto. *Intelectuales vs. revolución?: el caso del Centro de Estudios sobre América,* CEA. 1. edición. Colección Ciencias sociales cubanas. Montreal: Ediciones Arte D.T., 2001.

Amer Rodríguez, José. *Harold Gramatges: catálogo de obras.* Madrid: SGAE, 1997.

238 SELECT BIBLIOGRAPHY

Amnesty International. "Amnesty International Condemns the Sentences of Luis Manuel Otero Alcántara and Maykel 'Osorbo' Castillo," June 24, 2022. https://www.amnesty.org/en/latest/news/2022/06/cuba-amnesty-condemns-sentences-luis-manuel-otero-alcantara-maykel-osorbo-castillo/.

Ansari, Emily Abrams. "Musical Americanism, Cold War Consensus Culture, and the U.S.–USSR Composers' Exchange, 1958–60." *The Musical Quarterly* 97, no. 3 (2014): 360–389.

Ansari, Emily Abrams. *The Sound of a Superpower: Musical Americanism and the Cold War*. New York, NY: Oxford University Press, 2018.

Aponte Ledeé, Rafael. "Casals: Un Agente Para La Penetración Cultural." *Boletín Música*, no. 28 (1972): n.p.

Arcos, Betto. "'To Be Useful Is Something Incredible': Leo Brouwer Reflects On His Legacy." *NPR*, April 11, 2017, sec. Deceptive Cadence. https://www.npr.org/sections/deceptivecadence/2017/04/11/523317039/to-be-useful-is-something-incredible-leo-brouwer-reflects-on-his-legacy.

Ardévol, José. *Introducción a Cuba: La música*. Havana: Instituto del Libro, 1969.

Ardévol, José. *Música de cámara para seis instrumentos. Chamber music for six instruments*. Washington; New York: Pan American Union Peer International Corp., 1955.

Ardévol, José. *Música y revolución*. Havana, Cuba: UNEAC, 1966.

Ardévol, José. *Sonata no. 3 para piano*. Montevideo, Uruguay: Editorial Cooperativa Interamericana de Compositores, 1946.

Ardévol, José [Díaz, Clara, ed]. *José Ardévol: Correspondencia cruzada*. Havana, Cuba: Editorial Letras Cubanas, 2004.

Argeliers León. CD/DVD. Havana: Roldán/Producciones Colibrí, 2009.

Artaraz, Kepa. "Constructing Identities in a Contested Setting: Cuba's Intellectual Elite during and after the Revolution." *Oral History* 45, no. 2 (2017): 50–59.

Astley, Tom. *Outside the Revolution, Everything: A Redefinition of Left-Wing Identity in Contemporary Cuban Music Making*. Winchester, UK; Washington, USA: Zero Books, 2012.

Azicri, Max. *Cuba: Politics, Economics, and Society*. Marxist Regimes Series. London; New York: Pinter Publishers, 1988.

Bain, Mervyn J. "Cuba–Soviet Relations in the Gorbachev Era." *Journal of Latin American Studies* 37, no. 4 (2005): 769–791.

Beal, Amy C. "Negotiating Cultural Allies: American Music in Darmstadt, 1946–1956." *Journal of the American Musicological Society* 53, no. 1 (2000): 105–139.

Beezley, William H. *Cultural Nationalism and Ethnic Music in Latin America*. Albuquerque: University of New Mexico Press, 2018.

Benítez Rojo, Antonio. *The Repeating Island: The Caribbean and the Postmodern Perspective*. Second edition. Post-Contemporary Interventions. Durham, NC: Duke University Press, 1996.

Benson, Devyn Spence, Daisy Rubiera Castillo, and Inés María Martiatu Terry. *Afrocubanas: History, Thought, and Cultural Practices*. Lanham: Rowman & Littlefield, 2020.

Berroa, Jorge. "Encuentro de Música Latinoamericana. Septiembre de 1972." *Boletín Música*, no. 29 (1972): 10–19.

Birkenmaier, Anke. *Alejo Carpentier y la cultura del surrealismo en América Latina*. Madrid, España: Iberoamericana, 2006.

SELECT BIBLIOGRAPHY 239

Birkenmaier, Anke. *The Specter of Races: Latin American Anthropology and Literature between the Wars*. New World Studies. Charlottesville, VA; London: University of Virginia Press, 2016.

Blanco, Juan. *Contemporáneos 4*. LP. Vol. LD-3809. Contemporáneos. Havana, Cuba: EGREM-Areito, 1979.

Blanco, Juan. "Contrpunto Espacial III/Octagonales." Music Score MS. Museo Nacional de la Música Cubana, 1969. Juan Blanco Personal Collection.

Blanco, Juan. *Contrpunto Espacial No. 3*. Digitized Archival Recording, 1969.

Blanco, Juan. "La Música." *Revista Casa de las Américas*, no. 9 (December 1961): 117–123.

Blanco, Juan. *Música Electroacústica*. Vol. LD-4211. Havana, Cuba: Areito, 1986.

Blanco, Juan. *Música Electroacústica*. Vol. LD-4442. Havana, Cuba: Areito, 1987.

Blanco, Juan. *Quinteto para cuatro instrumentos de viento y violoncello*. Havana: Departmento de Música de la Biblioteca Nacional "José Martí", 1960.

Blanco, Juan and José Manuel García. "Monólogo de Cumpleaños." *Clave—Revista Cubana de Música*, no. 13 (1989): 3–5.

Blanco, Juan Marcos. *Caballos Música Electroacústica*. Vol. LD-4247. Havana, Cuba: Areito, 1984.

Blanco, Yurima. "Impronta del compositor cubano: Hilario González en la cultura venezolana (1947–1960)." *Boletín Música*, no. 50 (December 2018): 79–113.

Blanco, Yurima, and Ailer Pérez Gómez. "'Vanguardia' y 'retaguardia' musical en Cuba: relatos históricos y polémicas (1961–1971)." *El oído pensante* 8, no. 2 (August 6, 2020): 79–113.

Borges Triana, Joaquín. *Concierto cubano: la vida es un divino guión*. Diferencias. Barcelona: Linkgua Ediciones, 2009.

Borges Triana, Joaquín. "Música Cubana Alternativa: del margen al epicentro." IASPM-AL, 2012, 1–26.

Borges Triana, Joaquín. *Músicos de Cuba y del mundo: nadie se va del todo*. Cuba: Ediciones ConCierto Cubano, 2012.

Bourdieu, Pierre. *The Field of Cultural Production: Essays on Art and Literature*. New York: Columbia University Press, 1993.

Brandhorst, Rosa María, and Anna Lidia Beltrán Marín. "The Education System of Cuba." In *The Education Systems of the Americas*, edited by Sieglinde Jornitz and Marcelo Parreira do Amaral, 465–494. Global Education Systems. Cham: Springer International Publishing, 2021.

Bravo, Eva Silot. "Cubanidad 'In Between': The Transnational Cuban Alternative Music Scene." *Latin American Music Review / Revista de Música Latinoamericana* 38, no. 1 (May 23, 2017): 28–56.

Brennan, Timothy. *At Home in the World: Cosmopolitanism Now*. Convergences. Cambridge, MA: Harvard University Press, 1997.

Brennan, Timothy and Ester Blay. "El surrealismo y el son." *Guaraguao* 6, no. 15 (2002): 20–51.

Bringuez Acosta, Mirelys. "De mujeres y música, algo más que componer . . . ." Thesis, Instituto Superior de Arte, 2008.

Brouwer, Leo. "La improvisación aleatoria." *Boletín Música*, no. 38 (1973): 20–26.

Brouwer, Leo. "La tradición se rompe . . . pero cuesta trabajo." Score MS. Museo Nacional de la Música Cubana, 1969. Leo Brouwer Personal Collection.

Brouwer, Leo. *La música, lo cubano y la innovación*. Ensayo (Editorial Letras Cubanas). Havana, Cuba: Editorial Letras Cubanas, 1982.

240 SELECT BIBLIOGRAPHY

Brouwer, Leo. *La tradición se rompe . . . pero cuesta trabajo*. LP. Vol. LD 7009. Havana: Areito, 1970.

Brouwer, Leo. "La vanguardia en la música cubana." *Boletín Música*, no. 1 (1970): 2–6.

Brouwer, Leo. "Música, folclor, contemporaneidad y postmodernismo." *Clave—Revista Cubana de Música*, no. 13 (June 1989): 53–55.

Brouwer, Leo. *Sonata "pian e forte": für Klavier*. Mainz: Ars Viva, 1973.

Brouwer, Leo, and Juan Blanco. *Estructuras Conmutaciones*. Vol. LD 3652. Contemporáneos. EGREM, 1976.

"Brouwer & Chobanian Present Premieres." *Soundboard* 9, no. 4 (1982): 328.

Burton, Julianne. "The Camera as 'Gun': Two Decades of Culture and Resistance in Latin America." *Latin American Perspectives* 5, no. 1 (1978): 49–76.

Bustamante, Michael J. "Cold War Paquetería: Snail Mail Services Across and Around Cuba's 'Sugar Curtain', 1963–1969." *Journal of Latin American Cultural Studies* 30, no. 2 (April 3, 2021): 215–231.

Bustamante, Michael J. *Cuban Memory Wars: Retrospective Politics in Revolution and Exile*. Envisioning Cuba. Chapel Hill: University of North Carolina Press, 2021.

Bustamante, Michael J. "Cultural Politics and Political Cultures of the Cuban Revolution: New Directions in Scholarship." *Cuban Studies* 47, no. 1 (March 14, 2019): 3–18.

Bustamante, Michael J., and Jennifer L. Lambe. *The Revolution from Within: Cuba, 1959–1980*. Durham, NC: Duke University Press, 2019.

Busto Marín, Sandra M. "Carlos Fariñas, Compositor de Grandes Aportes a La Cultura." Accessed February 10, 2021. http://www.5septiembre.cu/carlos-farinas-composi tor-aportes-la-cultura/?fbclid=IwAR3L-c5m20QH1eHeS3YfoQHgKfKKfZRLOhOj mWRzdV8Bf3F8RUFbct5K76A.

Bylander, Cindy. "The Warsaw Autumn International Festival of Contemporary Music 1956–1961: Its Goals, Structures, Programs, and People." Ph.D. diss, The Ohio State University, 1989.

Cabezas Miranda, Jorge. *Proyectos poéticos en Cuba, 1959–2000: algunos cambios formales y temáticos*. San Vicente Raspeig: Publicaciones de la Universidad de Alicante, 2012.

Cairo Ballester, Ana. *El Grupo Minorista y su tiempo*. Havana: Editorial de Ciencias Sociales, 1978.

Calero Martín, José, and Leopoldo Valdés Quesada. *Cuba musical: album-resumen ilustrado de la historia y de la actual situación del arte musical en Cuba directores y gerentes*. Havana: Imprenta de Molina y Compañía, 1929.

Calero, Sonia. and University of Miami. Library. Cuban Heritage Collection, host institution. *Alberto Alonso and Sonia Calero papers, 1935–2002*. 1935.

Calico, Joy H. *Arnold Schoenberg's* A Survivor from Warsaw *in Postwar Europe*. California Studies in 20th-Century Music 17. Berkeley, CA: University of California Press, 2014.

Campbell, Alan Douglas. "The Binary Sonata Tradition in the Mid-Eighteenth Century: Bipartite and Tripartite 'First Halves' in the Venice XIII Collection of Keyboard Sonatas by Domenico Scarlatti." M.A. Thesis, McGill University, 2000.

Campbell, Jennifer L. "Shaping Solidarity: Music, Diplomacy, and Inter-American Relations, 1936–1946." Ph.D. diss, University of Connecticut, 2010.

Carballo, Erick. "De La Pampa al Cielo: The Development of Tonality in the Compositional Language of Alberto Ginastera." Ph.D. diss, Indiana University, 2006.

Carles Arribas, José Luis, and Cristina Palmese. "Los Paisajes Del Agua En El Discurrir de La Música." *Scherzo: Revista de Música* 23, no. 228 (March 2008): 114–125.

SELECT BIBLIOGRAPHY 241

Carpentier, Alejo. "El Grupo Musical Cubano-Norteamericano. Concierto de la Orquesta de Cámara." *Conservatorio* no. 5 (1945): 11–14.

Carpentier, Alejo. *El reino de este mundo*. Lima, Peru, 1948.

Carpentier, Alejo. *La música en Cuba*. Mexico: Fondo de Cultura Economica, 1946.

Carpentier, Alejo. "Panorama de la música en Cuba." Originally published in *Conservatorio* 1, no. 2 (1944): 5–10, reproduced in *La música en Cuba. Temas de la lira y del bongó*. Havana: Ediciones Museo de la Música, 2012, 354–364.

Carpentier, Alejo. *Temas de la lira y el bongó*. Mexico: Fondo de Cultura Economica, 2016.

Carpentier, Alejo, Radamés Giro, and Graziella Pogolotti. *La música en Cuba; Temas de la lira y del bongó*. Havana, Cuba: Ediciones Museo de la Música, 2012.

Carroll, Mark. *Music and Ideology in Cold War Europe*. Music in the Twentieth Century. Cambridge; New York: Cambridge University Press, 2003.

Carvajal, Mara Lioba Juan. *Leo Brouwer modernidad y vanguardia*. Mexico: Intercambio Cultural Latinoamericano Unicornio, 2006.

Carvajal, Mara Lioba Juan, and Dargen Tania Juan Carvajal. *Cuerdas Frotadas En Cuba: Medio Siglo de Creación*. Havana: CIDMUC, 2016.

Casanova, Nancy. *Nancy Casanova, piano*. LP. Vol. LD 3589. Havana, Cuba: Areito, 197AD.

Caso, Eduardo Morales. "Lo nacional en la obra para voz y piano de Gisela Hernández y Harold Gramatges. Análisis Compositivo." *Revista de Musicología* 37, no. 2 (2014): 724–731.

Cass, Jeremy Leeds. "Fashioning Afrocuba: Fernando Ortiz and the Advent of Afrocuban Studies, 1906–1957." Ph.D. diss, University of Kentucky, 2004.

Castro, Alina. "Acerca del estilo de creación en la obra de Gisela Hernández." Thesis, Instituto Superior de Arte, 1991.

Castro, Fidel. *Palabras a los intelectuales*. Havana: Consejo Nacional de Cultura, 1961.

Century, Paul. "Leo Brouwer: A Portrait of the Artist in Socialist Cuba." *Latin American Music Review / Revista de Música Latinoamericana* 8, no. 2 (1987): 151–171.

Chanan, Michael. *Cuban Cinema*. Minneapolis: University of Minnesota Press, 2004.

Guevara, Ernesto Che. *El socialismo y el hombre nuevo*. Mexico: Siglo Veintiuno, 1977.

Clásicos cubanos Orquesta Sinfónica Nacional. Havana: EGREM, 2000, compact disc.

Cohen, Brigid. *Musical Migration and Imperial New York: Early Cold War Scenes*. Chicago: University of Chicago Press, 2022.

Cole, Johnnetta B. "Race Toward Equality: The Impact of the Cuban Revolution on Racism." *The Black Scholar* 11, no. 8 (1980): 2–24.

Comisión Económica para América Latina y el Caribe. *La economía cubana: reformas estructurales y desempeño en los noventa*. CEPAL, 2000.

Congresso Nacional de Educacion y Cultura, Ministerio de Educación Cuba, and Instituto Cubano del Libro, eds. *Cuba '71*. Havana: Instituto Cubano del Libro Editorial Ambito, 1971.

Contemporáneos 1. LP. Vol. LD 3652. Contemporáneos. Havana, Cuba: EGREM, 1976.

Contemporáneos 12. LP. Vol. LD-4218. Contemporáneos. Havana, Cuba: EGREM, 1983.

Contemporáneos 13. LP. Vol. LD-4223. Contemporáneos. Havana, Cuba: EGREM, 1984.

Continuo's weblog. "Cuban Avantgarde – Continuo's Weblog." Accessed June 3, 2021. https://continuo.wordpress.com/category/cuban-avantgarde/.

Cornish, Gabrielle. "Sounding Socialist, Sounding Modern: Music, Technology, and Everyday Life in the Soviet Union, 1956–1975." Ph.D. diss, University of Rochester, 2020.

Corona fúnebre a la gloria de Ernesto Guevara. LP. Havana, Cuba: Areito, 196–.

242 SELECT BIBLIOGRAPHY

Cowell, Henry. *American Composers on American Music: A Symposium*. New York: F. Ungar, 1962.

Crook, Larry. "A Musical Analysis of the Cuban Rumba." *Latin American Music Review / Revista de Música Latinoamericana* 3, no. 1 (1982): 92–123.

Crooker, Matthew R. "Cool Notes in an Invisible War: The Use of Radio and Music in the Cold War from 1953 to 1968." Master's Thesis, Wright State University, 2019.

Meyer, Felix, Carol J. Oja, Wolfgang Rathert, and Anne Chatoney Shreffler, eds. *Crosscurrents: American and European Music in Interaction, 1900–2000*. Suffolk: The Boydell Press, 2014.

Cuban Culture and Cultural Relations, 1959–, Part 1: 'Casa y Cultura.' Boston: Brill, 1987.

Cushman, Gregory T. "'¿De qué color es el oro?': Race, Environment, and the History of Cuban National Music, 1898–1958." *Latin American Music Review / Revista de Música Latinoamericana* 26, no. 2 (Fall–Winter 2005): 164–194.

Dalton, David S. *Mestizo Modernity: Race, Technology, and the Body in Post-Revolutionary Mexico*. Gainesville, FL: University Press of Florida, 2018.

"DCubaMúsica - Empresa - Agencia Cubana de Derecho de Autor Musical (ACDAM)." Accessed January 17, 2022. http://dcubamusica.cult.cu/directorio/intitucion/agencia-cubana-de-derecho-de-autor-musical-acdam/.

De Ferrari, Guillermina. *Community and Culture in Post-Soviet Cuba*. Routledge Interdisciplinary Perspectives on Literature 23. New York, NY: Routledge, 2014.

De la Fuente, Alejandro. *A Nation for All: Race, Inequality, and Politics in Twentieth-Century Cuba*. Chapel Hill: University of North Carolina Press, 2011.

De la Fuente, Alejandro. "Race, National Discourse, and Politics in Cuba: An Overview." *Latin American Perspectives* 25, no. 3 (1998): 43–69.

De la Fuente, Alejandro. "The New Afro-Cuban Cultural Movement and the Debate on Race in Contemporary Cuba." *Journal of Latin American Studies* 40, no. 4 (November 2008): 697–720.

DeLapp-Birkett, Jennifer. "Aaron Copland and the Politics of Twelve-Tone Composition in the Early Cold War United States." *Journal of Musicological Research* 27, no. 1 (January 2008): 31–62.

"Derechos de Autores Musicales En Cuba." Accessed January 17, 2022. https://www.eumed.net/rev/cccss/18/amml2.html.

Díaz Ayala, Cristóbal. *Musica cubana: del areyto a la nueva trova*. Miami: Ediciones Universal, 1993.

Díaz, Javier. "Meaning Beyond Words: A Musical Analysis of Afro-Cuban Batá Drumming," DMA diss, City University of New York, 2019.

Diez Nieto, Alfredo. *Capricho Cubano*. CD. Havana, Cuba: Colibrí, 2011.

Dirlik, Arif, and Xudong Zhang. *Postmodernism & China*. Durham, NC: Duke University Press, 2000.

Djebbari, Elina. "Archive and Memory in Cuban Dances: The Performance of Memory and the Dancing Body as Archive in the Making." In *Cultural Memory and Popular Dance: Dancing to Remember, Dancing to Forget*, edited by Clare Parfitt, 193–209. Palgrave Macmillan Memory Studies. Cham: Springer International Publishing, 2021.

Domínguez, Yarelis. "En los 65 de Carlos Fariñas: No me visto de cubano para componer." *Clave—Revista Cubana de Música* 1, no. 2 (October 1999): 2–7.

Dopico Black, Georgina. "The Limits of Expression: Intellectual Freedom in Postrevolutionary Cuba." *Cuban Studies* 19 (1989): 107–142.

SELECT BIBLIOGRAPHY 243

Duchesne Cuzán, Manuel, and Orquesta Sinfónica Nacional de Cuba. *Contemporáneos 2*. LP. Vol. LD 3653. Contemporáneos. Havana, Cuba: EGREM, 1976.

Duchesne Cuzán, Manuel. *Contemporáneos 3*. LP. Vol. LD-3818. Contemporáneos. Havana, Cuba: EGREM, 2021.

Eckstein, Susan Eva. *The Immigrant Divide: How Cuban Americans Changed the U.S. and Their Homeland*. Taylor and Francis, 2009.

EcuRed. "Editora Musical de Cuba." Accessed January 17, 2022. https://www.ecured.cu/Editora_Musical_de_Cuba.

EcuRed. "Movimiento Cubano por la Paz y la Soberanía de los Pueblos." Accessed May 5, 2022. https://www.ecured.cu/index.php/Movimiento_Cubano_por_la_Paz_y_la_Soberan%C3%ADa_de_los_Pueblos.

Eli Rodríguez, Victoria. "Apuntes sobre la creación musical actual en Cuba." *Latin American Music Review / Revista de Música Latinoamericana* 10, no. 2 (1989): 287–297.

Eli Rodríguez, Victoria. "Convergencias y desencuentros en torno a la identidad nacional en la música (Cuba, 1920–1940)." *Boletín Música*, no. 36 (2014): 51–68.

Eli Rodríguez, Victoria. "Cuban Music and Ethnicity: Historical Considerations." In *Music and Black Ethnicity: The Caribbean and South America*, edited by Gerard Béhague, 91–108. Coral Gables, FL: North-South Center Press, University of Miami, 1994.

Eli Rodríguez, Victoria. "La creación musical de la Revolución (1959–1971)." Thesis, Instituto Superior de Arte, 1981.

Eli Rodríguez, Victoria. "Música e historia en Cuba (IV)." *Clave—Revista Cubana de Música*, no. 15 (1989): 12–15.

Eli Rodríguez, Victoria. *Roberto Valera*. Madrid: Fundación Autor, 1998.

Eli Rodríguez, Victoria, and Ileana Güeche. "Caminos de la electroacústica en Cuba." *Clave—Revista Cubana de Música* 4, no. 3 (2002): 21–30.

Eli Rodríguez, Victoria, Elena Torres, and Belén Vega Pichaco. *Música y construcción de identidades: poéticas, diálogos y utopías en Latinoamérica y España*. Madrid: Sociedad Española de Musicología, 2018.

Encuentro de Música Latinoamericana, Sep. 1972 Casa de las Américas. LP. Havana, Cuba: Casa de las Américas, 1973.

Fábrica de Arte Cubano. "Fábrica de Arte Cubano." Accessed January 19, 2022. http://www.fac.cu/.

Fairclough, Pauline. *Classics for the Masses: Shaping Soviet Musical Identity under Lenin and Stalin*. New Haven, CT: Yale University Press, 2016.

Falola, Toyin, and Matt D. Childs. *The Yoruba Diaspora in the Atlantic World*. Bloomington, IN: Indiana University Press, 2005.

Fariñas, Carlos. *Aguas Territoriales / Musica Electroacustica*. Vol. LD-4230. Havana, Cuba: Areito, 1981.

Fariñas, Carlos. "Reflexiones a un cuarto de siglo." *Clave—Revista Cubana de Música*, no. 1 (1986): 28–30.

Farra, Ricardo Dal. "El archivo de música electroacústica de compositores latinoamericanos." Fondation Daniel Langlois, 2004.

Fay, Brendan. *Classical Music in Weimar Germany: Culture and Politics before the Third Reich*. Bloomsbury Publishing, 2019.

Feldman, Morton. *Morton Feldman Says: Selected Interviews and Lectures 1964–1987*. Hyphen New Series. London: Hyphen Press, 2006.

Feller, Ross. "Juan Blanco: Nuestro Tiempo/Our Time." *Computer Music Journal* 38, no. 2 (June 1, 2014): 84–86.

244 SELECT BIBLIOGRAPHY

Fennell, Christopher C. *Crossroads and Cosmologies: Diasporas and Ethnogenesis in the New World*. Gainesville, FL: University Press of Florida, 2010.

Feraudy Espino, Heriberto. *Yo vi la música: vida y obra de Harold Gramatges*. Havana: Editorial de Ciencias Sociales, 2009.

Fernandes, Sujatha. *Cuba Represent!: Cuban Arts, State Power, and the Making of New Revolutionary Cultures*. Durham, NC: Duke University Press, 2006.

Fernandes, Sujatha. "Reinventing the Revolution: Artistic Public Spheres and the State in Contemporary Cuba." Ph.D. diss, University of Chicago, 2003.

Fernández, Frank, Orquesta Sinfónica Nacional de Cuba, Gonzalo Romeu, and Nancy Casanova. *Contemporáneos 7*. LP. Vol. LD-4134. Contemporáneos. Havana, Cuba: EGREM, 1983.

Fernández, Gastón A. "Race, Gender, and Class in the Persistence of the Mariel Stigma Twenty Years after the Exodus from Cuba." *The International Migration Review* 41, no. 3 (2007): 602–622.

Ferrando, Layda. "Juan Blano: cien años de música." *Boletín Música*, no. 51 (separata) (2019): 1–23.

Fornet, Ambrosio. "El quinquenio gris: revisitando el término." *Rebelión*, January 2007. https://rebelion.org/el-quinquenio-gris-revisitando-el-termino/.

Fosler-Lussier, Danielle. *Music in America's Cold War Diplomacy*. Berkeley, CA: University of California Press, 2015.

Inter-American Music Festival Foundation. "Inter-American Music Festival Foundation Records, 1961–1983." Mixed material. Washington, D.C.: Library of Congress Music Division, 1961–1983.

Fox, Christopher. "Darmstadt and the Institutionalisation of Modernism." *Contemporary Music Review* 26, no. 1 (February 2007): 115–123.

Frolova-Walker, Marina. "'National in Form, Socialist in Content': Musical Nation-Building in the Soviet Republics." *Journal of the American Musicological Society* 51, no. 2 (1998): 331–371.

Fugellie, Daniela. "Las relaciones de Luigi Nono con los compositores latinoamericanos de vanguardia." *Boletín Música*, no. 35 (2013): 3–29.

Fugellie, Daniela. "'Musiker Unserer Zeit': Internationale Avantgarde, Migration Und Wiener Schule in Südamerika." Ph.D. diss, Berlin University of the Arts, 2018.

Fugellie, Daniela, Ulrike Mühlschlegel, Matthias Pasdzierny, and Christina Richter-Ibañez, eds. *Trayectorias: Music between Latin America and Europe 1945–1970 / Trayectorias: Música Entre América Latina y Europa 1945–1970*. Berlin: Ibero-Online, 2019.

García Canclini, Néstor. *Culturas híbridas: estrategias para entrar y salir de la modernidad*. Nueva edición. Grijalbo, México: Consejo Nacional para la Cultura y las Artes, 2001.

García del Busto Arregui, José Luis. "Un escenario y dos propuestas." *Clave—Revista Cubana de Música*, no. 4 (January 1987): 9.

García, Fernando. "Harold Gramatges (1918–2008) y Juan Blanco (1919–2008)." *Revista musical chilena* 63, no. 211 (2009): 108–109.

García, José Manuel. "Cuando se rompe la clave." *Clave—Revista Cubana de Música*, no. 4 (January 1987): 38–40.

García, José Manuel. "Monólogo de cumpleaños." *Clave—Revista Cubana de Música*, no. 13 (April 1989): 3–5.

SELECT BIBLIOGRAPHY 245

García, Juan Antonio. *Cine cubano: la pupila insomne*. Havana: Ediciones Unión, 2012.

García Molina, Andrés Jacobo. "Aural Economies and Precarious Labor: Street-Vendor Songs in Cuba." Ph.D. diss, Columbia University, 2020.

García Yero, Cary Aileen. "The State within the Arts: A Study of Cuba's Cultural Policy, 1940–1958." *Cuban Studies* 47, no. 1 (March 14, 2019): 83–110.

Giro, Radamés, and Jesús Gómez Cairo. *Leo Brouwer: del rito al mito*. Havana, Cuba: Ediciones Museo de la Música, 2009.

Giro, Radamés, and Harold Gramatges. *Grupo Renovación Musical de Cuba*. Havana, Cuba: Ediciones Museo de la Música, 2009.

Gonçalves, João Felipe. "The Ajiaco in Cuba and Beyond." *HAU: Journal of Ethnographic Theory* 4, no. 3 (December 1, 2014): 445–454.

González Moreno, Liliana. *Federico Smith, cosmopolitismo y vanguardia*. Havana, Cuba: Ediciones CIDMUC, Centro de Investigación y Desarrollo de la Música Cubana, 2013.

Gott, Richard. *Cuba: A New History*. First edition. New Haven, CT: Yale University Press, 2004.

Gramatges, Harold. *Contemporáneos 11*. LP. Vol. LD-4219. Contemporáneos. Havana, Cuba: EGREM, 1986.

Gramatges, Harold. *Dos danzas cubanas: for piano*. New York: Peer International Corp., 1953.

Gramatges, Harold. *La muerte del guerrillero: para recitante y orquesta*. Havana: Editora Musical de Cuba, 1972.

Gramatges, Harold. *Obras para piano*. Madrid: Editorial de Música Española Contemporánea, 2008.

Gramatges, Harold. *Presencia de la Revolución en la música cubana*. Havana, Cuba: Editorial Letras Cubanas, 1983.

Gramatges, Harold. *Serenata, orquesta de cuerdas*. Havana: Editora Musical de Cuba, 1988.

Grenier, Yvon. *Culture and the Cuban State: Participation, Recognition, and Dissonance Under Communism*. Lanham: Lexington Books, 2017.

Grenier, Yvon. "The Politics of Culture and the Gatekeeper State in Cuba." *Cuban Studies* 46 (2018): 261–286.

Griffiths, Paul. "Discovering and Rediscovering Cuba." *New York Times*. 1999, sec. The Arts. Accessed September 28, 2020. https://www.nytimes.com/1999/03/18/arts/music-review-discovering-and-rediscovering-cuba.html.

Güeche, Ileana. "Breve caracterización de la música electroacústica en Cuba." *Pauta: Cuadernos de Teoría y Crítica Musical* 14, no. 53–54 (January 1995): 150–160.

Guerra, Lillian. "Gender Policing, Homosexuality and the New Patriarchy of the Cuban Revolution, 1965–70." *Social History* 35, no. 3 (2010): 268–289.

Guerra, Lillian. *Visions of Power in Cuba: Revolution, Redemption, and Resistance, 1959–1971*. Envisioning Cuba. Chapel Hill: University of North Carolina Press, 2012.

Guevara, Alfredo. *Alfredo Guevara en el ejercicio de la crítica en Hoy y Nuestro tiempo (1953–1957)*. Havana: Ediciones Nuevo Cine Latinoamericano, 2017.

Guldbrandsen, Erling E., and Julian Johnson. *Transformations of Musical Modernism*. Cambridge, United Kingdom: Cambridge University Press, 2015.

Guridi, Ricardo R. *Edgardo Martín/Alejo Carpentier correspondencia cruzada*. Havana, Cuba: Ediciones Museo de la Música, 2013.

246 SELECT BIBLIOGRAPHY

Guy, Jack. "An Introduction to Havana's Electronic Music Scene in 7 DJs." *Culture Trip*. Accessed November 19, 2019. https://theculturetrip.com/caribbean/cuba/articles/an-introduction-to-havanas-electronic-music-scene-in-7-djs/.

Guzmán Moré, Jorgelina. *De Dirección General a Instituto Nacional de Cultura*. Havana: Editora Historia, 2014.

Harris, Richard L. "Cuban Internationalism, Che Guevara, and the Survival of Cuba's Socialist Regime." *Latin American Perspectives* 36, no. 3 (2009): 27–42.

Hart, Armando. "La Música Cubana." *Bohemia*, February 11, 1977.

Hartman, Joseph R. *Dictator's Dreamscape: How Architecture and Vision Built Machado's Cuba and Invented Modern Havana*. Pittsburgh: University of Pittsburgh Press, 2019.

HavanaModerno. " 'Theremin En América Latina' Entrevista Con Edesio Alejandro Rodríguez." Accessed September 7, 2021. https://habanamoderno.blogspot.com/2021/08/theremin-en-america-latina-entrevista.html?m=1&fbclid=IwAR2cHMi6cuCl6IUEQ4lSnLvwRiF-C59J_74aQidS2HSP1-eey9dbNS4g3l8.

Hawk, Kate Dupes, and Bob Graham. *Florida and the Mariel Boatlift of 1980: The First Twenty Days*. Tuscaloosa, AL: The University of Alabama Press, 2014.

Head, Po Sim. "Cuban Women in Music: A Case Study of Ernestina Lecuona." Master's Thesis, University of Missouri-Kansas City, 2019.

Heile, Björn. "Darmstadt as Other: British and American Responses to Musical Modernism." *Twentieth-Century Music* 1, no. 2 (2004): 161–178.

Henken, Ted A. "The Opium of the Paquete: State Censorship, Private Self-Censorship, and the Content-Distribution Strategies of Cuba's Emergent, Independent Digital-Media Start-Ups." *Cuban Studies* 50, no. 1 (2021): 111–138.

Henthorne, Tony L. *Tourism in Cuba: Casinos, Castros, and Challenges*. Bingley, United Kingdom: Emerald Publishing Limited, 2018.

Hernández Baguer, Grizel. *Historias para una historia*. Havana, Cuba: Ediciones Museo de la Música, 2012.

Hernández, Henry Eric. "La censura bienintencionada: representaciones del peregrinaje político hacia la revolución cubana." *Iberoamericana (2001–)* 13, no. 50 (2013): 27–47.

Hernández, Isabelle. *Leo Brouwer*. Havana: Editora Musical de Cuba, 2000.

Hernández Otero, Ricardo Luis. *Revista Nuestro tiempo: compilación de trabajos publicados*. Havana: Editorial Letras Cubanas, 1989.

Hernández Otero, Ricardo Luis, and Sociedad Cultural Nuestro Tiempo. *Sociedad Cultural Nuestro Tiempo: resistencia y acción*. Ensayo. Havana, Cuba: Editorial Letras Cubanas, 2002.

Hernández-Reguant, Ariana. "Copyrighting Che: Art and Authorship under Cuban Late Socialism." *Public Culture* 16, no. 1 (2004): 1–29.

Herrera, Eduardo. *Elite Art Worlds: Philanthropy, Latin Americanism, and Avant-Garde Music*. New York: Oxford University Press, 2020.

Hess, Carol A. "From 'Greater America' to America's Music: Gilbert Chase and the Historiography of Borders." *Diagonal: An Ibero-American Music Review* 4, no. 2 (2019): 31–47.

Hess, Carol A. "Leopold Stokowski, 'Latin' Music, and Pan Americanism." *Inter-American Music Review* 18, no. 1–2 (2008): 395–401.

Hess, Carol A. *Manuel de Falla and Modernism in Spain, 1898–1936*. Chicago: University of Chicago Press, 2001.

SELECT BIBLIOGRAPHY   247

Hess, Carol A. *Representing the Good Neighbor: Music, Difference, and the Pan American Dream*. New York: Oxford University Press, 2013.

Hidalgo, Narciso. "Choteo, identidad y cultura cubana." *Afro-Hispanic Review* 32, no. 1 (2013): 55–70.

Hidalgo-Gato, Alfredo. "Presencia de los medios electroacústicos en la música cubana." *Boletín Música*, no. 21 (January 2008): 57–70.

Hobsbawm, E. J. *Nations and Nationalism since 1780: Programme, Myth, Reality*. Cambridge, United Kingdom; New York: Cambridge University Press, 1990.

Holland, Bernard. "Digging Up High Art from Ordinary Places." *New York Times*. 2005, sec. Weekend Arts Movies Performances.

Hope, William M. "'Donde nace lo cubano': Aesthetics, Nationalist Sentiment, and Cuban Music Making." Ph.D. diss, University of Illinois at Urbana-Champaign, 2009.

Humphreys, Laura-Zoë. *Fidel between the Lines: Paranoia and Ambivalence in Late Socialist Cuban Cinema*. Durham, NC: Duke University Press, 2019.

Humphreys, Laura-Zoë. "Utopia in a Package? Digital Media Piracy and the Politics of Entertainment in Cuba." *Boundary 2* 49, no. 1 (2022): 231–262.

Hyde, Martha MacLean. "Neoclassic and Anachronistic Impulses in Twentieth-Century Music." *Music Theory Spectrum: The Journal of the Society for Music Theory* 18, no. 2 (September 1996): 200–235.

Iber, Patrick. *Neither Peace nor Freedom: The Cultural Cold War in Latin America*. Cambridge, MA: Harvard University Press, 2015.

Iddon, Martin. "Darmstadt Schools: Darmstadt as a Plural Phenomenon." *Tempo: A Quarterly Review of Modern Music* 65, no. 256 (2011): 2–8.

Iverson, Jennifer. *Electronic Inspirations: Technologies of the Cold War Musical Avant-Garde*. New York: Oxford University Press, 2018.

Iverson, Jennifer. "Fraught Adjacencies: The Politics of German Electronic Music." *Acta Musicologica* 92, no. 1 (June 25, 2020): 93–111.

Jakelski, Lisa. "Górecki's Scontri and Avant-Garde Music in Cold War Poland." *The Journal of Musicology* 26, no. 2 (2009): 205–239.

Jakelski, Lisa. *Making New Music in Cold War Poland: The Warsaw Autumn Festival, 1956–1968*. California Studies in 20th-Century Music 19. Oakland, CA: University of California Press, 2017.

Janik, Elizabeth. *Recomposing German Music: Politics and Musical Tradition in Cold War Berlin*. Leiden; Boston: Brill, 2005.

John, Suki. *Contemporary Dance in Cuba: Técnica Cubana as Revolutionary Movement*. Jefferson, NC: McFarland & Co., 2012.

Kabous, Magali, and Carlos Paz. "'El ICAIC Presenta . . .' 1959–2009: Un Demi-Siècle de Cinéma Révolutionnaire à Cuba / 'El ICAIC Presenta . . . ' 1959–2009: Medio Siglo de Cine Revolucionario En Cuba." *Cinémas d'Amérique Latine*, no. 17 (2009): 145–158.

Kahn, Erminie. *English Biographies of Cuban Composers*. New York, NY: Cuban-American Music Group, 1946.

Kapcia, Antoni. *Havana: The Making of Cuban Culture*. Oxford; New York: Berg, 2005.

Kapcia, Antoni. "Revolution, the Intellectual and a Cuban Identity: The Long Tradition." *Bulletin of Latin American Research* 1, no. 2 (1982): 63–78.

Kent, James Clifford. *Aesthetics and the Revolutionary City: Real and Imagined Havana*. Cham, Switzerland: Palgrave Macmillan, 2019.

248 SELECT BIBLIOGRAPHY

Keyser, Joana, Luis Barreras, Carlos Fariñas, and Vessela Saucheva. *Contemporáneos 10.* LP. Vol. LD-4146. Havana, Cuba: EGREM, 2021.

Kirk, Emily J., Anna Clayfield, and Isabel Story, eds. *Cuba's Forgotten Decade: How the 1970s Shaped the Revolution.* Lanham, MD: Lexington Books, 2018.

Knight, Franklin W. *The Caribbean: The Genesis of a Fragmented Nationalism.* New York: Oxford University Press, 2012.

Kraglund, John. "Canadian Music Captures Esprit Contemporain." *The Globe and Mail.* February 24, 1983.

Kramer, Jonathan D. "The Nature and Origins of Musical Postmodernism." *Current Musicology*, no. 66 (Spring 1999): 7–20.

Kronenberg, Clive. "Guitar Composer Leo Brouwer: The Concept of a 'Universal Language.'" *Tempo: A Quarterly Review of Modern Music* 62, no. 245 (July 2008): 30–46.

La Cultura en Cuba socialista. Havana, Cuba: Editorial Letras Cubanas, 1982.

Laguna, Albert Sergio. "Aquí está Álvarez Guedes: Cuban Choteo and the Politics of Play." *Latino Studies* 8, no. 4 (Winter 2010): 509–531.

Lalau, Yllarramendiz Alfonso. "Para pensar una historia contemporánea." Museo Nacional de La Música Cubana (blog), November 25, 2021. https://museomusica-cuba.medium.com/para-pensar-una-historia-contempor%C3%A1nea-b8cb39802eaf.

Lanza, Alcides. "CLAEM [Centro LatinoAmericano de Altos Estudios Musicales]." *Colegio de Compositores Latinoamericanos de Música de Arte* (blog). Accessed February 14, 2020. http://www.colegiocompositores-la.org/en/articulo.php?art_id=65&orden=art_titulo. October 10, 2006.

Latner, Teishan. *Cuban Revolution in America: Havana and the Making of a United States Left, 1968–1992.* Chapel Hill: University of North Carolina Press, 2018.

Lavastida, Hamlet. *1970, Zafra de Los Diez Millones, Fragmentos ICAIC.* 2015. https://www.youtube.com/watch?v=4BAlsoBnzlQ.

Lent, John A. "Cuban Films and the Revolution." *Caribbean Studies* 20, no. 3/4 (1988): 59–68.

León, Argeliers. "Bolero, Guaguancó and Yammbú." Havana (1955–56). Collection Argeliers León. Museo Nacional de la Música Cubana.

León, Argeliers. "Del acto y el resultado." *Boletín Música*, no. 26 (1972): 9–21.

León, Argeliers. *Del canto y el tiempo.* Havana, Cuba: Editorial Letras Cubanas, 1984.

León, Argeliers. "[Review]." *Conservatorio* no. 8 (1947): 29.

León, Argeliers. *Sonatas de la Virgen del Cobre: para piano y orquesta de cuerdas.* Havana: Editora Musical de Cuba, 1988.

Leonard III, Neil. "Juan Blanco: Cuba's Pioneer of Electroacoustic Music." *Computer Music Journal* 21, no. 2 (June 1997): 10–20.

Lesman, Robert S. *Translating Cuba: Literature, Music, Film, Politics.* New York: Routledge, 2021.

Levine, Mike. "Sounding El Paquete: The Local and Transnational Routes of an Afro-Cuban Repartero." *Cuban Studies* 50, no. 1 (2021): 139–160.

Levitz, Tamara. "Experimental Music and Revolution: Cuba's Grupo de Experimentación Sonora Del ICAIC." In *Tomorrow Is the Question: New Directions in Experimental Music Studies*, edited by Benjamin Piekut, 180–210. Ann Arbor, MI: University of Michigan Press, 2014.

Lewis, George E. *A Power Stronger Than Itself: The AACM and American Experimental Music.* Chicago: University of Chicago Press, 2008.

SELECT BIBLIOGRAPHY 249

Lewis, George E., and Benjamin Piekut. "Introduction: On Critical Improvisation Studies." In *The Oxford Handbook of Critical Improvisation Studies*, edited by George E. Lewis and Benjamin Piekut, 1–35. New York: Oxford University Press, 2016.

Lewis, Zachary M. "Neo This, Neo That: An Attempt to Trace the Origins of Neo-Romanticism." NewMusicBox, September 1, 2003. https://nmbx.newmusicusa.org/Neo-This-Neo-That-An-Attempt-to-Trace-the-Origins-of-NeoRomanticism/

López, Iraida H. *Impossible Returns: Narratives of the Cuban Diaspora*. Gainesville, FL: University Press of Florida, 2015.

Lorenzino, Lisa. "Music Education in Cuban Schools." *Research Studies in Music Education* 33, no. 2 (December 1, 2011): 197–210.

Luis, William. *Literary Bondage: Slavery in Cuban Narrative*. Austin: University of Texas Press, 2021.

Lund, Joshua. *Mestizo State: Reading Race in Modern Mexico*. Minneapolis: University of Minnesota Press, 2012.

Lutjens, Sheryl L. "Reading between the Lines: Women, the State, and Rectification in Cuba." *Latin American Perspectives* 22, no. 2 (1995): 100–124.

Madrid, Alejandro L. *In Search of Julián Carrillo and Sonido 13*. New York: Oxford University Press, 2015.

Madrid, Alejandro L. *Sounds of the Modern Nation: Music, Culture, and Ideas in Post-Revolutionary Mexico*. Philadelphia: Temple University Press, 2008.

Madrid, Alejandro L. *Tania León's Stride: A Polyrhythmic Life*. Urbana: University of Illinois Press, 2021.

Madrid, Alejandro L., and Robin D. Moore. *Danzón: Circum-Carribean Dialogues in Music and Dance*. New York: Oxford University Press, 2013.

Mahler, Anne Garland. *From the Tricontinental to the Global South: Race, Radicalism, and Transnational Solidarity*. Durham, NC: Duke University Press, 2018.

Mañach, Jorge. *Indagación del choteo*. Barcelona: Editorial Linkgua, 2019.

Mañach, Jorge. *La crisis de la alta cultura en Cuba; Indagación del choteo*. Colección Cuba y sus jueces. Miami, FL: Ediciones Universal, 1991.

Manuel, Peter, ed. *Creolizing Contradance in the Caribbean*. Studies in Latin American and Caribbean Music. Philadelphia: Temple University Press, 2009.

Manuel, Peter. *Essays on Cuban Music: North American and Cuban Perspectives*. Lanham, MD: University Press of America, 1991.

Manuel, Peter. "From Contradanza to Son: New Perspectives on the Prehistory of Cuban Popular Music." *Latin American Music Review / Revista de Música Latinoamericana* 30, no. 2 (2009): 184–212.

Manuel, Peter. "The 'Guajira' between Cuba and Spain: A Study in Continuity and Change." *Latin American Music Review / Revista de Música Latinoamericana* 25, no. 2 (2004): 137–162.

Márquez Rodríguez, Alexis. "Alejo Carpentier: teorías del barroco y de lo real maravilloso." *Nuevo Texto Crítico* 3, no. 1 (1990): 95–121.

Martín, Edgardo. *Fugas para orquesta de cuerda Fugues for string orchestra*. Washington: New York: Pan American Union: Sole selling agent: Peer International Corp, 1954.

Martín, Edgardo. *Panorama histórico de la música en Cuba*. Havana: Universidad de La Habana, 1972.

Martínez, Andrew Michael. "An Archeology of Cuban Ballet: Reading State Discourse in Alicia Alonso's Ballet Nacional de Cuba." Master's Thesis, University of California, 2017.

250 SELECT BIBLIOGRAPHY

Martínez-Fernández, Luis. *Revolutionary Cuba: A History*. Gainesville, FL: University Press of Florida, 2014.

Martuza, Victor, and Abel Prieto. "A Conversation with Abel Prieto." *Journal of Reading* 25, no. 3 (1981): 261–269.

Masiello, Francine. "Rethinking Neocolonial Esthetics: Literature, Politics, and Intellectual Community in Cuba's 'Revista de Avance.'" *Latin American Research Review* 28, no. 2 (1993): 3–31.

Maynard, Olga. "Alicia Alonso and Ballet Nacional de Cuba." *Dance Magazine* (June 1978): 50–58.

McEwen, Abigail. *Revolutionary Horizons: Art and Polemics in 1950s Cuba*. New Haven, CT: Yale University Press, 2016.

McEwen, Abigail. "The Practice and Politics of Cuban Abstraction, c.1952–1963." Ph.D. diss, New York University, 2010.

McKenna, Constance. "An Interview with Leo Brouwer." *Guitar Review*, no. 75 (1988): 10–16.

Mead, Rita H. "Henry Cowell's New Music, 1925–1936: The Society, the Music Editions, and the Recordings." Ph.D. diss., City University of New York, 1978.

Menton, Seymour. *Prose Fiction of the Cuban Revolution*. Austin: University of Texas Press, 2021.

Mesa-Lago, Carmelo. *Cuba in the 1970s: Pragmatism and Institutionalization*. Revised edition. Albuquerque: University of New Mexico Press, 1978.

Messing, Scott. *Neoclassicism in Music: From the Genesis of the Concept through the Schoenberg/Stravinsky Polemic*. Ann Arbor: UMI Research Press, 1988.

Miller, Cait. "Copland as Good Neighbor: Cultural Diplomacy in Latin America During World War II." *In The Muse: Performing Arts Blog*. October 2, 2014. Accessed October 23, 2019. //blogs.loc.gov/music/2014/10/copland-as-good-neighbor-cultural-diplomacy-in-latin-america-during-world-war-ii/.

Miller, Erica L. "De choteos y choteadores en 'Indagación del choteo,' de Jorge Mañach." *Revista Canadiense de Estudios Hispánicos* 28, no. 2 (2004): 377–389.

Miller, Nicola. "A Revolutionary Modernity: The Cultural Policy of the Cuban Revolution." *Journal of Latin American Studies* 40, no. 4 (2008): 675–696.

Monal, Isabel. "Cuban Foundational Marxist Thought." *International Journal of Political Economy* 34, no. 4 (2004): 11–23.

Monasterio Barso, Freddy. "Music Production and Cultural Entrepreneurship in Today's Havana: Elephants in the Room." Ph.D. diss, Queen's University (Canada), 2018.

Montoya Deler, Whigman. *El Lyceum y Lawn Tennis Club. Su huella en la cultura cubana*. Houston: Ediciones Unos y Otros, 2017.

Moore, Robin D. "Poetic, Visual, and Symphonic Interpretations of the Cuban Rumba: Toward a Model of Integrative Studies." *Lenox Avenue: A Journal of Interarts Inquiry* 4 (1998): 93–112.

Moore, Robin D. "¿Revolución con pachanga?: Dance Music in Socialist Cuba." *Canadian Journal of Latin American and Caribbean Studies / Revue Canadienne Des Études Latino-Américaines et Caraïbes* 26, no. 52 (2001): 151–177.

Moore, Robin D. *Music and Revolution: Cultural Change in Socialist Cuba*. Berkeley, CA: University of California Press, 2006.

Moore, Robin D. *Nationalizing Blackness: Afrocubanismo and Artistic Revolution in Havana, 1920–1940*. Pittsburgh: University of Pittsburgh Press, 1998.

SELECT BIBLIOGRAPHY 251

Morales Flores, Iván César. "A 'Special Period in Times of Peace': Emergence, Exodus, and Evasion on the Cuban Music Map of the 1990s." *Lietuvos Muzikologija*, no. 21 (2020): 68–81.

Morales Flores, Iván César. "Música, ritual y sacrificio: una nueva estética afrocubana en 'Ebbó,' ópera-oratorio de Louis Aguirre." *Acta Musicologica* 90, no. 1 (2018): 95–115.

Morales Flores, Iván César. "Festival Internacional de Música Contemporánea de Camagüey: un hecho inédito en la Cuba de finales del siglo XX y principios del XXI." *Resonancias: Revista de Investigación Musical* 23, no. 44 (January 1, 2019): 161–173.

Morales Flores, Iván César. *Identidades en proceso. Cinco compositores cubanos de la diáspora (1990–2013).* Havana, Cuba: Fondo Editorial Casa de las Américas, 2018.

Morales Flores, Iván César. "Leo Brouwer y la re-territorialización de un modelo de dirección artística habanero en la Orquesta de Córdoba (1992–2001)." In *En, desde y hacia las Américas: músicas y migraciones transoceánicas,* edited by Belén Vega Pichaco, Javier Marín López, and Victoria Eli Rodríguez, 309–326. Madrid: Dykinson, 2021.

Morales Flores, Iván César. "Música, identidad y diáspora: jóvenes compositores cubanos en el cambio de siglo (1990–2010)." *Revista de Musicología* 38, no. 2 (2015): 748–756.

Morales Flores, Iván César. "Vanguardias mirando al este y al sur. los Festivales de Música Contemporánea en Cuba y su relación con la Europa oriental y Latinoamérica (1959–1990)." *Resonancias: Revista de Investigación Musical* 26, no. 20 (2022): 45–75.

Morales Flores, Iván César, and Malena Kuss. "Art Music and Transterritoriality: Reflections on Cuban Migrations to Europe during the 1990s." *Twentieth-Century Music* 17, no. 3 (October 2020): 291–309.

Moran, Dominic. "Carpentier's Stravinsky: Rites and Wrongs." *Bulletin of Spanish Studies* 79, no. 1 (2002): 81–104.

Moris, Judith. "¿Resolver o robar? Cubanos opinan sobre la 'lucha' diaria." *CiberCuba,* February 3, 2017. https://www.cibercuba.com/videos/noticias/2017-02-03-u129488-resolver-o-robar-cubanos-opinan-lucha-diaria.

Morris, Bernard S. "Continuity of Communist Strategic Doctrine Since the Twentieth Party Congress." *The Annals of the American Academy of Political and Social Science* 317 (1958): 130–137.

Mugía Santí, Zita. "Edesio Alejandro: co-autor y actor de la ópera-rock Violente." *Clave— Revista Cubana de Música,* no. 10 (July 1988): 45–46.

Murphy, Scott. "A Model of Melodic Expectation for Some Neo-Romantic Music of Penderecki." *Perspectives of New Music* 45, no. 1 (2007): 184–222.

Música Cubana Contemporánea. LP. Vol. babel 8529-4. Netherlands: Attacca, 1985.

Orbón, Julián. *Tocata [para] piano.* Montevideo: Editorial Cooperativa Interamericana de Compositores, 1945.

Ortega, Jesús. "Resumen de Cuarto Jornadas." *Clave—Revista Cubana de Música,* no. 15 (October 1989): 20–22.

Ortiz, Fernando. *Contrapunteo cubano del tabaco y el azúcar.* Barcelona: Editorial Linkgua, 2019.

Ortiz, Fernando. *Fernando Ortiz on Music: Selected Writing on Afro-Cuban Culture.* Edited by Robin D. Moore. Philadelphia, PA: Temple University Press, 2018.

Pacini Hernández, Deborah, and Reebee Garofalo. "Between Rock and a Hard Place: Negotiating Rock in Revolutionary Cuba, 1960–1980." In *Rockin' Las Américas: The Global Politics of Rock in Latin/o America,* edited by Deborah Pacini Hernández, Héctor D. Fernández l'Hoeste, and Eric Zolov, 43–67. Pittsburgh, PA: University of Pittsburgh Press, 2004.

252 SELECT BIBLIOGRAPHY

Padrón Nordase, Frank. "La música electrónica hacia nuevos horizontes (sobre el primer período en el Panorama de la Múisca Electrónica)." *El Caimán Barbudo*, no. 142 (October 1979): 28–31.

Padura Fuentes, Leonardo. *Un camino de medio siglo: Alejo Carpentier y la narrativa de lo real maravilloso*. Miramar, Playa: Ediciones Cubanas, 2016.

Pan American Union and Lyceum y Lawn Tennis Club. *33 artistas de las Américas: exposición organizada por la Unión Panamericana, Washington*. Washington: Secretaria General de la Organizacion de los Estados Americanos, 1949.

Parlamento Cubano. "Ley del derecho de autor," May 16, 2016. https://www.parlament ocubano.gob.cu/index.php/documento/ley-del-derecho-de-autor/.

Parrott, R. Joseph, and Mark Atwood Lawrence. *The Tricontinental Revolution*. Cambridge: Cambridge University Press, 2022.

Pedemonte, Rafael. "Birches Too Difficult to Cut down: The Rejection and Assimilation of the Soviet Reference in Cuban Culture." *International Journal of Cuban Studies* 9, no. 1 (Spring 2017): 127–141.

Peña, Juan Antonio. "Cuban and Afro-Cuban Musical Elements in the Classical Guitar Compositions by Héctor Angulo." DMA document, University of Miami, 2021.

Pérez Gómez, Ailer. *Música académica contemporánea cubana: catálogo de difusión (1961–1990)*. Havana, Cuba: Ediciones Centro de Investigación y Desarrollo de la Música Cubana, 2011.

Pérez, Louis A. *Cuba and the United States: Ties of Singular Intimacy*. 3rd ed. Athens, GA: University of Georgia Press, 2003.

Pérez, Louis A. *Cuba: Between Reform and Revolution*. New York: Oxford University Press, 2015.

Pérez, Louis A. *On Becoming Cuban: Identity, Nationality, and Culture*. Chapel Hill: University of North Carolina Press, 1999.

Perfiles culturales: Cuba 1977. Havana: Editorial Orbe, 1978.

Perfiles culturales: Cuba, 1978. Havana: Editorial Orbe, 1980.

Piekut, Benjamin. "Actor-Networks in Music History: Clarifications and Critiques." *Twentieth-Century Music* 11, no. 2 (September 2014): 191–215.

Piekut, Benjamin. *Experimentalism Otherwise: The New York Avant-Garde and Its Limits*. Berkeley, CA: University of California Press, 2011.

Pierobon, Chiara. *Music and Political Youth Organizations in Russia: The National Identity Issue*. Wiesbaden: Springer VS, 2014.

Pineda Barnet, Enrique. "Cámara Rápida." *Cuba Internacional*, February 1970, 69.

Pineda Barnet, Enrique. "José Massip." *Cuba Internacional*, March 1970, 65.

Piñera, Juan, Edesio Alejandro, Julio Roloff, and Juan Marcos Blanco. *Música Electroacústica*. LP. Vol. LD-4222. Havana, Cuba: Areito, 1984.

Prados Ortiz de Solórzano, Nicolás. *Cuba in the Caribbean Cold War*. Cham: Palgrave Macmillan, 2020.

Prieto, Abel Enrique. *El patrimonio cultural en defensa de la humanidad*. Colección Crisol. Bayamo, M.N., Granma: Ediciones Bayamo, 2009.

Punales Alpizar, Damaris. "Socialismo Mulato: Soviet Fascination with Race in Cuba." *PALARA*, no. 25 (Fall 2021): 1–10.

Quevedo, Marysol. "Cubanness, Innovation, and Politics in Art Music in Cuba, 1942–1979." Ph.D. diss, Indiana University, 2016.

SELECT BIBLIOGRAPHY 253

Quevedo, Marysol. "Exchanges: Modernist Approaches across Oceans and Borders." In *A Cultural History of Music in the Modern Age*, edited by William Cheng and Danielle Fosler-Lussier. Vol. 6 of *The Twentieth and Twenty-First Centuries*. New York: Bloomsbury, Forthcoming.

Quevedo, Marysol. "Experimental Music and the Avant-Garde in Post-1959 Cuba: Revolutionary Music for the Revolution." In *Experimentalisms in Practice: Music Perspectives from Latin America*, edited by Ana R. Alonso-Minutti, Eduardo Herrera, and Alejandro L. Madrid, 251–278. New York: Oxford University Press, 2018.

Quevedo, Marysol. "Music in Cuban Revolutionary Cinema: Musical Experimentation in the Service of Revolutionary Ideology." In *Experiencing Music and Visual Cultures: Threshold, Intermediality, and Synchresis*, edited by Antonio Cascelli and Denis Condon, 131–141. Oxford, United Kingdom: Routledge, 2021.

Quevedo, Marysol. "The Orquesta Sinfónica Nacional de Cuba and Its Role in the Cuban Revolution's Cultural Project." *Cuban Studies* 47, no. 1 (March 14, 2019): 19–34.

Quintero-Herencia, Juan Carlos. *Fulguración del espacio: letras e imaginario institucional de la Revolución Cubana, 1960–1971*. 1st edición. Ensayos críticos Rosario, Argentina: Beatriz Viterbo, 2002.

Quiroga, Jose. *Cuban Palimpsests*. Minneapolis: University of Minnesota Press, 2005.

Rae, Caroline. "In Havana and Paris: The Musical Activities of Alejo Carpentier." *Music and Letters* 89, no. 3 (August 1, 2008): 373–395.

Raines, Robert. *Composition in the Digital World: Conversations with 21st Century American Composers*. New York: Oxford University Press, 2015.

Ramírez, Marta. "Juan Blanco: aún a la vanguardia." *Clave—Revista Cubana de Música* 4, no. 3 (2002): 35–36.

Recio, Milena. "X Alfonso: la Fábrica de Arte Cubano, una sinfonía en constante creación." *OnCubaNews* (blog), September 4, 2017. https://oncubanews.com/cultura/musica/x-alfonso-la-fabrica-arte-cubano-una-sinfonia-constante-creacion/.

Reid, Marc Olivier. "Esta fiesta se acabó: vida nocturna, orden y desorden social en P.M. y Soy Cuba." *Hispanic Research Journal* 18, no. 1 (February 2017): 30–44.

Rexach, Rosario. "La revista de Avance publicada en Habana, 1927–1930." *Caribbean Studies* 3, no. 3 (1963): 3–16.

Rey, Mario. "The Rhythmic Component of 'Afrocubanismo' in the Art Music of Cuba." *Black Music Research Journal* 26, no. 2 (2006): 181–212.

Rich, Alan, Andrew W. Imbrie, Frederick Dorian, Irving Lowens, and Richard Franko Goldman. "Current Chronicle." *The Musical Quarterly* 44, no. 3 (1958): 367–384.

Ritter, Archibald R. M., and Nicholas Rowe. "Cuba: 'Dollarization' and 'Dedollarization.'" In *The Dollarization Debate*, edited by Dominick Salvatore, James W. Dean, and Thomas D. Willett, 425–448. New York: Oxford University Press, 2003.

Rivera, Zoia, and Dayilien Lazcano. "Biblioteca pública del Lyceum Lawn Tennis Club: promotora de la cultura en la Cuba republicana." *Bibliotecas*, no. 1–2 (December 2001): 1–14.

Robbins, Dylon Lamar. *Audible Geographies in Latin America: Sounds of Race and Place*. London: Palgrave Macmillan, 2019.

Roca, Octavio. *Cuban Ballet*. Layton, UT: Gibbs Smith, 2010.

Rockwell, John. *All American Music: Composition in the Late Twentieth Century*. New York: Vintage Books, 1984.

254 SELECT BIBLIOGRAPHY

Rodríguez Alpízar, Fernando A. "Juan Blanco y la profecía del sonido futuro." *Boletín Música*, no. 39 (Enero-Abril 2015): 43–57.

Rodríguez Alpízar, Fernando A., "Juan Blanco, pionero de la música electrónica cubana cultura, política e ideología en Cuba (1960–1970)," Ph.D. diss, Universidad Complutense de Madrid, and Facultad de Geografía e Historia, 2019.

Rodríguez Cuervo, Marta, and Victoria Eli Rodríguez. *Leo Brouwer, caminos de la creación: edición homenaje por su 70mo aniversario*. Madrid: Ediciones y Publicaciones Autor, 2009.

Rodríguez, Fernando, José Manuel García Suárez, Miguel Bonachea, and Mirtha De la Torre. *Música Electroacústica (TIME) - Jóvenes Compositores Cubanos*. LP. Vol. LD-4411. Havana, Cuba: Areito, 1987.

Rodríguez, Milvia. "Eclecticism in Modern Cuban Music as Reflected in Selected Piano Works by Harold Gramatges: An Investigative Analysis." DMA document, University of Nebraska-Lincoln, 2006.

Rodríguez-Mangual, Edna M. *Lydia Cabrera and the Construction of an Afro-Cuban Cultural Identity*. Chapel Hill: University of North Carolina Press, 2004.

Rogers, Charlotte. "Carpentier, Collecting, and 'Lo Barroco Americano.'" *Hispania* 94, no. 2 (2011): 240–251.

Rojas, Rafael. *Tumbas sin sosiego: revolución, disidencia y exilio del intelectual cubano*. Barcelona: Editorial Anagrama, 2006.

Romeu, Rafael, Carmelo Mesa-Lago, Woodrow Wilson International Center for Scholars, Latin American Program, and Jorge F. Pérez-López. *The Cuban Economy Recent Trends*. Washington, D.C.: Woodrow Wilson International Center for Scholars, 2011.

Rooney, Isabella. "Gendering the Revolution: *Bohemia*, Power and Culture in Post-Revolutionary Cuba, 1960–85." *Radical Americas* 7, no. 1 (February 24, 2022): 1–29.

Root, Deane L. "The Pan American Association of Composers (1928–1934)." *Anuario Interamericano de Investigación Musical: Yearbook for Inter-American Musical Research/Anuário Interamericano de Pesquisa Musical* 8 (January 1, 1972): 49–70.

Ruiz, Magaly. "El ISA, '45 Aniversario' . . . La Facultad de Música. Memorias como alumna de composición y profesora." *Del canto y el tiempo* (blog), June 28, 2021. https://cid mucmusicacubana.wordpress.com/2021/06/28/el-isa-45-aniversario-la-facultad-de-musica-memorias-como-alumna-de-composicion-y-profesora/

Ryer, Paul. *Beyond Cuban Waters: África, La Yuma, and the Island's Global Imagination*. Nashville, TN: Vanderbilt University Press, 2018.

Salazar Rebolledo, Juan Alberto. "La rosa y la espina: expresiones musicales de solidaridad antiimperialista en Latinoamérica. El Primer Encuentro de la Canción Protesta en La Habana, Cuba, 1967." *Secuencia*, no. 108 (2020): 1–26.

"Salir de Cuba por primera vez y aterrizar en el mundo," *Gatopardo*. January 27, 2022.

Samson, Anna. "A History of the Soviet-Cuban Alliance (1960–1991)." *Politeja*, no. 10/2 (2008): 89–108.

Sánchez Cabrera, Maruja. *Orquesta filarmónica de La Habana: memoria, 1924–1959*. Havana, Ministerio de Cultura: Editorial Orbe, 1979.

Sandoval, Chela. *Methodology of the Oppressed*. Minneapolis: University of Minnesota Press, 2000.

Sandu-Dediu, Valentina. "Dodecaphonic Composition in 1950s and 1960s Europe: The Ideological Issue of Rightist or Leftist Orientation." *Journal of Musicological Research* 26, no. 2–3 (June 5, 2007): 177–192.

SELECT BIBLIOGRAPHY   255

Saunders, Tanya L. *Cuban Underground Hip Hop: Black Thoughts, Black Revolution, Black Modernity*. Austin: University of Texas Press, 2015.

Schloss, Walter Andrew. "Report on the Second International Conference of Electroacoustic Music, Varadero, Cuba." *Computer Music Journal* 10, no. 4 (1986): 89–90.

Schmelz, Peter John. "Andrey Volkonsky and the Beginnings of Unofficial Music in the Soviet Union." *Journal of the American Musicological Society* 58, no. 1 (January 1, 2005): 139–207.

Schmelz, Peter John. "From Scriabin to Pink Floyd: The ANS Synthesizer and the Politics of Soviet Music between Thaw and Stagnation." In *Sound Commitments: Avant-Garde Music and the Sixties*, edite by Robert Adlington, 254–278. New York: Oxford University Press, 2009.

Schmelz, Peter John. *Sonic Overload: Alfred Schnittke, Valentin Silvestrov, and Polystylism in the Late USSR*. New York: Oxford University Press, 2020.

Schmelz, Peter John. *Such Freedom, If Only Musical: Unofficial Soviet Music during the Thaw*. New York: Oxford University Press, 2009.

Schneider, David E. *Bartók, Hungary, and the Renewal of Tradition: Case Studies in the Intersection of Modernity and Nationality* 1st edition. Berkeley, CA: University of California Press, 2006.

Schreiber, Rebecca M. *Cold War Exiles in Mexico: U.S. Dissidents and the Culture of Critical Resistance*. Minneapolis: University of Minnesota Press, 2008.

Schwall, Elizabeth B. "Dancing with the Revolution: Cuban Dance, State, and Nation, 1930–1990." Ph.D. diss, Columbia University, 2016.

Schwall, Elizabeth B. *Dancing with the Revolution: Power, Politics, and Privilege in Cuba*. Chapel Hill: University of North Carolina Press, 2021.

Searcy, Anne. *Ballet in the Cold War: A Soviet-American Exchange*. New York: Oxford University Press, 2020.

Serra, Ana. *The "New Man" in Cuba: Culture and Identity in the Revolution*. Gainesville, FL: University Press of Florida, 2007.

Shadle, Douglas. "Louis Moreau Gottschalk's Pan-American Symphonic Ideal." *American Music* 29, no. 4 (2011): 443–471.

Shreffler, Anne Chatoney. "Ideologies of Serialism: Stravinsky's 'Threni' and the Congress for Cultural Freedom." In *Music and the Aesthetics of Modernity*, edited by Karol Berger, Anthony Newcomb, and Reinhold Brinkmann, 217–245. Cambridge, MA: Harvard University Press, 2005.

Sigal, Rodrigo. "Implementación de ideas en el lenguaje, discurso y significado en la música electroacústica." *Boletín Música*, no. 39 (January 2015): 3–24.

Silverberg, Laura. "Between Dissonance and Dissidence: Socialist Modernism in the German Democratic Republic." *The Journal of Musicology* 26, no. 1 (2009): 44–84.

Simón, Pedro, and Juan Blanco. "Hacia otra nueva música? Entrevista realizada al compositor cubano Juan Blanco." *Boletín Música*, no. 22 (1972): 11–15.

Smith, Anthony D. *Nationalism and Modernism: A Critical Survey of Recent Theories of Nations and Nationalism*. New York: Routledge, 1998.

Soares, Thiago. "Beyond Nostalgic Havana: Music and Identity in the Fábrica de Arte Cubano." In *Music Cities: Evaluating a Global Cultural Policy Concept*, edited by Christina Ballico and Allan Watson, 63–79. Cham: Springer International Publishing, 2020.

256 SELECT BIBLIOGRAPHY

Sofer, Danielle. "Categorising Electronic Music." *Contemporary Music Review* 39, no. 2 (March 3, 2020): 231–251.

Staff, Rialta. "Declaración del Primer Congreso Nacional de Educación y Cultura." *Rialta* (blog), May 9, 2018. Accessed July 23, 2019. http://rialta-ed.com/declaracion-del-pri mer-congreso-nacional-de-educacion-y-cultura/.

Stallings, Stephanie N. "Collective Difference: The PanAmerican Association of Composers and Pan-American Ideology in Music, 1925–1945." Ph.D. diss, The Florida State University, 2009.

Storhoff, Timothy P. "Beyond the Blockade: An Ethnomusicological Study of the Policies and Aspirations for U.S.-Cuban Musical Interaction." Ph.D. diss, The Florida State University, 2014.

Straus, Joseph N. "A Revisionist History of Twelve-Tone Serialism in American Music." *Journal of the Society for American Music* 2, no. 3 (August 2008): 355–395.

Taruskin, Richard. "Back to Whom? Neoclassicism as Ideology." *19th-Century Music* 16, no. 3 (1993): 286–302.

Taruskin, Richard. "Darmstadt: Music in the Late Twentieth Century." Accessed October 30, 2019. https://www.oxfordwesternmusic.com/view/Volume5/actrade-9780195384 857-div1-001008.xml.

The UNESCO Works of Art Collection. "Pedro, Luís Martínez (1910–1989): Territorial Waters, 1967." Accessed June 14, 2021. http://www.unesco.org/artcollection/Navigatio nAction.do?idOeuvre=3074.

Thomas, Susan. "Cosmopolitan, International, Transnational: Locating Cuban Music." In *Cuba Transnational*, edited by Damián Fernández, 104–120. Gainesville, FL: University Press of Florida, 2005.

Thomas, Susan. *Cuban Zarzuela: Performing Race and Gender on Havana's Lyric Stage.* Urbana: University of Illinois Press, 2009.

Thomas, Susan. "Musical Cartographies of the Transnational City: Mapping Havana in Song." *Latin American Music Review / Revista de Música Latinoamericana* 31, no. 2 (2010): 210–240.

Tomé, Lester. "'Music in the Blood': Performance and Discourse of Musicality in Cuban Ballet Aesthetics." *Dance Chronicle* 36, no. 2 (May 1, 2013): 218–242.

Tomé, Lester. "The Racial Other's Dancing Body in El Milagro de Anaquillé (1927): Avant-Garde Ballet and Ethnography of Afro-Cuban Performance." *Cuban Studies* 46, no. 1 (2019): 185–227.

Tompkins, David G. "The Rise and Decline of Socialist Realism in Music." In *Composing the Party Line: Music and Politics in Early Cold War Poland and East Germany*, 15–94. West Lafayette: Purdue University Press, 2013.

Torres Rivera, Noel. "The Making of an Avant-Gardist: A Study of Rafael Aponte-Ledée's Early Life and Works (1957–1966)." Ph.D. diss, City University of New York, 2021.

Torres Zayas, Ramón. "Afrocubanismo: algo más que una opción." *Comparative Cultural Studies—European and Latin American Perspectives* 7, no. 14 (March 15, 2022): 61–69.

Torres-Santos, Raymond, ed. *Music Education in the Caribbean and Latin America: A Comprehensive Guide.* Lanham: Rowman & Littlefield Publishers, 2017.

Town, Sarah. "Cuba Dances: Popular Dance, Documentary Film and the Construction of the Revolutionary State." *Studies in Spanish & Latin-American Cinemas* 14, no. 2 (June 1, 2017): 171–91.

Triay, Victor Andres. *The Mariel Boatlift: A Cuban-American Journey.* Gainesville, FL: University Press of Florida, 2019.

SELECT BIBLIOGRAPHY 257

Trujillo, Iraida, Maria Victoria Oliver, Rolando Estévez Jordán, and José White. *José White*. Matanzas, Cuba: Ediciones Vigía, 2005.

Turino, Thomas. "Nationalism and Latin American Music: Selected Case Studies and Theoretical Considerations." *Latin American Music Review / Revista de Música Latinoamericana* 24, no. 2 (2003): 169–209.

Union Panamericana, Departamento de Asuntos Culturales. *Boletín de música y artes visuales*. 11. Departamento de Asuntos Culturales, Unión Panamericana, 1951.

Uy, Michael Sy. *Ask the Experts: How Ford, Rockefeller, and the NEA Changed American Music*. New York: Oxford University Press, 2020.

Valera, Roberto. *Devenir*. Havana: Editora Musical de Cuba, 1979.

Valera, Roberto. "Posibilidades de la técnica musical en la nueva sociedad." *Boletín Música*, no. 20 (1972): n.p.

Van den Toorn, Pieter C. *Music, Politics, and the Academy*. Berkeley, CA: University of California Press, 1995.

Vázquez, Hernán G. "Alberto Ginastera, el surgimiento del CLAEM, la producción musical de los primeros becarios y su recepción critica en el campo musical de Buenos Aires." *Revista Argentina de Musicología* 10 (January 1, 2009): 137–164.

Vázquez, Hernán G. *Conversaciones en torno al CLAEM. Entrevistas a compositores becarios del Centro Latinoamericano de Altos Estudios Musicales del Instituto Torcuato Di Tella*. Buenos Aires: Instituto Nacional de Musicología Carlos Vega, 2015.

Vega Pichaco, Belén. "La construcción de la música nueva en Cuba (1927–1946): del Afrocubanismo al neoclasicismo." *Revista de Musicología* 37, no. 2 (2014): 715–723.

Vega Pichaco, Belén. "La evolución discursiva del Grupo de Renovación Musical de Cuba en las revistas Conservatorio (1943–1947) y La Música (1948): hacia la superación de neoclasicismo e hispanismo." *Journal of Music Criticism* 4 (2020): 85–127.

Vega Pichaco, Belén. *Ni la lira, ni el bongó . . .: La construcción de la música nueva en Cuba desde la órbita de Musicalia*. 1st edition. Granada: Editorial Comares, 2021.

Verdery, Katherine. *National Ideology under Socialism: Identity and Cultural Politics in Ceaușescu's Romania*. Berkeley, CA: University of California Press, 1995.

Vest, Lisa Cooper. *Awangarda: Tradition and Modernity in Postwar Polish Music*. Berkeley, CA: University of California Press, 2020.

Vilar Payá, Luisa, and Ana Ruth Alonso Minutti. "Estrategias de Diferenciación En La Composición Musical: Mario Lavista y El México de Fines de Los Sesenta y Comienzos de Los Setenta." *Revista Argentina de Musicología* 12–13 (2012): 267–290.

Von Eschen, Penny M. *Satchmo Blows up the World Jazz Ambassadors Play the Cold War*. Cambridge, MA: Harvard University Press, 2006.

Wahlström, Victor. "Lo real maravilloso y lo barroco americano." M.A. Thesis, Medier vid Lunds Universitet, 2012.

Weppler-Grogan, Doreen. "Cultural Policy, the Visual Arts, and the Advance of the Cuban Revolution in the Aftermath of the Gray Years." *Cuban Studies* 41, no. 1 (2010): 143–165.

West, Alan. *Cuba*. Detroit: Charles Scribner's Sons, 2012.

White, Charles W. *Alejandro García Caturla: A Cuban Composer in the Twentieth Century*. Lanham, MD: Scarecrow Press, 2003.

White, Charles W. "Report on Music in Cuba Today." *Latin American Music Review / Revista de Música Latinoamericana* 13, no. 2 (September 1992): 234–242.

Willson, Rachel Beckles. *Ligeti, Kurtág, and Hungarian Music during the Cold War*. Cambridge: Cambridge University Press, 2007.

258 SELECT BIBLIOGRAPHY

Wirtz, Kristina. *Performing Afro-Cuba: Image, Voice, Spectacle in the Making of Race and History*. Chicago: University of Chicago Press, 2021.

Wistuba-Álvarez, Vladimir. "Lluvia, rumba y campanas en los paisajes cubanos de Leo Brouwer y otros temas (una conversación con Leo Brouwer)." *Latin American Music Review / Revista de Música Latinoamericana* 10, no. 1 (1989): 135–147.

Yaffe, Helen. *We Are Cuba!: How a Revolutionary People Have Survived in a Post-Soviet World*. New Haven, CT: Yale University Press, 2020.

Yost, Austin. "Exposiciones Soviéticas: Selling Socialist Modernity in the US's Backyard." M.A. Thesis, University of Chapel Hill, 2015.

Zieliński, Tadeusz A. "The Penderecki Controversy." *Studies in Penderecki* 2 (2003): 29–40.

Index

For the benefit of digital users, indexed terms that span two pages (e.g., 52–53) may, on occasion, appear on only one of those pages.

1933 Revolution 3–4, 32
1940 Constitution 3–4, 32, 154
1959 Revolution. *See* Cuban Revolution
1976 Constitution 150–51, 154, 181
1991 Dissolution of Soviet Union 3–4, 210–11, 212–13

Abakuá 14, 71–72, 198
Abbate, Luigi 201–2
Acosta, Leonardo 101–2, 163–64
Ades, Moisés 93
Afro-Cuban religion 10–11, 59–60, 71–72, 82–83, 206
Afrocubanismo, Afrocubanista 6–8, 9, 23, 44, 45–46, 66–67
Águila, Orestes 197
Aguirre, Louis 217
Aguirre, Mirta 40–41
Akademie der Kunst, East Berlin 207–8
aleatoric/aleatorism 109, 126–27, 130, 157–59, 178–79
Alejandro, Edesio 185, 196–97, 202–3
Alfonso, Carlos 230–31
Alfonso, X 230–32
Allied Forces 33
Alonso, Alberto 40–41, 67–70, 71–72
Alonso, Alicia 67–69, 70
Alonso, Fernando 67–69, 72
Álvarez del Río, María 169–70
Álvarez, Calixto 121–23, 196–97
American Steel Corporation of Cuba 50–51
American Tropical Products Corporation of Cuba 50–51
Amnesty International 233
amphibrac 62
Angulo, Héctor 121–23, 141–42, 170, 173–75, 195, 196–97, 220–21
Antes del Alba 71–72
Apollo 11 Moon landing 190–92
Appleton, Jon 201–2
Ardévol, José 3–4, 9, 10, 16–17, 27–30, 31–32, 35, 39–49, 50–51, 52–57, 63–64, 65, 67–69,
72, 80–81, 83, 102–3, 105, 106–8, 113, 117–19, 121–23, 130–31, 138–40, 141–42, 165–66, 169–70, 180, 184
Ardévol, José, *Concerto Grosso* 35
Ardévol, José, *Music for Little Orchestra* 102–3, 106–7
Ardévol, José, *Música de cámara* 41–43
Argentina 16–17, 20–21, 41, 58–59
Arrufat, Antón 148–49, 154
artista(s) comprometido(s) 67–69, 100, 117, 123–24, 130–31, 135–36, 189–90
Asociación Hermanos Saíz 123–24, 183–84, 187–88
avant-garde/avant-gardist 1–2, 5–9, 11–13, 15–16, 19–21, 95–97, 103–5, 107–8, 109–10, 114, 115–17, 118–19, 121–24, 125–28, 133–34, 136–37, 138–43

Bacewicz, Grażyna 121–23, 125–26, 128
Bach, J.S. 39–40, 65–66, 69–70, 133–34, 157–59
Baird, Tadeusz 121–23, 125–26
Ballagas, Emilio 40–41
Ballet Nacional 69–70, 71–72, 73, 95–96, 148–49
Ballet of the Society Pro-Arte Musical 41–42
Ballet Russes 69–70
Ballet Theater 69–70
Baragaño, José A. 109, 124
Baralt, Luis A. 40–41
Bartholomew, Marshall 35
Bartók, Béla 41, 60–62, 83–85, 119–20, 144, 163–64
batá drums/toque(s) 204–5, 206
Batista, Fulgencio 2–4, 5–6, 32, 35–38, 63–64, 66–69, 72, 74–76, 77–78, 79–80, 81, 93, 96–97, 98, 100, 104, 105, 114, 139–40, 141–42
Beethoven, Ludwig von 65–66, 133–34, 156–57
Benítez Rojo, Antonio 235–36
Berger, Arthur 46–49

260 INDEX

Bergman, Ingmar 203–4
Berio, Luciano 133–34, 157
Berklee College of Music 229
Berkshire Music Festival 25–26, 27–30
Berliner Künstlerprogramm 204–5
Bernstein, Leonard 63–64
Berrien, William 35
Berroa, Jorge 165–66, 170
Biblioteca Nacional José Martín (no n) 82–83, 182–83, 192–93
Black Mountain College 74–75
Blanco, Juan 1–2, 4, 40–41, 65–66, 74–79, 80–81, 83–87, 91–93, 95–97, 98–99, 104, 106, 107–8, 109–14, 116–17, 118–19, 121–34, 136, 137–42, 144, 147, 150–51, 154, 161–62, 165, 166, 170–72, 173–76, 177–80, 182–83, 184, 188–206, 207–8, 219–21, 229
Blanco, Juan, *Cirkus Toccata* 188–89, 198–99
Blanco, Juan, *Contrapunto Espacial III* 128–30, 132, 136, 138, 147, 150–51
Blanco, Juan, *Desde su voz amada* 189–90, 192
Blanco, Juan, *Estructuras* 189–90, 192
Blanco, Juan, *Galaxia M-50* 189–92
Blanco, Juan, *Música para un joven mártir* 189–90, 192
Blanco, Juan, *Quinteto* 80–81, 83–87, 91, 92–93
Blanco, Juan, *Texturas* 96–97
Blank, Olga de 38–39
Bohemia 38–39, 180
bolero 62, 204–5
Bolivia 58–59, 144, 151–52, 176–77, 234
Bonachea, Miguel 196–97
Bonilla, Diego 27–30
boogie-woogie 95–96
Borodin, Alexander 65–66
Boulanger, Nadia 51–52
Bowles, Paul 50–51
Braga, Francisco 101
Brazil 16–17, 20–21, 25–26, 41
Brecht, Bertolt 137–38
Brigadas Hermanos Saíz 123–24
British Broadcasting Corporation 100–1
Britos, Federico 176–77
Brncic, Gabriel 201–2
Brouwer, Leo 1–2, 4, 8–9, 107–8, 115–17, 121–42, 144–45, 146–47, 154–62, 165, 166, 170–72, 173–76, 177–80, 182–83, 184, 185, 188–89, 190, 193–94, 195, 196, 204–6, 207–10, 216–17, 218, 225, 234
Brouwer, Leo, *Canción de Gesta* 208–9

Brouwer, Leo, *La tradición se rompe. . .pero cuesta trabajo* 128–30, 133–38, 147, 156–57, 190, 208–9
Brouwer, Leo, *Manuscrito encontrado en una botella* 188–89, 208–9
Brouwer, Leo, *Sonata pian e forte* 23–24, 144–45, 155–60, 161, 175–76, 177
Brouwer, Leo, *Sonograma I* 121–23, 125–27, 195
Bueno, Descemer 233
Bulgaria 25–26, 164–65, 167

Cabrera Infante, Alberto 127–28, 154
Cabrera, Lydia 40–41
Cage, John 50–51, 74–75, 136–37
Calcavecchia, Anunciata 169–70
Calígula 92–93
Canada 200
Cárdenas, Lázaro 120–21
Carnegie Corporation 34
Carpentier, Alejo 8–13, 14, 27, 31–32, 40–41, 43, 45, 46–49, 50–53, 57–58, 63–64, 66–69, 101, 109, 124, 163–64, 165–66, 195–96, 220
Carteles 51–52
Carter, Jimmy 185–86, 193–94, 201–2
Carvajal, Ailem 197, 217
Casa de las Américas 109, 111–12, 121, 141, 142–43, 148–49, 167, 180, 222–23
Casanova, Nancy 160–61
Caso Padilla 148–49
Castro, Fidel 3–4, 104, 117–18, 128–29, 150–53, 170–72, 185–86, 213
Castro, Juan J. 101, 107
Castro, Raul 228
Castroite heresy 151–52
CEA Affair (Caso CEA) 222
Centro de Estudios sobre América 222
Centro de Investigación y Desarrollo de la Música Cubana (CIDMUC) 17–18, 220–21
Centro Latinoamericano de Altos Estudios Musicales (CLAEM) 20–21
Cervantes, Ignacio 65, 66–67, 155–56
Chávez, Carlos 86–87
Chile 16–17, 20–21, 58–59, 164–65, 166, 234
Chomón, Faure 98–99
Choral Society of Havana 38–39
choteo 8–9, 135–36, 159–60, 208–9
Christian Science Monitor 77–78
cinquillo 57–58, 62, 83–85, 86–87, 89–90
Clark, Evans 35
CMBF Radio Station 138

INDEX 261

CMZ Radio Station 98–99, 106, 113
Cold War 7–8, 19–21, 49–50, 67–69, 80, 115–
16, 117–18, 173, 190–92
collectivism 116–17, 134–35, 136–37,
154, 168–69
Colombia 16–17
Coloquio Internacional de Musicología Casa de
las Américas 221
Comité Cubano del Consejo Internacional de la
Música de la UNESCO (CIM) 200
Composers Union of Poland 160–61, 170
Congress on Education and Culture,
1972 151–54
Conjunto Folklórico Nacional 164–65
Consejo de Ayuda Mutua Económica. *See*
Council for Mutual Economic Assistance
Consejo Nacional de Cultura (CNC) 23–24,
25–26, 128–29, 137–38, 139–40, 149, 152–
53, 154–55, 167, 223–24
Conservatorio Alejandro García Caturla 113,
130–31, 196–97
Conservatorio Amadeo Roldán 102–3, 114–
15, 160–61, 199–200
Conservatorio Municipal de "Félix Alpízar." *See*
Conservatorio Municipal de La Habana
Conservatorio Municipal de La Habana 10,
22–23, 27–30, 31–32, 38–39, 40–42,
44–45, 65–66, 67–69, 74–75, 105, 114–
15, 220–21
contradanza 38–39, 53–60, 62–63, 92–93
Contrapunteo Cubano del tabaco y el
azucar 10–11
Copland, Aaron 25–26, 27–30, 35, 38–39,
50–51, 63–64, 74–75, 86–88, 92–93, 95–96,
101, 121, 130–31, 155–56
Cordero, Roque, *Segunda Sinfonía* 101–2
Corelli, Arcangelo 39–40, 42–43
Corona, Beatriz 225
Council for Mutual Economic Assistance
(CMEA or COMECON) 148–49, 151–52
Cowell, Henry 3–4, 35, 50–51, 74–75, 87–
88, 157
Cruz, Celia 22
Cubadisco 226–27
Cuban-American Music Group 38–39, 46–51
Cuban Assets Control Regulations 227–28
Cuban Democracy Act/Torricelli Act 213
Cuban diaspora 210–11, 212, 217–18
cubanía 6–7, 155–56, 222–23
Cuban Missile Crisis 117–18, 151–52
Cuban Rafter Crisis 213
Cuban Revolution 2–5, 11–13, 31–32, 67–69,
76–77, 100, 102–3, 104, 107–8, 110–11,

121, 123, 127–28, 134–36, 140–41, 148–49,
164–65, 213, 230, 234
Cueto, Elena de 69–70
Cultural and Scientific Conference for World
Peace 63–64
Cultural Congress 1968 151–52
Cunningham, Merce 74–75
Czechoslovakia 25–26, 125–26, 151–52, 160–
61, 167

danzón 57, 58, 65–66
Decreto 349 223–24, 232–35
Denisov, Edison 173–75
Department of Treasury's Office of Foreign
Assets Control 227–28
Desnos, Robert 51–52
Di, Leonid 169–70
Díaz Ayala, Crirstóbal 218
Díaz-Canel, Miguel 233
Diez Nieto, Alfredo 1–2, 169–70, 220–21
Dirección de Cultura of the Ministry of
Education 46–49, 67–69, 152–53
Dirección de Música de Casa de las Américas
17–18, 111–12, 221
Division of Cultural Relations of the State
Department 34
Dobrowolski, Andrzej 146–47
dodecaphony/dodecaphonic. *See*
twelve-tone
Dominican Republic 57–58
Drake, Ñica 82–83
Duchesne Cuzán, Manuel 4, 112, 118–19,
121–23, 126–27, 128, 129–30, 178–79,
195, 196

Eastern Europe 19–21, 23, 25–26, 103, 104,
123–24, 136, 160–61, 215
Editora Musical de Cuba 62–63,
147, 225
EDM (electronic dance music) 199–200, 210–
11, 229, 231–32
EGREM, Empresa de Grabación y Ediciones
Musicales 121–23, 138, 172–76, 183–84,
189–90, 193–94, 196–97, 199–200, 202–3,
210–11, 225, 226–28
Ejército Rebelde (Rebel Army) 113, 130–31
electroacoustic/electronic music 4, 21, 24–
25, 81, 96–97, 107–8, 109, 121–23, 124,
125, 126–28, 129–31, 138–39, 140–41,
150–51, 164–65, 173, 177, 178–80,
182–85, 188–211, 225–26, 227–28,
229, 230
El Funky 233

262 INDEX

El Mégano 93–97, 127–28, 201–2
Elósegui, Juan 65–66, 169–70
El reino de este mundo 11–13, 52–53
Encuentro de Música Latinoamericana 1972
  23–24, 144–45, 147, 163–65, 166
Escalante Chernova, Irina 197
Escuela Nacional de Arte (ENA) 16–17, 102–3,
  169–72, 199–200
Escuela Normal de Maestros 65, 74–75
Espinosa, Guillermo 101–2
Estudio de Música Electroacústica y por
  Computadoras (EMEC) 197
Estudios Abdala 226
Experimental Music International
  Competition, Bourges 196–97
experimental, experimentalism 1–2, 4, 5–9,
  11–13, 15–16, 19–21, 23, 81, 96–97, 104,
  107–8, 109–10, 111–12, 114, 115–17, 118–
  19, 123, 124, 125, 127–30, 132–41, 142–43,
  144–45, 146–48, 149–51, 154–57, 159–60,
  161–66, 175–76, 177–79, 180–81, 188–89,
  193–94, 195, 196–97, 198–99, 210–11
extended techniques 92–93, 133–34, 150–51,
  156–57, 163–64

Fábrica de Arte Cubano 229–32
Fall of the Berlin Wall 213
Falla, Manuel de 41–42, 55–57, 60–
  62, 155–56
  Falla, Manuel de, Harpsichord
    Concerto 55–57
Fariñas, Carlos 1–2, 4, 121–24, 125–26, 128–
  31, 133–34, 136, 137–38, 140–42, 144, 147,
  166, 169–70, 178–79, 184, 188–89, 193–94,
  195, 197, 202–3, 204–7, 217, 220–21, 229
  Fariñas, Carlos, *Aguas territoriales* 198,
    202–3, 204–7
  Fariñas, Carlos, *Relieves* 128–32, 138, 147
Fayad, Jamís 109, 124
Feldman, Morton 136, 157, 159–60
Fere, Vladimir 110
Fernández Barroso, Sergio 121–23, 169–70
Fernández Retamar, Roberto 109, 117, 124
Fernández-Brito, Ninowska 92–93, 150–51
Fernández, Pablo Armando 109, 124
Festival de Música Contemporánea de La
  Habana 184–85, 234–35
Festival de Música Contemporánea de los Países
  Socialistas 25–26, 166–69, 184–85
Festival de Música Cubana 166–67
Festival de Música Electrónica Primavera en
  Varadeo/Primavera en La Habana 183–
  85, 192–93, 199–203, 210–11, 229

Festival Internacional de Música
  Contemporánea de Camagüey 166–67
Fleites, Virginia 27–30, 44–45
Fokine, Michel 69–70
Folklore Department at the National Theater of
  Cuba 82–83
Fornet, Ambrosio 23–24, 148–49
Foyo, Guillermina 35–38
France 98–99, 100–1, 160, 179–80, 216–17
Freed, Isadore 139–40
Frescobaldi, Girolamo 39–40
Fuentes, Norberto 148–49

Gabinetede Patrimonio Musical Esteban
  Salas 17–18
Gabrieli, Giovanni 39–40, 42–43, 156–57
Gagarin, Yuri 190–92
Galería Nuestro Tiempo 82–83
Galindo, Blas 101, 107, 117–18, 119–
  21, 141–42
García Caturla, Alejandro 3–4, 9, 41–42,
  43–44, 45–46, 51–52, 53–54, 65–67, 81,
  104, 113, 117–18, 125–26, 147–48, 163–64,
  165–66, 196–97
  García Caturla, Alejandro, *Primera suite
    cubana* 40–41
García Espinosa, Julio 93–95
García Espinosa, Pedro 93
García Ruda, Julio 197–98
García, Fernando 166
García, José M. 196–97
García, Orlando Jacinto 212
Garrido-Lecca, Celso 166
Gente de Zona 233
German Democratic Republic, *See* Easter
  Germany 107–8, 109, 110, 125–26, 164–65, 167
Ginastera, Alberto 49–50, 58–59, 92–93, 101,
  107, 117–18, 119–20, 141–42
  Ginastera, Alberto, *Estancia* 58–59
  Ginastera, Alberto, *Malambo* 86–87
  Ginastera, Alberto, *Toccata Concertante* 89–90
Giuliano, Maurizio 222
globalization 8–9, 24–25, 181, 183–84, 188–89
Goehr, Walter 100–1
González Mantici, Enrique 100–1, 112, 118–
  19, 125–26, 130–31, 141–42
González, Hilario 44–45, 50–51, 52–53, 71–72,
  121–23, 141–42, 220–21, 227–28
Good Neighbor Policy 34, 46–49
Gottschalk, Louis Moreau 57–58, 155–56
Gramatges, Harold 1–2, 23–24, 31–32, 35,
  38–39, 44–45, 50–51, 52–54, 60–64, 67–69,
  74–81, 83–85, 88–93, 98–99, 100–1, 104,

INDEX   263

109, 111–12, 118–19, 124, 126–27, 130–31, 144–47, 149–50, 155–56, 160–64, 165, 166, 169–72, 173–75, 179–80, 184, 217, 220–21, 227–28
Gramatges, Harold, *Dos invenciones* 35
Gramatges, Harold, *La muerte del guerrillero* 144–46, 147, 149–50, 160
Gramatges, Harold, *Móvil I* 23–24, 144–45, 155–56, 160–64, 166
Gramatges, Harold, *Serenata* 31–32, 53–55, 60–63, 100–1
Gramatges, Harold, *Tres preludios a modo de toccata* 88–93
graphic score/notation 92–93, 96–97, 127–28, 146–47, 150–51, 156–57, 161–62, 165, 166, 196
Grupo de Experimentación Sonora del ICAIC (GESI) 121–23, 164–65, 193–94
Grupo de Renovación Musical (GRM) 1–2, 9, 10–11, 21, 22–23, 27, 30–32, 39–41, 44–46, 50–54, 63–64, 83–85, 87–88, 102–3, 114–15, 155–56, 195–96, 220–21, 227–28
Grupo Minorista 51–52, 67–69
guajira/punto guajiro 44, 54–55, 57, 58–59, 60–63, 90–91, 92–93
Guerrero, Félix 124
Guerrero, Félix, *Homenaje al sóngoro consongo* 100–1
Guevara, Alfredo 93, 98–99
Guevara, Ernesto Che 4, 98–99, 117, 144, 146, 151–52, 182–83
Guillén, Nicolás 109, 124, 146, 149–50
Gutiérrez Alea, Tomás 92–93, 94–95
Gutiérrez Alea, Tomás, *Historias de la Revolución* 92–93

habanera 42–44, 57, 62, 89–90, 106, 196
Haiti 52–53, 57–58
Halffter, Rodolfo 101
Hall of the Americas 88–89
Hallet, Robert M. 77–78
happening 4, 75–76, 132–35, 136–38
Harris, Roy, Trio 35
Hart Dávalos, Armando 149, 154–55, 169–72, 222–23
Hartt College of Music 121–23, 139–40
Haydu, Jorge 93
Helms-Burton Act 213
Henríquez, Antonieta 124
Henry, Pierre 196
Henze, Hans Werner 156–57, 159–60
Heras León, Eduardo 148–49
Hernández Catá, Sara 40–41

Herñandez, Gisela 27–30, 38–39, 44–45, 52–53
Hernández, Ivette 124
Hiller, Lejaren 201–2
Hindemith, Paul 41, 60–62, 119–20, 178
hip hop 214–15, 230–31
hombre nuevo 4, 114, 116–17, 134–35, 152–53, 192
Hotel Internacional of Varadero 200
House Un-American Activities Committee (HUAC) 63–64
Hungary 25–26, 125–26, 164–65, 167

Ichaso, Francisco 46–49
Imprenta Nacional de Cuba 172–73
improvisation/improvisatory 60–62, 127–28, 156–59, 161, 163–64, 177
indeterminacy 92–93, 101–2, 121–24, 126–27, 130, 132–34, 136, 156–57, 159–60, 161–64, 165, 166, 195, 196, 198–99
Institute of Ethnology and Folklore at the Academy of Sciences of Cuba 82–83
Instituto Cubano de Amistad con los Pueblos (ICAP) 196–97, 199–200, 201–2
Instituto Cubano de Artes e Industrias Cinematográficas (ICAIC, Cuban Film Institute) 92–93, 94–97, 121–23, 139–41, 142–43, 180, 189–90, 193–94
Instituto Cubano de la Música 199–200, 223–24
Instituto Cubano de Radio y Televisión (ICRT) 200
Instituto Musical de Barcelona 41–42
Instituto Nacional de Cultura (INC) 65, 66–69, 71–72, 75–78, 97, 98
Instituto Superior de Arte (ISA) 16–17, 130–31, 169–72, 196–97, 215, 217, 229
Instituto Superior de Artes' Electroacoustic and Computer Music Laboratory 130–31
Inter-American Music Association 101
Inter-American Music Festival (IAMF) 88–89, 101–3, 106–7, 108, 110–11, 113, 117–21
International Dance Festival in Paris 170
International House of New Orleans 102–3, 106
International Popular Song Contest, Sopot, Poland 170
International Society for Contemporary Music (ISCM) 100–1
Interpodium Music Fstival 160–61, 170
Italy 164–65, 170, 200
Ives, Charles 55–57

Jagger, Mick 230–31

264 INDEX

jazz 35–38, 46–49, 95–96, 157–59, 204–5,
214–15, 227–28
Jiménez García, Ernesto 229–30
Jiménez Leal, Orlando 127–28
Jornadas de Música Contemporánea de La
Habana 184–85
joropo 58–59
Juárez, Benito 120–21
Julliard School of Music 121–23
Junco, Teresita 169–70

Kabalevsky, Dmitry 130–31
Kahn, Ermine 50–51
Kalatozov, Mikhail 130–31
Kessler, Tomas 201–2
Khachaturian, Aram 141–42
Khrushchev, Nikita 117–18
Kleiber, Erich 79
Klopov, Vladimir 169–70
Kochan, Gunther 110
Koussevitzky, Serge 27–30
Kupper, Leo 201–2

Laboratorio Nacional de Música Electroacústica
(LNME) 196–97, 198, 199–200, 201–2,
210–11, 229
Lady Gaga 230–31
Laika 190–92
Lam, Wifredo 40–41, 163–64
La música en Cuba 9, 13–14, 17–18, 31–32,
51–53, 57–58, 59–60, 66–67, 138–39
Latin American Music Center 212
Latin American Music Festival (Cuba) 25–26,
107–8, 117–21
Latin American Music Festival, Caracas 67–
69, 101–2, 117–18
Lavista, Mario 20–21
Lecuona, Ernesto 22
Lenin, Vladimir 151–52, 190
León, Argeliers 10–11, 31–32, 44–45, 52–60,
62–63, 71–72, 75–76, 82–85, 109, 121–23,
124, 126–27, 165, 173–75, 184, 188–89,
220–21, 227–28
León, Argeliers, *Sonatas a la Virgen del Cobre*
31–32, 53–60
León, Argeliers, *Toque* 71–72
León, Ithiel 65–67, 74–75
León, Tania 16, 20–21, 212, 214–15
Leonard III, Neil 74–75, 137–38, 201–2
Lezama Lima, José 109, 124, 148–49, 218
Ligeti, György 136–37
Linares, María Teresa 82–83
lo barroco americano 11–14, 208–9

lo criollo 8–9, 208–9
López Gavilán, Guido 228–29, 231–32
López Rovirosa, María Isabel, Suite 35
lo real maravilloso 8–9, 11–13, 14, 52–53, 155–
56, 163–64
Los Papines 219
Loyola, José 123–24, 169–70
Lucumí 14, 54–55
Luening, Otto 46–49
Lutłosławski, Witold 125–26, 128, 133–34
Lyceum Lawn and Tennis Club 27–30, 31–32,
35, 38–39, 42–43, 46–49, 74–75, 82–
83, 101

Machado, Gerardo 32, 51–52
Macías, Segried 229
magnetic tape 96–97, 127–28, 129–30, 132,
136, 182, 188–89, 194, 196, 204–5, 206
malambo 58–59
Malcolm, Carlos 121–24, 173–75
Maletá, Jorge 196–97
Mañach, Jorge 8–9
Mariel Boatlift, 184, 185–86, 201–2, 214–15
Martí, José 1, 24–25, 114–15, 208–9
Martín, Edgardo 38–39, 44–45, 46–49, 52–53,
65, 67–69, 72–73, 95, 104, 108, 119–23,
125–28, 139–40, 141–42, 165–66, 170,
177–79, 180, 184, 188–89, 220–21
Martín, Edgardo, *(Cuatro) Fugas (para
cuerdas)* 54–55, 65, 69–72, 74, 83, 88–89,
92–93, 95–96, 100–1
Martínez Pedro, Luis 109, 124, 206, 207
Massip, José 93, 130–31
McBride, Robert 46–49
McClure, Henry 88–89
mestizaje 10–11, 13
Mexico 16–17, 20–21, 25–26, 41, 58, 100–1,
102–3, 115–16, 120–21, 164–65, 200, 201–
2, 203–4, 228
Mexico-Cuba Electronic Music
Festival 203–4
Milanés, Pablo 193–94
Milhaud, Darius 41, 163–64
Mini Moog 198
minimalism/minimalist 8–9, 185, 206
Ministerio de Cultura/Ministry of Cultue (of
Cuba) 23–24, 149, 154–55, 169–72, 181,
200, 226, 232–33
Moncayo, José Pablo 117
Monier, Conrado 225
Monteverdi, Claudio 39–40
Monumento a José Martí 182–83
Moog Sonic Six 198

INDEX 265

Moore, Douglas 46–49
Morales, Jesús 197
Morales(–Caso), Eduardo 197, 217
Moscow Conservatory 130–31
Movimiento por la Paz 81
Movimiento San Isidro (MSI) 233–35
multimedia 193–94, 204–5
multiórgano 193
Muñoz de Quevedo, María 27–30, 38–
39, 59–60
Museo Nacional de la Música Cubana 16–18,
50–51, 225–26
Music and Theater Festival in Berlin 170
Music Department at Casa de las Américas
82–83, 111–12, 139–40, 164–65
Music Department of the José Martí National
Library 82–83
Music Festival of Socialist Countries. *See*
Festival de Música Contemporánea de los
Países Socialistas
musique concrète 193, 198

N27 Movement 233, 234–35
neoclassical, neoclassicism 1–2, 5–8, 10, 22–
23, 31–32, 35, 41–43, 45–50, 53–57, 59–64,
65, 69–70, 71–72, 80–81, 83, 86–87, 88–89,
155–56, 196
new man. *See* hombre nuevo
New Music Society 3–4, 35
NeXT 198
Nicaragua 176–77
Nín Castellanos, Joaquín 27–30
Nín-Culmell, Joaquín 50–51
Nono, Luigi 20–21, 164–65, 176–77,
196, 201–2
Notowicz, Nathan 110
nueva trova 193–94, 226, 232–33
Núñez Jiménez, Antonio 98–99
Núñez, Teresa 197

Obama, Barack 227–28
Obama, Michelle 230–31
Ofensiva Revolucionaria 151–52
Office of Inter-American Affairs (OIAA) 27–
30, 34–35
Office of Inter-American Affairs Music
Committee 27–30, 34–35
Ono, Yoko 136
Orbón, Julián 44–45, 50–51, 52–53, 55–57,
101–3, 214–15
O'Reilly, Mónica 197
Organization of American States (OAS) 88–
89, 101–2, 117–18, 121

Orozco, Keyla 217
Orquesta de Cámara de La Habana 39–40, 46–
50, 55–57, 62–63, 118–19
Orquesta de Córdoba 216–17
Orquesta de Música Eterna 231–32
Orquesta Ensueño 35–38
Orquesta Filarmónica de La Habana (OFLH)
31–32, 76–77, 78–80, 118–19
Orquesta Sinfónica Nacional de Cuba (OSN)
16–17, 96–97, 107–8, 112–13, 117–19,
121–23, 125–26, 128–30, 137–41, 142–43,
144, 145–46, 147–48, 154–55, 166, 167–75,
180, 196, 215–17, 228–29
Orrego-Salas, Juan 101
Ortega, Jesús 150–51, 170, 196–97
Ortiz, Fernando 10–13, 14, 40–41, 59–60, 62–
63, 71–72, 82–83, 222–23
oscillator 198
Oshún 54–55
Osorbo, Maykel 233
Otero Alcántara, Luis Manuel 233
Otero, Lisandro 109, 124

P.M. incident 127–28
Padilla, Heberto 148–49, 154
Padrón Nordase, Frank 182–83, 190–92
Padura Fuentes, Leonardo 13
Palabras a los intelectuales 116–17, 170–72
Palacios, Inocente 101
Pan American Association of Composers 3–4,
34, 35, 50–51
Pan American Union 38–39, 42–43, 74, 88–
89, 121
Pan American Union, Music Division 34,
42–43, 101–2
Pan American/Pan Americanist 5–6, 19,
31–41, 49–50, 87–88, 100–1, 102–3, 113,
117–18, 121
paquete semanal 225–26
Paris Conservatoire 3–4
Partido Comunista de Cuba (PCC) 105, 129–
30, 222
Partido Socialista Popular (PSP) 40–41, 67–69,
75–78, 79–80, 81, 88–89
Patria y vida 233
pavonato 154
Pavón Tamayo, Luis 154
Paz, Octavio 207–8
Penderecki, Krzysztof 125–26, 128, 133–34
Pensamiento crítico 154
Pérez Sentenat, César 27–30, 124
Pérez Velázquez, Ileana 197, 212, 217
Perfiles Culturales 170–72

266 INDEX

período especial (en tiempos de paz) 212–13, 215–17, 225–26, 229
Persichetti, Vincent 121–23, 139–40
Peru 58–59, 164–65, 166
Peruvian embassy 185–86
Picasso, [Pablo] 38–39
Piñera, Juan 196–97, 202–3, 227–28
Piñera, Virgilio 148–49
Pinilla, Enrique 166
Pirumov, Alexander 130–31
Platt Amendment 32
Plaza de la Revolución 182–83
Poland 5–6, 23, 25–26, 103, 123–24, 125–26, 139–40, 142–43, 146–47, 167, 169–70, 173–75, 176–77, 201–2
Polish avant-garde 5–6, 19, 123–24, 125–26, 128, 146–47
polystylism, polystylistic 135–36, 193–94
Port of Mariel 185–86
Portocarrero, René 69–72, 109
postminimalism/postminimalist 8–9, 185, 206
postmodern, postmodernism 6–7, 8–9, 24–25, 136, 183–84, 185, 188–89, 198–99, 205, 207–11
Prague Spring 151–52
pregón 85–86
Premio de Composición Casa de las Américas 221
Premio de Musicología Casa de las Américas 221
prepared piano 121–23, 195
Prieto, Abel 222–23, 232–33
Prío Socarrás, Carlos 66–67
Pro, Serafín 44–45, 83, 166
Producciones Colibrí 1–2, 226, 227–28
Prokofieff, Sergei 52–53, 119–20
Puerto Rico 17–18, 57–58, 164–65, 212
Puig, Carlos 197

Quevedo, Antonio 38–39
quinquenio gris 23–24, 128–29, 144–45, 148–49, 151–52, 154–55, 175–76, 181, 233, 234–35

Rauschenberg, Robert 74–75
Ravel, Maurice 133–34, 155–56
Reagan, Ronald 185–86, 201–2
Registro de Marcas y Patentes 193
retaguardia 121–23, 125–26, 139–40
Revista Avance 51–52
Revista Bimestre Cubana 10–11

Revolution, Cuban 2–5, 31–32, 67–69, 93, 98–100, 104, 107–8, 110–11, 123, 213, 234
Revueltas, Silvestre 83–85, 86–87, 117–18
Revueltas, Silvestre, *Ocho por radio* 83–85
Revueltas, Silvestre, *Toccata sin fuga* 89–90
Robaina, Rita 65–66
Robins, Jerome 69–70, 71–72
Rockefeller, Nelson 34–35
Rodríguez, Fernando 21, 196–97, 202–4
Rodríguez, Fernando, *El otro huevo de la serpiente* 203–4
Rodríguez, Janet 197
Rodríguez, Nilo 65–66, 83, 166
Rodríguez, Silvio 193–94, 225, 226, 230–31, 232–33
Roig, Gonzalo 65
Roland Jupiter 8 198
Roldán, Amadeo 3–4, 9, 40–42, 44–46, 51–52, 53–54, 65–67, 74–75, 78–79, 81, 104, 114–15, 117–18, 125–26, 147–48, 160–61, 163–64, 165–66, 170
Roldán, Amadeo, *Rítmicas* 40–41
Roldán, Amadeo, *Tres pequeños poemas* 100–1
Roloff, Julio 196–97, 202–4
Roloff, Julio, *Halley 86* 203–4
Romeu, Gonzalo 169–70
Roosevelt, Franklin D. 34–35
Rudziński, Witold 146–47
Ruggles, Carl 50–51
Ruiz, Magaly 169–70, 196–97
Rumania 164–65, 167

Salon de Mai 151–52
sampling technique 198
San Martín, Grau 35–38, 79–80
Santamaría, Haydée 111–12
Saumell, Manuel 38–39, 66–67, 155–56
Schaeffer, Bogusław 136–37, 157
Schaffer, Pierre 196
Scherchen, Hermann 41–42
Schloss, Andrew 201–2
Schoenberg, Arnold 20–21, 41–42, 45, 52–53, 60–62, 127–28, 144, 178, 203–4
Seeger, Charles 34
serialism/serial technique 6–7, 20–21, 100, 101–2, 106–7, 108, 110, 113, 119–20, 126–28, 144–46, 179–80, 196, 198–99
Silva, Electo 225
Simón, Moisés 35–38
Síntesis 230–31

INDEX 267

Smith, Federico 21
socialist realism 23–24, 149–50, 214–15
Sociedad Amadeo Roldán 65, 67–69, 74–75
Sociedad Cultural Nuestro Tiempo (SCNT)
1–3, 23, 67–69, 72, 74–79, 80–83, 86–90,
92–101, 104, 113, 118–19, 139–40
Sociedad de la Orquesta de Cámara de La
Habana/Sociedad Música de Cámara
27–30, 31–32, 38–42, 50–51, 54–55, 63–64,
65, 74–75
Sociedad General de Autores y Editores
(SGAE) 223–24
Sojo, Vicente 101
son (Cuban) 53–55, 83–85, 90–91, 92–93, 95–
96, 166, 204–5
son (Mexican) 58–59
sonorization 177, 193–94, 200
Sony Music Entertainment 227–28
Soviet Composers Union 128
Soviet Exhibition of Science, Technology, and
Culture 115–16
Soviet Intercosmos program 190–92
Sovietization 23–24, 144–45
Soviet Union 3–4, 19, 25–26, 108–9, 110, 115–
16, 117–18, 125–26, 128–29, 130–31, 149–
53, 167, 169–70, 183–84, 185–86, 190–92,
210–11, 212–13, 214–15
Soyuz 38 190–92
Spain 5–6, 7–9, 21, 43, 52–53, 170, 200, 216–
17, 221
Spargue Smith, Carleton 35
Spassov, Ivan 173–75
special period (in times of peace). *See* período
especial (en tiempos de paz)
Sputnik 190–92
Stalin, Joseph 19, 108, 128
Stalinist 110, 152–53
Stalinization 149–50
Steiner, Max 216–17
Stockhausen, Karlheinz 133–34, 136–37, 157,
178, 196
Stravinsky, Igor 39–40, 41–43, 44–45, 60–62,
83–85, 86–87, 119–20, 125–26, 128, 133–
34, 178
surrealism/surrealist 51–52, 163–64

Taller de Composición e Interpretación Casa de
las Américas 221
Taller ICAP de Música Electroacústica (TIME)
183–84, 189–90, 192–93, 196–97, 199–200,
202–3, 210–11
Tamayo Méndez, Arnaldo 190–92

Tanglewood 27–30, 35, 44–45, 50–
51, 130–31
Tchaikovsky, Pytor Ilyich 65–66, 133–34
Teatro "Normal" (Teatro de la Escuela Normal
de Maestros) 65, 74–75
Thaw 19
Torcuato Di Tella Institute 20–21
Torre, Mirta de la 196–97, 202–3
Torres, Dolores 44–45, 169–70
Tosar, Héctor 101, 164–65, 166
tourism 185–87, 213, 229–30, 234
transculturation 10–11, 13, 57–58, 62–
63, 179–80
tres (string instrument) 60–62, 90–91
tresillo 57, 62, 83–85, 89–90
Triple Balance Empresarial Model 230–31
twelve-tone 6–7, 20–21, 45–46, 63–64, 92–93,
100–2, 108, 109, 119–20, 126–28, 134–35,
144, 145–47

Unidades Militares de Apoyo a la Producción
(UMAP) 149
Unión Nacional de Escritores y Artistas de
Cuba (UNEAC, National Union of Writers
and Artists of Cuba) 82–83, 98–99, 107–
8, 109, 113, 121–25, 142–43, 147, 148–49,
150–51, 160–61, 167–68, 170, 178–79,
187–88, 192–93, 194, 195, 196–97, 200
Universidad de La Habana 10–11, 59–60
Universidad de Oriente 77–78
Urfé, Odilio 65–66
Uruguay 25–26, 164–65, 166, 176–77
US-imposed embargo 5–6, 23, 24–26, 103,
108, 110–12, 139–40, 185, 201–2, 223–24
US Military interventions 33

Valdés Arnau, Roberto 124
Valdés, Ele 230–31
Valdés, Gilberto 125–26
Valera, Roberto 121–24, 140–42, 144, 146–47,
149–50, 165–66, 169–72, 175–78, 180, 184,
193–94, 198, 205, 217, 225, 227–28
Valera, Roberto, *Devenir* 144, 146–
47, 165–66
vanguardia/vanguardismo 6–7, 100, 107–8,
115–17, 121–23, 129–30, 135–37, 139–41,
142–43, 144, 146–47, 163–64, 168–69, 173,
176–77, 178–80, 190, 195, 198–99
Varèse, Edgar 3–4, 51–52, 163–64
Vázquez Millares, Angel 129–30, 146–47
Vega, Aurelio de la 40–41, 102–3, 117–
18, 214–15

268 INDEX

Veulens, Marieta 196–97
Villafranca, Elio 197
Villalba, Fico 69–70
Villa-Lobos, Heitor 86–87, 92–93, 117–18, 119–20, 141–42
  Villa-Lobos, Heitor, *Bachianas Brasileiras No. 2* 89–90
Vitali, Tomaso Antonio 42–43

Warsaw Autumn Music Festival 5–6, 121–23, 139–40, 156–57, 173–75, 196, 201
Wet-foot/dry-foot policy 213
White, José 3–4
Williams, John 216–17

Woodward, Roger 156–57
World Peace Council 81
World War II 5–6, 32–35, 46–50, 63–64, 67–69, 79–80

Xenakis, Iannis 136–37

Yamaha CS 70 M 198
Yotuel 233
Young, La Monte 136

zafra de los 10 millones 128–29, 136, 148–49, 154–55, 186–87
Zhdanovist/Zhdanovism 110